CASE CLOSED

VOLUME 68

Gosho Aoyama

Case Briefing:

Subject:
Occupation:
Special Skills:
Equipment:

Jimmy Kudo, a.k.a. Conan Edogawa
High School Student/Detective
Analytical thinking and deductive reasoning, Soccer
Bow Tie Voice Transmitter, Super Sneakers,
Homing Glasses, Stretchy Suspenders

The subject is hot on the trail of a pair of suspicious men in black when he is attacked from behind and administered a strange substance which physically transforms him into a first grader. When the subject confides in the eccentric inventor Dr. Agasa, they decide to keep the subject's true identity a secret for the safety of everyone around him. Assuming the new identity of first grader Conan Edogawa, the subject continues to assist the police force on their most baffling cases. The only problem is that most crime-solving professionals won't take a little kid's advice!

Table of Contents

CONFIDEN

CASE CLOSED
Volume 68
Shonen Sunday Edition

Story and Art by GOSHO AOYAMA

MEITANTEI CONAN Vol. 68
by Gosho AOYAMA
© 1994 Gosho AOYAMA
All rights reserved.
Original Japanese edition published by SHOGAKUKAN.
English translation rights in the United States of America, Canada,
the United Kingdom and Ireland arranged with SHOGAKUKAN.

Translation
Tetsuichiro Miyaki

Touch-up & Lettering
Freeman Wong

Cover & Graphic Design
Andrea Rice

Editor
Shaenon K. Garrity

Printed in the U.S.A.

Published by VIZ Media, LLC
P.O. Box 77010
San Francisco, CA 94107

10 9 8 7 6 5 4 3 2 1
First printing, October 2018

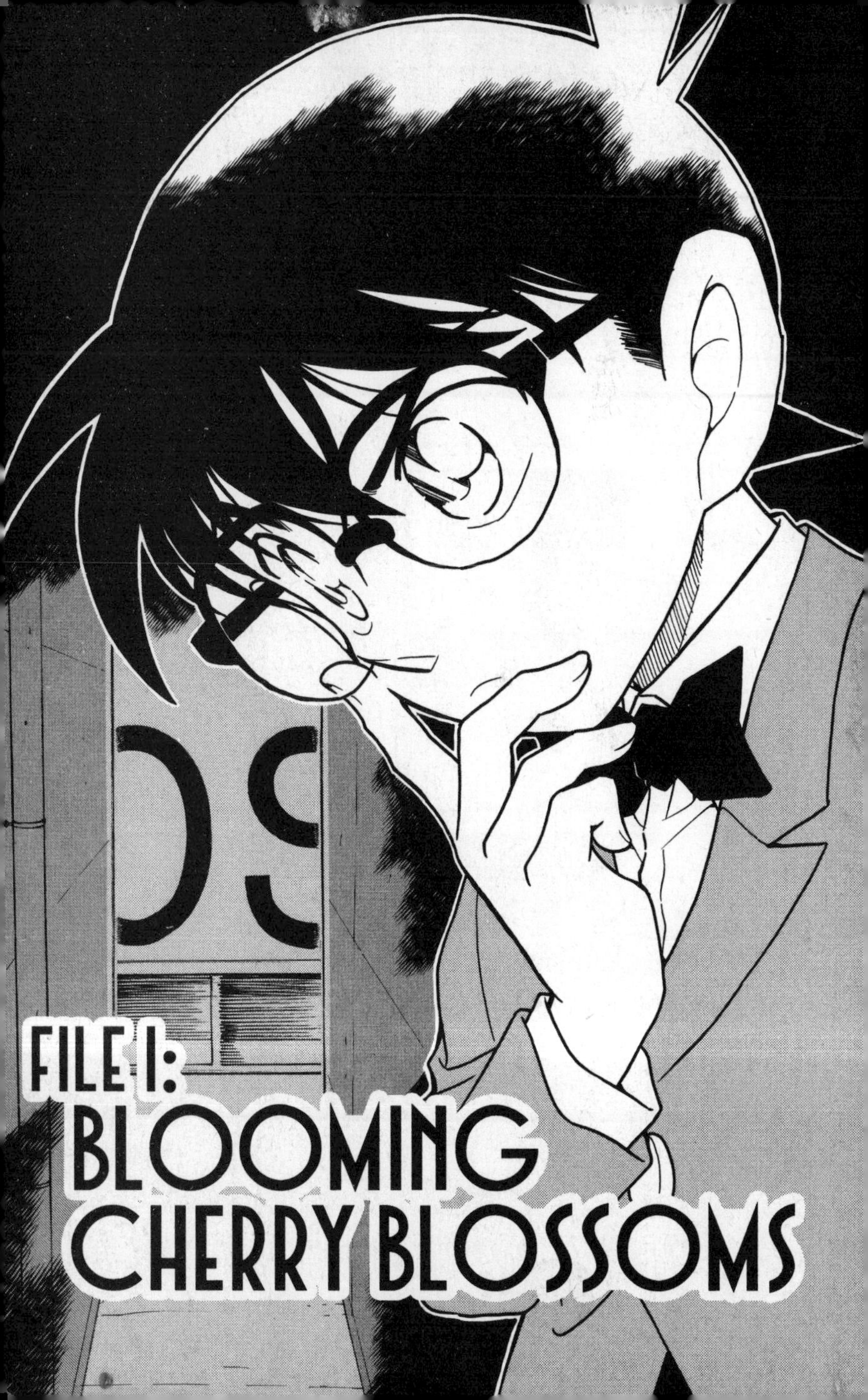
FILE 1:
BLOOMING CHERRY BLOSSOMS

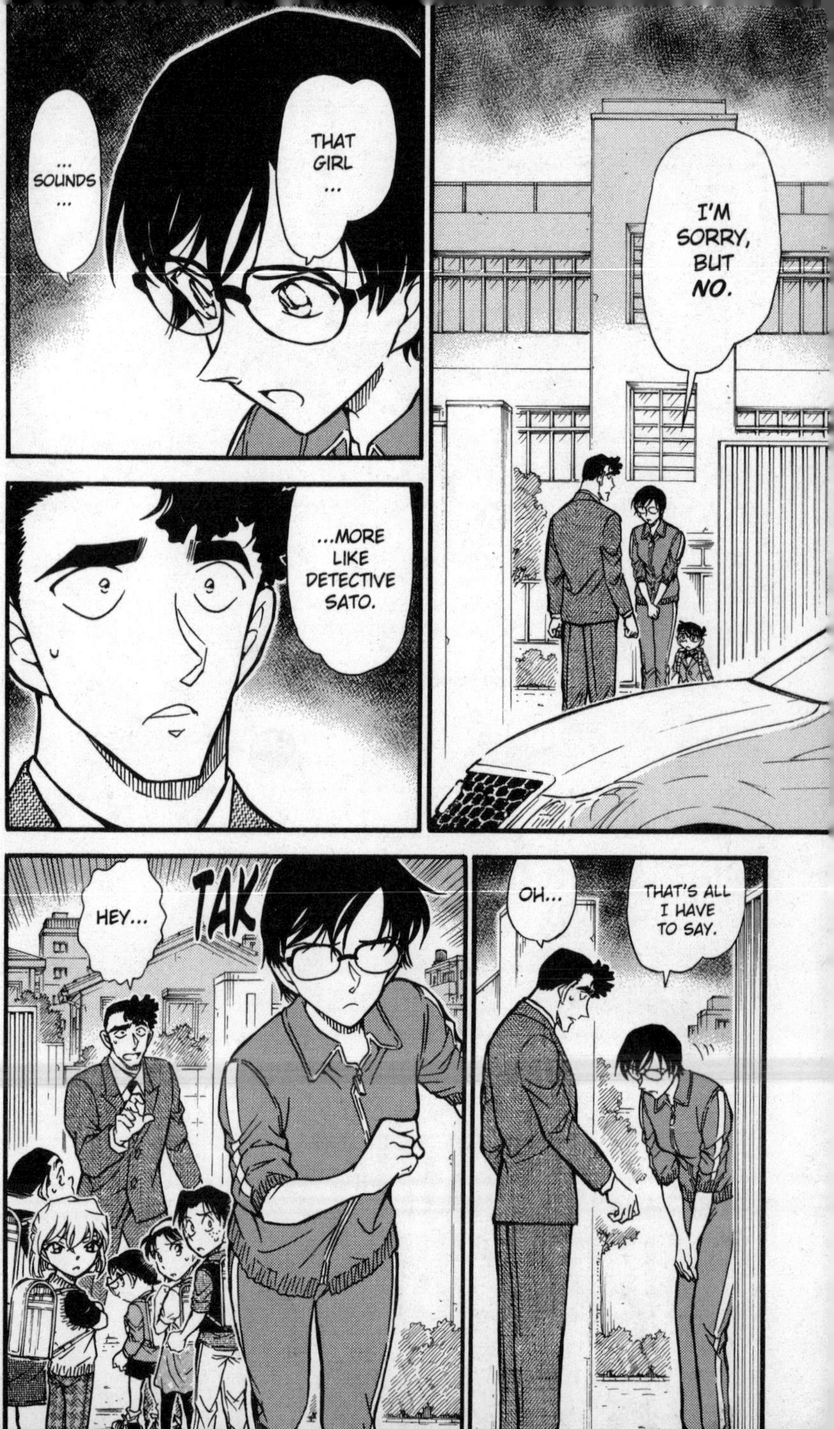

I'M SORRY, BUT NO.
THAT GIRL ...
... SOUNDS ...
...MORE LIKE DETECTIVE SATO.
THAT'S ALL I HAVE TO SAY.
OH...
TAK
HEY...

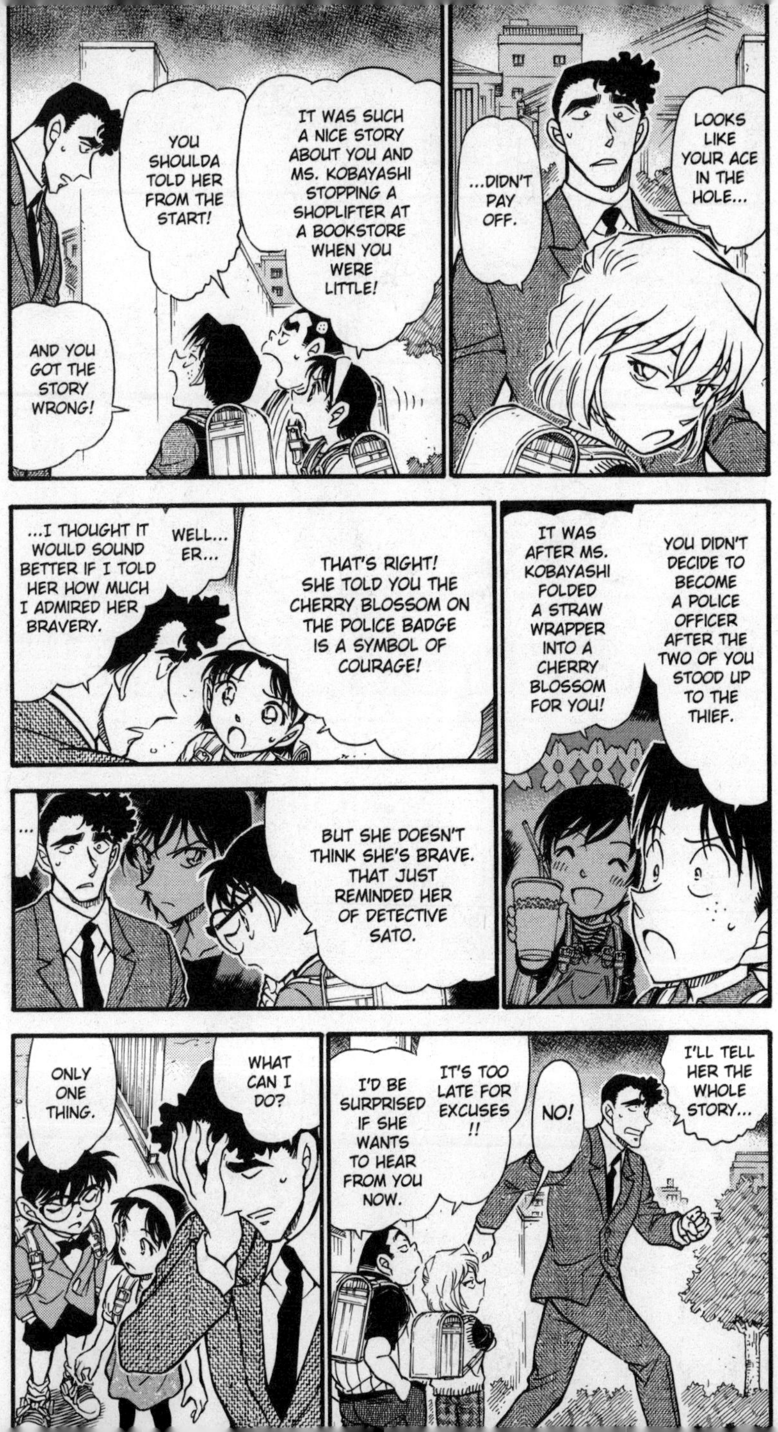
LOOKS LIKE YOUR ACE IN THE HOLE...
...DIDN'T PAY OFF.
IT WAS SUCH A NICE STORY ABOUT YOU AND MS. KOBAYASHI STOPPING A SHOPLIFTER AT A BOOKSTORE WHEN YOU WERE LITTLE!
YOU SHOULDA TOLD HER FROM THE START!
AND YOU GOT THE STORY WRONG!
YOU DIDN'T DECIDE TO BECOME A POLICE OFFICER AFTER THE TWO OF YOU STOOD UP TO THE THIEF.
IT WAS AFTER MS. KOBAYASHI FOLDED A STRAW WRAPPER INTO A CHERRY BLOSSOM FOR YOU!
THAT'S RIGHT! SHE TOLD YOU THE CHERRY BLOSSOM ON THE POLICE BADGE IS A SYMBOL OF COURAGE!
WELL... ER...
...I THOUGHT IT WOULD SOUND BETTER IF I TOLD HER HOW MUCH I ADMIRED HER BRAVERY.
BUT SHE DOESN'T THINK SHE'S BRAVE. THAT JUST REMINDED HER OF DETECTIVE SATO.
...
I'LL TELL HER THE WHOLE STORY...
NO!
IT'S TOO LATE FOR EXCUSES!!
I'D BE SURPRISED IF SHE WANTS TO HEAR FROM YOU NOW.
WHAT CAN I DO?
ONLY ONE THING.

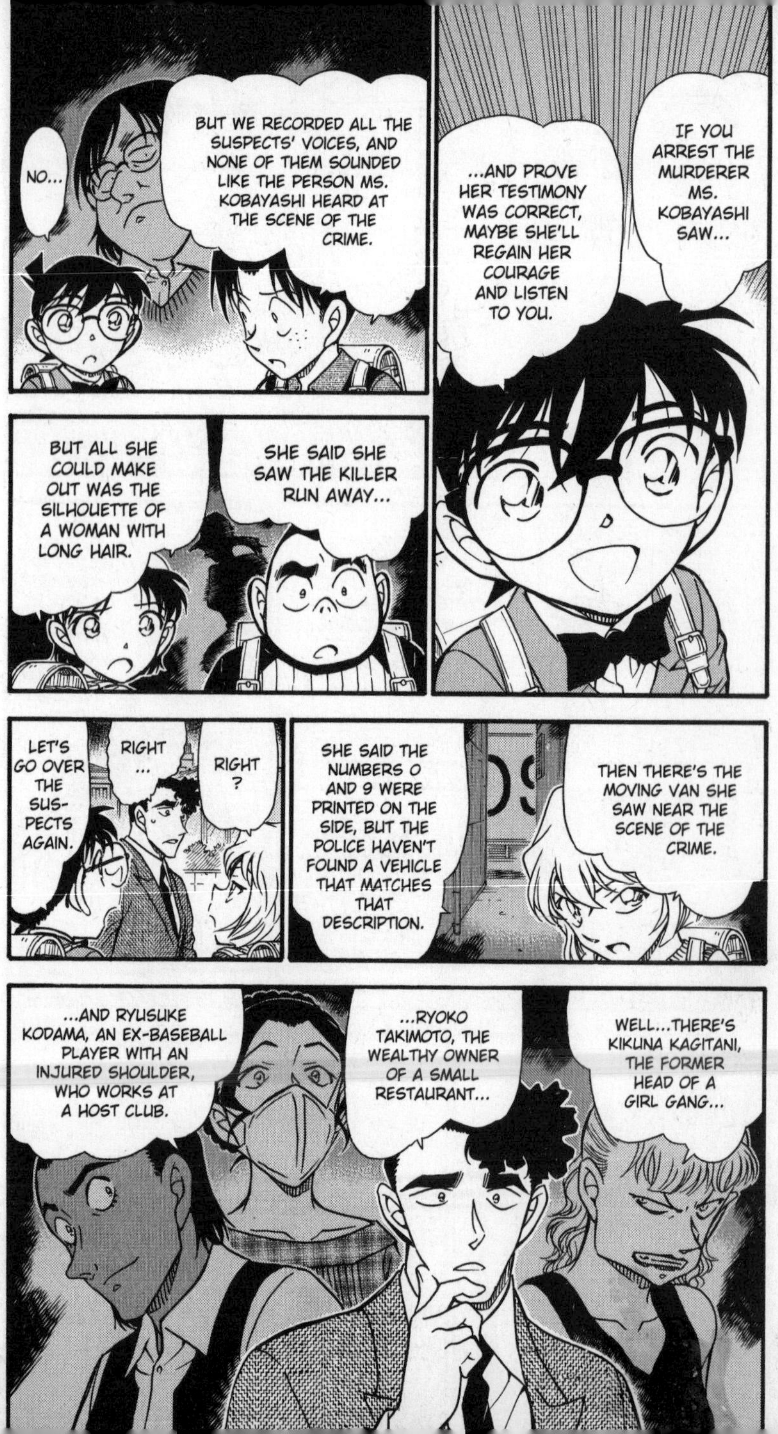
IF YOU ARREST THE MURDERER MS. KOBAYASHI SAW...
...AND PROVE HER TESTIMONY WAS CORRECT, MAYBE SHE'LL REGAIN HER COURAGE AND LISTEN TO YOU.
BUT WE RECORDED ALL THE SUSPECTS' VOICES, AND NONE OF THEM SOUNDED LIKE THE PERSON MS. KOBAYASHI HEARD AT THE SCENE OF THE CRIME.
NO...
SHE SAID SHE SAW THE KILLER RUN AWAY...
BUT ALL SHE COULD MAKE OUT WAS THE SILHOUETTE OF A WOMAN WITH LONG HAIR.
THEN THERE'S THE MOVING VAN SHE SAW NEAR THE SCENE OF THE CRIME.
09
SHE SAID THE NUMBERS 0 AND 9 WERE PRINTED ON THE SIDE, BUT THE POLICE HAVEN'T FOUND A VEHICLE THAT MATCHES THAT DESCRIPTION.
RIGHT ?
RIGHT ...
LET'S GO OVER THE SUS-PECTS AGAIN.
WELL...THERE'S KIKUNA KAGITANI, THE FORMER HEAD OF A GIRL GANG...
...RYOKO TAKIMOTO, THE WEALTHY OWNER OF A SMALL RESTAURANT...
...AND RYUSUKE KODAMA, AN EX-BASEBALL PLAYER WITH AN INJURED SHOULDER, WHO WORKS AT A HOST CLUB.

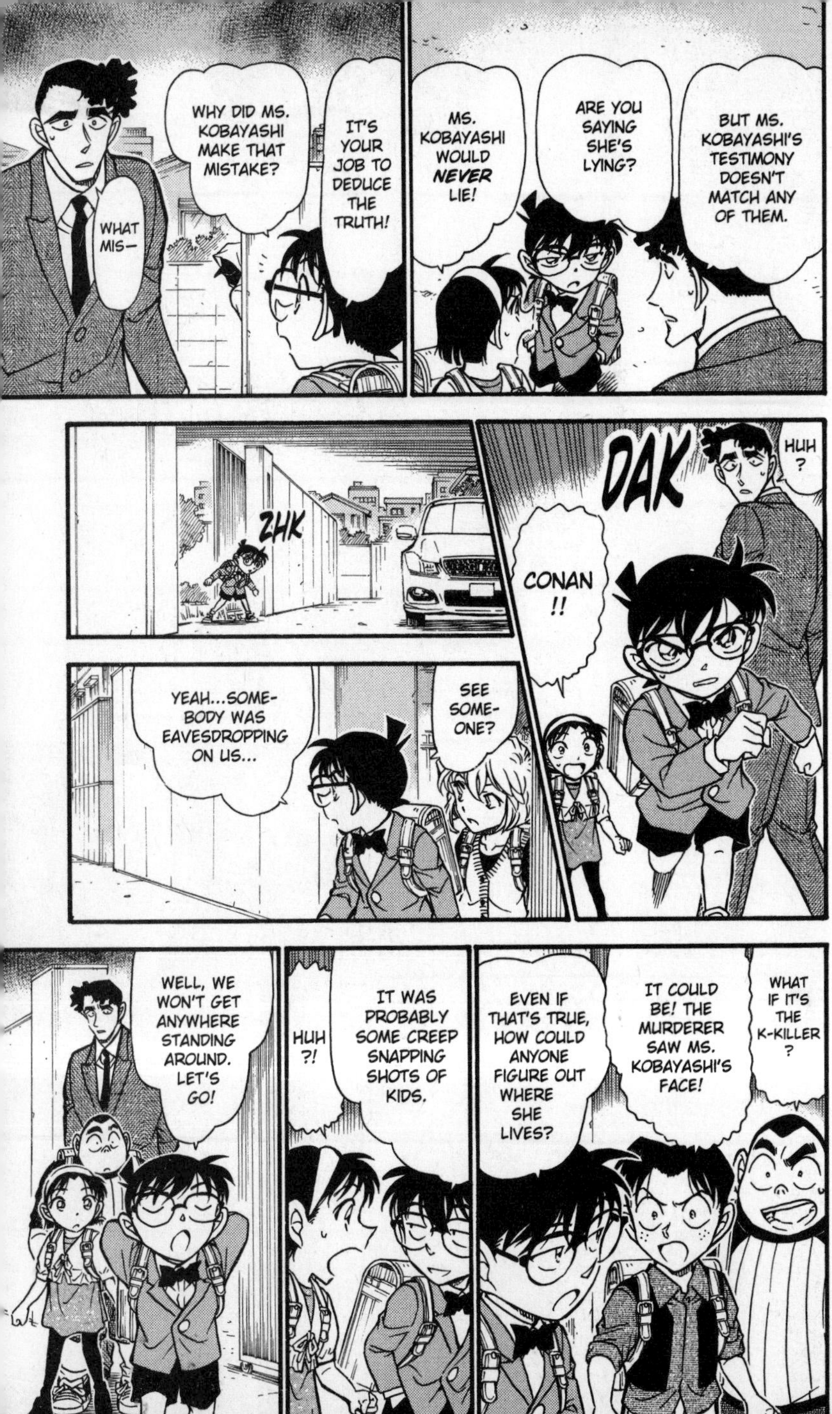
BUT MS. KOBAYASHI'S TESTIMONY DOESN'T MATCH ANY OF THEM.
ARE YOU SAYING SHE'S LYING?
MS. KOBAYASHI WOULD **NEVER** LIE!
IT'S YOUR JOB TO DEDUCE THE TRUTH!
WHY DID MS. KOBAYASHI MAKE THAT MISTAKE?
WHAT MIS—
DAK
HUH?
CONAN!!
ZHK
SEE SOME-ONE?
YEAH...SOME-BODY WAS EAVESDROPPING ON US...
WHAT IF IT'S THE K-KILLER?
IT COULD BE! THE MURDERER SAW MS. KOBAYASHI'S FACE!
EVEN IF THAT'S TRUE, HOW COULD ANYONE FIGURE OUT WHERE SHE LIVES?
IT WAS PROBABLY SOME CREEP SNAPPING SHOTS OF KIDS.
HUH?!
WELL, WE WON'T GET ANYWHERE STANDING AROUND. LET'S GO!

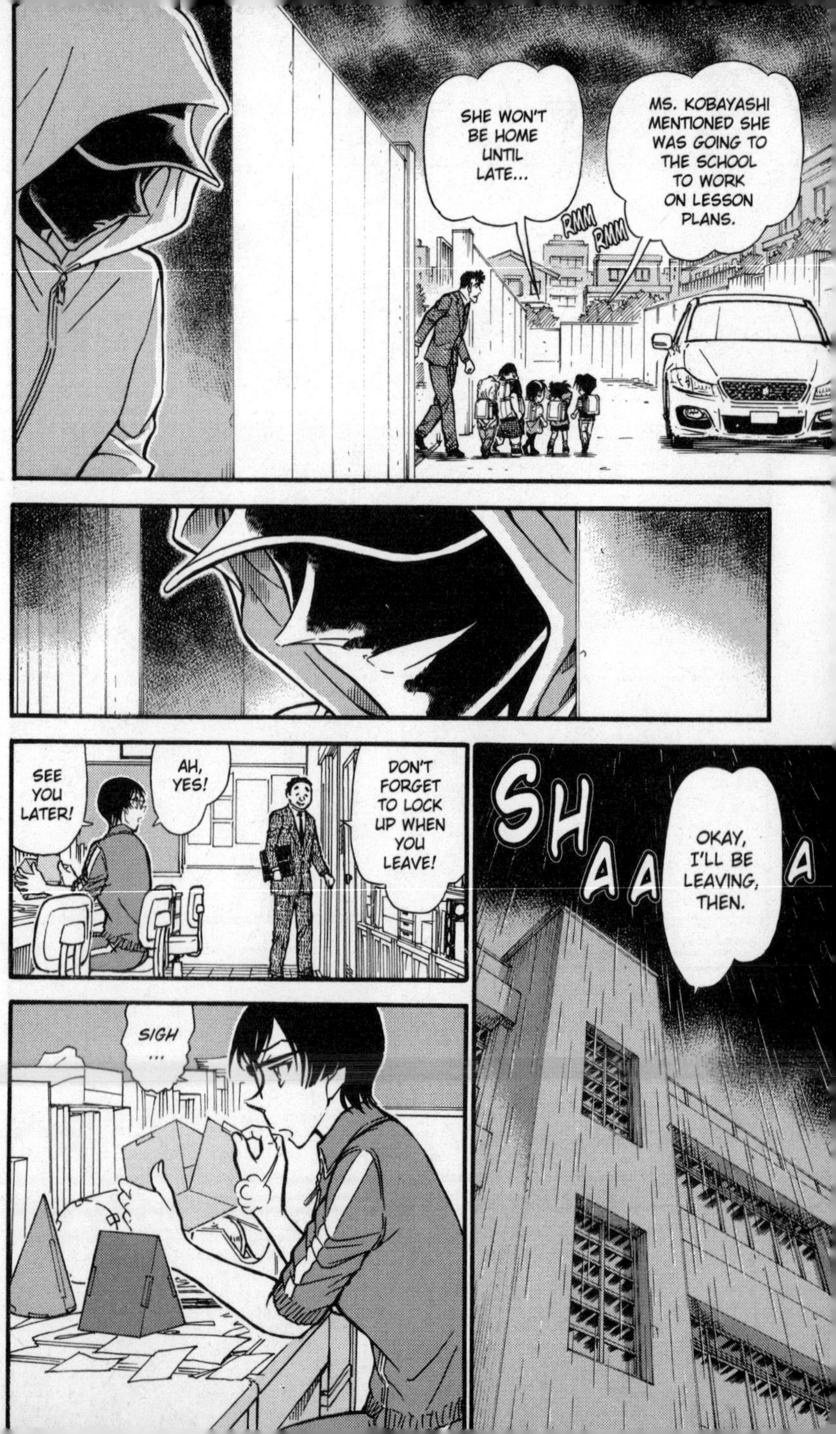
MS. KOBAYASHI MENTIONED SHE WAS GOING TO THE SCHOOL TO WORK ON LESSON PLANS.
RMM RMM
SHE WON'T BE HOME UNTIL LATE...
SHAAAA
OKAY, I'LL BE LEAVING, THEN.
DON'T FORGET TO LOCK UP WHEN YOU LEAVE!
AH, YES!
SEE YOU LATER!
SIGH...

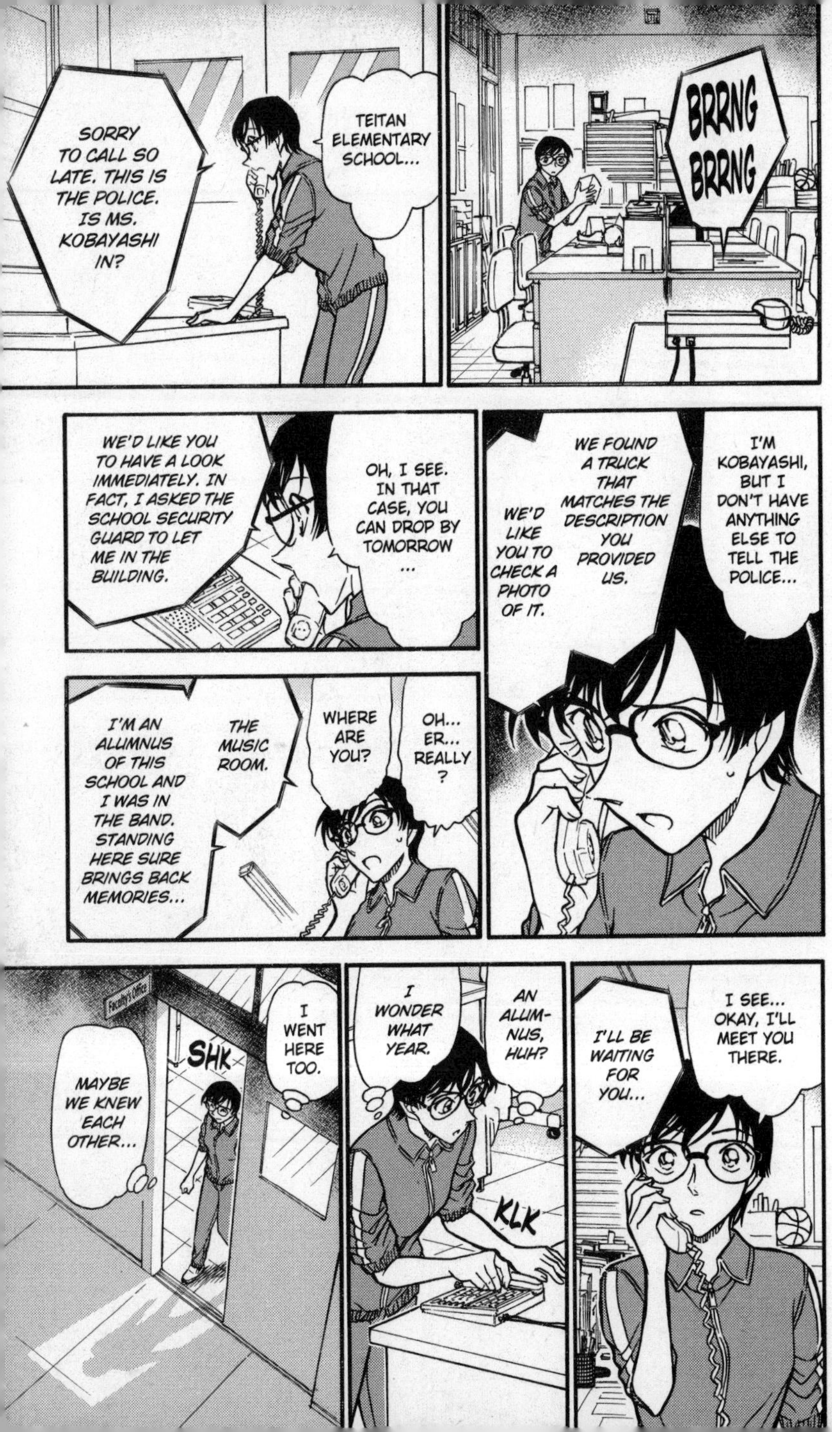
BRRNG BRRNG
TEITAN ELEMENTARY SCHOOL...
SORRY TO CALL SO LATE. THIS IS THE POLICE. IS MS. KOBAYASHI IN?
I'M KOBAYASHI, BUT I DON'T HAVE ANYTHING ELSE TO TELL THE POLICE...
WE FOUND A TRUCK THAT MATCHES THE DESCRIPTION YOU PROVIDED US.
WE'D LIKE YOU TO CHECK A PHOTO OF IT.
OH, I SEE. IN THAT CASE, YOU CAN DROP BY TOMORROW...
WE'D LIKE YOU TO HAVE A LOOK IMMEDIATELY. IN FACT, I ASKED THE SCHOOL SECURITY GUARD TO LET ME IN THE BUILDING.
OH... ER... REALLY?
WHERE ARE YOU?
THE MUSIC ROOM.
I'M AN ALUMNUS OF THIS SCHOOL AND I WAS IN THE BAND. STANDING HERE SURE BRINGS BACK MEMORIES...
I SEE... OKAY, I'LL MEET YOU THERE.
I'LL BE WAITING FOR YOU...
AN ALUMNUS, HUH?
I WONDER WHAT YEAR.
KLK
I WENT HERE TOO.
Faculty's Office
SHK
MAYBE WE KNEW EACH OTHER...

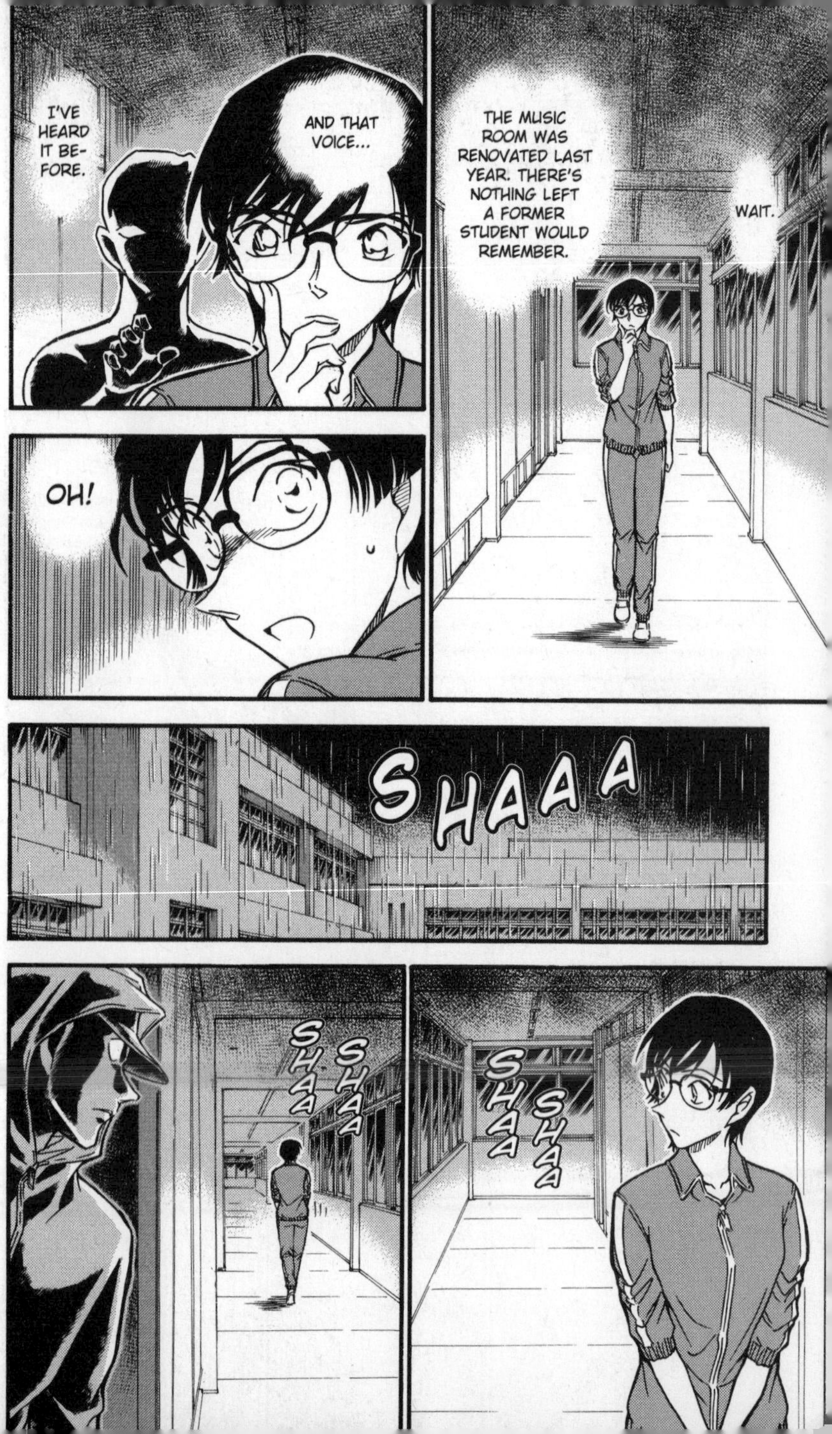
THE MUSIC ROOM WAS RENOVATED LAST YEAR. THERE'S NOTHING LEFT A FORMER STUDENT WOULD REMEMBER.
WAIT.
AND THAT VOICE...
I'VE HEARD IT BE-FORE.
OH!
SHAAA
SHAA
SHAA
SHAA
SHAA

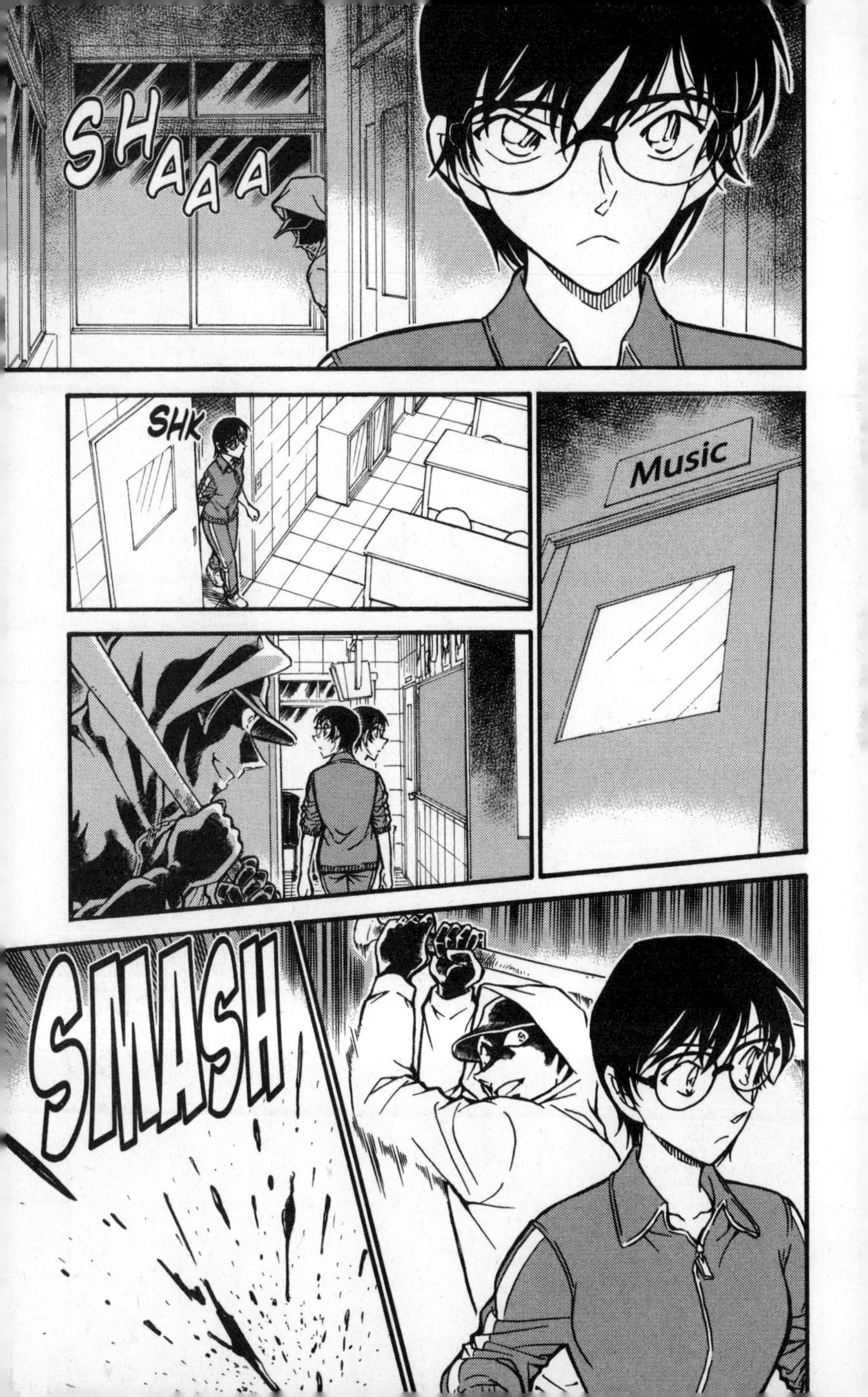
SHAAAA
Music
SHK
SMASH

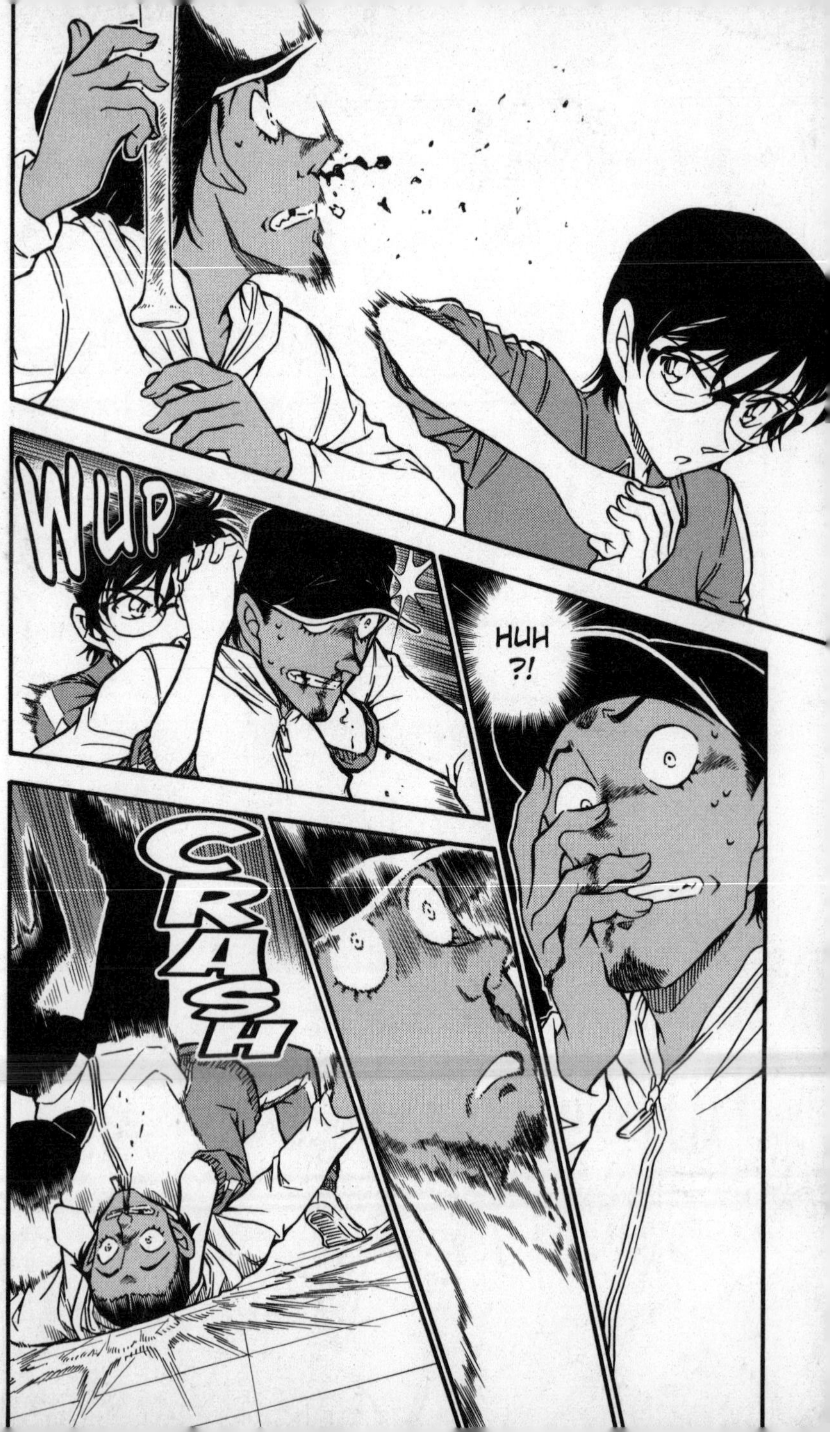
WUP
HUH ?!
CRASH

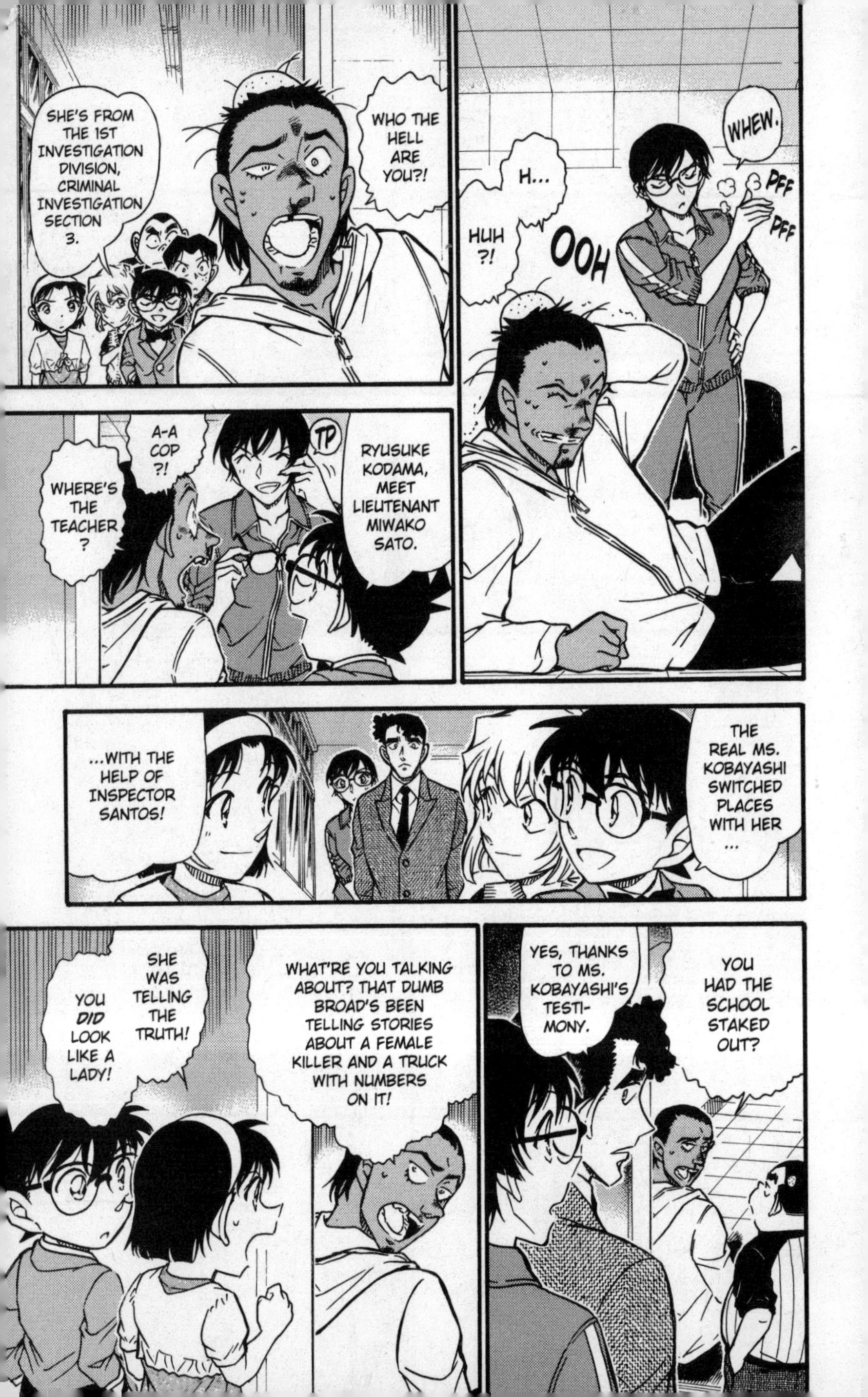
WHEW.
PFF
PFF
H...
OOH
HUH ?!
WHO THE HELL ARE YOU?!
SHE'S FROM THE 1ST INVESTIGATION DIVISION, CRIMINAL INVESTIGATION SECTION 3.
TP
RYUSUKE KODAMA, MEET LIEUTENANT MIWAKO SATO.
A-A COP ?!
WHERE'S THE TEACHER ?
THE REAL MS. KOBAYASHI SWITCHED PLACES WITH HER ...
...WITH THE HELP OF INSPECTOR SANTOS!
YOU HAD THE SCHOOL STAKED OUT?
YES, THANKS TO MS. KOBAYASHI'S TESTI-MONY.
WHAT'RE YOU TALKING ABOUT? THAT DUMB BROAD'S BEEN TELLING STORIES ABOUT A FEMALE KILLER AND A TRUCK WITH NUMBERS ON IT!
SHE WAS TELLING THE TRUTH!
YOU *DID* LOOK LIKE A LADY!

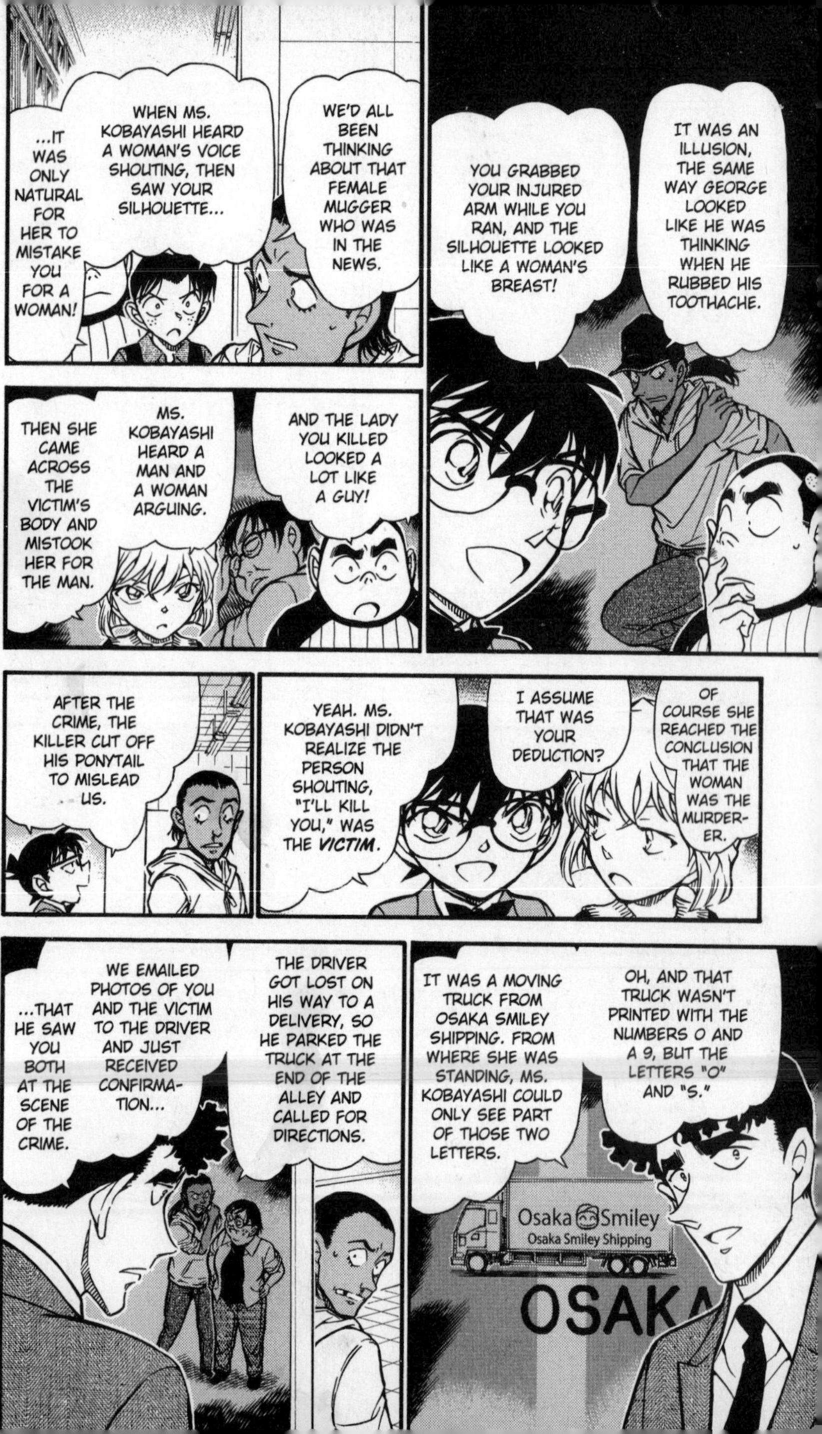
IT WAS AN ILLUSION, THE SAME WAY GEORGE LOOKED LIKE HE WAS THINKING WHEN HE RUBBED HIS TOOTHACHE.
YOU GRABBED YOUR INJURED ARM WHILE YOU RAN, AND THE SILHOUETTE LOOKED LIKE A WOMAN'S BREAST!
WE'D ALL BEEN THINKING ABOUT THAT FEMALE MUGGER WHO WAS IN THE NEWS.
WHEN MS. KOBAYASHI HEARD A WOMAN'S VOICE SHOUTING, THEN SAW YOUR SILHOUETTE...
...IT WAS ONLY NATURAL FOR HER TO MISTAKE YOU FOR A WOMAN!
AND THE LADY YOU KILLED LOOKED A LOT LIKE A GUY!
MS. KOBAYASHI HEARD A MAN AND A WOMAN ARGUING.
THEN SHE CAME ACROSS THE VICTIM'S BODY AND MISTOOK HER FOR THE MAN.
OF COURSE SHE REACHED THE CONCLUSION THAT THE WOMAN WAS THE MURDERER.
I ASSUME THAT WAS YOUR DEDUCTION?
YEAH. MS. KOBAYASHI DIDN'T REALIZE THE PERSON SHOUTING, "I'LL KILL YOU," WAS THE *VICTIM*.
AFTER THE CRIME, THE KILLER CUT OFF HIS PONYTAIL TO MISLEAD US.
OH, AND THAT TRUCK WASN'T PRINTED WITH THE NUMBERS 0 AND A 9, BUT THE LETTERS "O" AND "S."
IT WAS A MOVING TRUCK FROM OSAKA SMILEY SHIPPING. FROM WHERE SHE WAS STANDING, MS. KOBAYASHI COULD ONLY SEE PART OF THOSE TWO LETTERS.
Osaka Smiley
Osaka Smiley Shipping
OSAKA
THE DRIVER GOT LOST ON HIS WAY TO A DELIVERY, SO HE PARKED THE TRUCK AT THE END OF THE ALLEY AND CALLED FOR DIRECTIONS.
WE EMAILED PHOTOS OF YOU AND THE VICTIM TO THE DRIVER AND JUST RECEIVED CONFIRMATION...
...THAT HE SAW YOU BOTH AT THE SCENE OF THE CRIME.

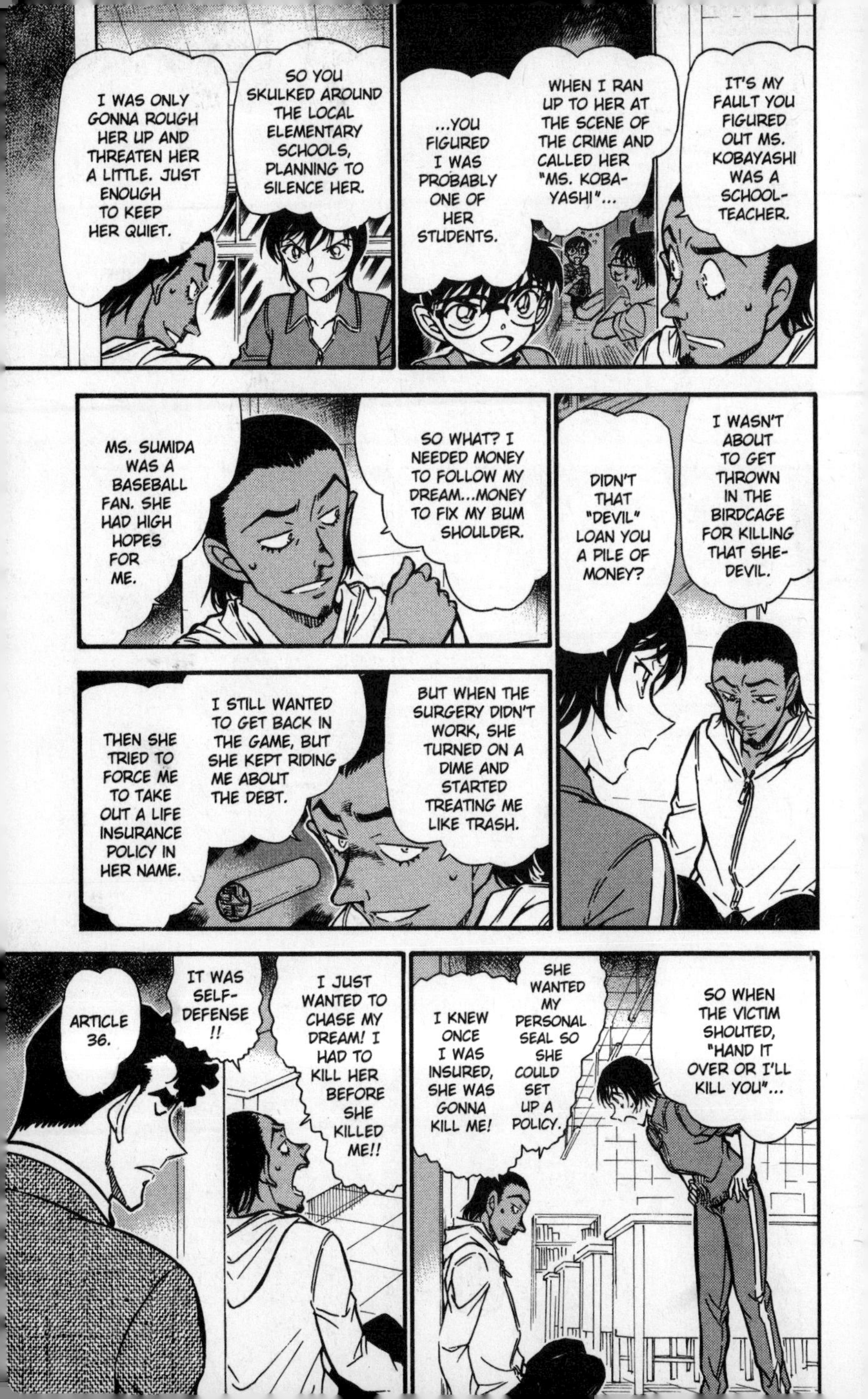
IT'S MY FAULT YOU FIGURED OUT MS. KOBAYASHI WAS A SCHOOL-TEACHER.
WHEN I RAN UP TO HER AT THE SCENE OF THE CRIME AND CALLED HER "MS. KOBA-YASHI"...
...YOU FIGURED I WAS PROBABLY ONE OF HER STUDENTS.
SO YOU SKULKED AROUND THE LOCAL ELEMENTARY SCHOOLS, PLANNING TO SILENCE HER.
I WAS ONLY GONNA ROUGH HER UP AND THREATEN HER A LITTLE. JUST ENOUGH TO KEEP HER QUIET.
I WASN'T ABOUT TO GET THROWN IN THE BIRDCAGE FOR KILLING THAT SHE-DEVIL.
DIDN'T THAT "DEVIL" LOAN YOU A PILE OF MONEY?
SO WHAT? I NEEDED MONEY TO FOLLOW MY DREAM...MONEY TO FIX MY BUM SHOULDER.
MS. SUMIDA WAS A BASEBALL FAN. SHE HAD HIGH HOPES FOR ME.
BUT WHEN THE SURGERY DIDN'T WORK, SHE TURNED ON A DIME AND STARTED TREATING ME LIKE TRASH.
I STILL WANTED TO GET BACK IN THE GAME, BUT SHE KEPT RIDING ME ABOUT THE DEBT.
THEN SHE TRIED TO FORCE ME TO TAKE OUT A LIFE INSURANCE POLICY IN HER NAME.
SO WHEN THE VICTIM SHOUTED, "HAND IT OVER OR I'LL KILL YOU"...
SHE WANTED MY PERSONAL SEAL SO SHE COULD SET UP A POLICY.
I KNEW ONCE I WAS INSURED, SHE WAS GONNA KILL ME!
I JUST WANTED TO CHASE MY DREAM! I HAD TO KILL HER BEFORE SHE KILLED ME!!
IT WAS SELF-DEFENSE!!
ARTICLE 36.

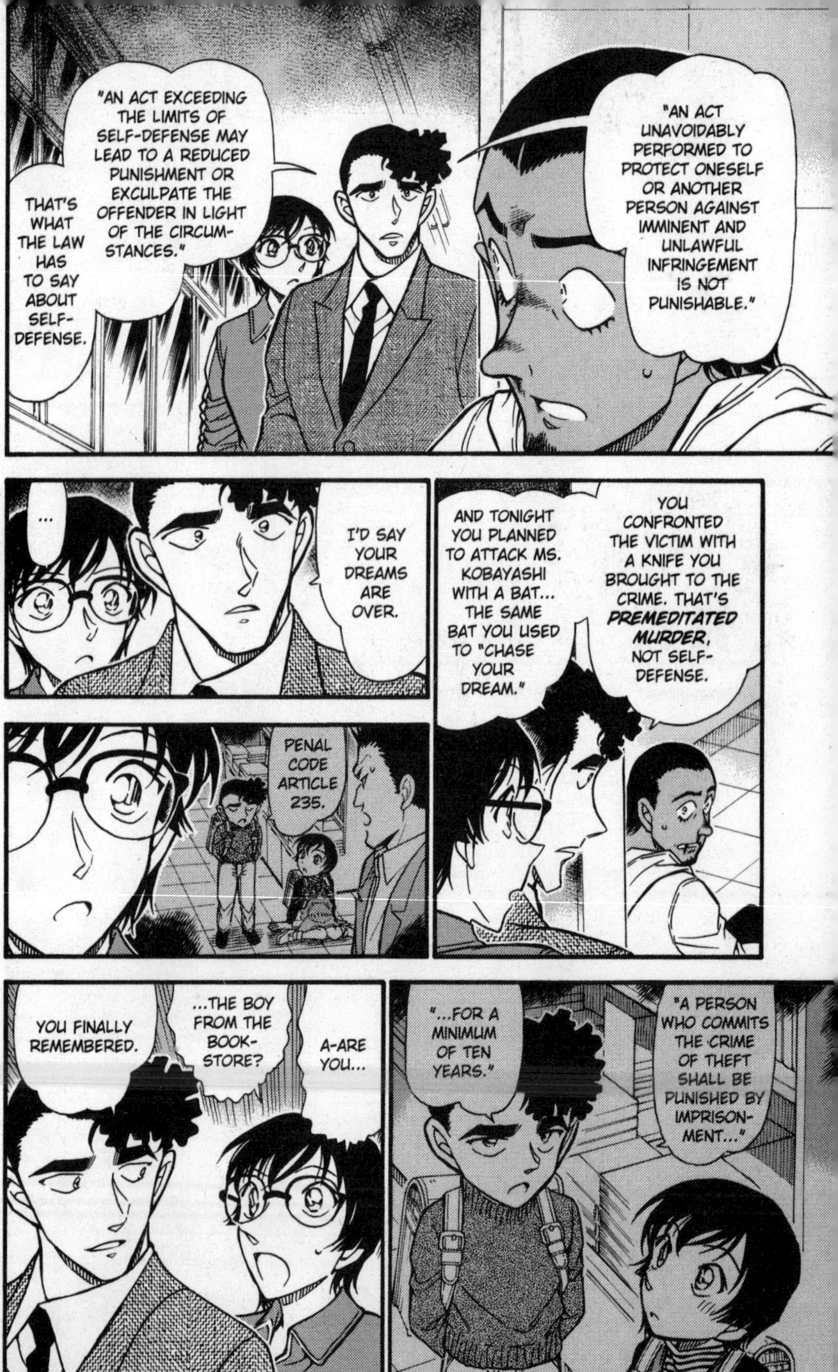
"AN ACT UNAVOIDABLY PERFORMED TO PROTECT ONESELF OR ANOTHER PERSON AGAINST IMMINENT AND UNLAWFUL INFRINGEMENT IS NOT PUNISHABLE."
"AN ACT EXCEEDING THE LIMITS OF SELF-DEFENSE MAY LEAD TO A REDUCED PUNISHMENT OR EXCULPATE THE OFFENDER IN LIGHT OF THE CIRCUM-STANCES."
THAT'S WHAT THE LAW HAS TO SAY ABOUT SELF-DEFENSE.
YOU CONFRONTED THE VICTIM WITH A KNIFE YOU BROUGHT TO THE CRIME. THAT'S ***PREMEDITATED MURDER***, NOT SELF-DEFENSE.
AND TONIGHT YOU PLANNED TO ATTACK MS. KOBAYASHI WITH A BAT... THE SAME BAT YOU USED TO "CHASE YOUR DREAM."
I'D SAY YOUR DREAMS ARE OVER.
...
PENAL CODE ARTICLE 235.
"A PERSON WHO COMMITS THE CRIME OF THEFT SHALL BE PUNISHED BY IMPRISON-MENT..."
"...FOR A MINIMUM OF TEN YEARS."
A-ARE YOU...
...THE BOY FROM THE BOOK-STORE?
YOU FINALLY REMEMBERED.

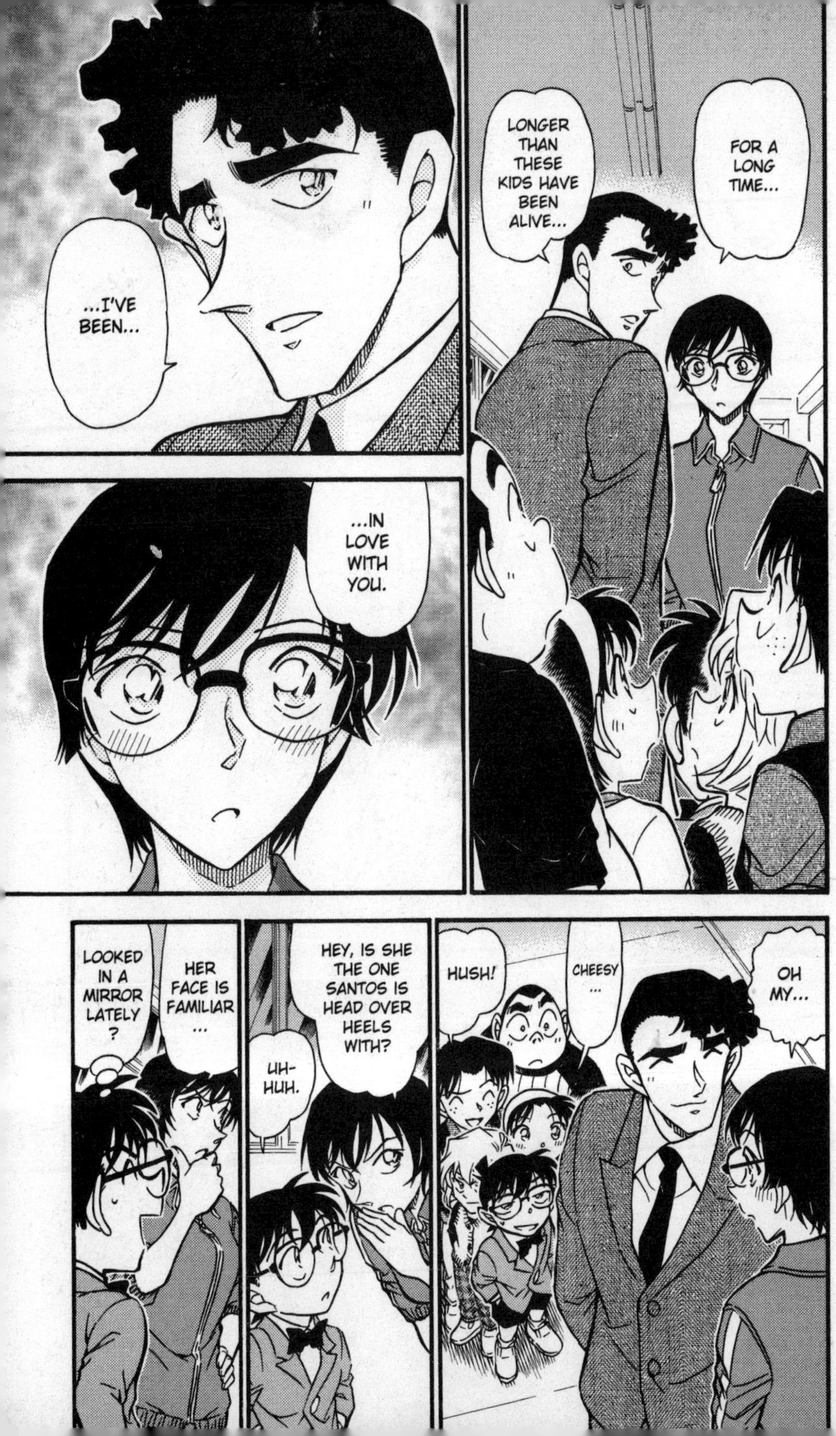
FOR A LONG TIME...
LONGER THAN THESE KIDS HAVE BEEN ALIVE...
...I'VE BEEN...
...IN LOVE WITH YOU.
OH MY...
CHEESY...
HUSH!
HEY, IS SHE THE ONE SANTOS IS HEAD OVER HEELS WITH?
UH-HUH.
HER FACE IS FAMILIAR...
LOOKED IN A MIRROR LATELY?

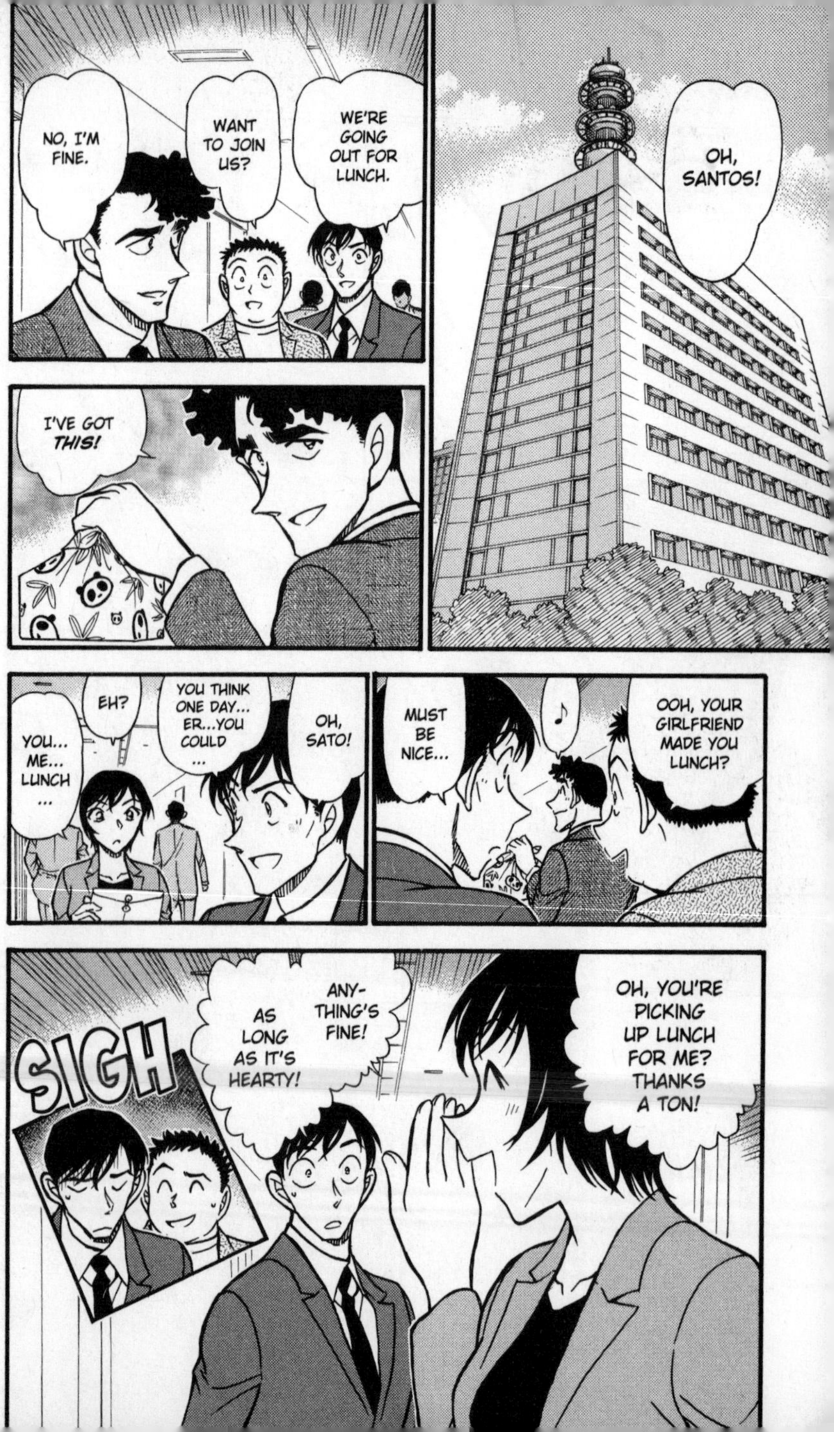
OH, SANTOS!
WE'RE GOING OUT FOR LUNCH.
WANT TO JOIN US?
NO, I'M FINE.
I'VE GOT *THIS!*
OOH, YOUR GIRLFRIEND MADE YOU LUNCH?
♪
MUST BE NICE...
OH, SATO!
YOU THINK ONE DAY... ER...YOU COULD ...
EH?
YOU... ME... LUNCH ...
OH, YOU'RE PICKING UP LUNCH FOR ME? THANKS A TON!
ANY-THING'S FINE!
AS LONG AS IT'S HEARTY!
SIGH

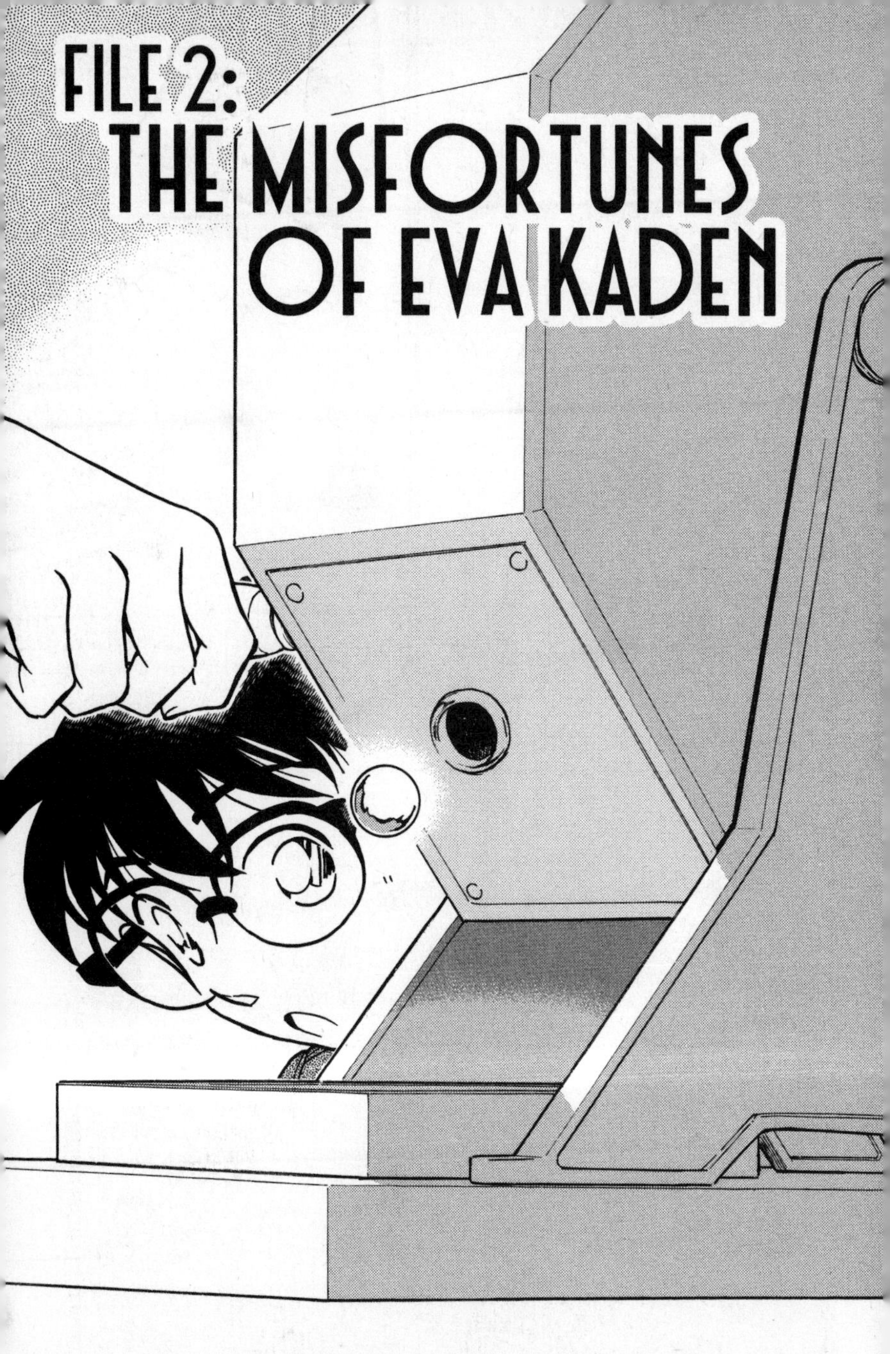
FILE 2:
THE MISFORTUNES OF EVA KADEN

YUP!!

ISN'T THERE A HOLIDAY COMING UP?

SAY, RACHEL...

Nichiuri News

Sun	Mon.	Tue.	Wed.	Thu.	Fri.	Sat.
				1	2	3
4	5	6	7	8	9	10
11	12	13	14	15	16	17
	19	20	21	22	23	24
		27	28	29	30	31

10 October

HEALTH AND SPORTS DAY, ON THE 12TH.

IT'S ON A MONDAY, SO WE HAVE A THREE-DAY WEEKEND.

HEY, MR. MOORE! DID YOU GET TICKETS FOR THE NEIGHBORHOOD LOTTERY?

OH... I SEE...

NAH, JUST ASKING.

YOU PLANNING TO TAKE US SOMEWHERE COOL?

WHY?

OH, DAD...

YEAH, GRAB MY WALLET, RACHEL. I'VE GOT 'EM IN THERE.

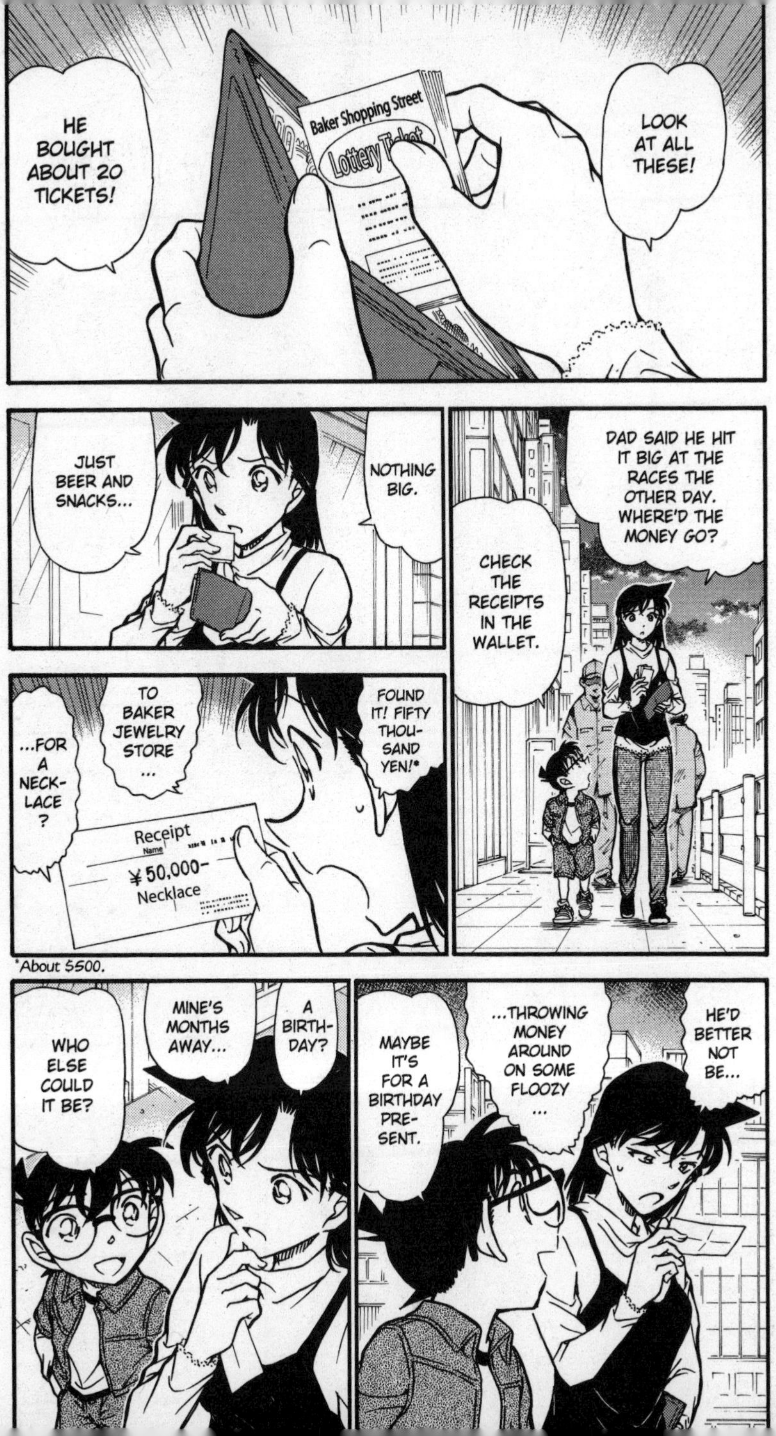
LOOK AT ALL THESE!
Baker Shopping Street
Lottery Ticket
HE BOUGHT ABOUT 20 TICKETS!
DAD SAID HE HIT IT BIG AT THE RACES THE OTHER DAY. WHERE'D THE MONEY GO?
CHECK THE RECEIPTS IN THE WALLET.
NOTHING BIG.
JUST BEER AND SNACKS...
FOUND IT! FIFTY THOUSAND YEN!*
TO BAKER JEWELRY STORE...
...FOR A NECKLACE?
Receipt
Name
¥50,000-
Necklace
HE'D BETTER NOT BE...
...THROWING MONEY AROUND ON SOME FLOOZY...
MAYBE IT'S FOR A BIRTHDAY PRESENT.
A BIRTHDAY?
MINE'S MONTHS AWAY...
WHO ELSE COULD IT BE?

*About $500.

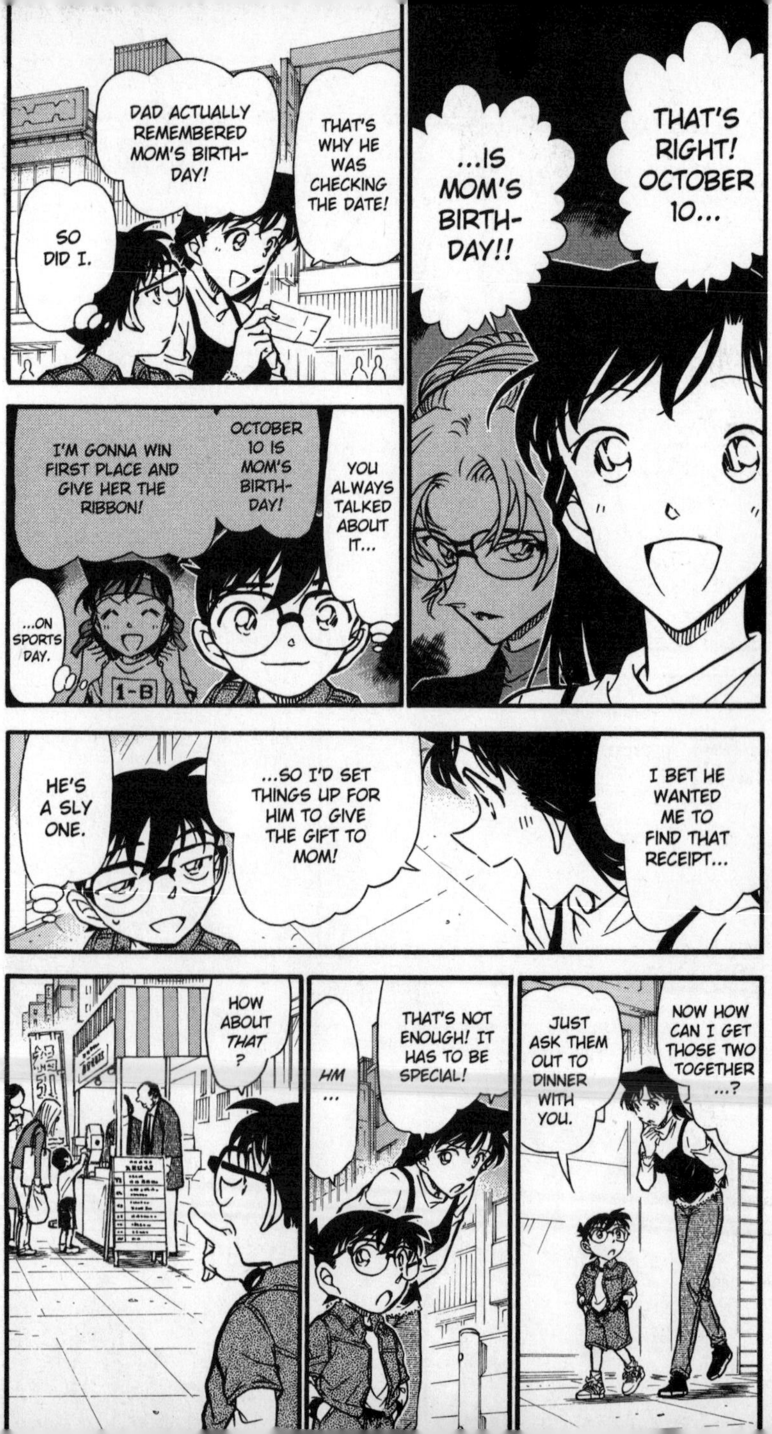
THAT'S RIGHT! OCTOBER 10...
...IS MOM'S BIRTH-DAY!!
THAT'S WHY HE WAS CHECKING THE DATE!
DAD ACTUALLY REMEMBERED MOM'S BIRTH-DAY!
SO DID I.
YOU ALWAYS TALKED ABOUT IT...
OCTOBER 10 IS MOM'S BIRTH-DAY!
I'M GONNA WIN FIRST PLACE AND GIVE HER THE RIBBON!
...ON SPORTS DAY.
I BET HE WANTED ME TO FIND THAT RECEIPT...
...SO I'D SET THINGS UP FOR HIM TO GIVE THE GIFT TO MOM!
HE'S A SLY ONE.
NOW HOW CAN I GET THOSE TWO TOGETHER ...?
JUST ASK THEM OUT TO DINNER WITH YOU.
THAT'S NOT ENOUGH! IT HAS TO BE SPECIAL!
HM ...
HOW ABOUT THAT ?
1-B

DONE!!

DON'T GET YOUR HOPES UP...

	Baker Shopping Street	
	Lottery	
Grand Prize	SONY Large-Screen LCD TV	
1st Prize	Shizuoka Seaside Hotel Getaway Voucher for Two	
2nd Prize	Perfect for Novices Golf Set	
3rd	Bathroom Scale	

YOU WON A HOTEL GETAWAY FOR TWO?

WHAT ?!

RICHARD MOORE

UH...

HUH?

THE THREE OF US CAN SPEND THE HOLIDAY WEEKEND THERE!

CONAN'S A KID, SO THE HOTEL WILL LET HIM STAY FOR FREE.

AND IT COMES WITH A GOURMET DINNER!

GOOD GIRL!

TALK ABOUT LUCKY.

ER...

HUH?

AND IF THERE'S *SOMETHING SPECIAL* YOU WANT TO BRING...

Shizuoka Seaside Hotel Voucher

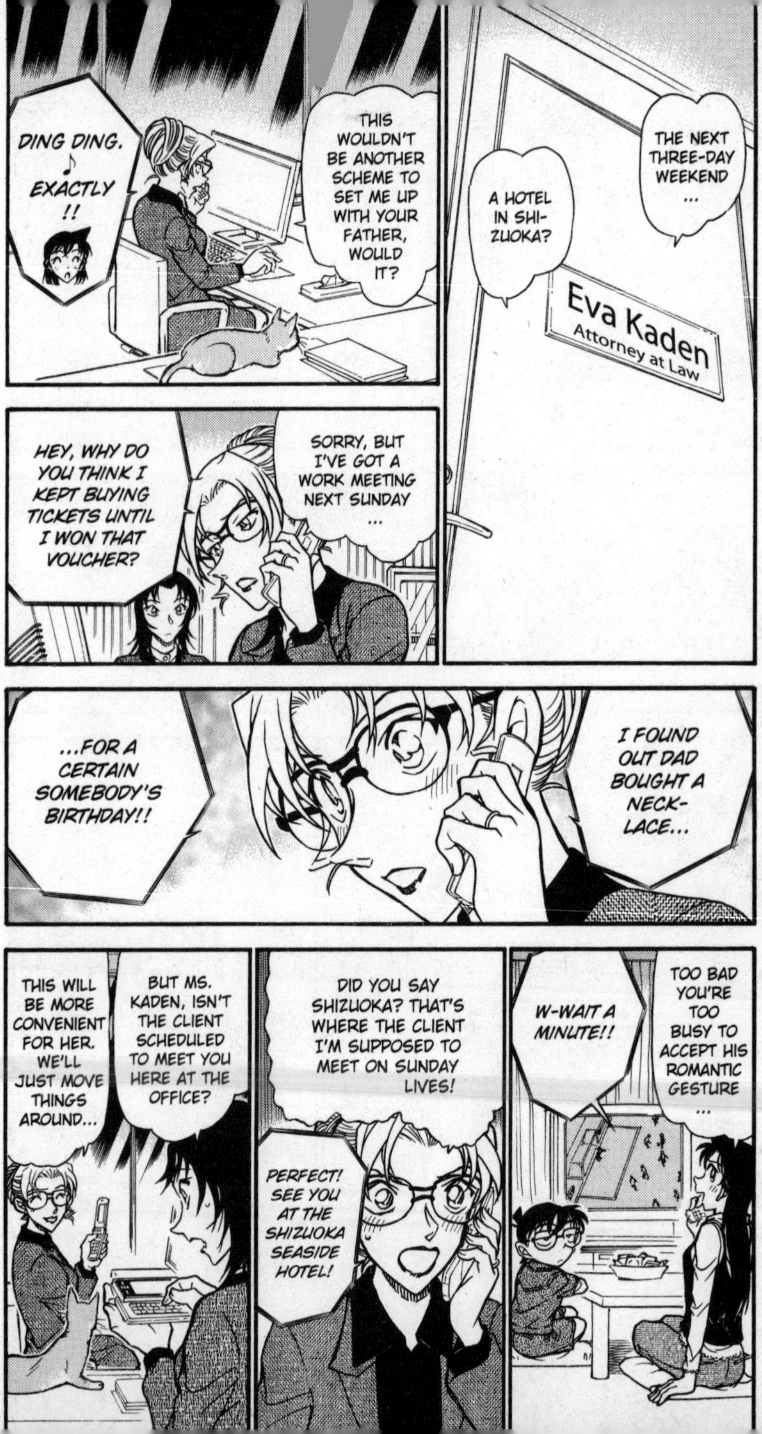
THE NEXT THREE-DAY WEEKEND ...
A HOTEL IN SHIZUOKA?
Eva Kaden
Attorney at Law
THIS WOULDN'T BE ANOTHER SCHEME TO SET ME UP WITH YOUR FATHER, WOULD IT?
DING DING. ♪ EXACTLY!!
SORRY, BUT I'VE GOT A WORK MEETING NEXT SUNDAY ...
HEY, WHY DO YOU THINK I KEPT BUYING TICKETS UNTIL I WON THAT VOUCHER?
I FOUND OUT DAD BOUGHT A NECKLACE...
...FOR A CERTAIN SOMEBODY'S BIRTHDAY!!
TOO BAD YOU'RE TOO BUSY TO ACCEPT HIS ROMANTIC GESTURE ...
W-WAIT A MINUTE!!
DID YOU SAY SHIZUOKA? THAT'S WHERE THE CLIENT I'M SUPPOSED TO MEET ON SUNDAY LIVES!
PERFECT! SEE YOU AT THE SHIZUOKA SEASIDE HOTEL!
BUT MS. KADEN, ISN'T THE CLIENT SCHEDULED TO MEET YOU HERE AT THE OFFICE?
THIS WILL BE MORE CONVENIENT FOR HER. WE'LL JUST MOVE THINGS AROUND...

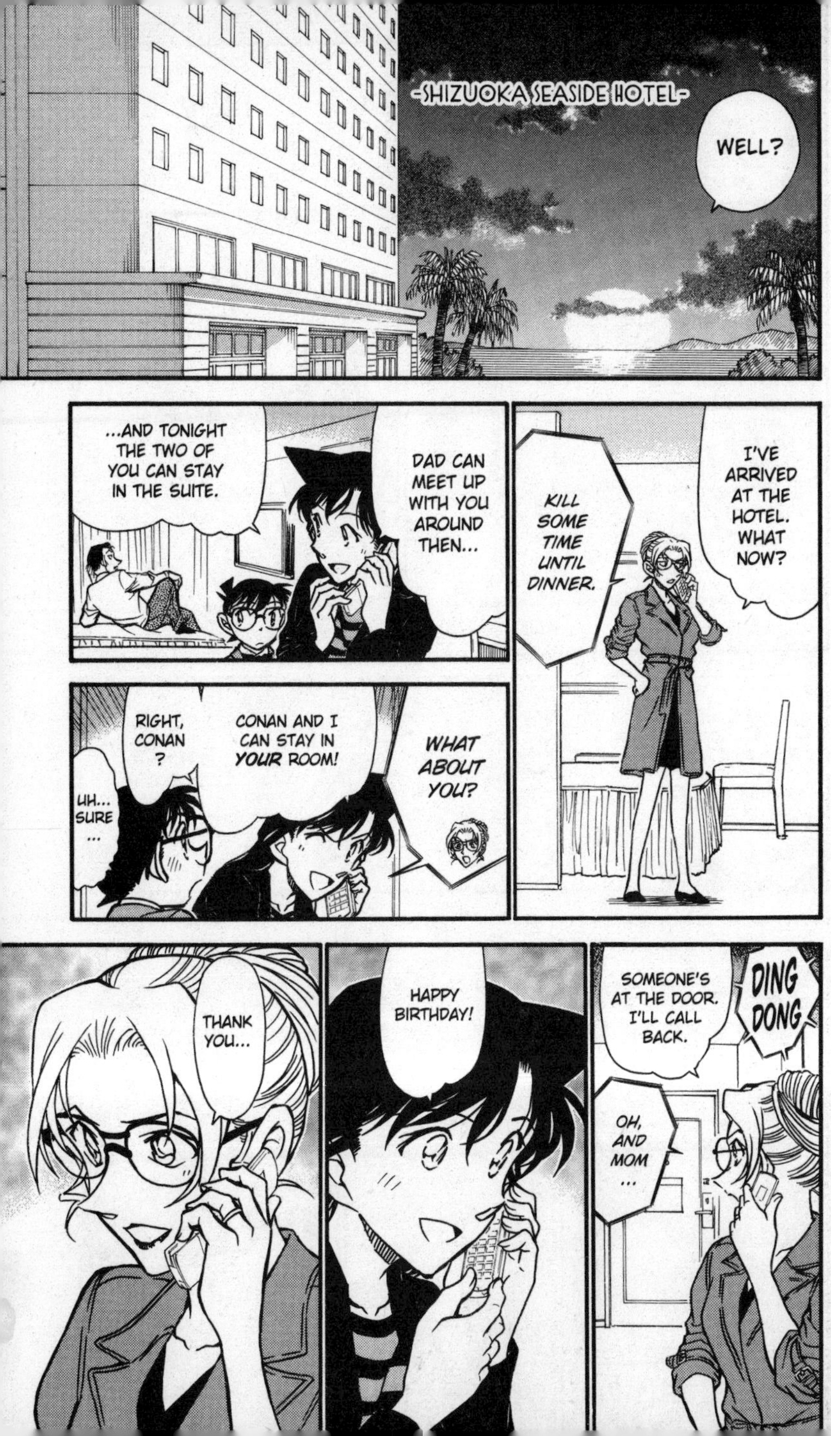
-SHIZUOKA SEASIDE HOTEL-
WELL?
I'VE ARRIVED AT THE HOTEL. WHAT NOW?
KILL SOME TIME UNTIL DINNER.
DAD CAN MEET UP WITH YOU AROUND THEN...
...AND TONIGHT THE TWO OF YOU CAN STAY IN THE SUITE.
WHAT ABOUT YOU?
CONAN AND I CAN STAY IN *YOUR* ROOM!
RIGHT, CONAN?
UH... SURE...
DING DONG
SOMEONE'S AT THE DOOR. I'LL CALL BACK.
OH, AND MOM...
HAPPY BIRTHDAY!
THANK YOU...

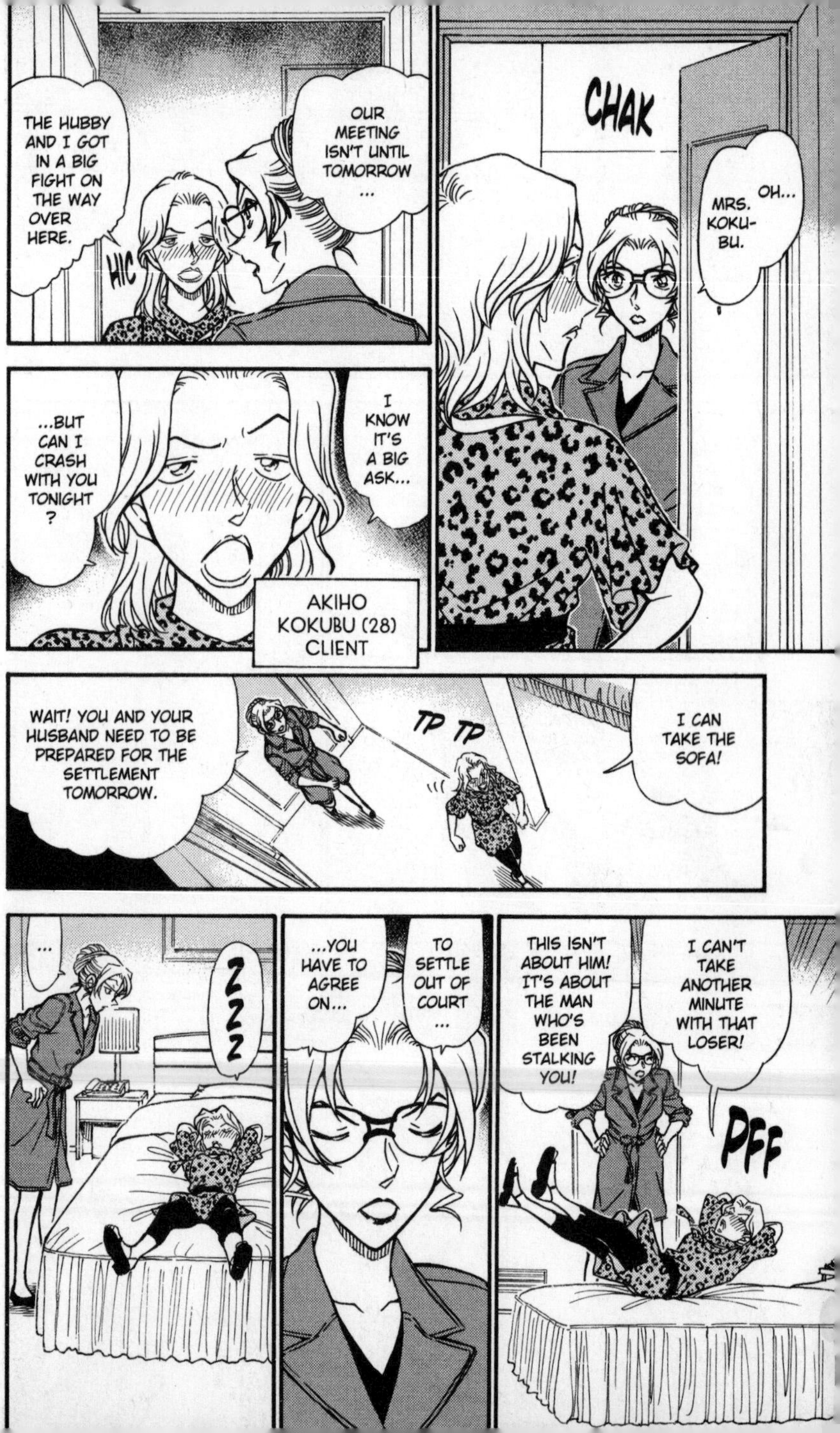
CHAK
OH... MRS. KOKUBU.
OUR MEETING ISN'T UNTIL TOMORROW...
THE HUBBY AND I GOT IN A BIG FIGHT ON THE WAY OVER HERE.
HIC
I KNOW IT'S A BIG ASK...
...BUT CAN I CRASH WITH YOU TONIGHT?
AKIHO KOKUBU (28) CLIENT
I CAN TAKE THE SOFA!
TP TP
WAIT! YOU AND YOUR HUSBAND NEED TO BE PREPARED FOR THE SETTLEMENT TOMORROW.
I CAN'T TAKE ANOTHER MINUTE WITH THAT LOSER!
PFF
THIS ISN'T ABOUT HIM! IT'S ABOUT THE MAN WHO'S BEEN STALKING YOU!
TO SETTLE OUT OF COURT...
...YOU HAVE TO AGREE ON...
ZZZ
...

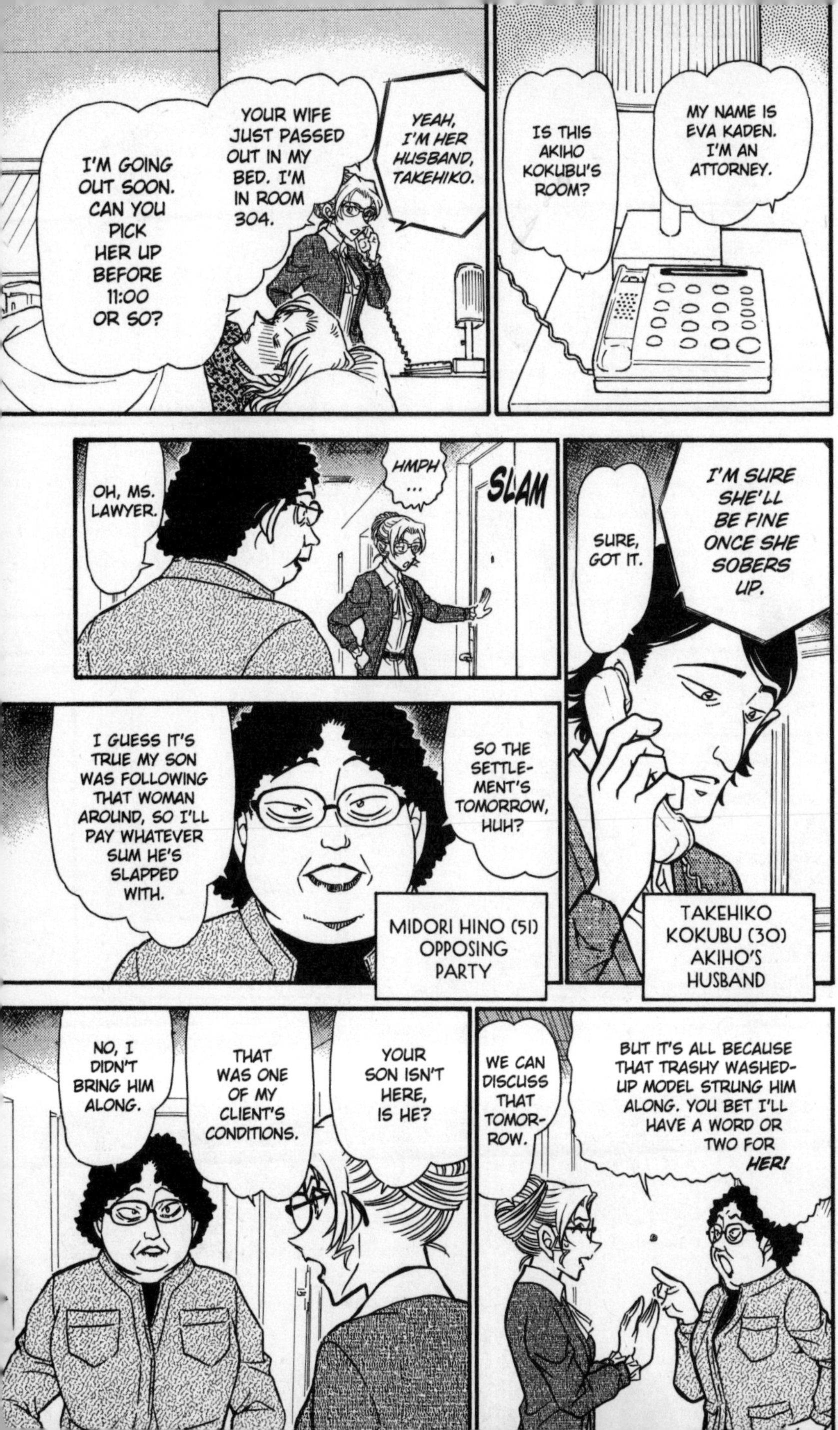
MY NAME IS EVA KADEN. I'M AN ATTORNEY.
IS THIS AKIHO KOKUBU'S ROOM?
YEAH, I'M HER HUSBAND, TAKEHIKO.
YOUR WIFE JUST PASSED OUT IN MY BED. I'M IN ROOM 304.
I'M GOING OUT SOON. CAN YOU PICK HER UP BEFORE 11:00 OR SO?
I'M SURE SHE'LL BE FINE ONCE SHE SOBERS UP.
SURE, GOT IT.
TAKEHIKO KOKUBU (30) AKIHO'S HUSBAND
SLAM
HMPH ...
OH, MS. LAWYER.
SO THE SETTLEMENT'S TOMORROW, HUH?
I GUESS IT'S TRUE MY SON WAS FOLLOWING THAT WOMAN AROUND, SO I'LL PAY WHATEVER SUM HE'S SLAPPED WITH.
MIDORI HINO (51) OPPOSING PARTY
BUT IT'S ALL BECAUSE THAT TRASHY WASHED-UP MODEL STRUNG HIM ALONG. YOU BET I'LL HAVE A WORD OR TWO FOR HER!
WE CAN DISCUSS THAT TOMORROW.
YOUR SON ISN'T HERE, IS HE?
THAT WAS ONE OF MY CLIENT'S CONDITIONS.
NO, I DIDN'T BRING HIM ALONG.

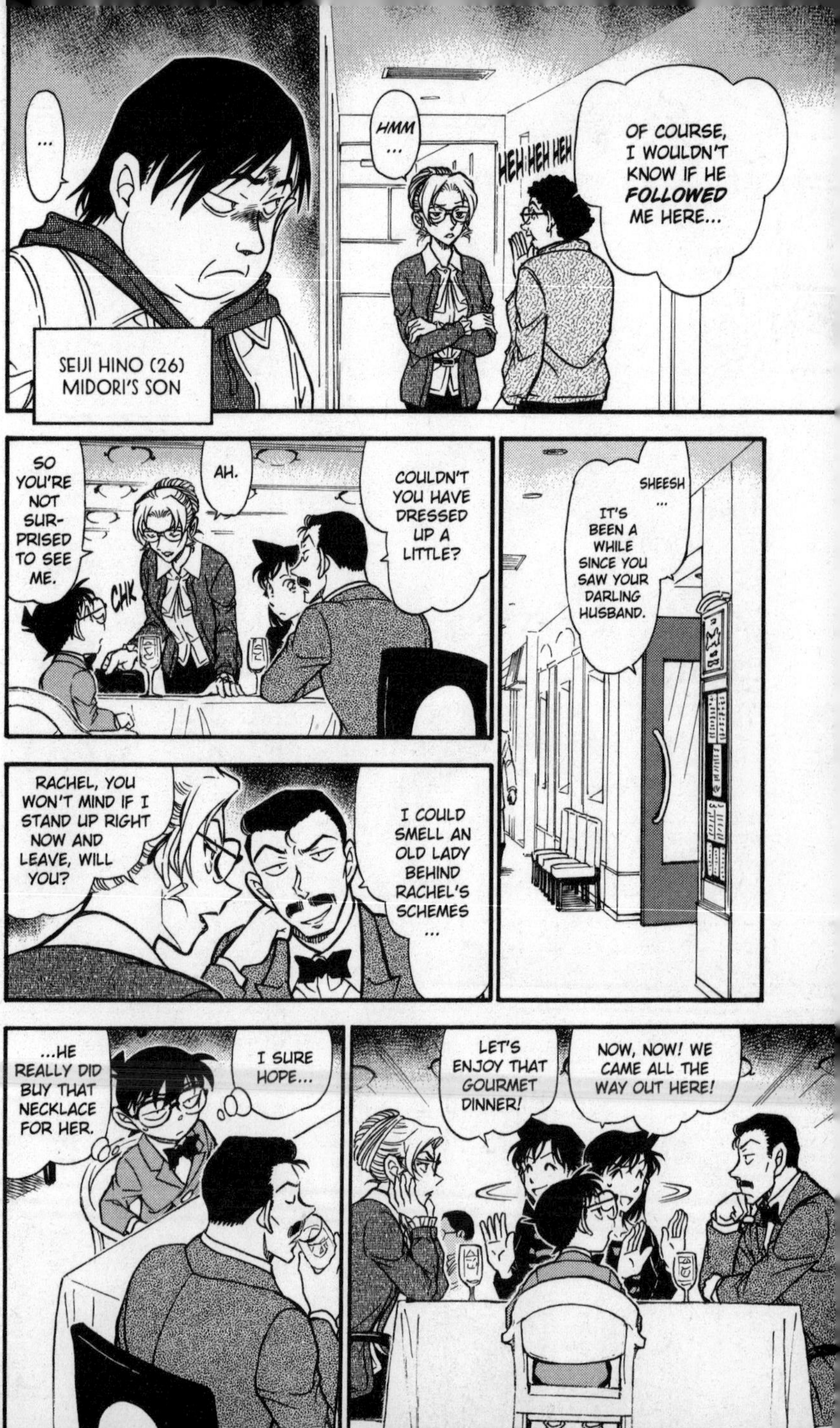
OF COURSE, I WOULDN'T KNOW IF HE FOLLOWED ME HERE...
HEH HEH HEH
HMM ...
...
SEIJI HINO (26) MIDORI'S SON
SHEESH ...
IT'S BEEN A WHILE SINCE YOU SAW YOUR DARLING HUSBAND.
COULDN'T YOU HAVE DRESSED UP A LITTLE?
AH.
SO YOU'RE NOT SUR-PRISED TO SEE ME.
CHK
I COULD SMELL AN OLD LADY BEHIND RACHEL'S SCHEMES ...
RACHEL, YOU WON'T MIND IF I STAND UP RIGHT NOW AND LEAVE, WILL YOU?
NOW, NOW! WE CAME ALL THE WAY OUT HERE!
LET'S ENJOY THAT GOURMET DINNER!
I SURE HOPE...
...HE REALLY DID BUY THAT NECKLACE FOR HER.

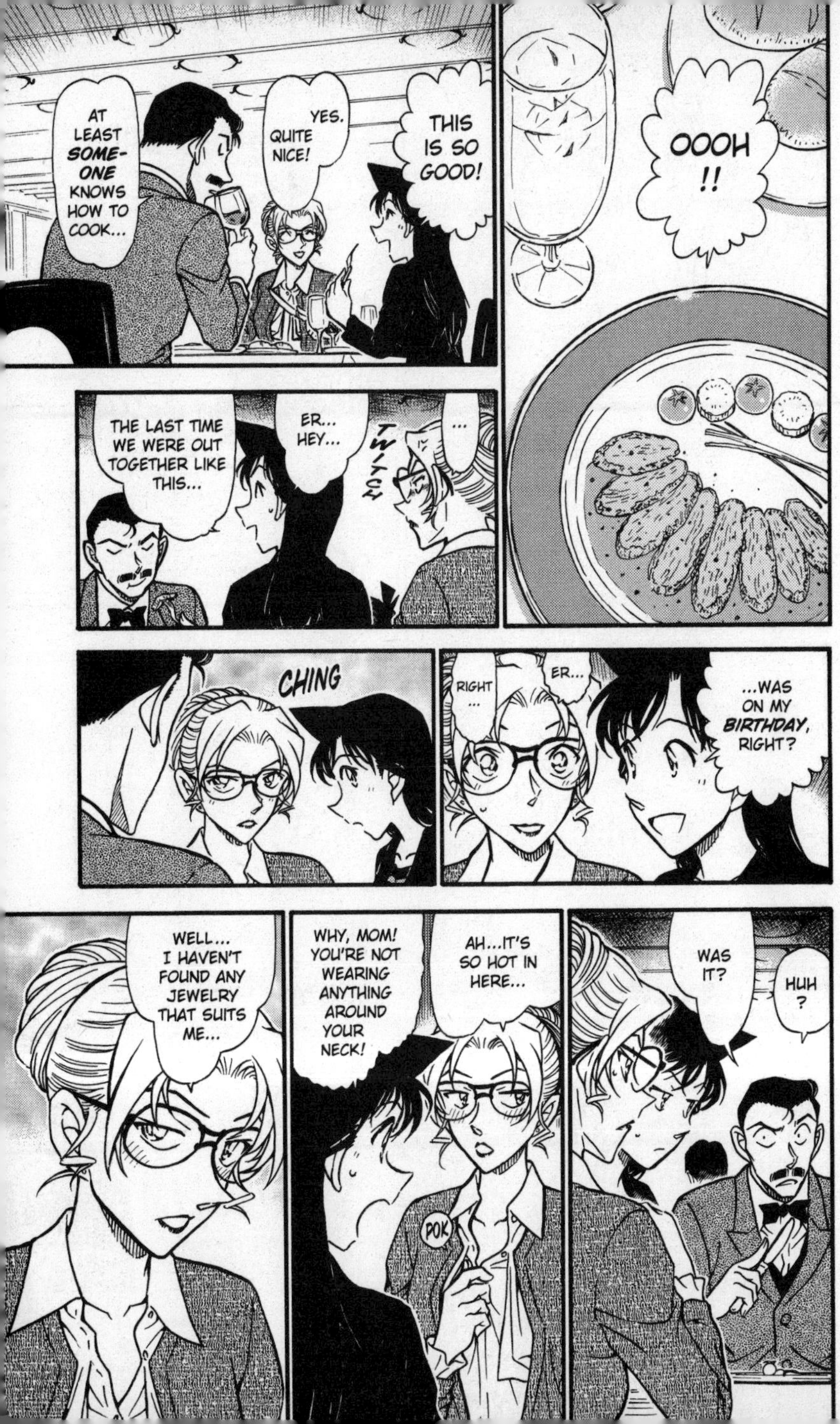
OOOH !!
THIS IS SO GOOD!
YES. QUITE NICE!
AT LEAST SOMEONE KNOWS HOW TO COOK...
...
TWITCH
ER... HEY...
THE LAST TIME WE WERE OUT TOGETHER LIKE THIS...
...WAS ON MY BIRTHDAY, RIGHT?
ER...
RIGHT ...
CHING
HUH ?
WAS IT?
AH...IT'S SO HOT IN HERE...
POK
WHY, MOM! YOU'RE NOT WEARING ANYTHING AROUND YOUR NECK!
WELL... I HAVEN'T FOUND ANY JEWELRY THAT SUITS ME...

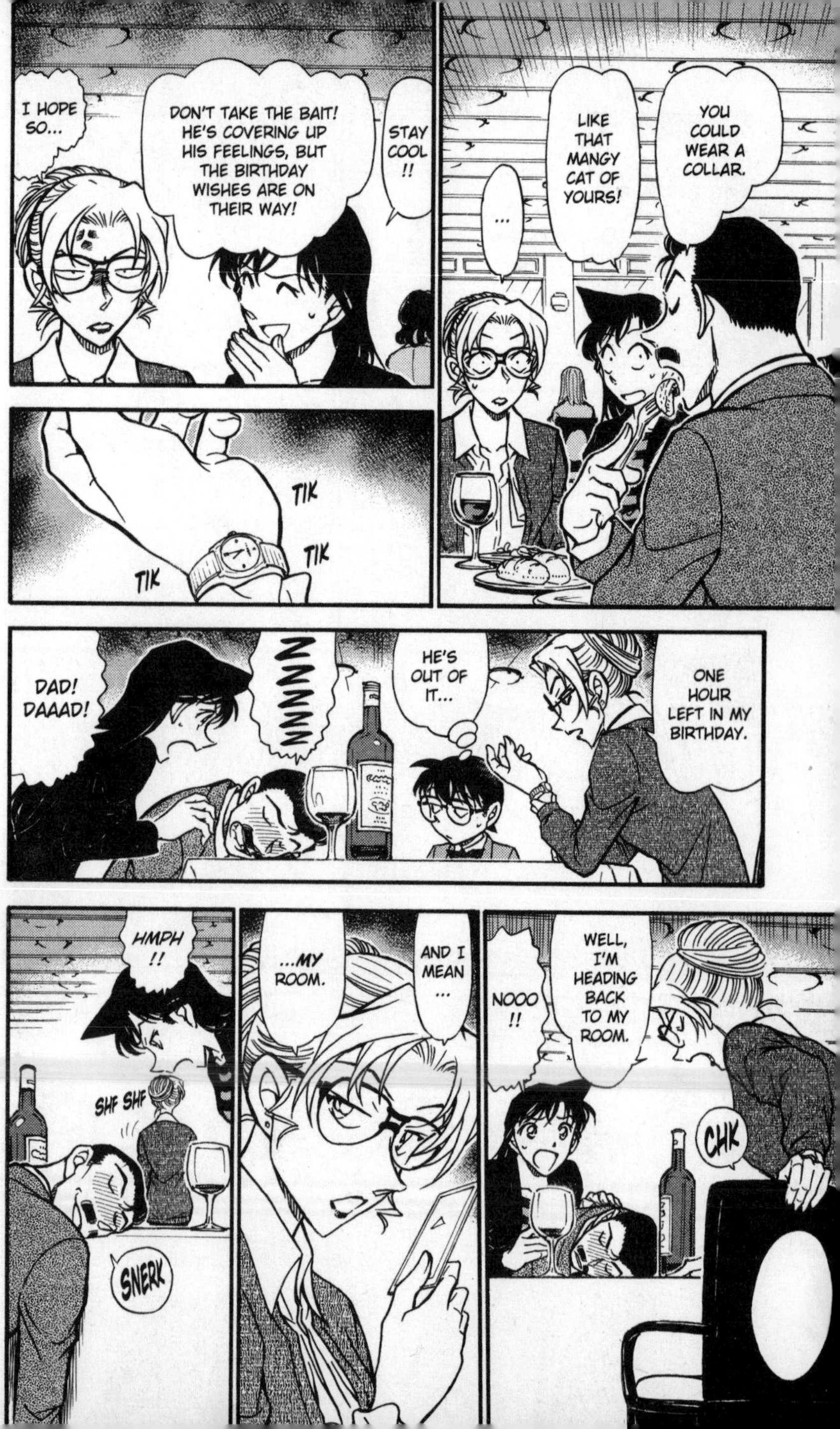
YOU COULD WEAR A COLLAR.
LIKE THAT MANGY CAT OF YOURS!
...
STAY COOL!!
DON'T TAKE THE BAIT! HE'S COVERING UP HIS FEELINGS, BUT THE BIRTHDAY WISHES ARE ON THEIR WAY!
I HOPE SO...
TIK
TIK
TIK
ONE HOUR LEFT IN MY BIRTHDAY.
HE'S OUT OF IT...
DAD! DAAAD!
WELL, I'M HEADING BACK TO MY ROOM.
NOOO!!
CHK
AND I MEAN...
...MY ROOM.
HMPH!!
SHF SHF
SNERK

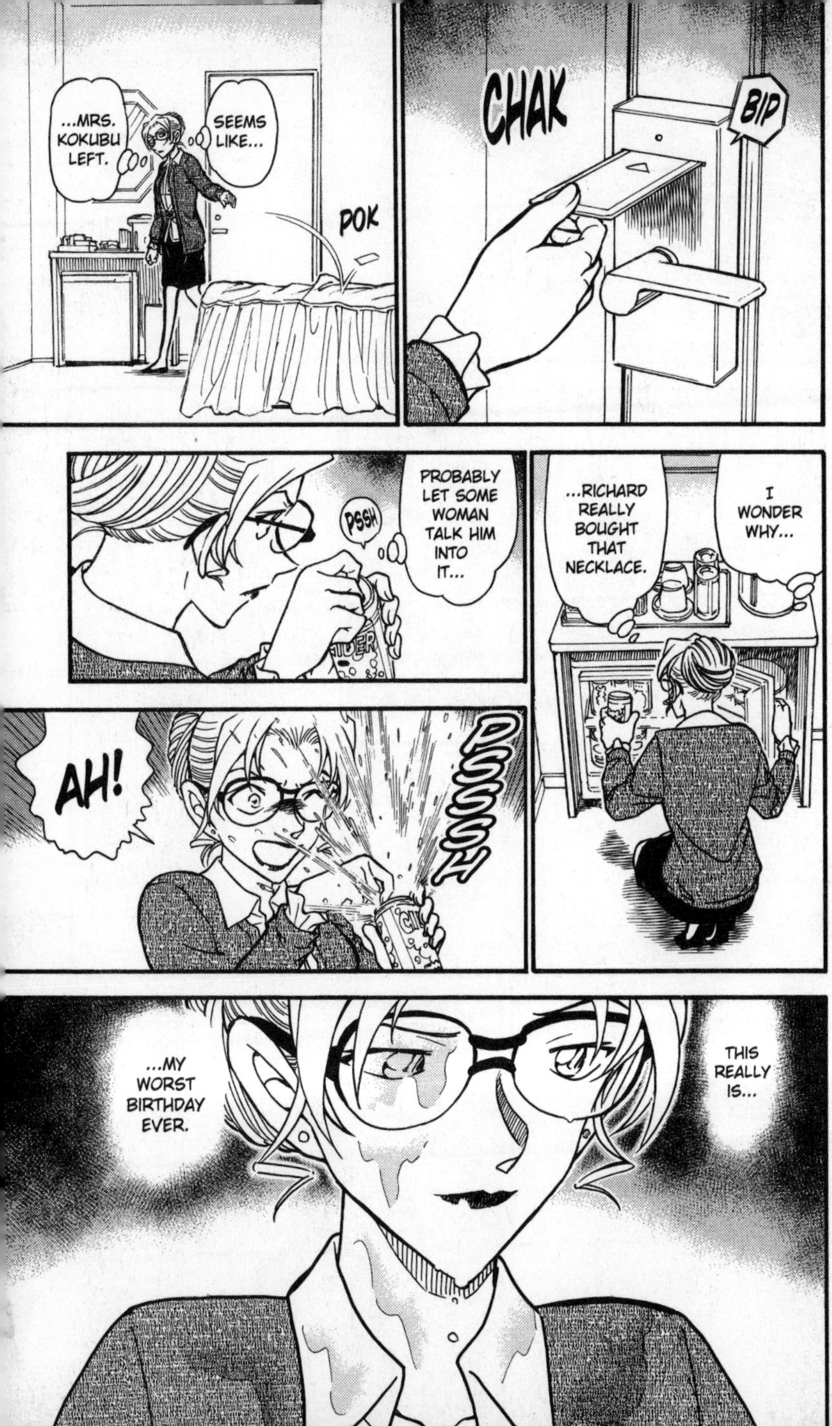
BIP
CHAK
SEEMS LIKE...
...MRS. KOKUBU LEFT.
POK
I WONDER WHY...
...RICHARD REALLY BOUGHT THAT NECKLACE.
PROBABLY LET SOME WOMAN TALK HIM INTO IT...
PSSH
PSSSH
AH!
THIS REALLY IS...
...MY WORST BIRTHDAY EVER.

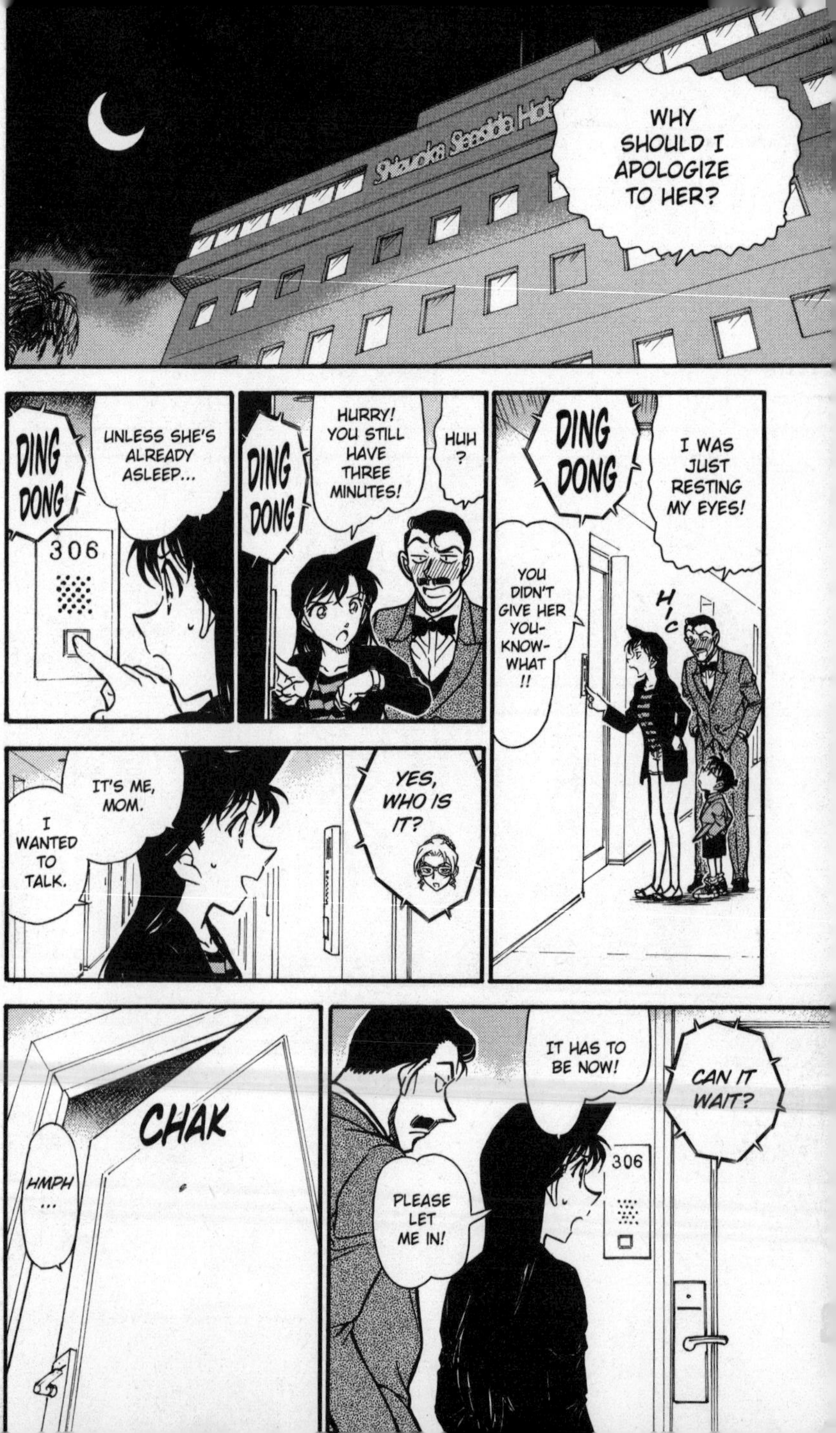
WHY SHOULD I APOLOGIZE TO HER?
I WAS JUST RESTING MY EYES!
DING DONG
HIC
YOU DIDN'T GIVE HER YOU-KNOW-WHAT!!
HUH?
HURRY! YOU STILL HAVE THREE MINUTES!
DING DONG
UNLESS SHE'S ALREADY ASLEEP...
DING DONG
306
YES, WHO IS IT?
IT'S ME, MOM.
I WANTED TO TALK.
CAN IT WAIT?
IT HAS TO BE NOW!
306
PLEASE LET ME IN!
CHAK
HMPH...

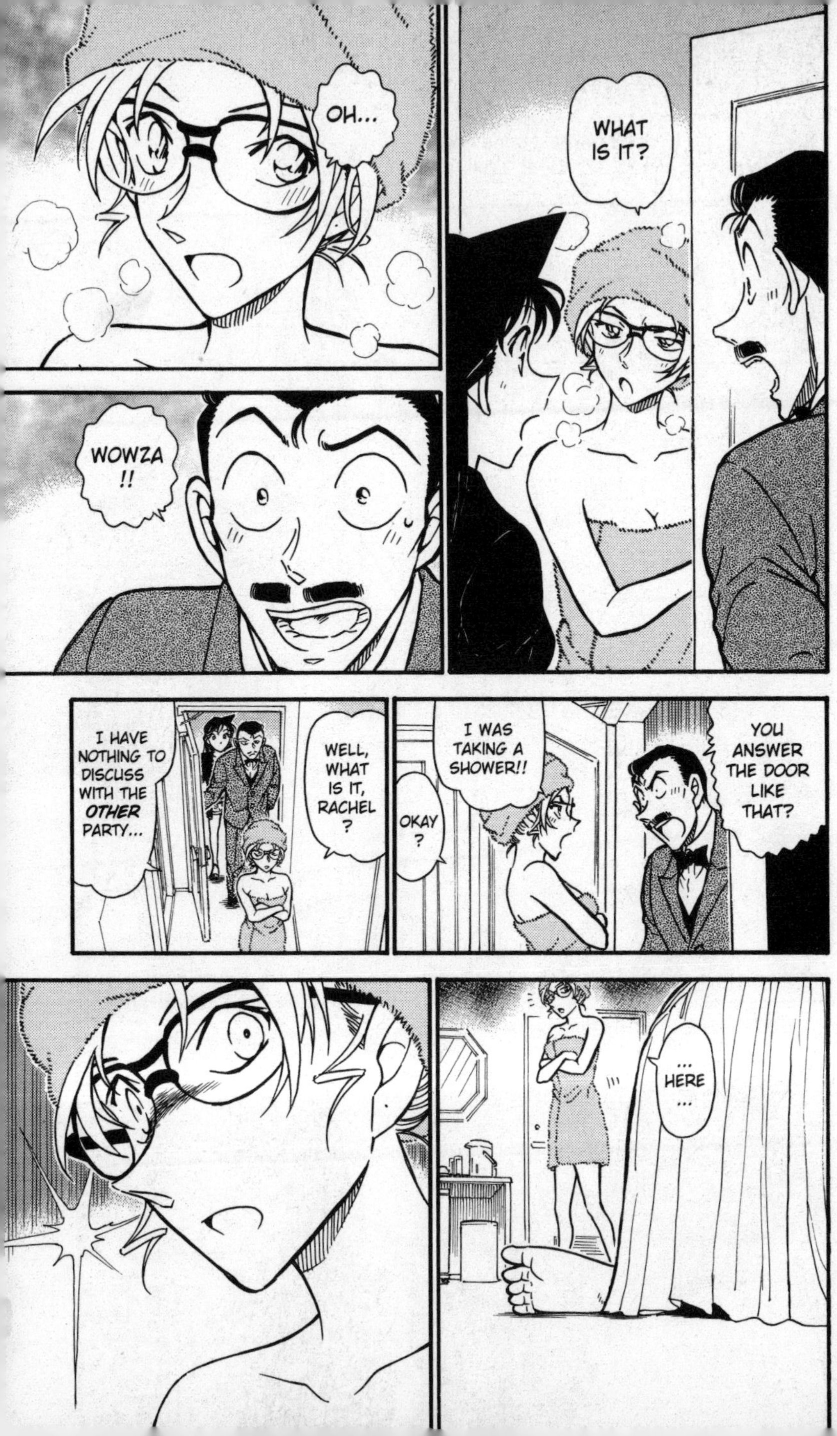
WHAT IS IT?
OH...
WOWZA !!
YOU ANSWER THE DOOR LIKE THAT?
I WAS TAKING A SHOWER!!
OKAY ?
WELL, WHAT IS IT, RACHEL ?
I HAVE NOTHING TO DISCUSS WITH THE *OTHER* PARTY...
... HERE ...

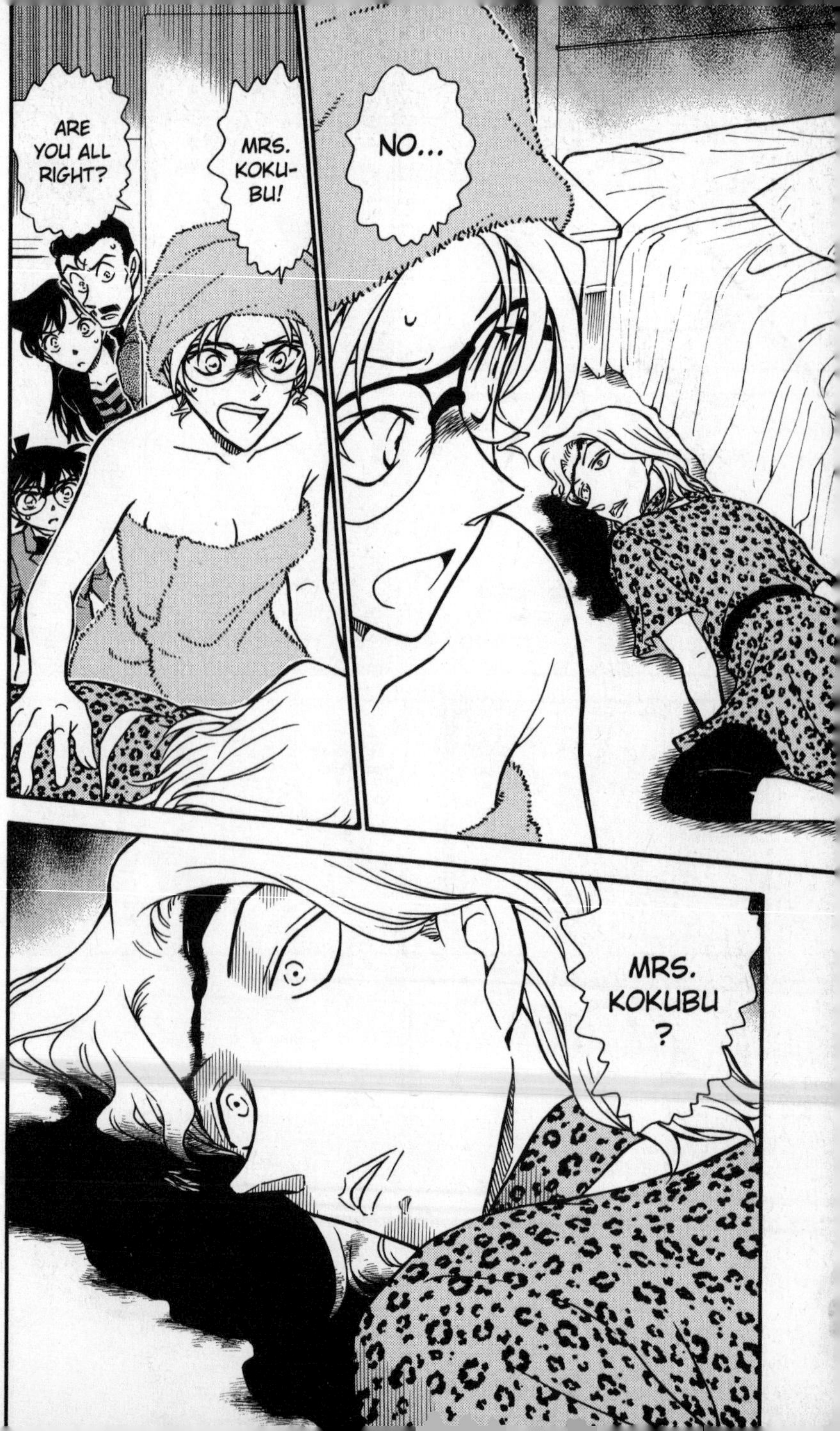
NO...
MRS. KOKU-BU!
ARE YOU ALL RIGHT?
MRS. KOKUBU ?

FILE 3: HIGH HOPES AND DISAPPOINTMENTS

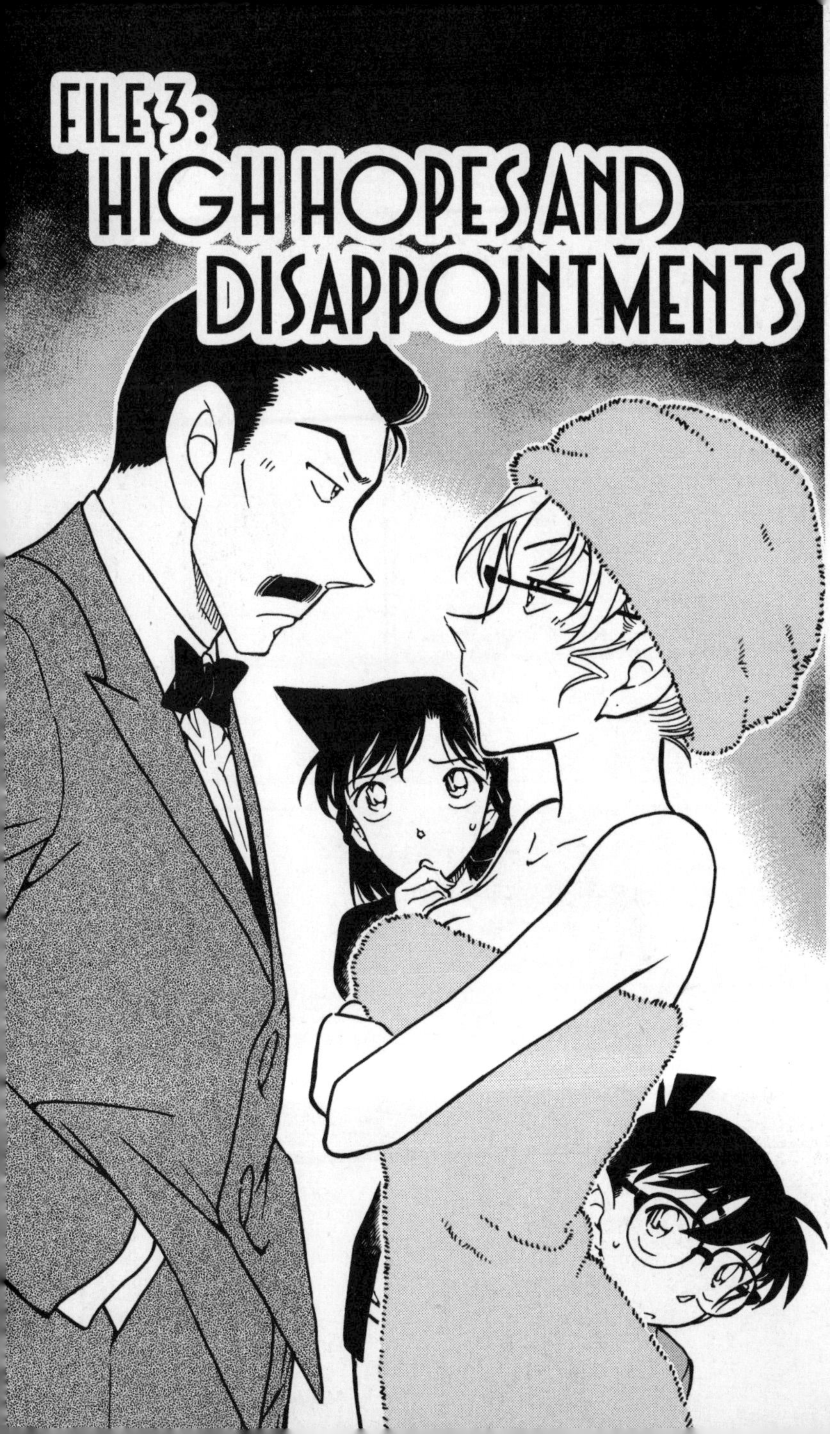

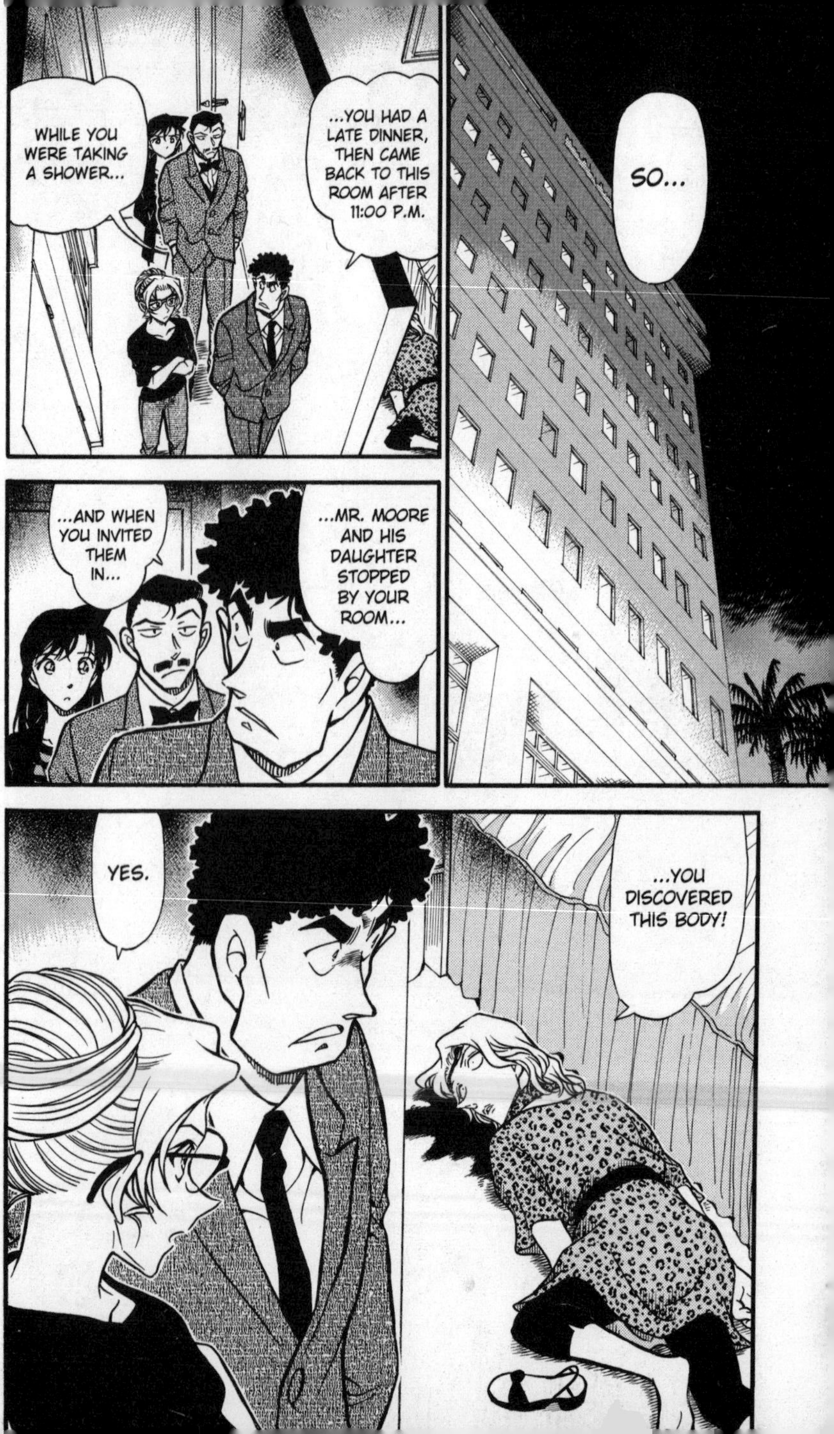
SO...
...YOU HAD A LATE DINNER, THEN CAME BACK TO THIS ROOM AFTER 11:00 P.M.
WHILE YOU WERE TAKING A SHOWER...
...MR. MOORE AND HIS DAUGHTER STOPPED BY YOUR ROOM...
...AND WHEN YOU INVITED THEM IN...
...YOU DISCOVERED THIS BODY!
YES.

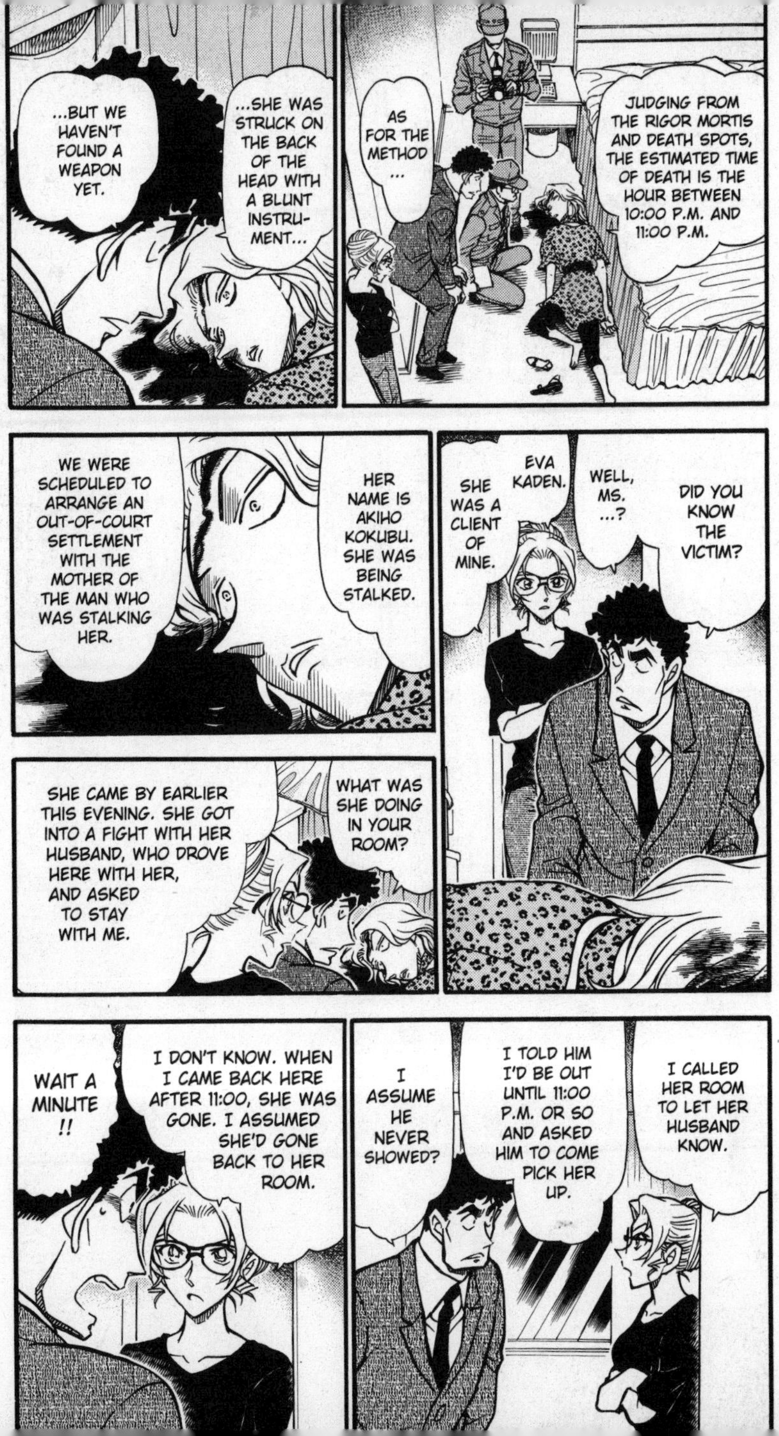
JUDGING FROM THE RIGOR MORTIS AND DEATH SPOTS, THE ESTIMATED TIME OF DEATH IS THE HOUR BETWEEN 10:00 P.M. AND 11:00 P.M.
AS FOR THE METHOD...
...SHE WAS STRUCK ON THE BACK OF THE HEAD WITH A BLUNT INSTRU-MENT...
...BUT WE HAVEN'T FOUND A WEAPON YET.
DID YOU KNOW THE VICTIM?
WELL, MS. ...?
EVA KADEN.
SHE WAS A CLIENT OF MINE.
HER NAME IS AKIHO KOKUBU. SHE WAS BEING STALKED.
WE WERE SCHEDULED TO ARRANGE AN OUT-OF-COURT SETTLEMENT WITH THE MOTHER OF THE MAN WHO WAS STALKING HER.
WHAT WAS SHE DOING IN YOUR ROOM?
SHE CAME BY EARLIER THIS EVENING. SHE GOT INTO A FIGHT WITH HER HUSBAND, WHO DROVE HERE WITH HER, AND ASKED TO STAY WITH ME.
I CALLED HER ROOM TO LET HER HUSBAND KNOW.
I TOLD HIM I'D BE OUT UNTIL 11:00 P.M. OR SO AND ASKED HIM TO COME PICK HER UP.
I ASSUME HE NEVER SHOWED?
I DON'T KNOW. WHEN I CAME BACK HERE AFTER 11:00, SHE WAS GONE. I ASSUMED SHE'D GONE BACK TO HER ROOM.
WAIT A MINUTE!!

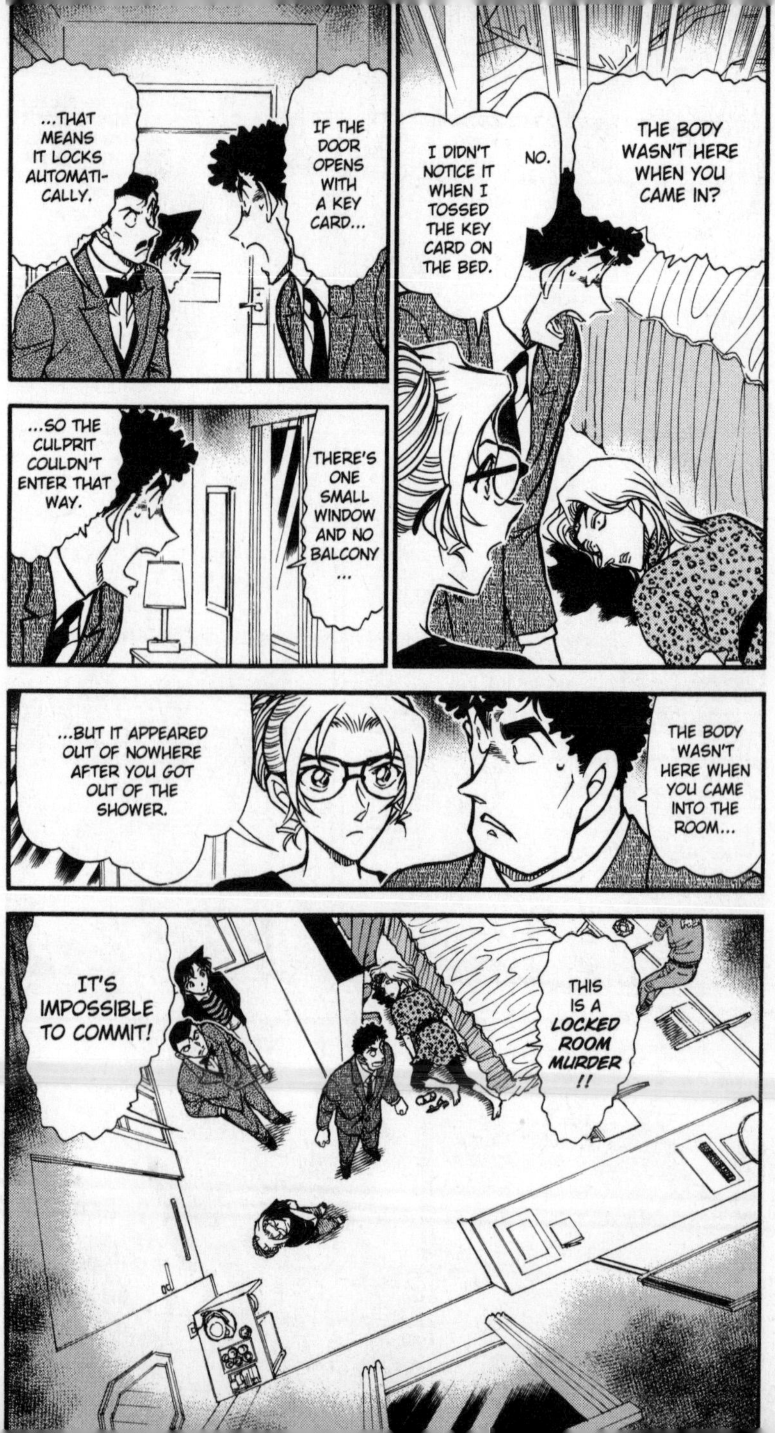
THE BODY WASN'T HERE WHEN YOU CAME IN?
NO.
I DIDN'T NOTICE IT WHEN I TOSSED THE KEY CARD ON THE BED.
IF THE DOOR OPENS WITH A KEY CARD...
...THAT MEANS IT LOCKS AUTOMATICALLY.
THERE'S ONE SMALL WINDOW AND NO BALCONY...
...SO THE CULPRIT COULDN'T ENTER THAT WAY.
THE BODY WASN'T HERE WHEN YOU CAME INTO THE ROOM...
...BUT IT APPEARED OUT OF NOWHERE AFTER YOU GOT OUT OF THE SHOWER.
THIS IS A *LOCKED ROOM MURDER* !!
IT'S IMPOSSIBLE TO COMMIT!

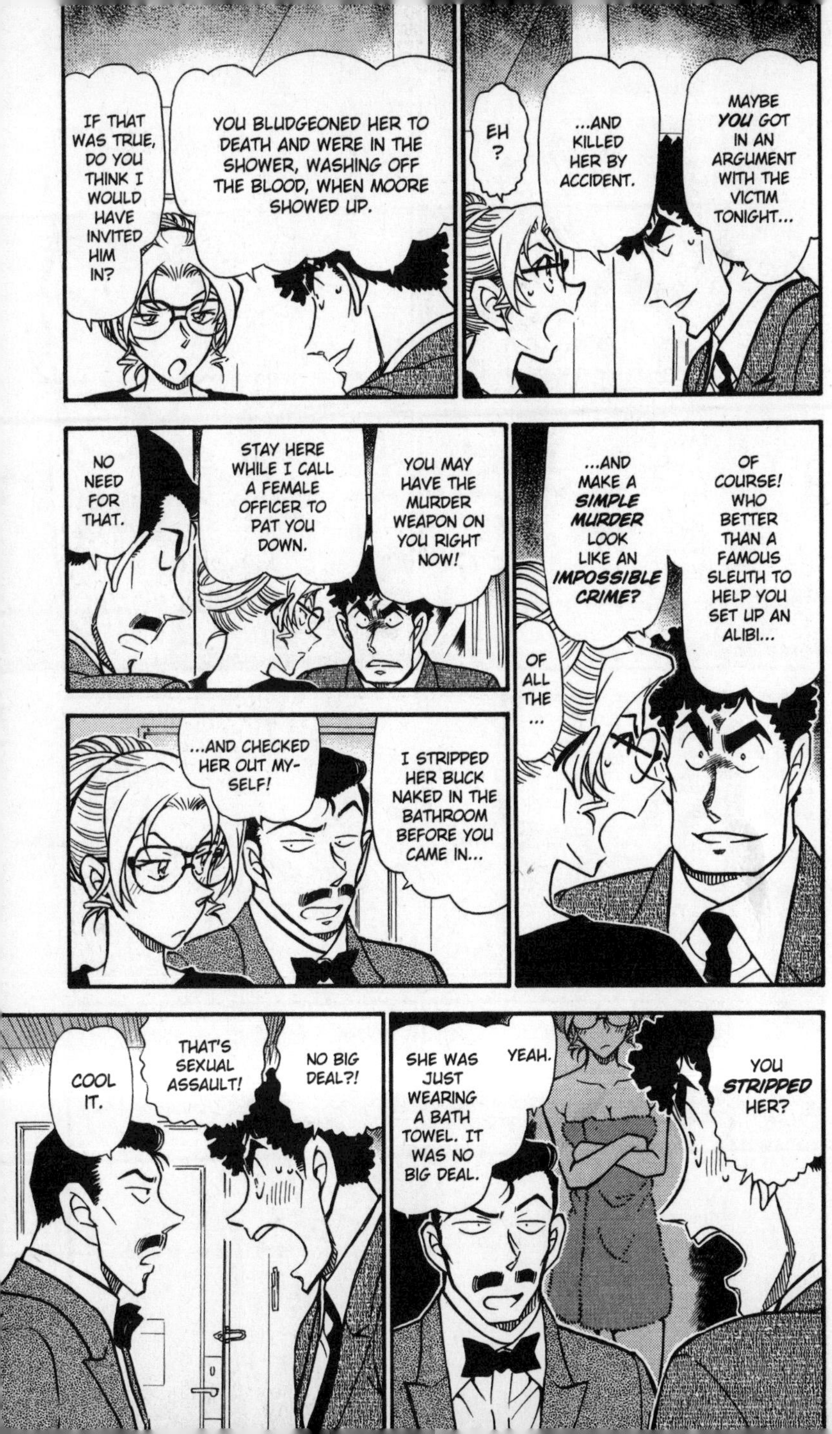
MAYBE *YOU* GOT IN AN ARGUMENT WITH THE VICTIM TONIGHT...
...AND KILLED HER BY ACCIDENT.
EH?
YOU BLUDGEONED HER TO DEATH AND WERE IN THE SHOWER, WASHING OFF THE BLOOD, WHEN MOORE SHOWED UP.
IF THAT WAS TRUE, DO YOU THINK I WOULD HAVE INVITED HIM IN?
OF COURSE! WHO BETTER THAN A FAMOUS SLEUTH TO HELP YOU SET UP AN ALIBI...
...AND MAKE A *SIMPLE MURDER* LOOK LIKE AN *IMPOSSIBLE CRIME?*
OF ALL THE...
YOU MAY HAVE THE MURDER WEAPON ON YOU RIGHT NOW!
STAY HERE WHILE I CALL A FEMALE OFFICER TO PAT YOU DOWN.
NO NEED FOR THAT.
I STRIPPED HER BUCK NAKED IN THE BATHROOM BEFORE YOU CAME IN...
...AND CHECKED HER OUT MY-SELF!
YOU *STRIPPED* HER?
YEAH.
SHE WAS JUST WEARING A BATH TOWEL. IT WAS NO BIG DEAL.
NO BIG DEAL?!
THAT'S SEXUAL ASSAULT!
COOL IT.

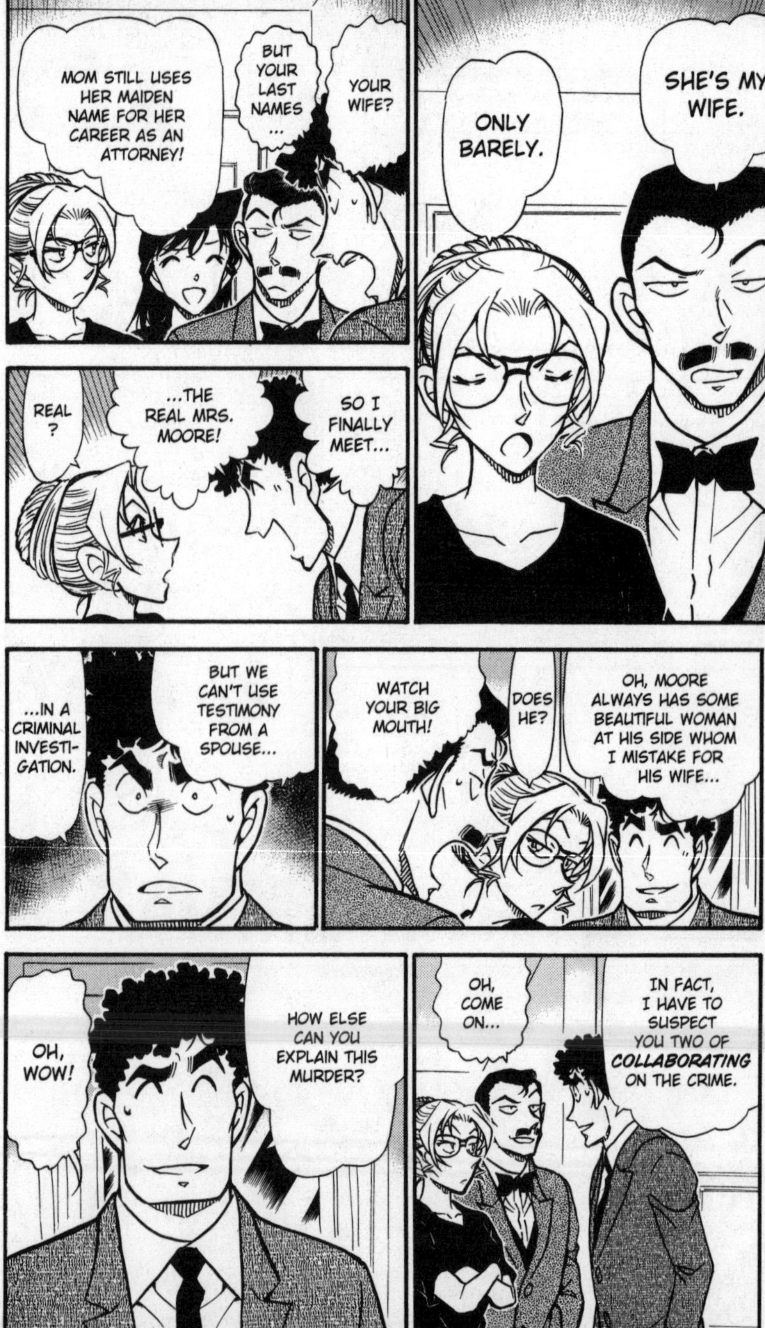
SHE'S MY WIFE.
ONLY BARELY.
YOUR WIFE?
BUT YOUR LAST NAMES ...
MOM STILL USES HER MAIDEN NAME FOR HER CAREER AS AN ATTORNEY!
SO I FINALLY MEET...
...THE REAL MRS. MOORE!
REAL ?
OH, MOORE ALWAYS HAS SOME BEAUTIFUL WOMAN AT HIS SIDE WHOM I MISTAKE FOR HIS WIFE...
DOES HE?
WATCH YOUR BIG MOUTH!
BUT WE CAN'T USE TESTIMONY FROM A SPOUSE...
...IN A CRIMINAL INVESTIGATION.
IN FACT, I HAVE TO SUSPECT YOU TWO OF *COLLABORATING* ON THE CRIME.
OH, COME ON...
HOW ELSE CAN YOU EXPLAIN THIS MURDER?
OH, WOW!

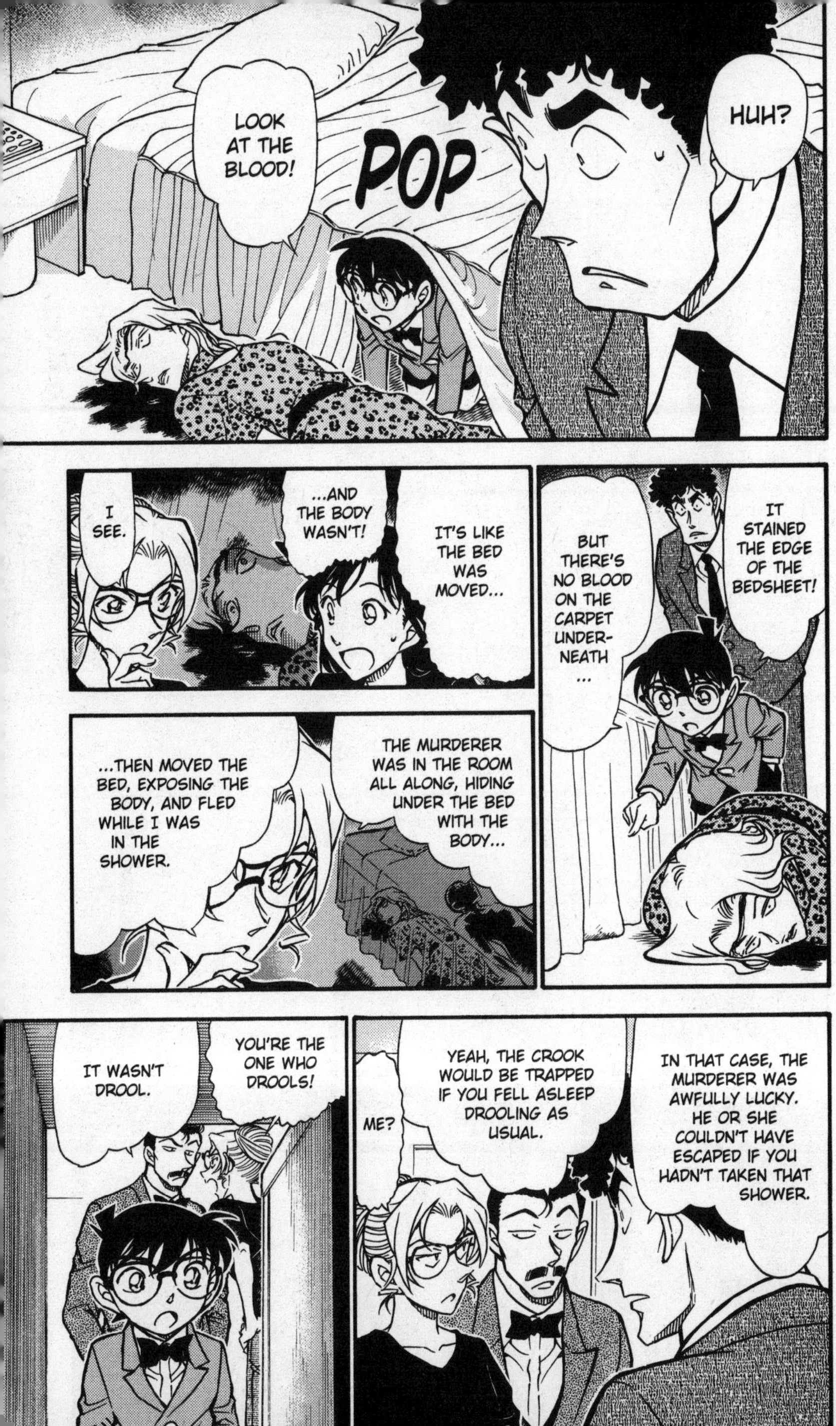
HUH?
POP
LOOK AT THE BLOOD!
IT STAINED THE EDGE OF THE BEDSHEET!
BUT THERE'S NO BLOOD ON THE CARPET UNDERNEATH...
IT'S LIKE THE BED WAS MOVED...
...AND THE BODY WASN'T!
I SEE.
THE MURDERER WAS IN THE ROOM ALL ALONG, HIDING UNDER THE BED WITH THE BODY...
...THEN MOVED THE BED, EXPOSING THE BODY, AND FLED WHILE I WAS IN THE SHOWER.
IN THAT CASE, THE MURDERER WAS AWFULLY LUCKY. HE OR SHE COULDN'T HAVE ESCAPED IF YOU HADN'T TAKEN THAT SHOWER.
YEAH, THE CROOK WOULD BE TRAPPED IF YOU FELL ASLEEP DROOLING AS USUAL.
ME?
YOU'RE THE ONE WHO DROOLS!
IT WASN'T DROOL.

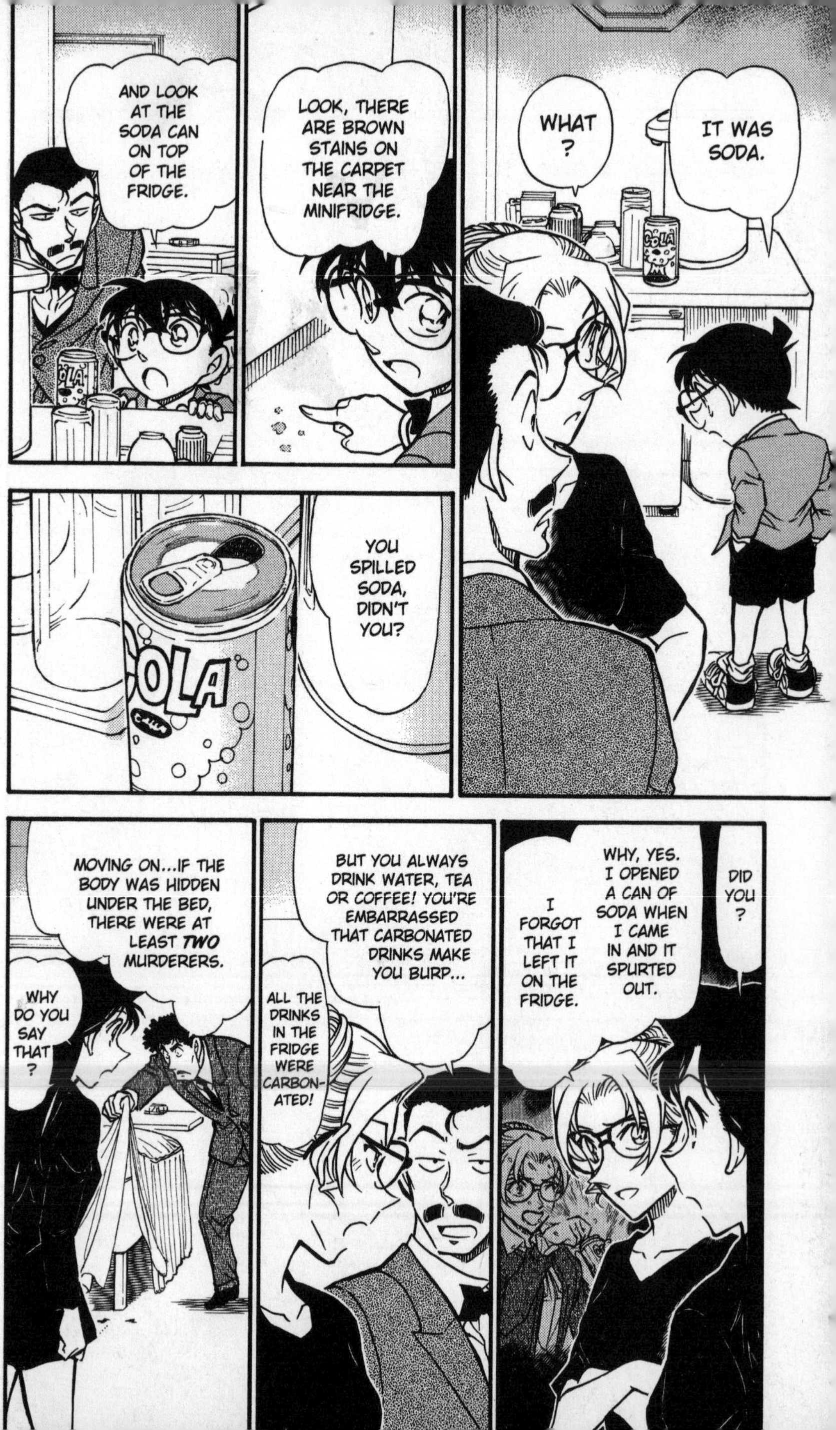
IT WAS SODA.
WHAT?
LOOK, THERE ARE BROWN STAINS ON THE CARPET NEAR THE MINIFRIDGE.
AND LOOK AT THE SODA CAN ON TOP OF THE FRIDGE.
YOU SPILLED SODA, DIDN'T YOU?
COLA
DID YOU?
WHY, YES. I OPENED A CAN OF SODA WHEN I CAME IN AND IT SPURTED OUT.
I FORGOT THAT I LEFT IT ON THE FRIDGE.
BUT YOU ALWAYS DRINK WATER, TEA OR COFFEE! YOU'RE EMBARRASSED THAT CARBONATED DRINKS MAKE YOU BURP...
ALL THE DRINKS IN THE FRIDGE WERE CARBONATED!
MOVING ON...IF THE BODY WAS HIDDEN UNDER THE BED, THERE WERE AT LEAST *TWO* MURDERERS.
WHY DO YOU SAY THAT?

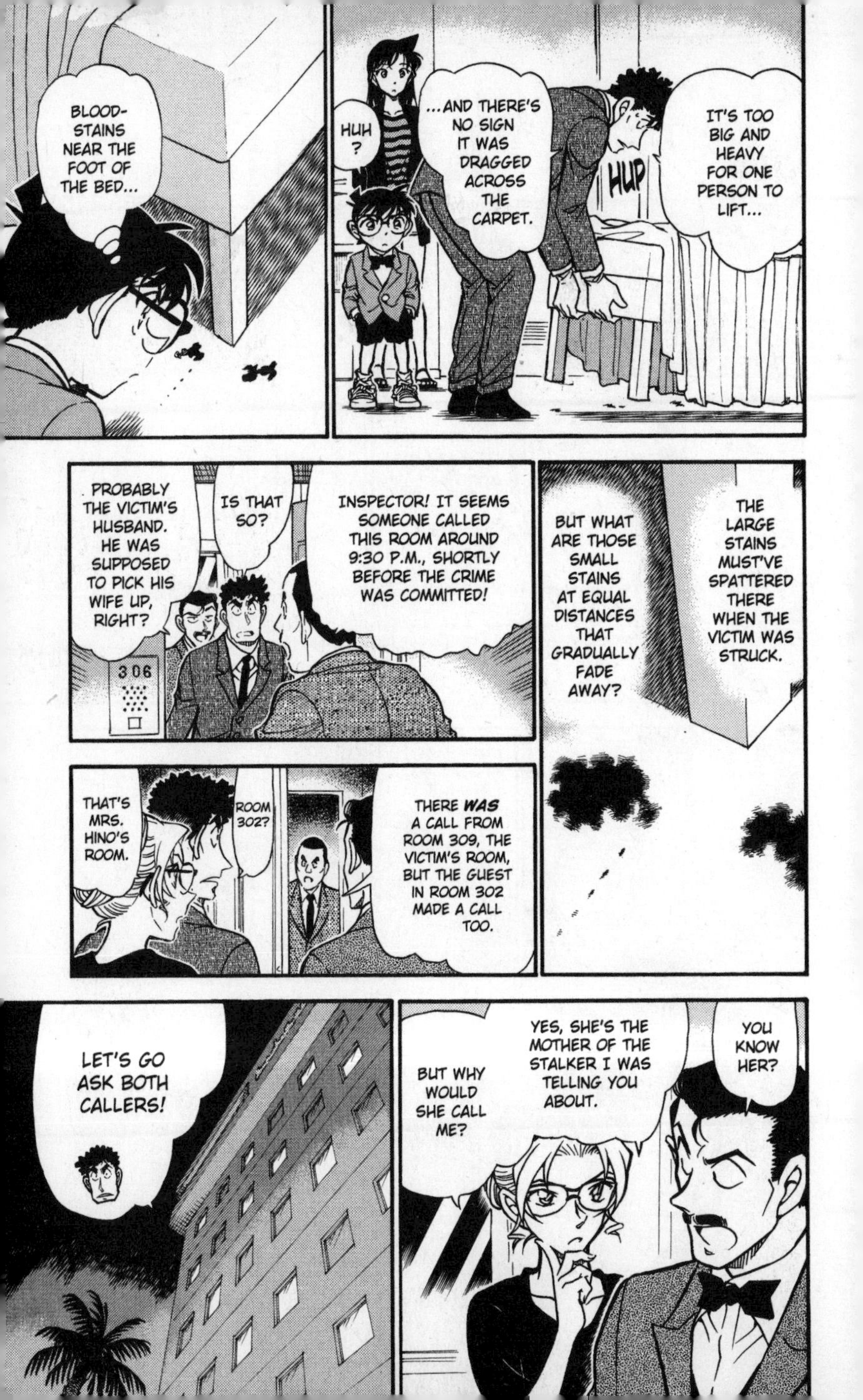
IT'S TOO BIG AND HEAVY FOR ONE PERSON TO LIFT...
HUP
...AND THERE'S NO SIGN IT WAS DRAGGED ACROSS THE CARPET.
HUH?
BLOOD-STAINS NEAR THE FOOT OF THE BED...
THE LARGE STAINS MUST'VE SPATTERED THERE WHEN THE VICTIM WAS STRUCK.
BUT WHAT ARE THOSE SMALL STAINS AT EQUAL DISTANCES THAT GRADUALLY FADE AWAY?
INSPECTOR! IT SEEMS SOMEONE CALLED THIS ROOM AROUND 9:30 P.M., SHORTLY BEFORE THE CRIME WAS COMMITTED!
IS THAT SO?
PROBABLY THE VICTIM'S HUSBAND. HE WAS SUPPOSED TO PICK HIS WIFE UP, RIGHT?
306
THERE *WAS* A CALL FROM ROOM 309, THE VICTIM'S ROOM, BUT THE GUEST IN ROOM 302 MADE A CALL TOO.
ROOM 302?
THAT'S MRS. HINO'S ROOM.
YOU KNOW HER?
YES, SHE'S THE MOTHER OF THE STALKER I WAS TELLING YOU ABOUT.
BUT WHY WOULD SHE CALL ME?
LET'S GO ASK BOTH CALLERS!

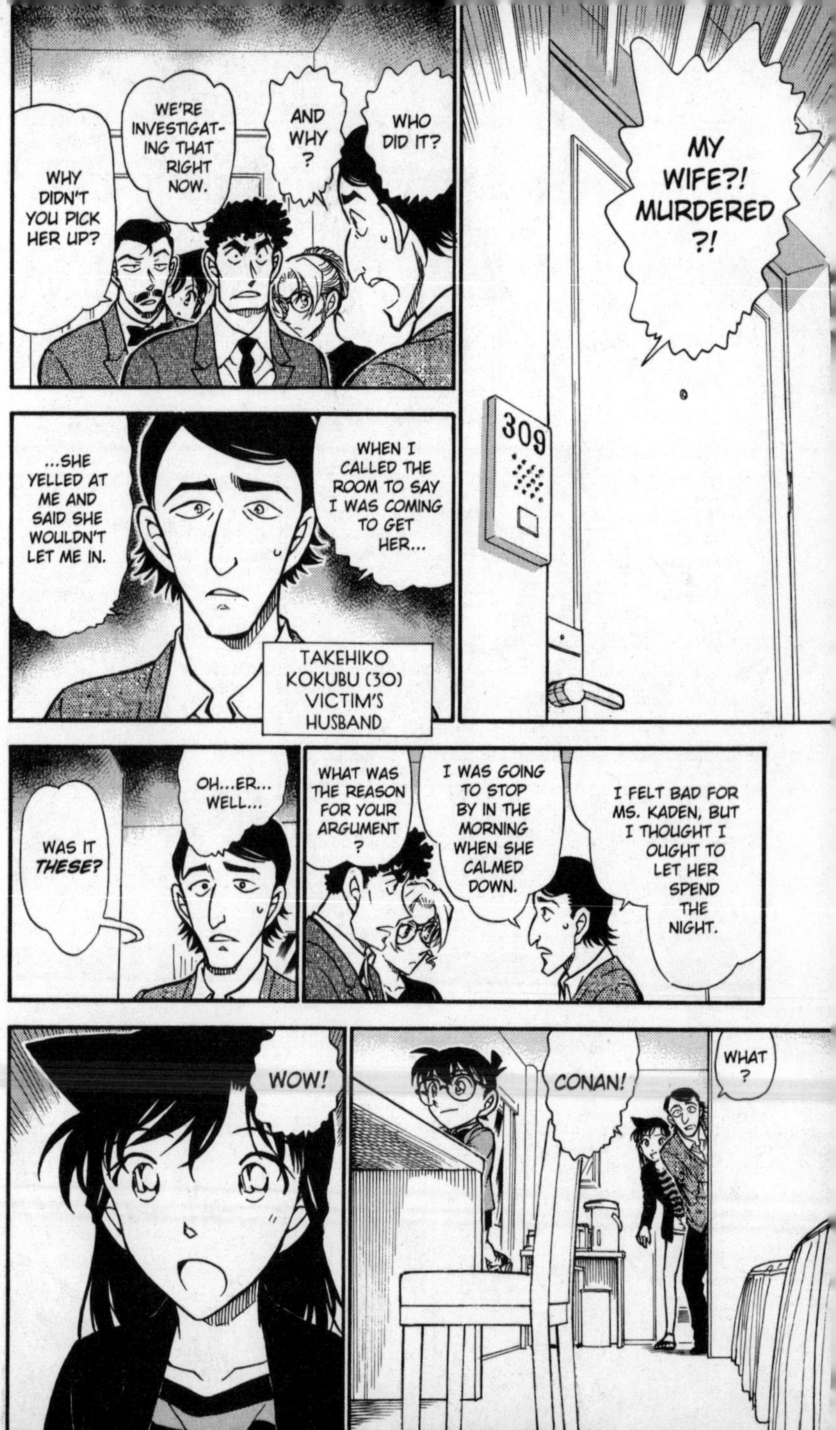
MY WIFE?! MURDERED ?!
309
WHO DID IT?
AND WHY ?
WE'RE INVESTIGATING THAT RIGHT NOW.
WHY DIDN'T YOU PICK HER UP?
WHEN I CALLED THE ROOM TO SAY I WAS COMING TO GET HER...
...SHE YELLED AT ME AND SAID SHE WOULDN'T LET ME IN.
TAKEHIKO KOKUBU (30) VICTIM'S HUSBAND
I FELT BAD FOR MS. KADEN, BUT I THOUGHT I OUGHT TO LET HER SPEND THE NIGHT.
I WAS GOING TO STOP BY IN THE MORNING WHEN SHE CALMED DOWN.
WHAT WAS THE REASON FOR YOUR ARGUMENT ?
OH...ER... WELL...
WAS IT *THESE?*
WHAT ?
CONAN!
WOW!

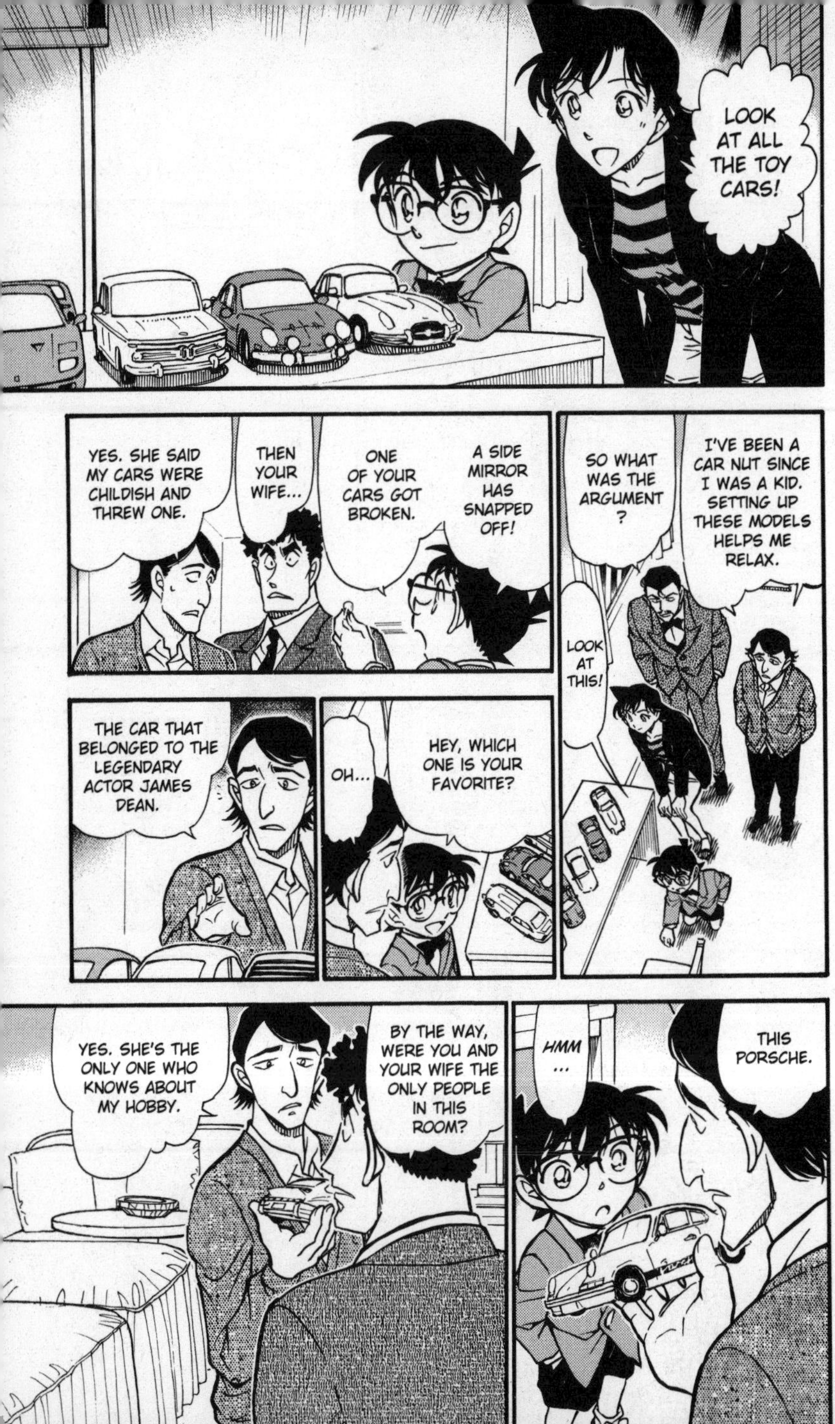
LOOK AT ALL THE TOY CARS!
I'VE BEEN A CAR NUT SINCE I WAS A KID. SETTING UP THESE MODELS HELPS ME RELAX.
SO WHAT WAS THE ARGUMENT?
LOOK AT THIS!
A SIDE MIRROR HAS SNAPPED OFF!
ONE OF YOUR CARS GOT BROKEN.
THEN YOUR WIFE...
YES. SHE SAID MY CARS WERE CHILDISH AND THREW ONE.
HEY, WHICH ONE IS YOUR FAVORITE?
OH...
THE CAR THAT BELONGED TO THE LEGENDARY ACTOR JAMES DEAN.
THIS PORSCHE.
HMM...
BY THE WAY, WERE YOU AND YOUR WIFE THE ONLY PEOPLE IN THIS ROOM?
YES. SHE'S THE ONLY ONE WHO KNOWS ABOUT MY HOBBY.

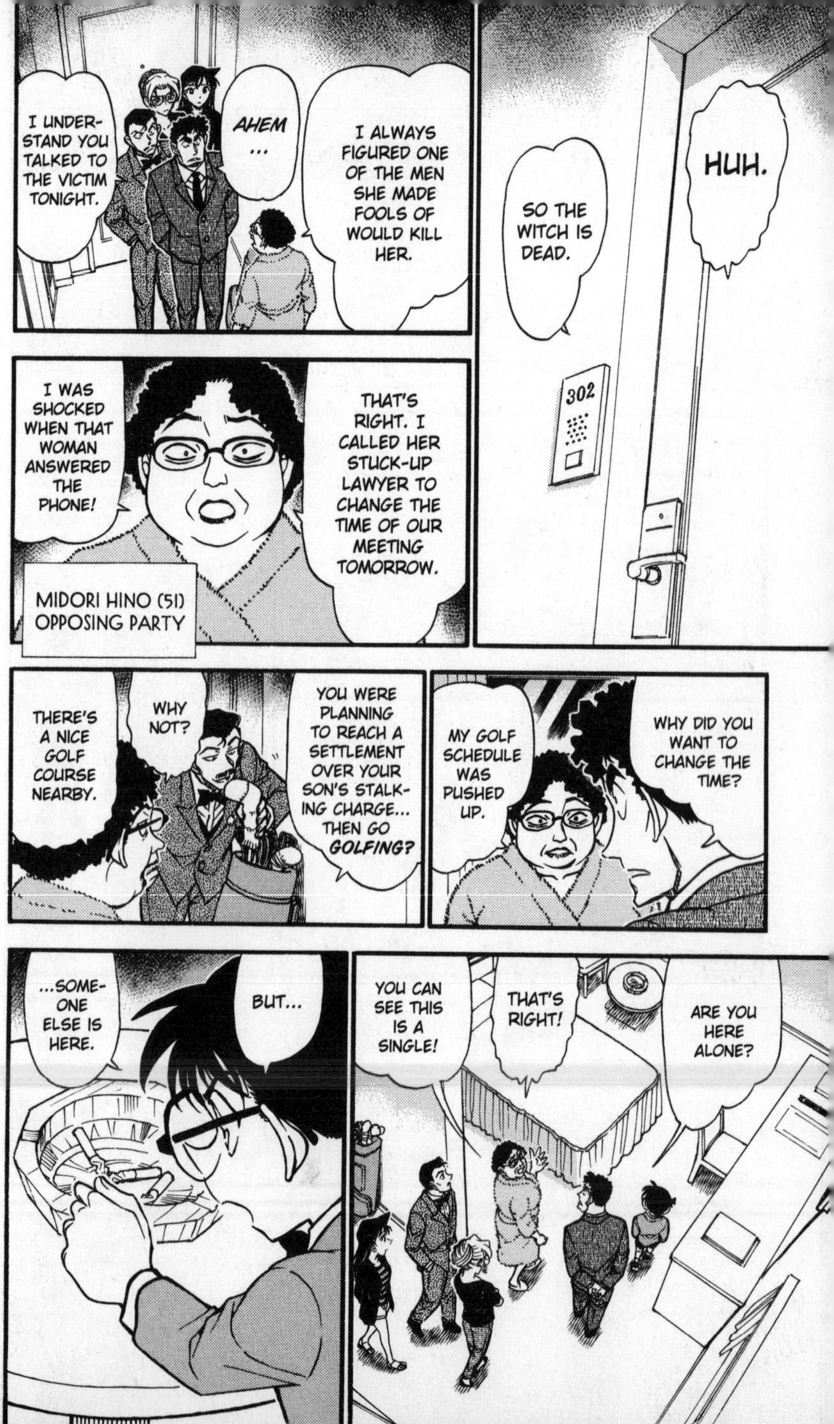
HUH.
SO THE WITCH IS DEAD.
302
I ALWAYS FIGURED ONE OF THE MEN SHE MADE FOOLS OF WOULD KILL HER.
AHEM ...
I UNDER-STAND YOU TALKED TO THE VICTIM TONIGHT.
THAT'S RIGHT. I CALLED HER STUCK-UP LAWYER TO CHANGE THE TIME OF OUR MEETING TOMORROW.
I WAS SHOCKED WHEN THAT WOMAN ANSWERED THE PHONE!
MIDORI HINO (51) OPPOSING PARTY
WHY DID YOU WANT TO CHANGE THE TIME?
MY GOLF SCHEDULE WAS PUSHED UP.
YOU WERE PLANNING TO REACH A SETTLEMENT OVER YOUR SON'S STALK-ING CHARGE... THEN GO GOLFING?
WHY NOT?
THERE'S A NICE GOLF COURSE NEARBY.
ARE YOU HERE ALONE?
THAT'S RIGHT!
YOU CAN SEE THIS IS A SINGLE!
BUT...
...SOME-ONE ELSE IS HERE.

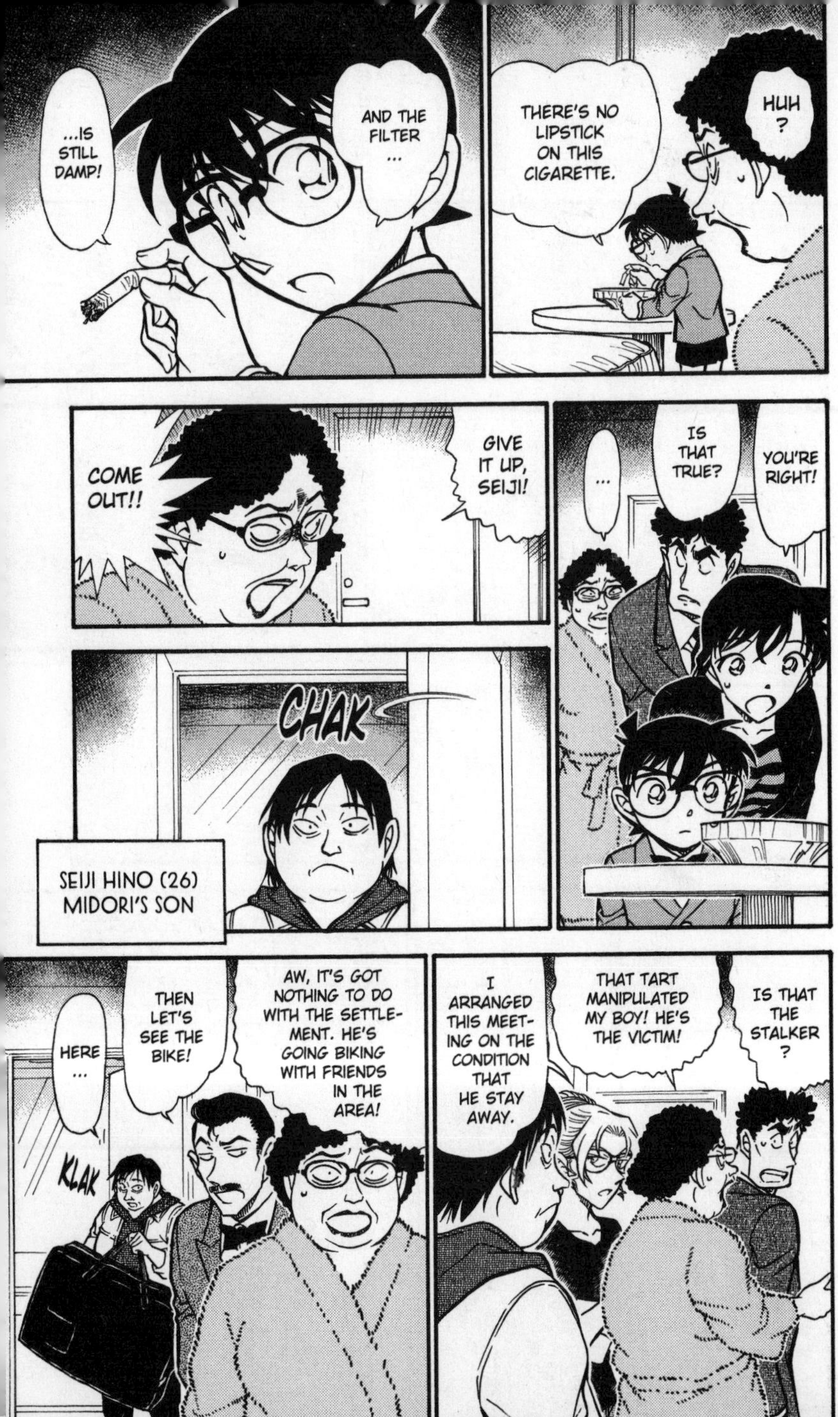
HUH ?
THERE'S NO LIPSTICK ON THIS CIGARETTE.
AND THE FILTER ...
...IS STILL DAMP!
YOU'RE RIGHT!
IS THAT TRUE?
...
GIVE IT UP, SEIJI!
COME OUT!!
CHAK
SEIJI HINO (26) MIDORI'S SON
IS THAT THE STALKER ?
THAT TART MANIPULATED MY BOY! HE'S THE VICTIM!
I ARRANGED THIS MEETING ON THE CONDITION THAT HE STAY AWAY.
AW, IT'S GOT NOTHING TO DO WITH THE SETTLEMENT. HE'S GOING BIKING WITH FRIENDS IN THE AREA!
THEN LET'S SEE THE BIKE!
HERE ...
KLAK

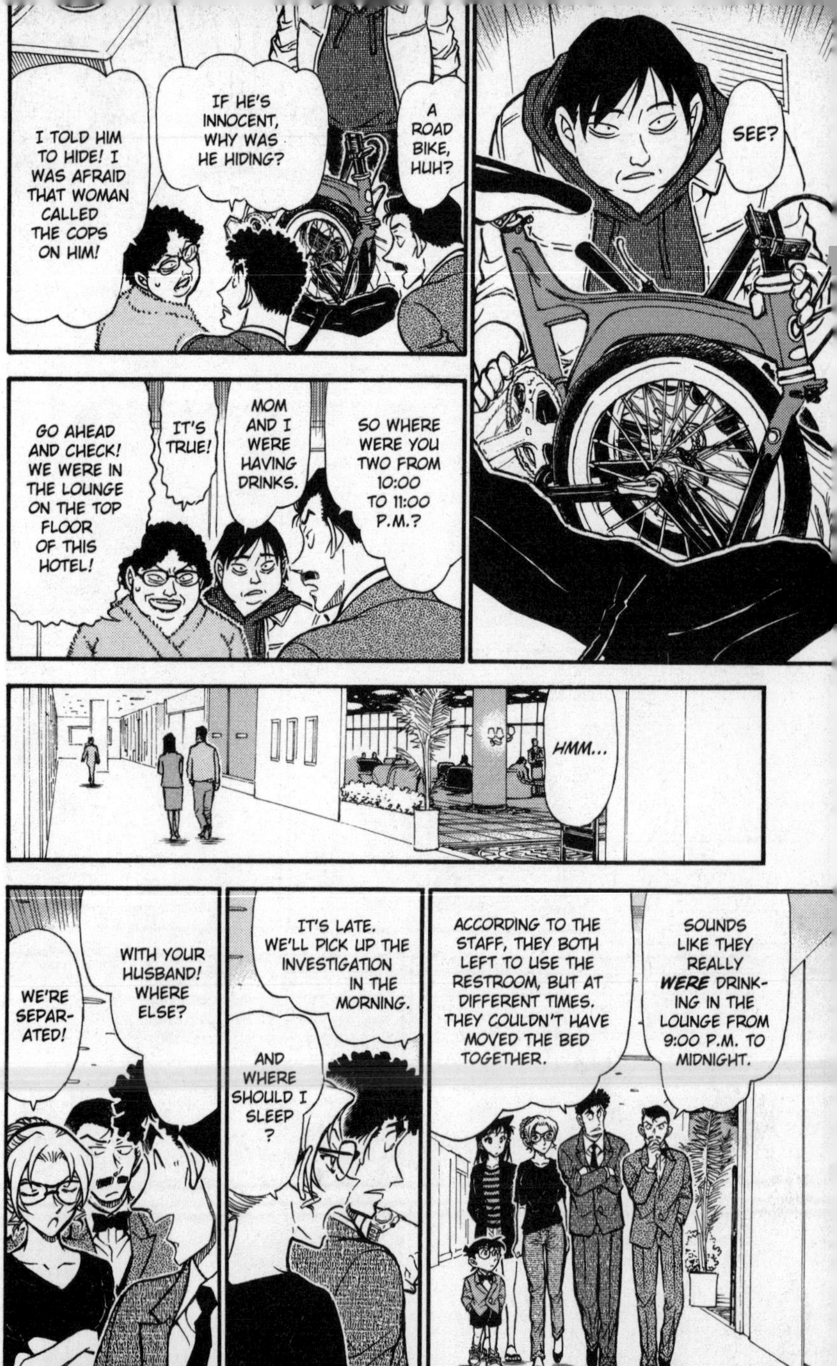
SEE?
A ROAD BIKE, HUH?
IF HE'S INNOCENT, WHY WAS HE HIDING?
I TOLD HIM TO HIDE! I WAS AFRAID THAT WOMAN CALLED THE COPS ON HIM!
SO WHERE WERE YOU TWO FROM 10:00 TO 11:00 P.M.?
MOM AND I WERE HAVING DRINKS.
IT'S TRUE!
GO AHEAD AND CHECK! WE WERE IN THE LOUNGE ON THE TOP FLOOR OF THIS HOTEL!
HMM...
SOUNDS LIKE THEY REALLY *WERE* DRINKING IN THE LOUNGE FROM 9:00 P.M. TO MIDNIGHT.
ACCORDING TO THE STAFF, THEY BOTH LEFT TO USE THE RESTROOM, BUT AT DIFFERENT TIMES. THEY COULDN'T HAVE MOVED THE BED TOGETHER.
IT'S LATE. WE'LL PICK UP THE INVESTIGATION IN THE MORNING.
AND WHERE SHOULD I SLEEP?
WITH YOUR HUSBAND! WHERE ELSE?
WE'RE SEPARATED!

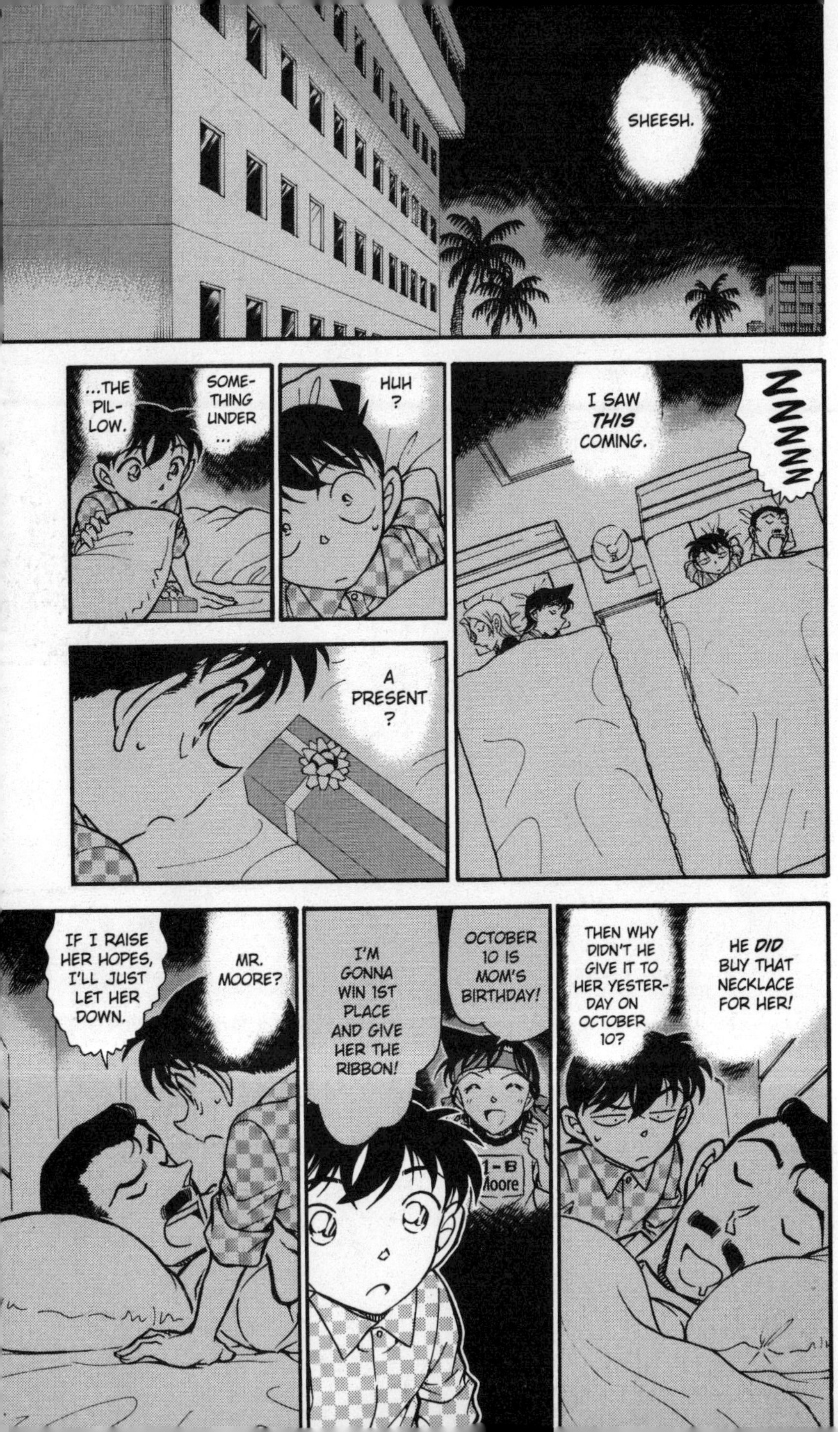
SHEESH.
ZZZZZ
I SAW THIS COMING.
HUH ?
SOME-THING UNDER ...
...THE PIL-LOW.
A PRESENT ?
HE DID BUY THAT NECKLACE FOR HER!
THEN WHY DIDN'T HE GIVE IT TO HER YESTER-DAY ON OCTOBER 10?
OCTOBER 10 IS MOM'S BIRTHDAY!
I'M GONNA WIN 1ST PLACE AND GIVE HER THE RIBBON!
1-B Moore
MR. MOORE?
IF I RAISE HER HOPES, I'LL JUST LET HER DOWN.

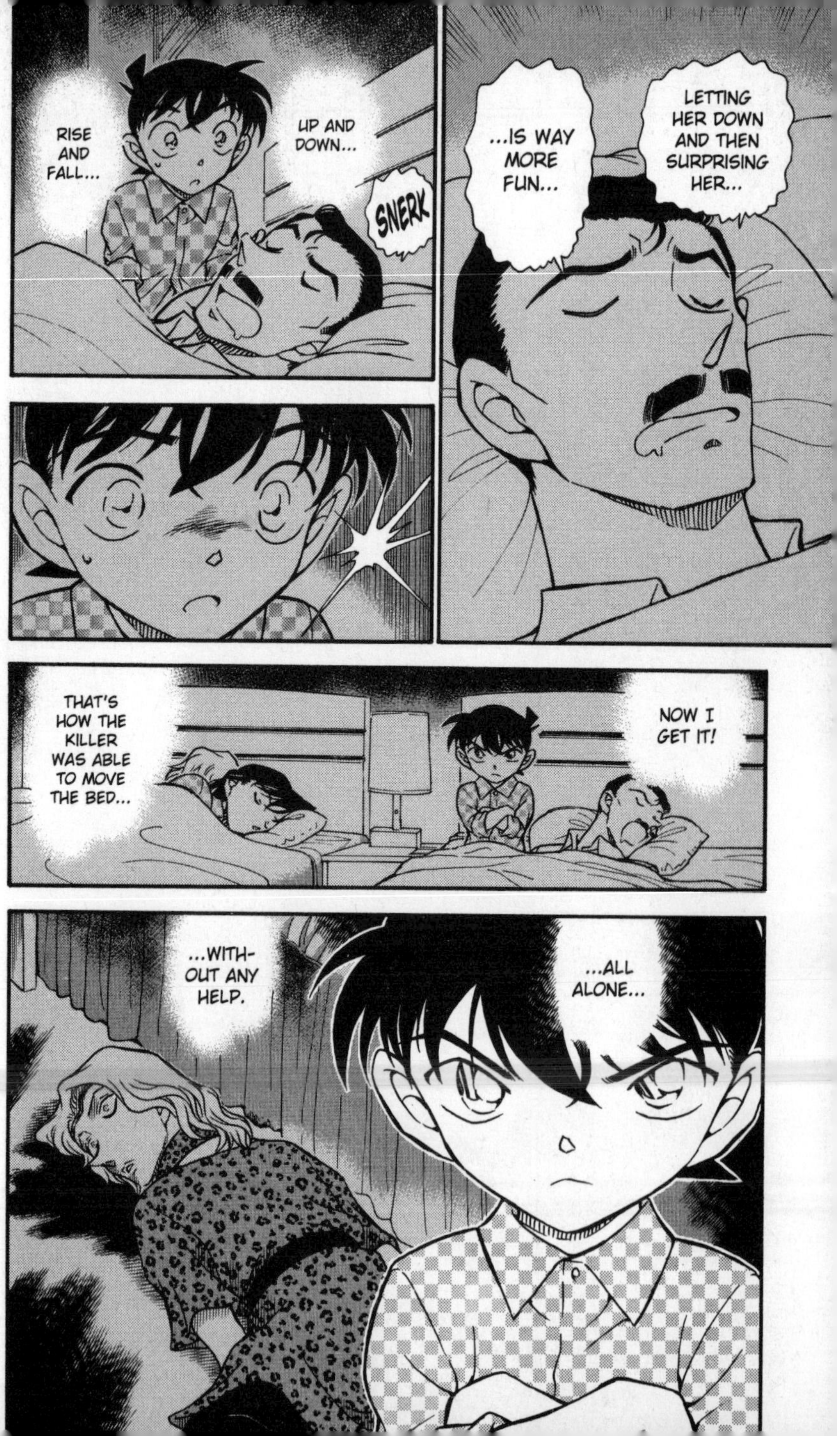
LETTING HER DOWN AND THEN SURPRISING HER...
...IS WAY MORE FUN...
UP AND DOWN...
RISE AND FALL...
SNERK
NOW I GET IT!
THAT'S HOW THE KILLER WAS ABLE TO MOVE THE BED...
...ALL ALONE...
...WITH-OUT ANY HELP.

THE BEST BIRTHDAY

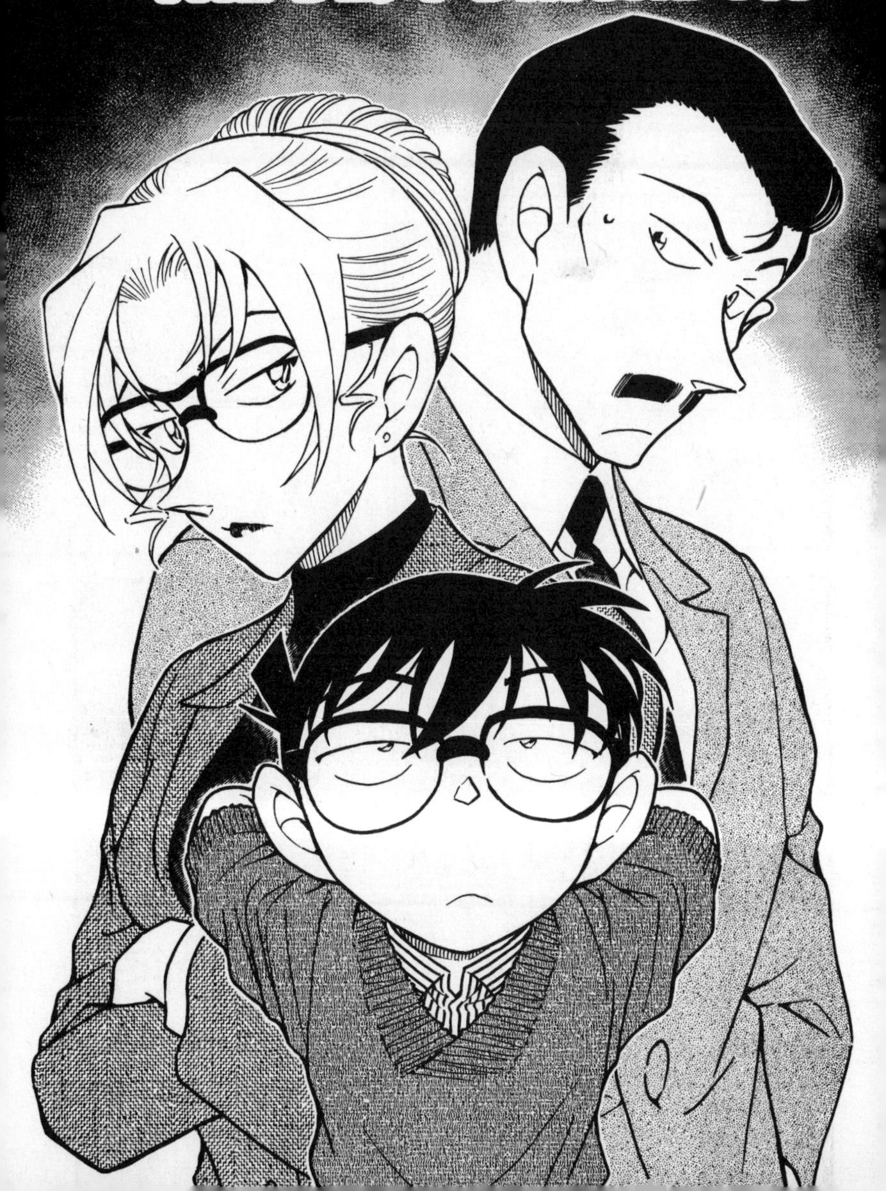

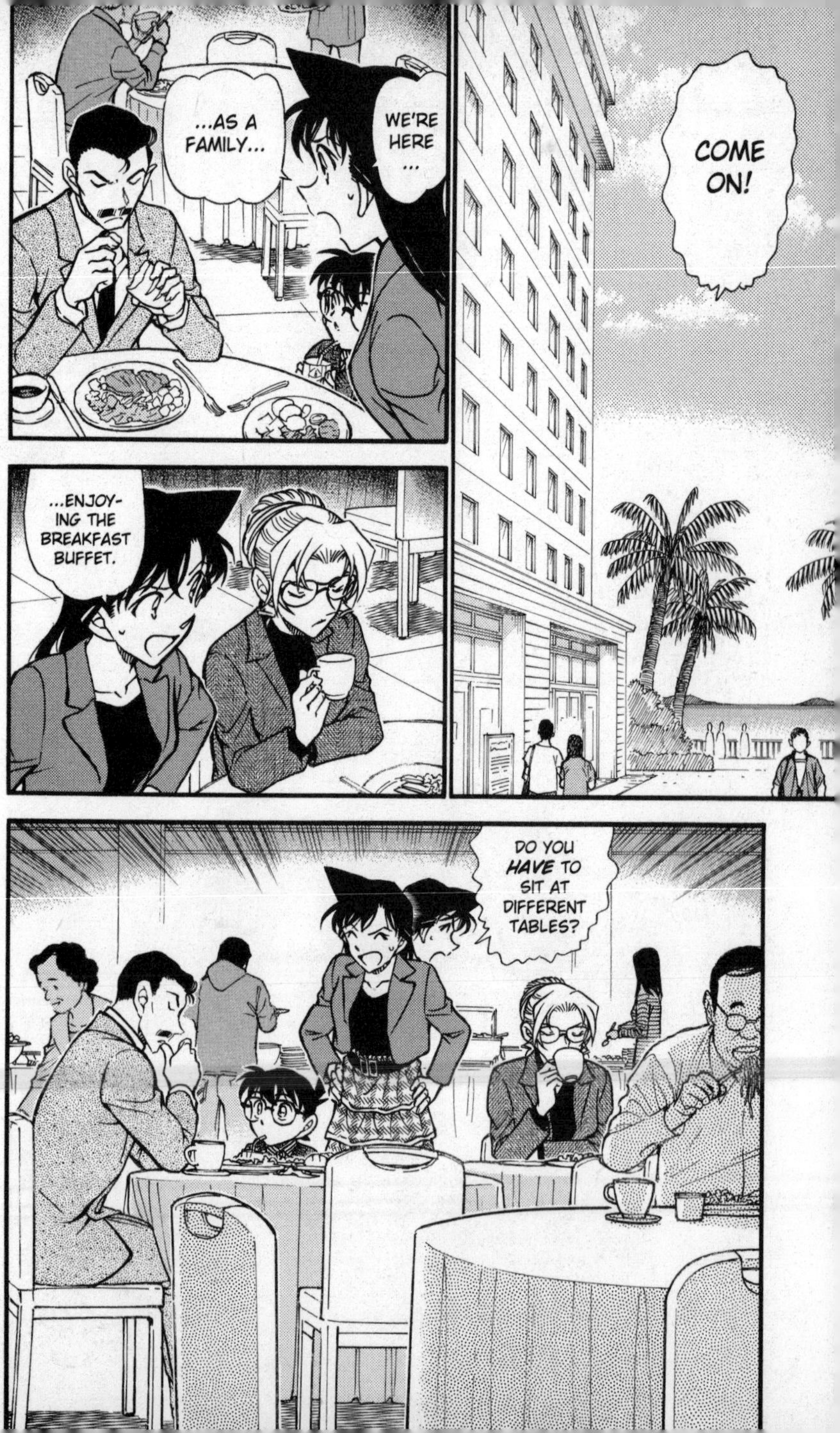
COME ON!
WE'RE HERE...
...AS A FAMILY...
...ENJOYING THE BREAKFAST BUFFET.
DO YOU *HAVE* TO SIT AT DIFFERENT TABLES?

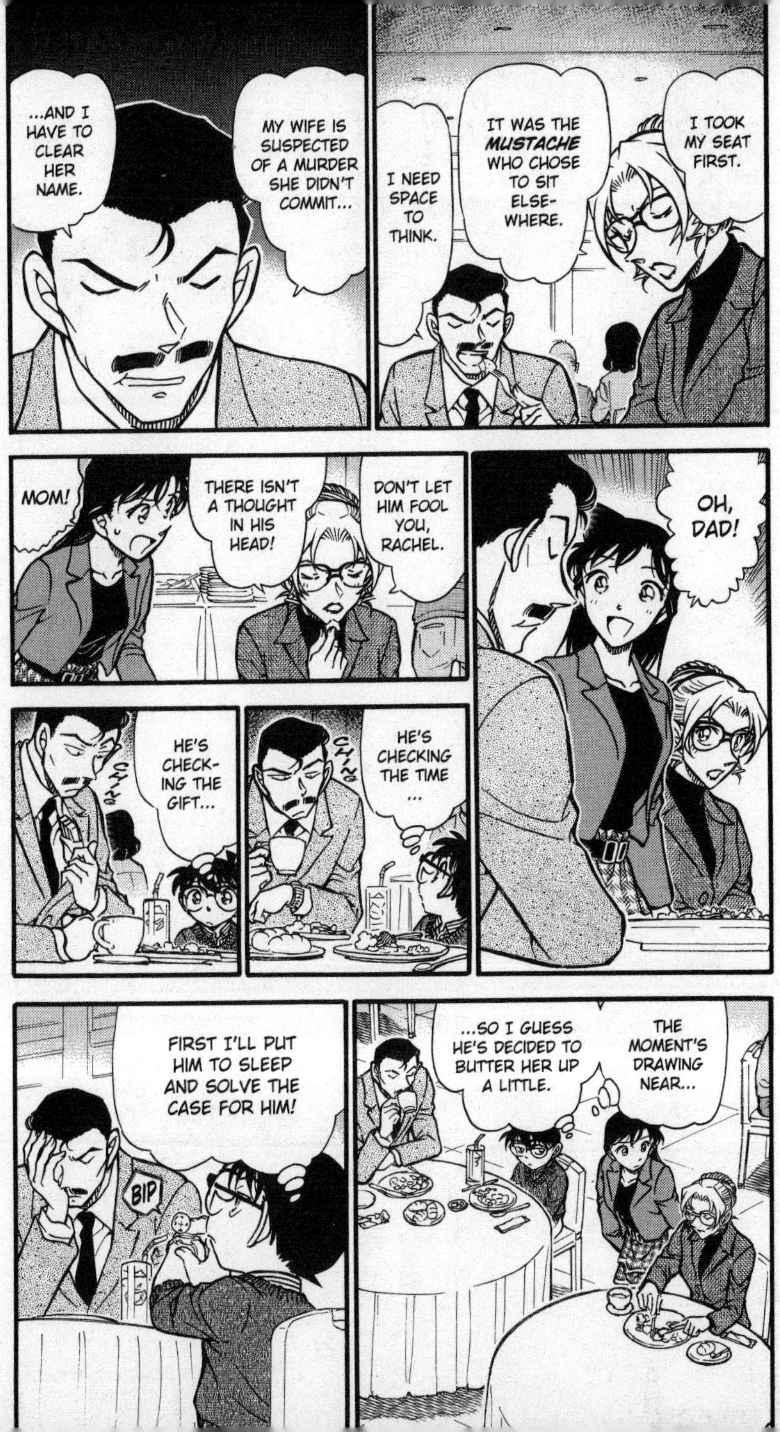
I TOOK MY SEAT FIRST.
IT WAS THE MUSTACHE WHO CHOSE TO SIT ELSE-WHERE.
I NEED SPACE TO THINK.
MY WIFE IS SUSPECTED OF A MURDER SHE DIDN'T COMMIT...
...AND I HAVE TO CLEAR HER NAME.
OH, DAD!
DON'T LET HIM FOOL YOU, RACHEL.
THERE ISN'T A THOUGHT IN HIS HEAD!
MOM!
CHING
HE'S CHECKING THE TIME...
CHING
HE'S CHECK-ING THE GIFT...
THE MOMENT'S DRAWING NEAR...
...SO I GUESS HE'S DECIDED TO BUTTER HER UP A LITTLE.
FIRST I'LL PUT HIM TO SLEEP AND SOLVE THE CASE FOR HIM!
BIP

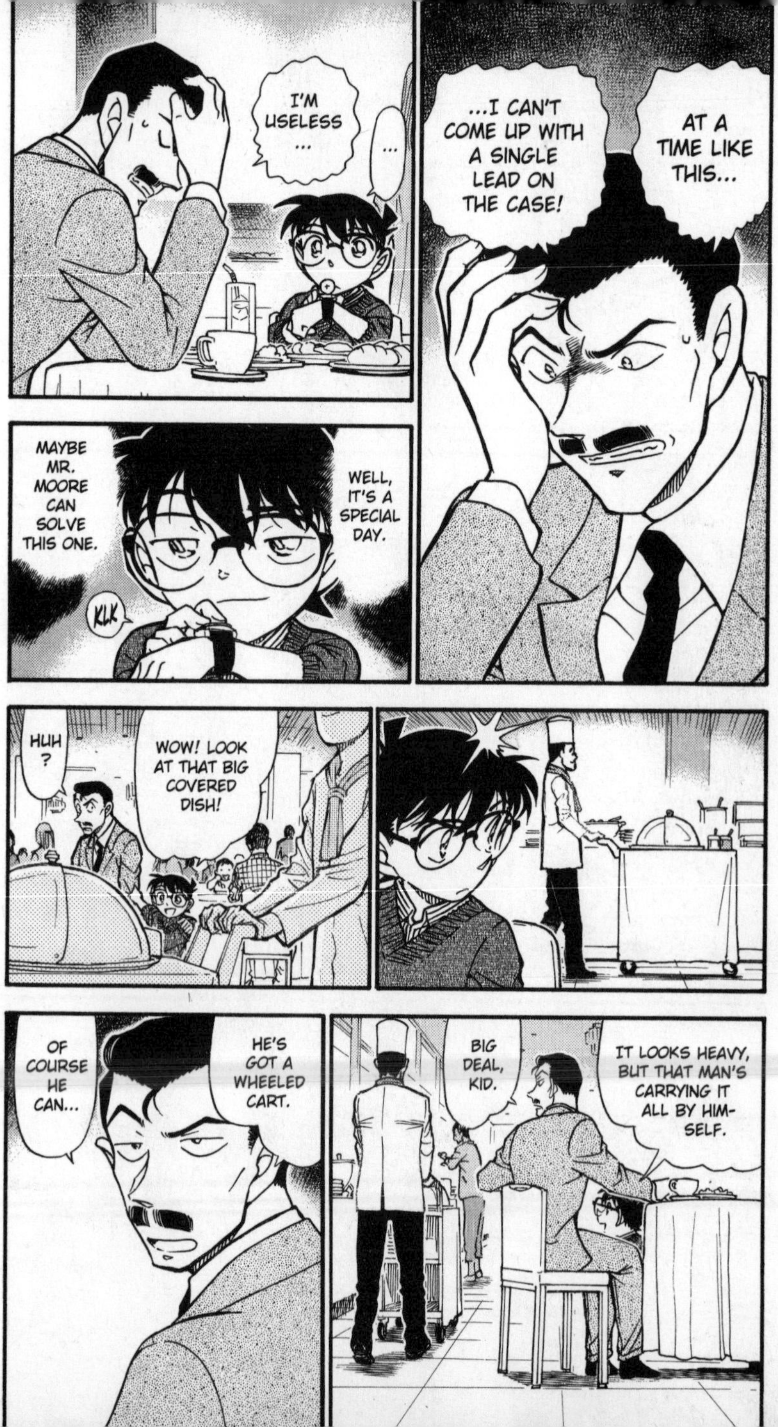
AT A TIME LIKE THIS...
...I CAN'T COME UP WITH A SINGLE LEAD ON THE CASE!
...
I'M USELESS ...
WELL, IT'S A SPECIAL DAY.
MAYBE MR. MOORE CAN SOLVE THIS ONE.
KLK
WOW! LOOK AT THAT BIG COVERED DISH!
HUH?
IT LOOKS HEAVY, BUT THAT MAN'S CARRYING IT ALL BY HIM-SELF.
BIG DEAL, KID.
HE'S GOT A WHEELED CART.
OF COURSE HE CAN...

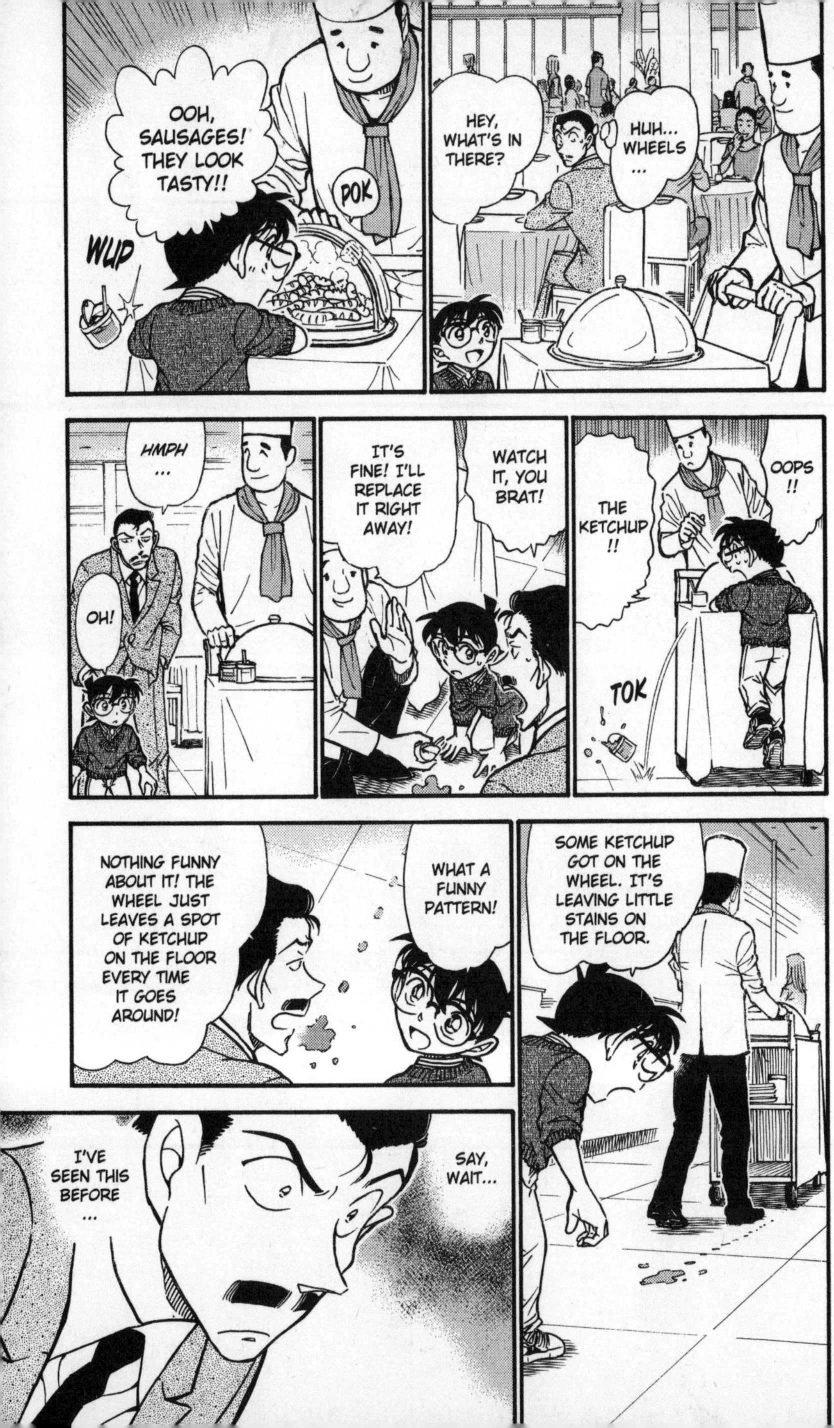
HUH... WHEELS ...
HEY, WHAT'S IN THERE?
OOH, SAUSAGES! THEY LOOK TASTY!!
POK
WUP
OOPS !!
THE KETCHUP !!
TOK
WATCH IT, YOU BRAT!
IT'S FINE! I'LL REPLACE IT RIGHT AWAY!
HMPH ...
OH!
SOME KETCHUP GOT ON THE WHEEL. IT'S LEAVING LITTLE STAINS ON THE FLOOR.
WHAT A FUNNY PATTERN!
NOTHING FUNNY ABOUT IT! THE WHEEL JUST LEAVES A SPOT OF KETCHUP ON THE FLOOR EVERY TIME IT GOES AROUND!
SAY, WAIT...
I'VE SEEN THIS BEFORE ...

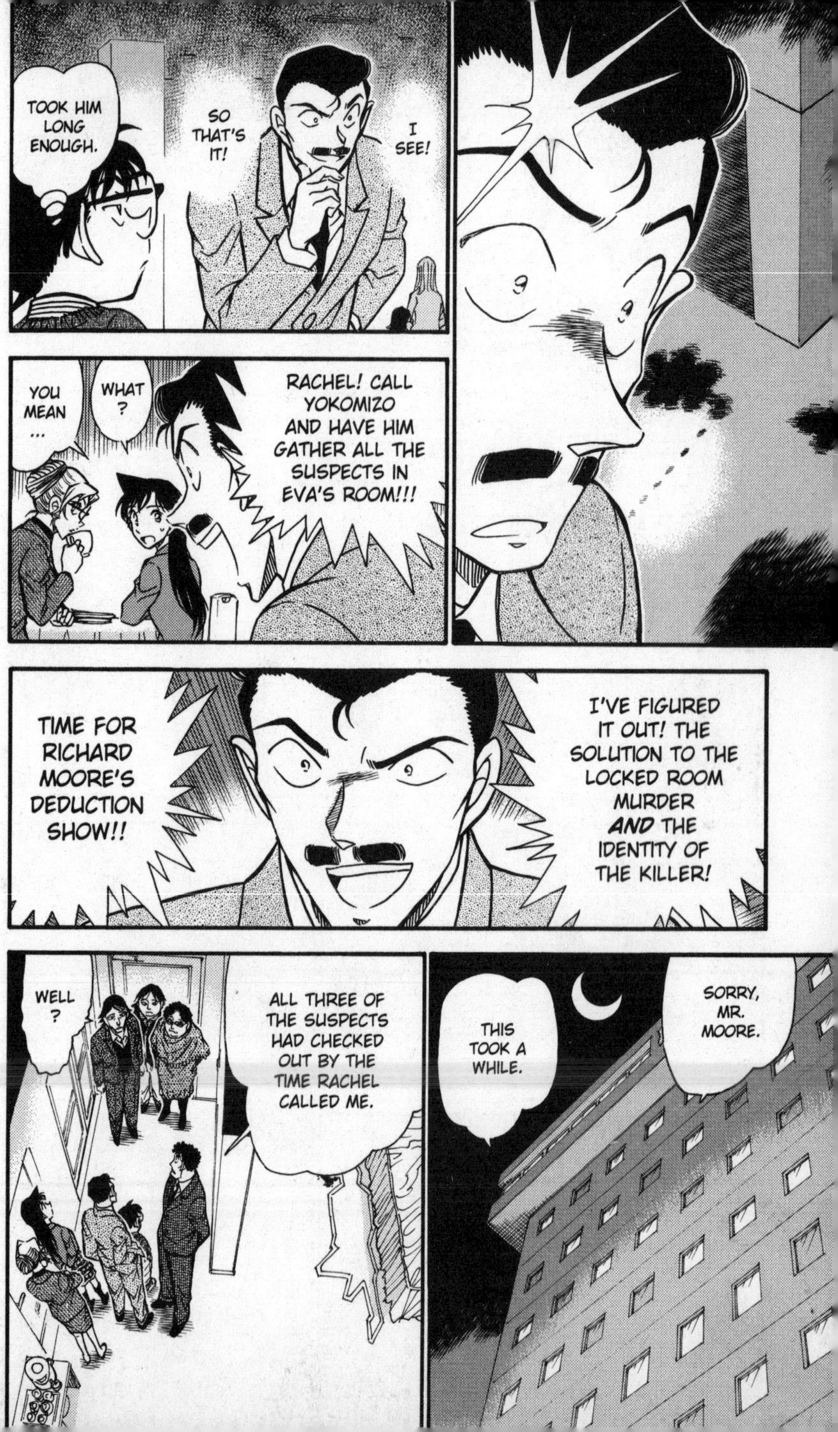
I SEE!
SO THAT'S IT!
TOOK HIM LONG ENOUGH.
RACHEL! CALL YOKOMIZO AND HAVE HIM GATHER ALL THE SUSPECTS IN EVA'S ROOM!!!
WHAT?
YOU MEAN...
I'VE FIGURED IT OUT! THE SOLUTION TO THE LOCKED ROOM MURDER AND THE IDENTITY OF THE KILLER!
TIME FOR RICHARD MOORE'S DEDUCTION SHOW!!
SORRY, MR. MOORE.
THIS TOOK A WHILE.
ALL THREE OF THE SUSPECTS HAD CHECKED OUT BY THE TIME RACHEL CALLED ME.
WELL?

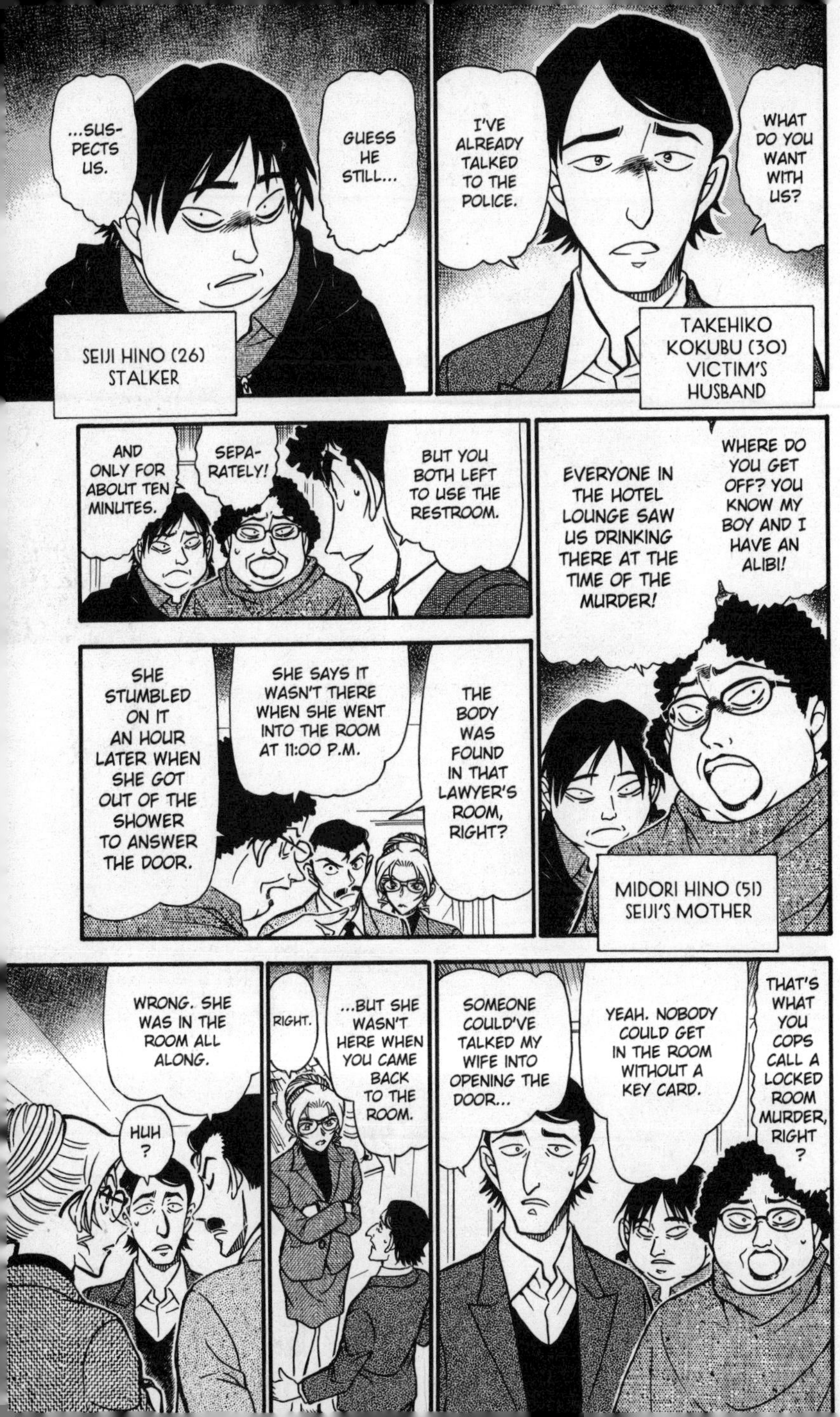
WHAT DO YOU WANT WITH US?
I'VE ALREADY TALKED TO THE POLICE.
TAKEHIKO KOKUBU (30) VICTIM'S HUSBAND
GUESS HE STILL...
...SUS-PECTS US.
SEIJI HINO (26) STALKER
WHERE DO YOU GET OFF? YOU KNOW MY BOY AND I HAVE AN ALIBI!
EVERYONE IN THE HOTEL LOUNGE SAW US DRINKING THERE AT THE TIME OF THE MURDER!
MIDORI HINO (51) SEIJI'S MOTHER
BUT YOU BOTH LEFT TO USE THE RESTROOM.
SEPA-RATELY!
AND ONLY FOR ABOUT TEN MINUTES.
THE BODY WAS FOUND IN THAT LAWYER'S ROOM, RIGHT?
SHE SAYS IT WASN'T THERE WHEN SHE WENT INTO THE ROOM AT 11:00 P.M.
SHE STUMBLED ON IT AN HOUR LATER WHEN SHE GOT OUT OF THE SHOWER TO ANSWER THE DOOR.
THAT'S WHAT YOU COPS CALL A LOCKED ROOM MURDER, RIGHT?
YEAH. NOBODY COULD GET IN THE ROOM WITHOUT A KEY CARD.
SOMEONE COULD'VE TALKED MY WIFE INTO OPENING THE DOOR...
...BUT SHE WASN'T HERE WHEN YOU CAME BACK TO THE ROOM.
RIGHT.
WRONG. SHE WAS IN THE ROOM ALL ALONG.
HUH?

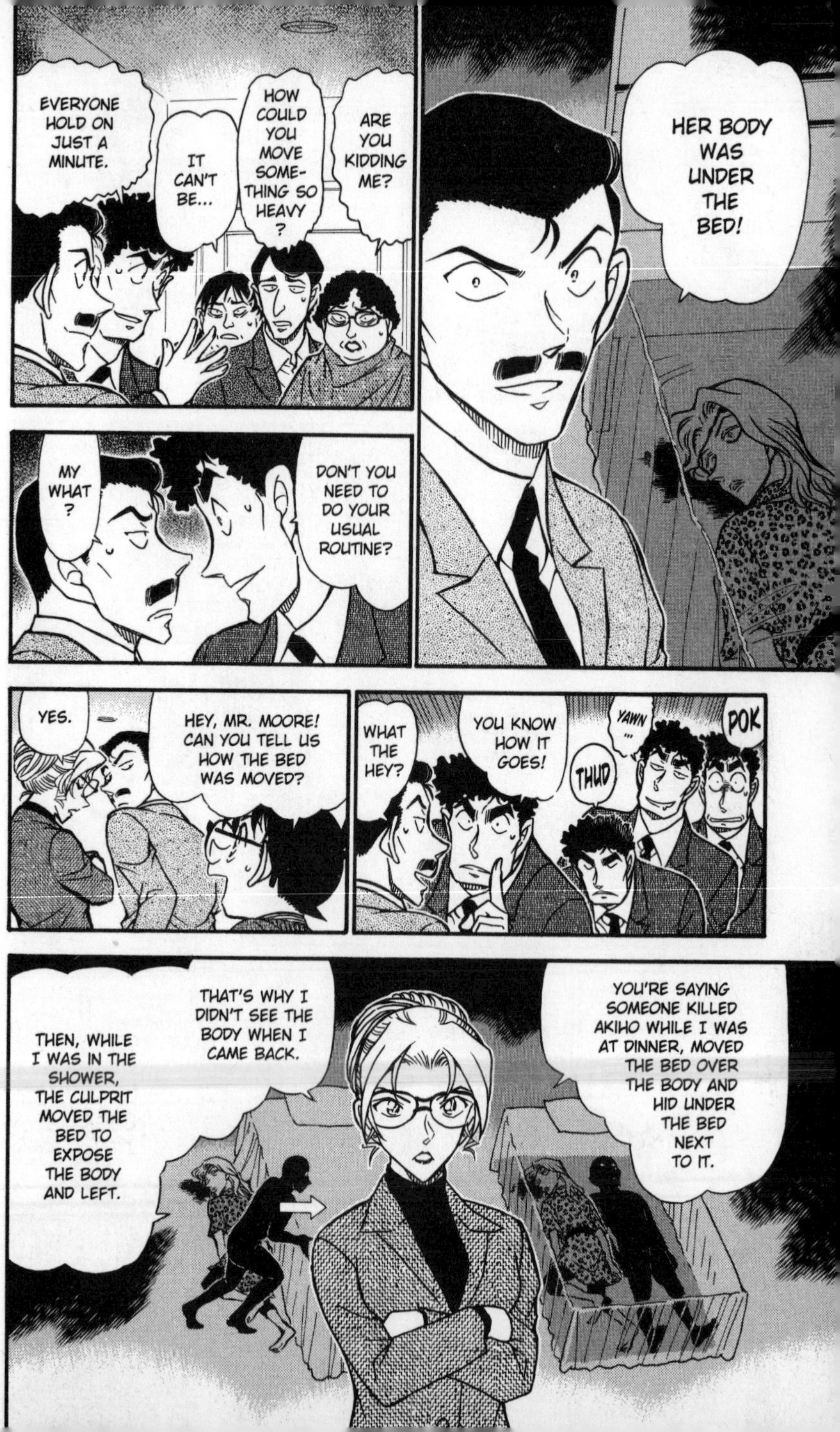
HER BODY WAS UNDER THE BED!
ARE YOU KIDDING ME?
HOW COULD YOU MOVE SOME-THING SO HEAVY?
IT CAN'T BE...
EVERYONE HOLD ON JUST A MINUTE.
DON'T YOU NEED TO DO YOUR USUAL ROUTINE?
MY WHAT?
POK
YAWN...
THUD
YOU KNOW HOW IT GOES!
WHAT THE HEY?
HEY, MR. MOORE! CAN YOU TELL US HOW THE BED WAS MOVED?
YES.
YOU'RE SAYING SOMEONE KILLED AKIHO WHILE I WAS AT DINNER, MOVED THE BED OVER THE BODY AND HID UNDER THE BED NEXT TO IT.
THEN, WHILE I WAS IN THE SHOWER, THE CULPRIT MOVED THE BED TO EXPOSE THE BODY AND LEFT.
THAT'S WHY I DIDN'T SEE THE BODY WHEN I CAME BACK.

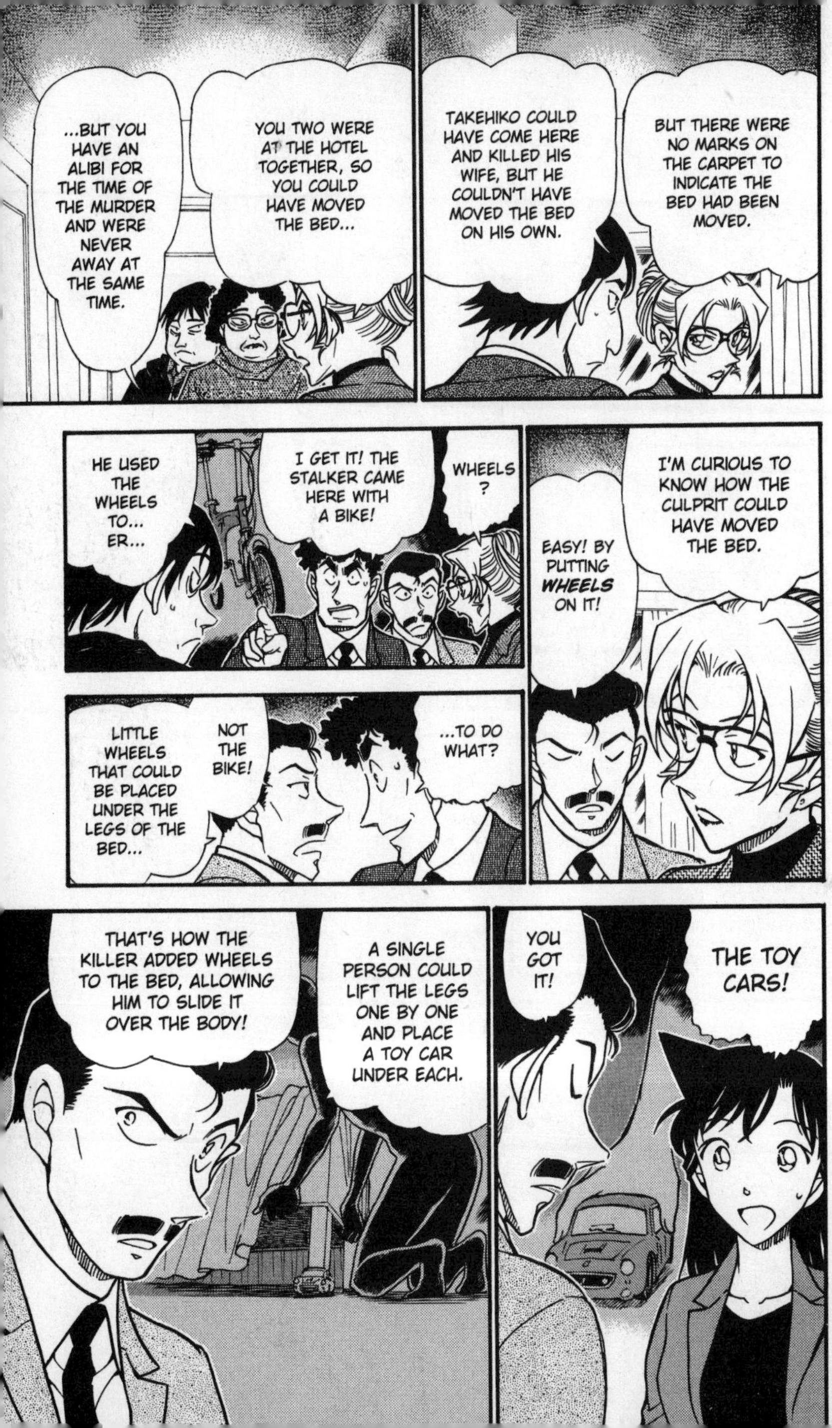
BUT THERE WERE NO MARKS ON THE CARPET TO INDICATE THE BED HAD BEEN MOVED.
TAKEHIKO COULD HAVE COME HERE AND KILLED HIS WIFE, BUT HE COULDN'T HAVE MOVED THE BED ON HIS OWN.
YOU TWO WERE AT THE HOTEL TOGETHER, SO YOU COULD HAVE MOVED THE BED...
...BUT YOU HAVE AN ALIBI FOR THE TIME OF THE MURDER AND WERE NEVER AWAY AT THE SAME TIME.
I'M CURIOUS TO KNOW HOW THE CULPRIT COULD HAVE MOVED THE BED.
EASY! BY PUTTING *WHEELS* ON IT!
WHEELS?
I GET IT! THE STALKER CAME HERE WITH A BIKE!
HE USED THE WHEELS TO... ER...
...TO DO WHAT?
NOT THE BIKE!
LITTLE WHEELS THAT COULD BE PLACED UNDER THE LEGS OF THE BED...
THE TOY CARS!
YOU GOT IT!
A SINGLE PERSON COULD LIFT THE LEGS ONE BY ONE AND PLACE A TOY CAR UNDER EACH.
THAT'S HOW THE KILLER ADDED WHEELS TO THE BED, ALLOWING HIM TO SLIDE IT OVER THE BODY!

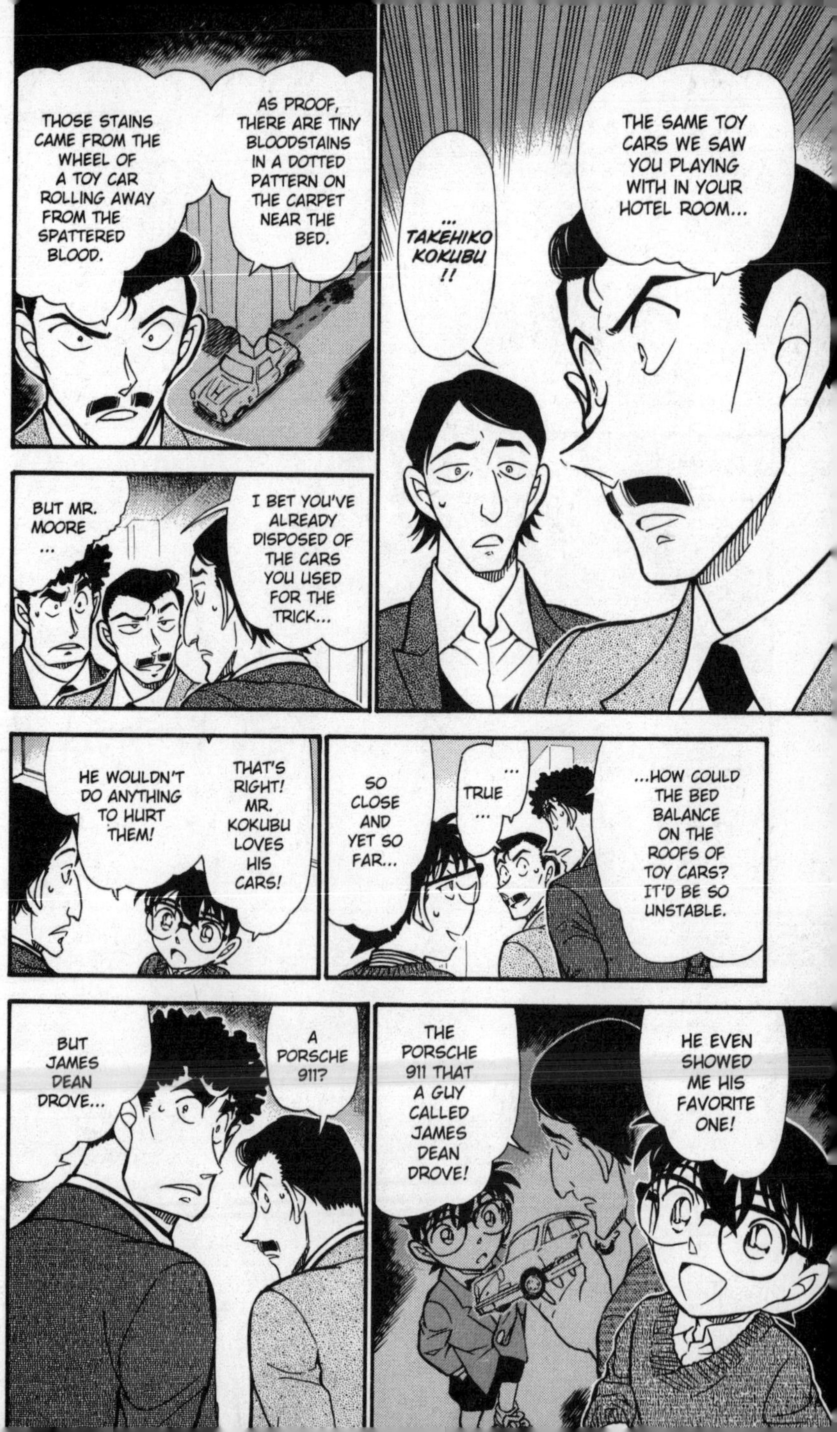
THE SAME TOY CARS WE SAW YOU PLAYING WITH IN YOUR HOTEL ROOM...
... TAKEHIKO KOKUBU !!
AS PROOF, THERE ARE TINY BLOODSTAINS IN A DOTTED PATTERN ON THE CARPET NEAR THE BED.
THOSE STAINS CAME FROM THE WHEEL OF A TOY CAR ROLLING AWAY FROM THE SPATTERED BLOOD.
I BET YOU'VE ALREADY DISPOSED OF THE CARS YOU USED FOR THE TRICK...
BUT MR. MOORE ...
...HOW COULD THE BED BALANCE ON THE ROOFS OF TOY CARS? IT'D BE SO UNSTABLE.
... TRUE ...
SO CLOSE AND YET SO FAR...
THAT'S RIGHT! MR. KOKUBU LOVES HIS CARS!
HE WOULDN'T DO ANYTHING TO HURT THEM!
HE EVEN SHOWED ME HIS FAVORITE ONE!
THE PORSCHE 911 THAT A GUY CALLED JAMES DEAN DROVE!
A PORSCHE 911?
BUT JAMES DEAN DROVE...

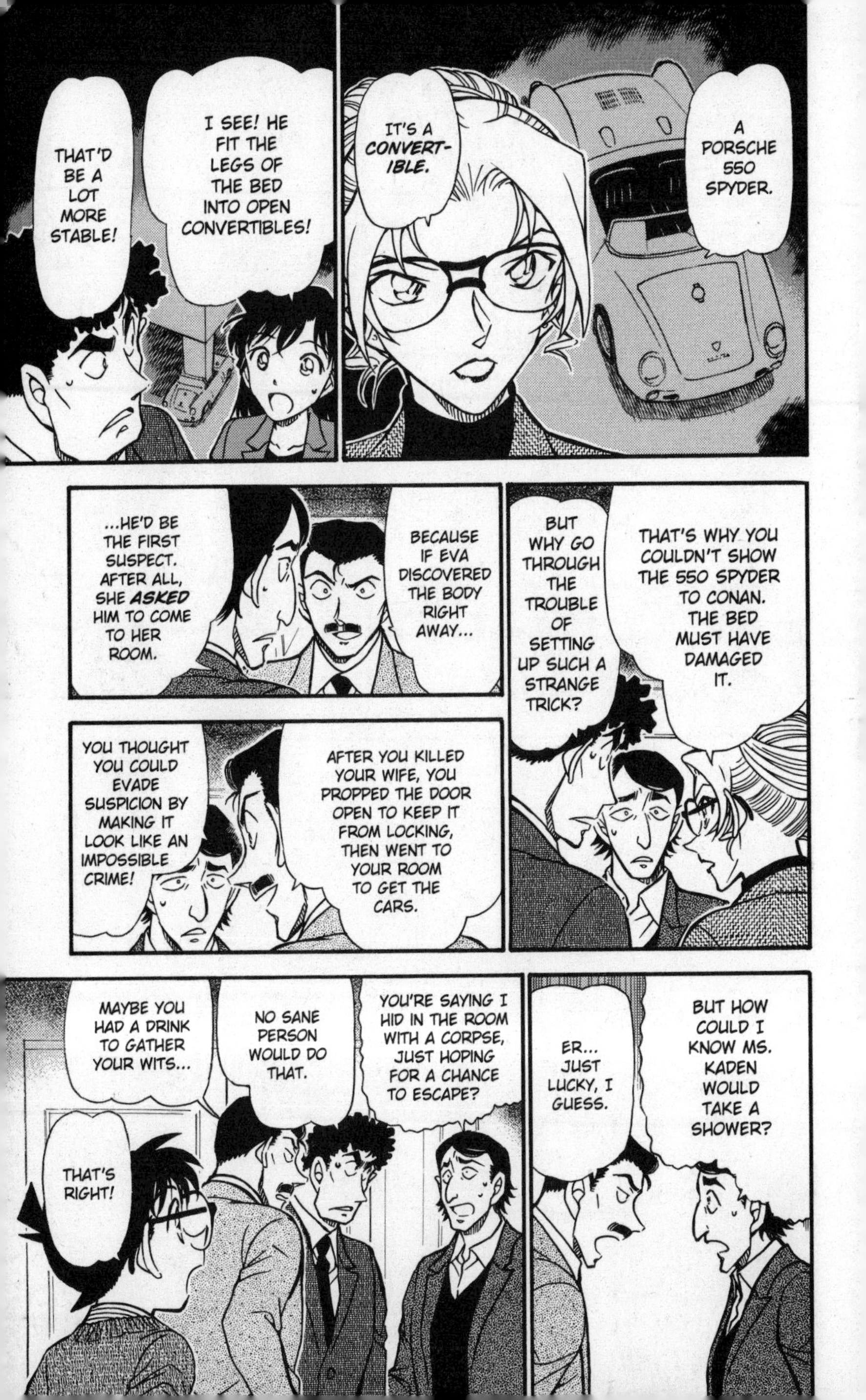
A PORSCHE 550 SPYDER.
IT'S A *CONVERTIBLE.*
I SEE! HE FIT THE LEGS OF THE BED INTO OPEN CONVERTIBLES!
THAT'D BE A LOT MORE STABLE!
THAT'S WHY YOU COULDN'T SHOW THE 550 SPYDER TO CONAN. THE BED MUST HAVE DAMAGED IT.
BUT WHY GO THROUGH THE TROUBLE OF SETTING UP SUCH A STRANGE TRICK?
BECAUSE IF EVA DISCOVERED THE BODY RIGHT AWAY...
...HE'D BE THE FIRST SUSPECT. AFTER ALL, SHE *ASKED* HIM TO COME TO HER ROOM.
AFTER YOU KILLED YOUR WIFE, YOU PROPPED THE DOOR OPEN TO KEEP IT FROM LOCKING, THEN WENT TO YOUR ROOM TO GET THE CARS.
YOU THOUGHT YOU COULD EVADE SUSPICION BY MAKING IT LOOK LIKE AN IMPOSSIBLE CRIME!
BUT HOW COULD I KNOW MS. KADEN WOULD TAKE A SHOWER?
ER... JUST LUCKY, I GUESS.
YOU'RE SAYING I HID IN THE ROOM WITH A CORPSE, JUST HOPING FOR A CHANCE TO ESCAPE?
NO SANE PERSON WOULD DO THAT.
MAYBE YOU HAD A DRINK TO GATHER YOUR WITS...
THAT'S RIGHT!

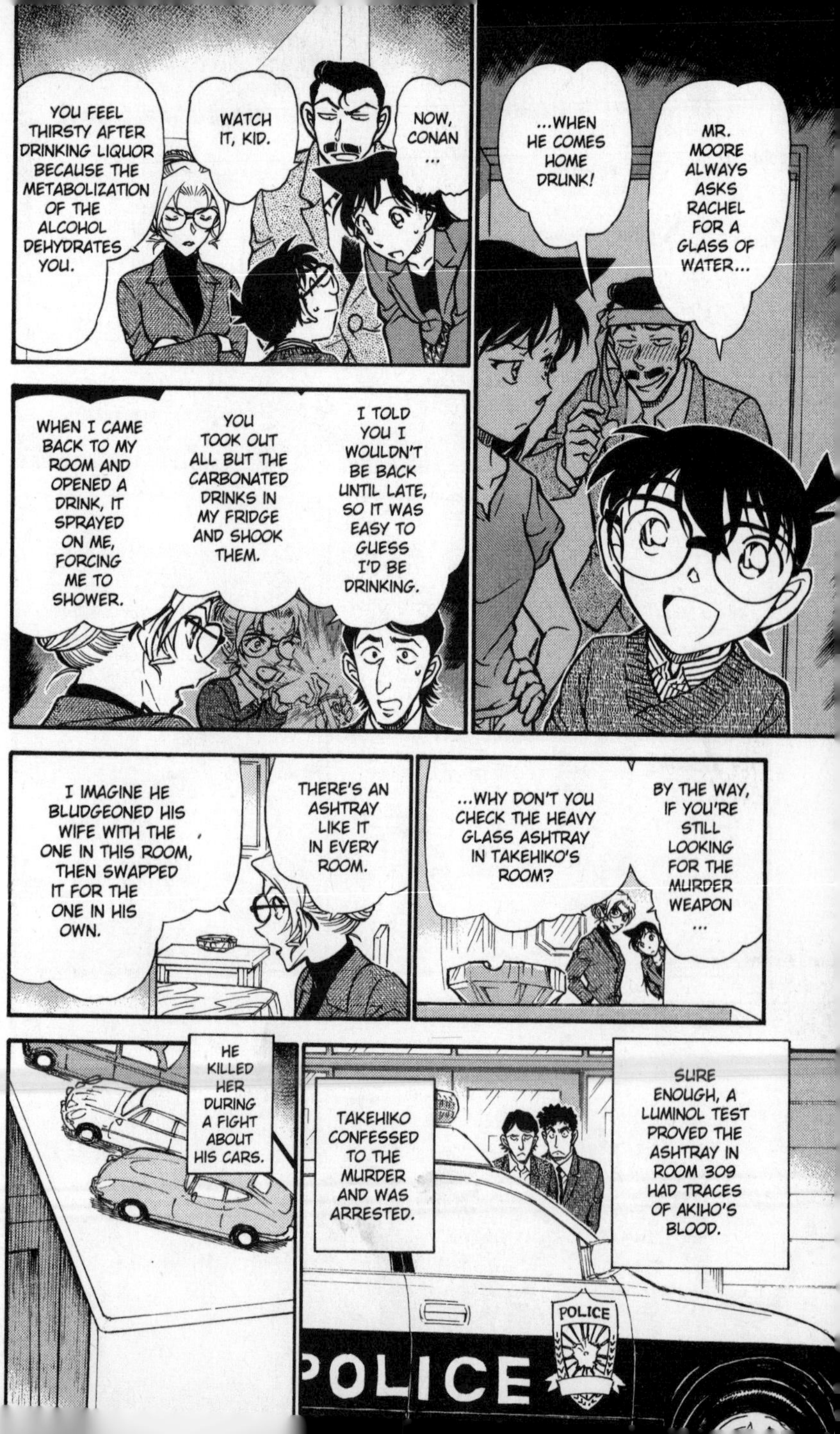
MR. MOORE ALWAYS ASKS RACHEL FOR A GLASS OF WATER...
...WHEN HE COMES HOME DRUNK!
NOW, CONAN ...
WATCH IT, KID.
YOU FEEL THIRSTY AFTER DRINKING LIQUOR BECAUSE THE METABOLIZATION OF THE ALCOHOL DEHYDRATES YOU.
I TOLD YOU I WOULDN'T BE BACK UNTIL LATE, SO IT WAS EASY TO GUESS I'D BE DRINKING.
YOU TOOK OUT ALL BUT THE CARBONATED DRINKS IN MY FRIDGE AND SHOOK THEM.
WHEN I CAME BACK TO MY ROOM AND OPENED A DRINK, IT SPRAYED ON ME, FORCING ME TO SHOWER.
BY THE WAY, IF YOU'RE STILL LOOKING FOR THE MURDER WEAPON ...
...WHY DON'T YOU CHECK THE HEAVY GLASS ASHTRAY IN TAKEHIKO'S ROOM?
THERE'S AN ASHTRAY LIKE IT IN EVERY ROOM.
I IMAGINE HE BLUDGEONED HIS WIFE WITH THE ONE IN THIS ROOM, THEN SWAPPED IT FOR THE ONE IN HIS OWN.
SURE ENOUGH, A LUMINOL TEST PROVED THE ASHTRAY IN ROOM 309 HAD TRACES OF AKIHO'S BLOOD.
TAKEHIKO CONFESSED TO THE MURDER AND WAS ARRESTED.
HE KILLED HER DURING A FIGHT ABOUT HIS CARS.
POLICE
POLICE

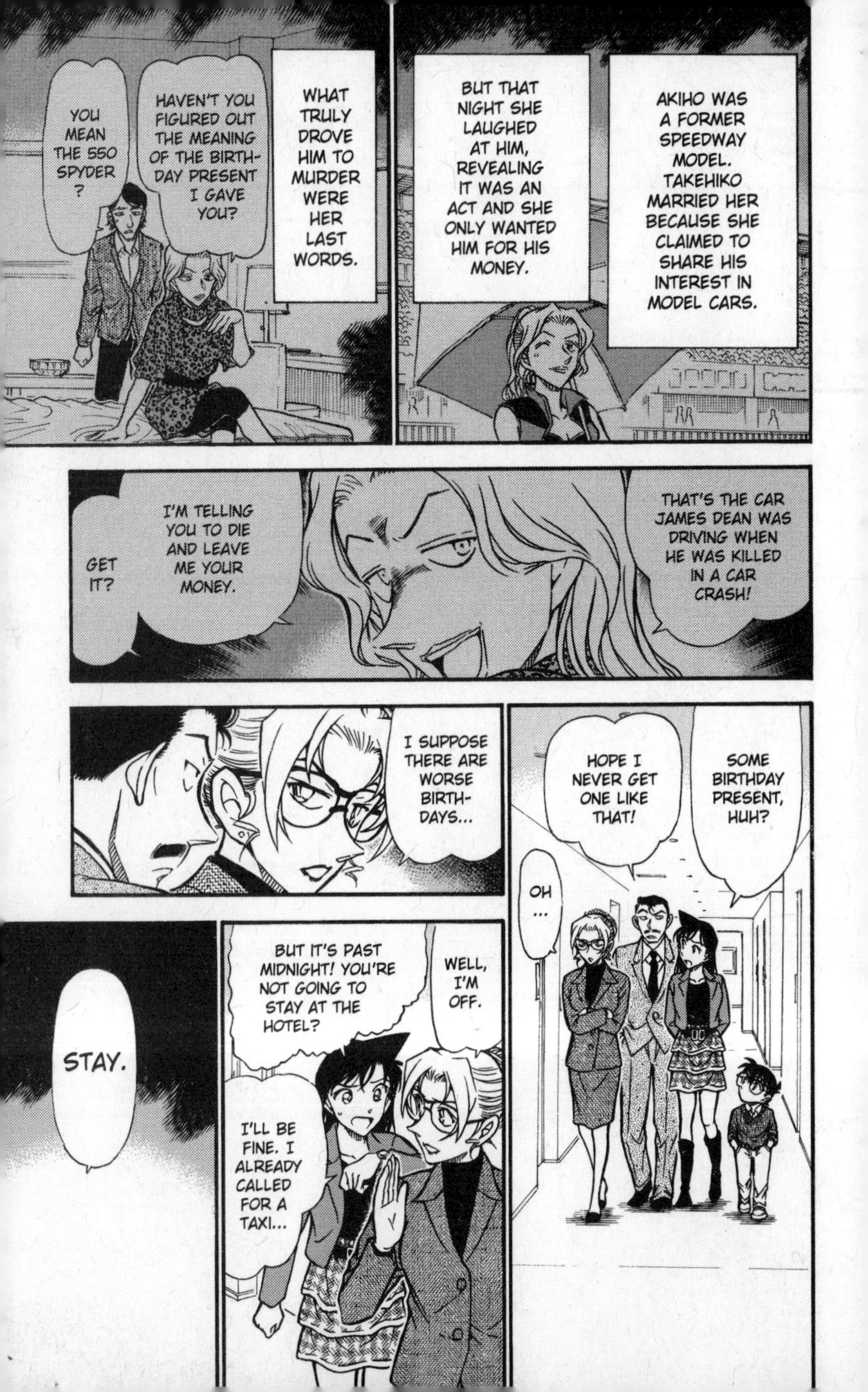
AKIHO WAS A FORMER SPEEDWAY MODEL. TAKEHIKO MARRIED HER BECAUSE SHE CLAIMED TO SHARE HIS INTEREST IN MODEL CARS.
BUT THAT NIGHT SHE LAUGHED AT HIM, REVEALING IT WAS AN ACT AND SHE ONLY WANTED HIM FOR HIS MONEY.
WHAT TRULY DROVE HIM TO MURDER WERE HER LAST WORDS.
HAVEN'T YOU FIGURED OUT THE MEANING OF THE BIRTH-DAY PRESENT I GAVE YOU?
YOU MEAN THE 550 SPYDER?
THAT'S THE CAR JAMES DEAN WAS DRIVING WHEN HE WAS KILLED IN A CAR CRASH!
I'M TELLING YOU TO DIE AND LEAVE ME YOUR MONEY.
GET IT?
SOME BIRTHDAY PRESENT, HUH?
HOPE I NEVER GET ONE LIKE THAT!
OH...
I SUPPOSE THERE ARE WORSE BIRTH-DAYS...
WELL, I'M OFF.
BUT IT'S PAST MIDNIGHT! YOU'RE NOT GOING TO STAY AT THE HOTEL?
I'LL BE FINE. I ALREADY CALLED FOR A TAXI...
STAY.

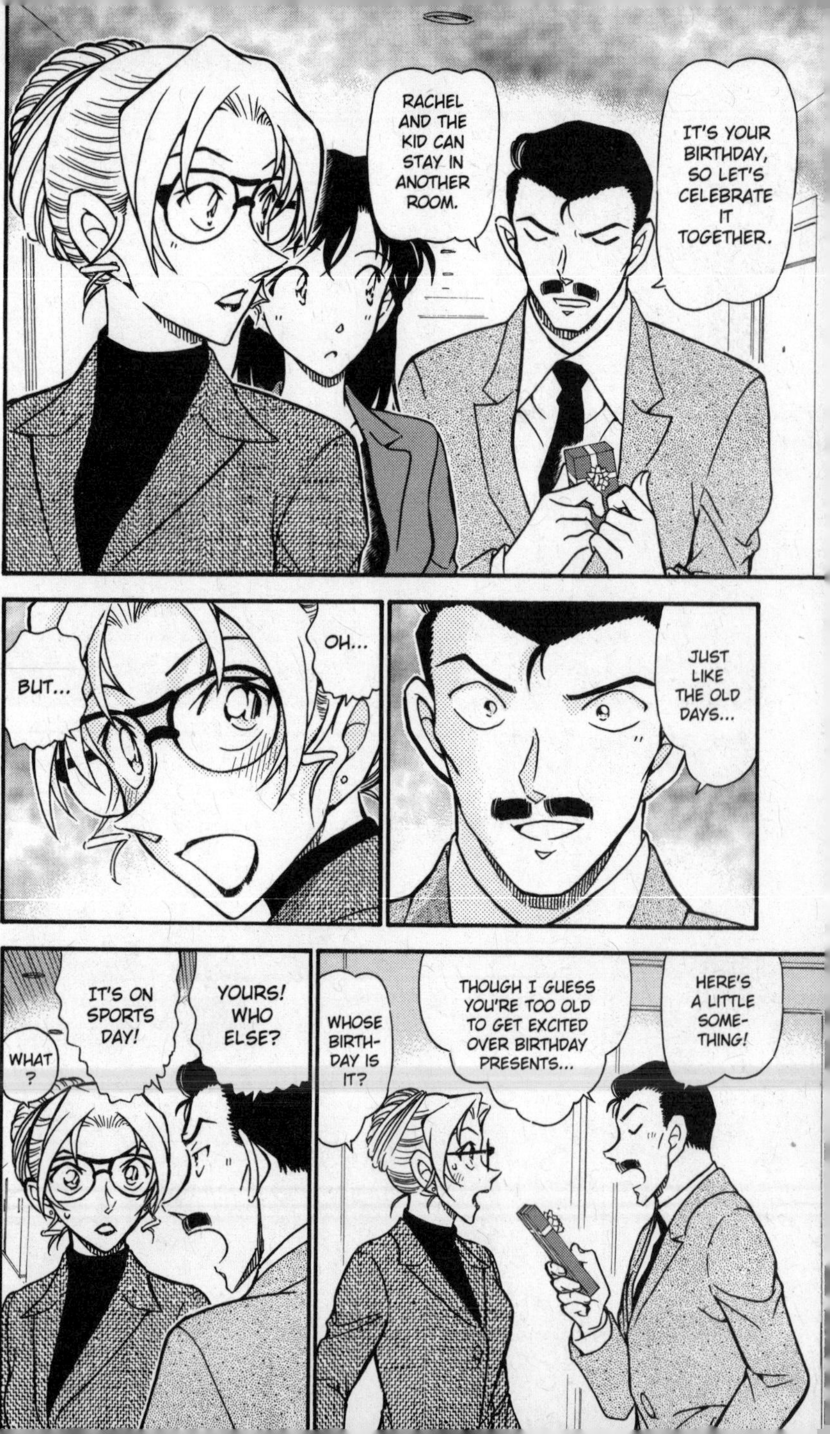
IT'S YOUR BIRTHDAY, SO LET'S CELEBRATE IT TOGETHER.
RACHEL AND THE KID CAN STAY IN ANOTHER ROOM.
JUST LIKE THE OLD DAYS...
OH...
BUT...
HERE'S A LITTLE SOME-THING!
THOUGH I GUESS YOU'RE TOO OLD TO GET EXCITED OVER BIRTHDAY PRESENTS...
WHOSE BIRTH-DAY IS IT?
YOURS! WHO ELSE?
IT'S ON SPORTS DAY!
WHAT?

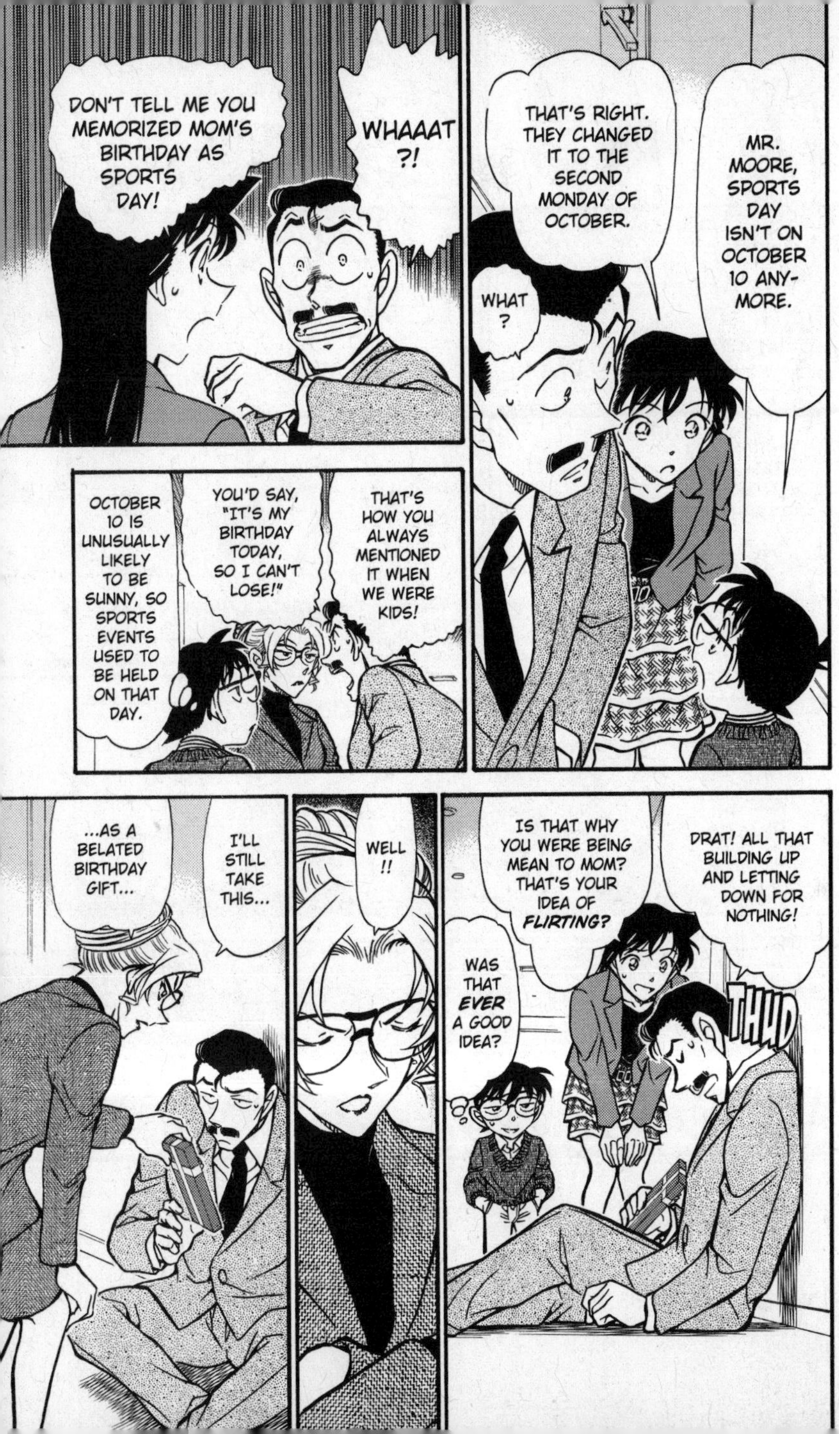
MR. MOORE, SPORTS DAY ISN'T ON OCTOBER 10 ANY-MORE.
THAT'S RIGHT. THEY CHANGED IT TO THE SECOND MONDAY OF OCTOBER.
WHAT?
WHAAAT?!
DON'T TELL ME YOU MEMORIZED MOM'S BIRTHDAY AS SPORTS DAY!
THAT'S HOW YOU ALWAYS MENTIONED IT WHEN WE WERE KIDS!
YOU'D SAY, "IT'S MY BIRTHDAY TODAY, SO I CAN'T LOSE!"
OCTOBER 10 IS UNUSUALLY LIKELY TO BE SUNNY, SO SPORTS EVENTS USED TO BE HELD ON THAT DAY.
DRAT! ALL THAT BUILDING UP AND LETTING DOWN FOR NOTHING!
THUD
IS THAT WHY YOU WERE BEING MEAN TO MOM? THAT'S YOUR IDEA OF *FLIRTING?*
WAS THAT *EVER* A GOOD IDEA?
WELL!!
I'LL STILL TAKE THIS...
...AS A BELATED BIRTHDAY GIFT...

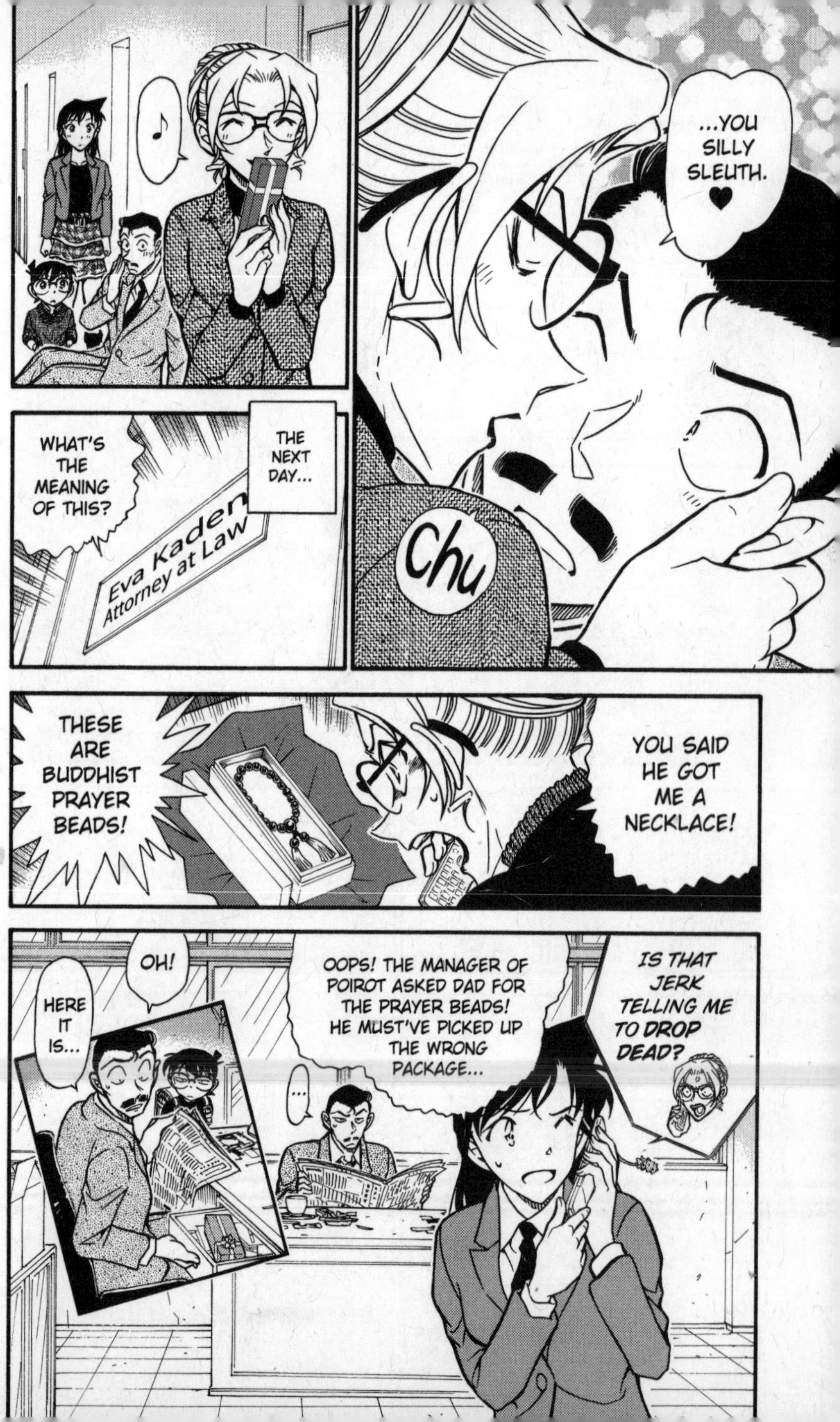
...YOU SILLY SLEUTH. ♥
Chu
♪
THE NEXT DAY...
WHAT'S THE MEANING OF THIS?
Eva Kaden
Attorney at Law
YOU SAID HE GOT ME A NECKLACE!
THESE ARE BUDDHIST PRAYER BEADS!
IS THAT JERK TELLING ME TO *DROP DEAD*?
OOPS! THE MANAGER OF POIROT ASKED DAD FOR THE PRAYER BEADS! HE MUST'VE PICKED UP THE WRONG PACKAGE...
OH!
HERE IT IS...
...

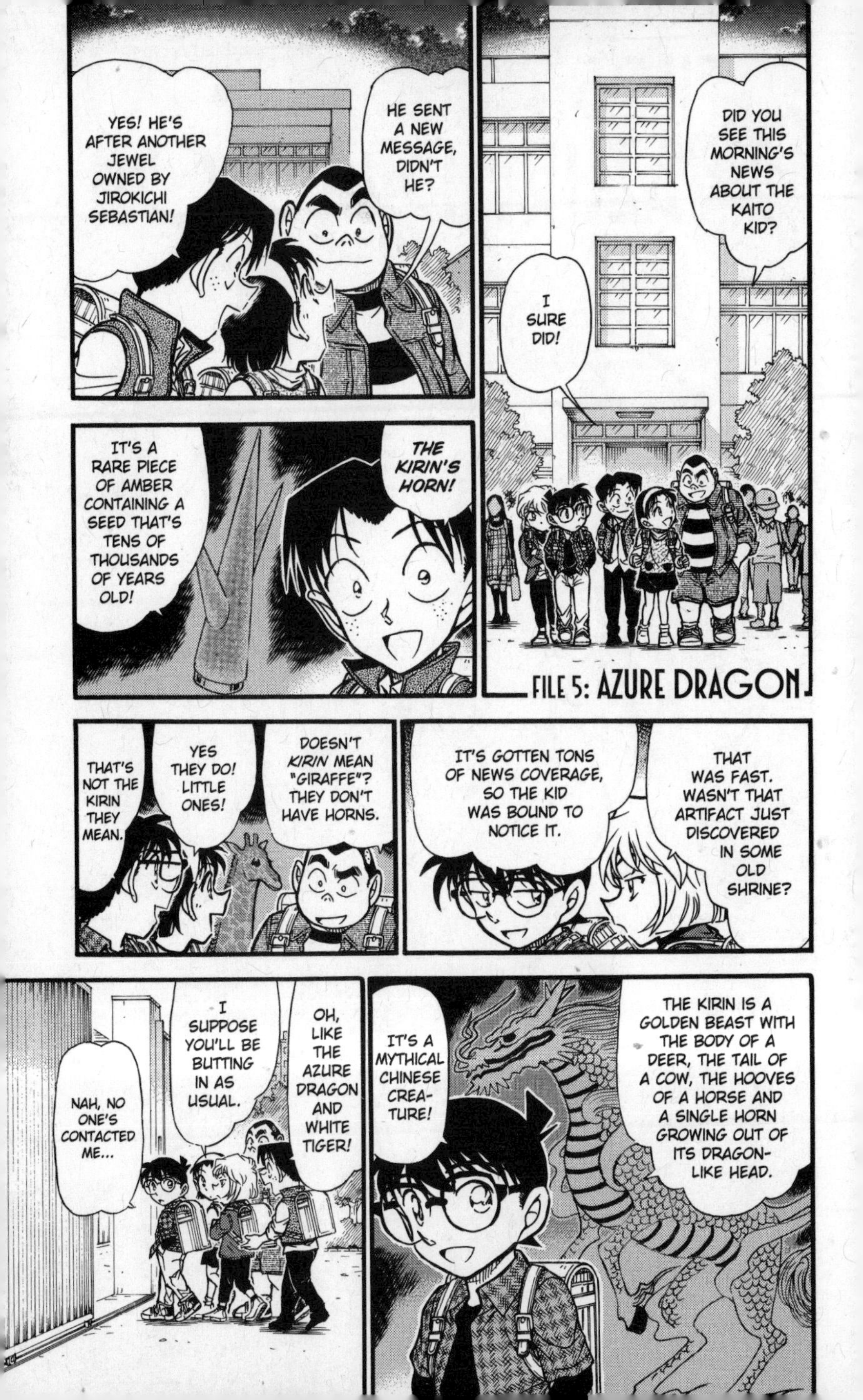
DID YOU SEE THIS MORNING'S NEWS ABOUT THE KAITO KID?
I SURE DID!
FILE 5: AZURE DRAGON
HE SENT A NEW MESSAGE, DIDN'T HE?
YES! HE'S AFTER ANOTHER JEWEL OWNED BY JIROKICHI SEBASTIAN!
THE KIRIN'S HORN!
IT'S A RARE PIECE OF AMBER CONTAINING A SEED THAT'S TENS OF THOUSANDS OF YEARS OLD!
THAT WAS FAST. WASN'T THAT ARTIFACT JUST DISCOVERED IN SOME OLD SHRINE?
IT'S GOTTEN TONS OF NEWS COVERAGE, SO THE KID WAS BOUND TO NOTICE IT.
DOESN'T *KIRIN* MEAN "GIRAFFE"? THEY DON'T HAVE HORNS.
YES THEY DO! LITTLE ONES!
THAT'S NOT THE KIRIN THEY MEAN.
THE KIRIN IS A GOLDEN BEAST WITH THE BODY OF A DEER, THE TAIL OF A COW, THE HOOVES OF A HORSE AND A SINGLE HORN GROWING OUT OF ITS DRAGON-LIKE HEAD.
IT'S A MYTHICAL CHINESE CREA-TURE!
OH, LIKE THE AZURE DRAGON AND WHITE TIGER!
I SUPPOSE YOU'LL BE BUTTING IN AS USUAL.
NAH, NO ONE'S CONTACTED ME...

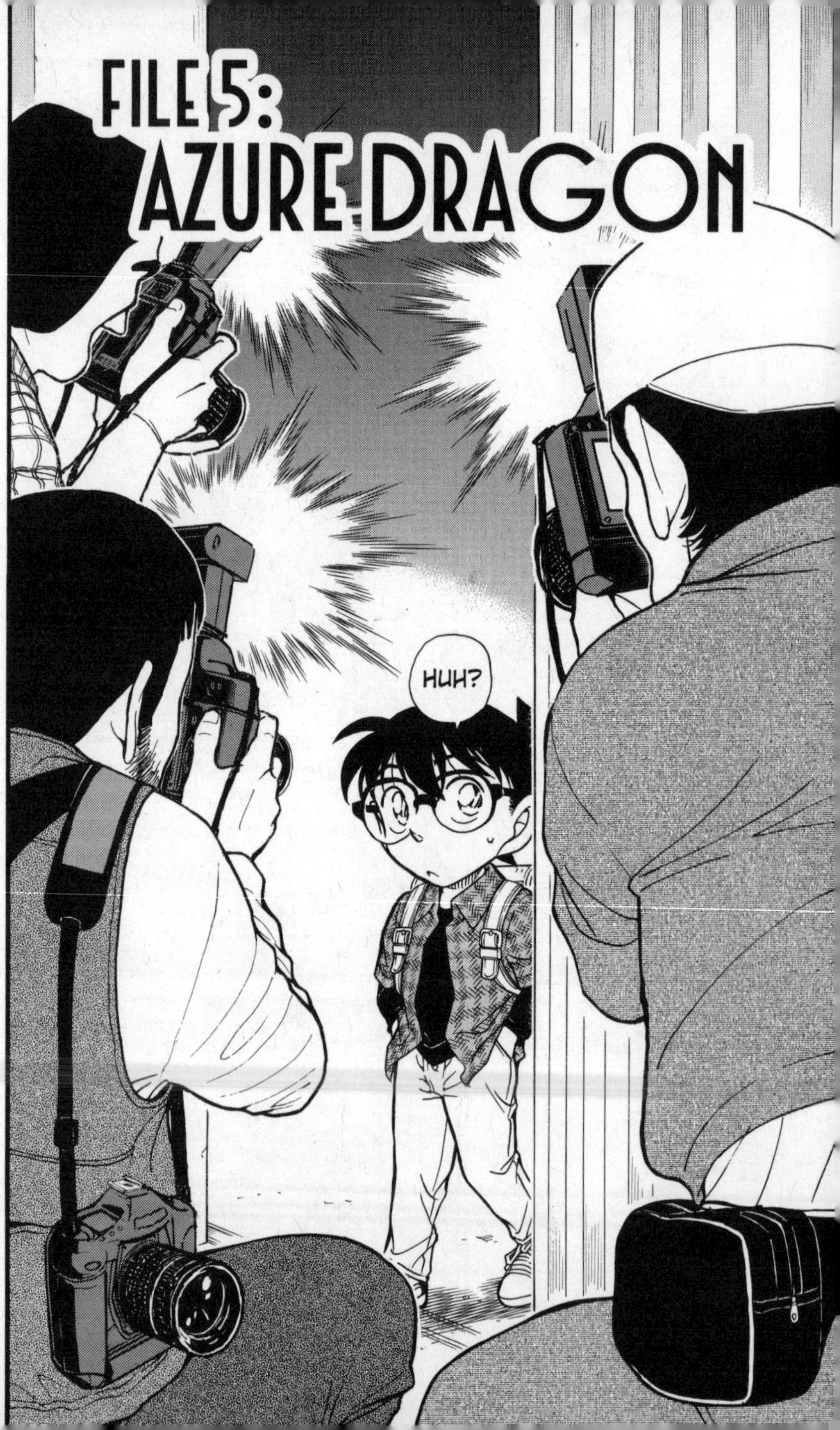
FILE 5:
AZURE DRAGON
HUH?

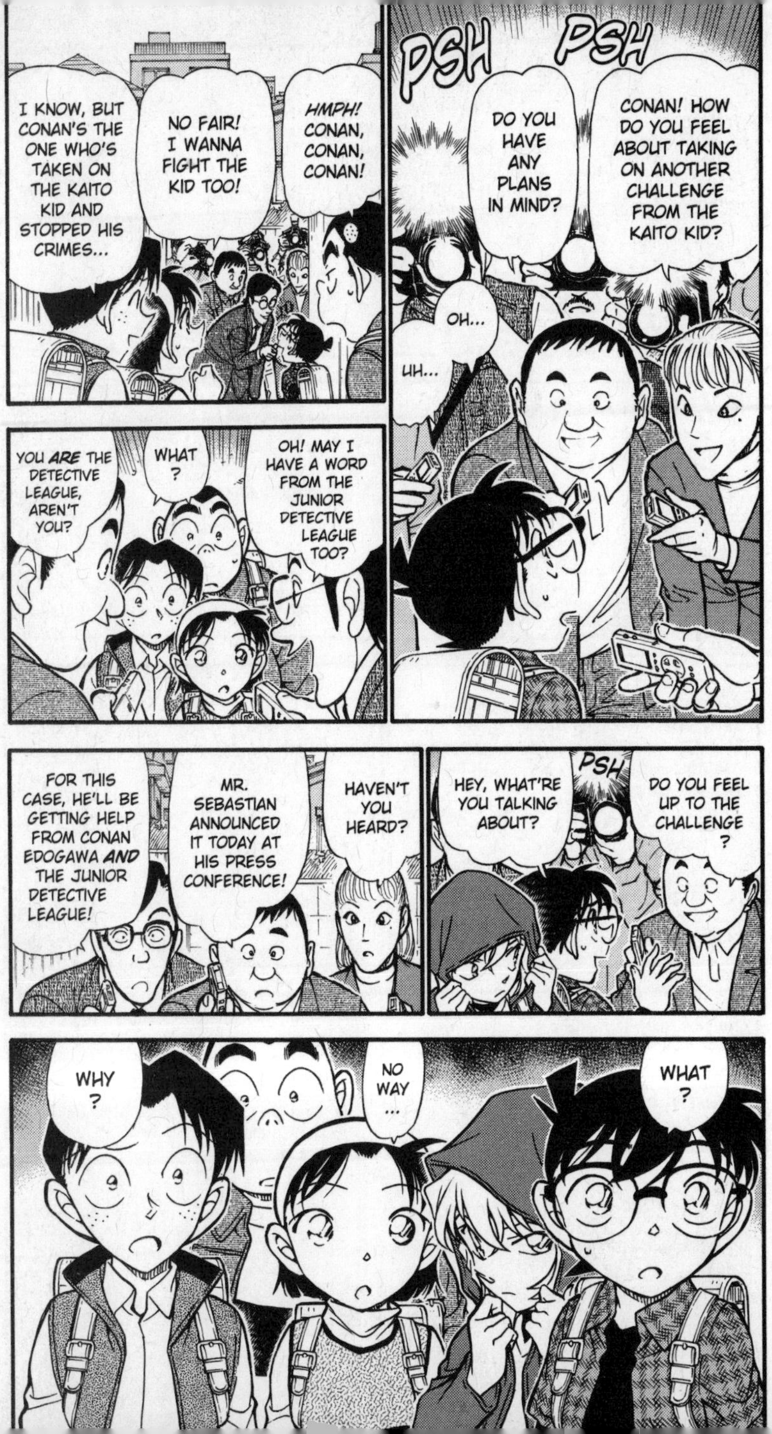
PSH PSH
CONAN! HOW DO YOU FEEL ABOUT TAKING ON ANOTHER CHALLENGE FROM THE KAITO KID?
DO YOU HAVE ANY PLANS IN MIND?
OH...
UH...
HMPH! CONAN, CONAN, CONAN!
NO FAIR! I WANNA FIGHT THE KID TOO!
I KNOW, BUT CONAN'S THE ONE WHO'S TAKEN ON THE KAITO KID AND STOPPED HIS CRIMES...
OH! MAY I HAVE A WORD FROM THE JUNIOR DETECTIVE LEAGUE TOO?
WHAT?
YOU ***ARE*** THE DETECTIVE LEAGUE, AREN'T YOU?
PSH
DO YOU FEEL UP TO THE CHALLENGE?
HEY, WHAT'RE YOU TALKING ABOUT?
HAVEN'T YOU HEARD?
MR. SEBASTIAN ANNOUNCED IT TODAY AT HIS PRESS CONFERENCE!
FOR THIS CASE, HE'LL BE GETTING HELP FROM CONAN EDOGAWA ***AND*** THE JUNIOR DETECTIVE LEAGUE!
WHAT?
NO WAY...
WHY?

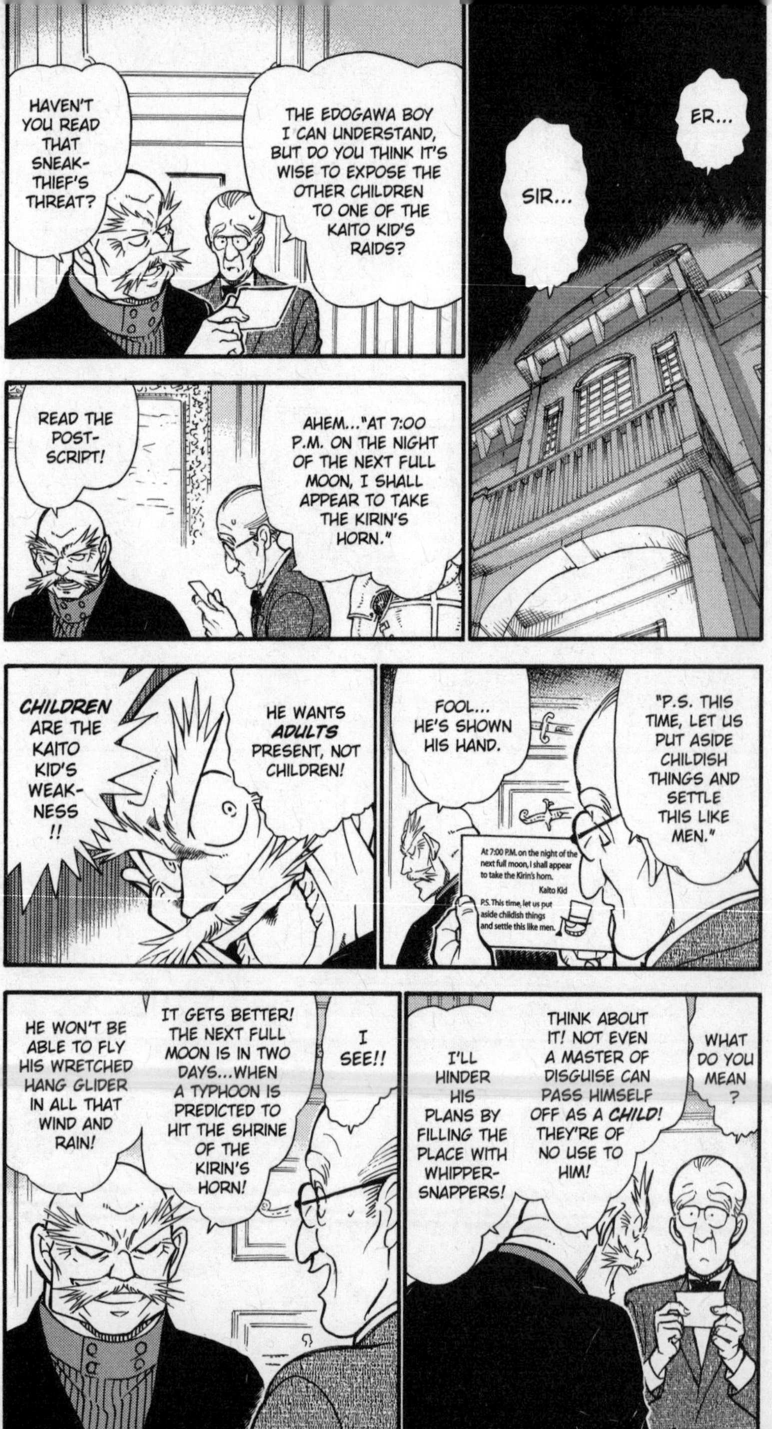

ER...
SIR...
THE EDOGAWA BOY I CAN UNDERSTAND, BUT DO YOU THINK IT'S WISE TO EXPOSE THE OTHER CHILDREN TO ONE OF THE KAITO KID'S RAIDS?
HAVEN'T YOU READ THAT SNEAK-THIEF'S THREAT?
AHEM..."AT 7:00 P.M. ON THE NIGHT OF THE NEXT FULL MOON, I SHALL APPEAR TO TAKE THE KIRIN'S HORN."
READ THE POST-SCRIPT!
"P.S. THIS TIME, LET US PUT ASIDE CHILDISH THINGS AND SETTLE THIS LIKE MEN."
FOOL... HE'S SHOWN HIS HAND.
At 7:00 P.M. on the night of the next full moon, I shall appear to take the Kirin's horn.
Kaito Kid
P.S. This time, let us put aside childish things and settle this like men.
HE WANTS ADULTS PRESENT, NOT CHILDREN!
CHILDREN ARE THE KAITO KID'S WEAK-NESS !!
WHAT DO YOU MEAN ?
THINK ABOUT IT! NOT EVEN A MASTER OF DISGUISE CAN PASS HIMSELF OFF AS A CHILD! THEY'RE OF NO USE TO HIM!
I'LL HINDER HIS PLANS BY FILLING THE PLACE WITH WHIPPER-SNAPPERS!
I SEE!!
IT GETS BETTER! THE NEXT FULL MOON IS IN TWO DAYS...WHEN A TYPHOON IS PREDICTED TO HIT THE SHRINE OF THE KIRIN'S HORN!
HE WON'T BE ABLE TO FLY HIS WRETCHED HANG GLIDER IN ALL THAT WIND AND RAIN!

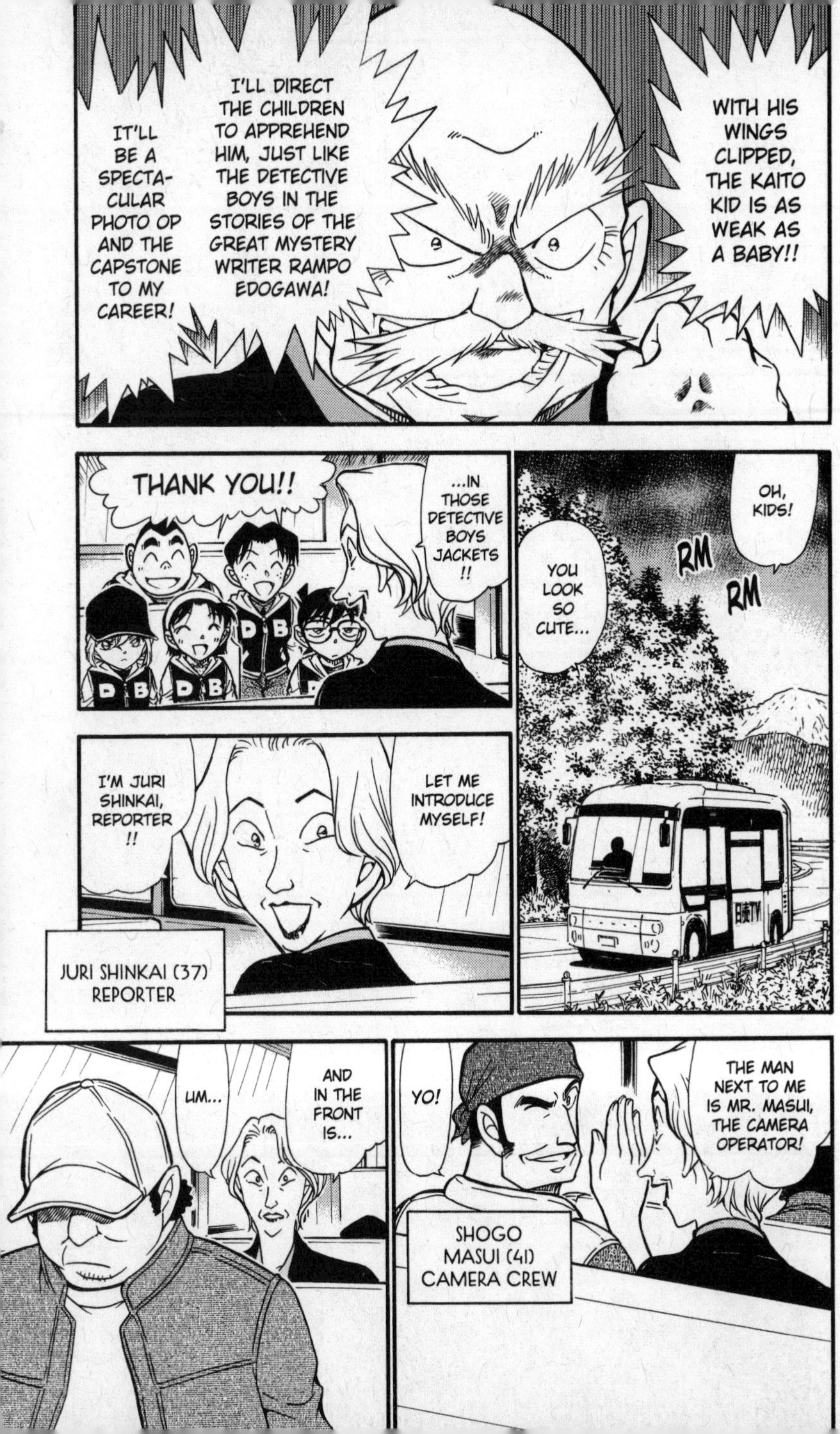
WITH HIS WINGS CLIPPED, THE KAITO KID IS AS WEAK AS A BABY!!
I'LL DIRECT THE CHILDREN TO APPREHEND HIM, JUST LIKE THE DETECTIVE BOYS IN THE STORIES OF THE GREAT MYSTERY WRITER RAMPO EDOGAWA!
IT'LL BE A SPECTACULAR PHOTO OP AND THE CAPSTONE TO MY CAREER!
OH, KIDS!
RM
RM
YOU LOOK SO CUTE...
...IN THOSE DETECTIVE BOYS JACKETS!!
THANK YOU!!
LET ME INTRODUCE MYSELF!
I'M JURI SHINKAI, REPORTER!!
JURI SHINKAI (37) REPORTER
THE MAN NEXT TO ME IS MR. MASUI, THE CAMERA OPERATOR!
YO!
SHOGO MASUI (41) CAMERA CREW
AND IN THE FRONT IS...
UM...

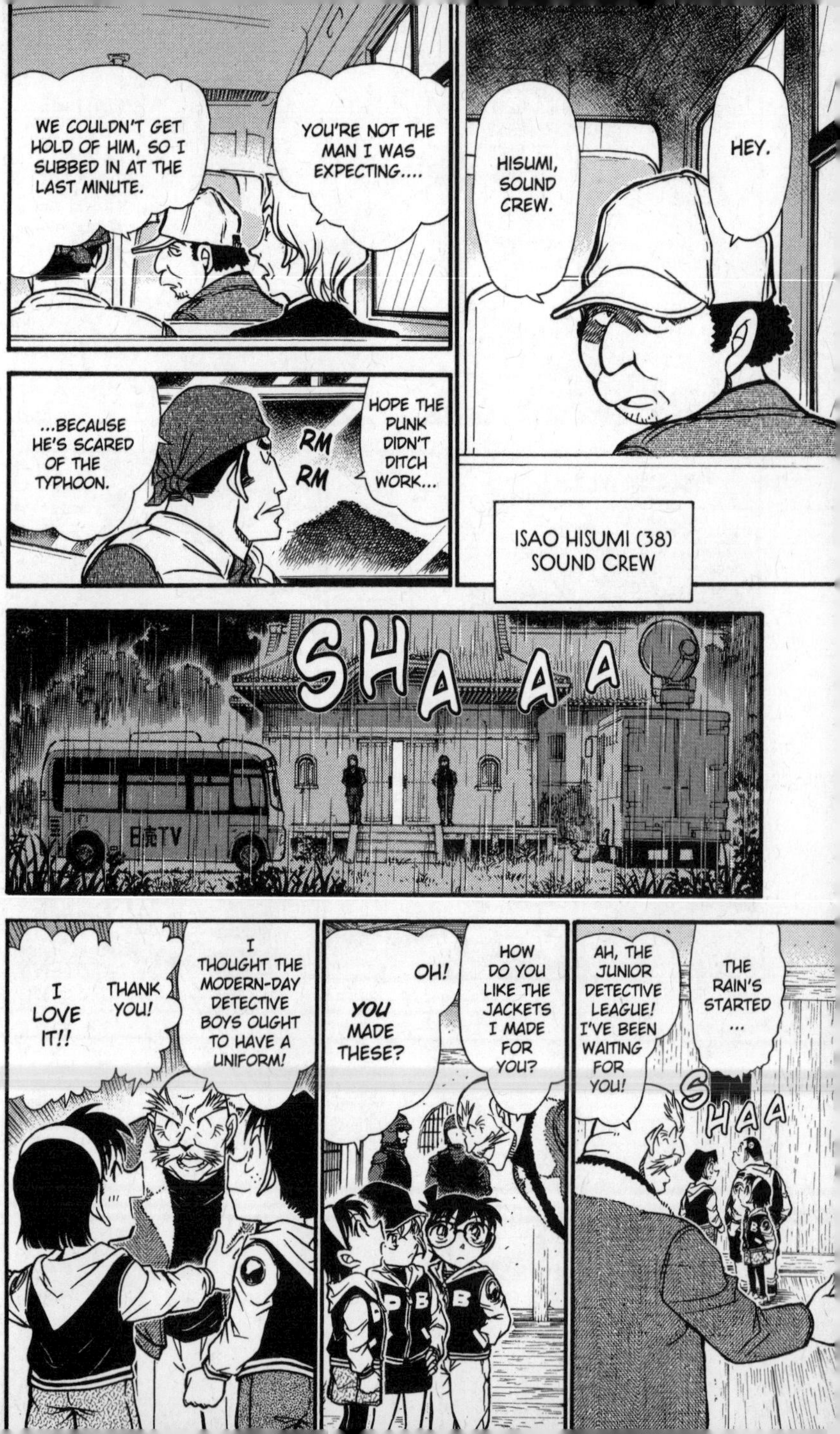
HEY.
HISUMI, SOUND CREW.
ISAO HISUMI (38) SOUND CREW
YOU'RE NOT THE MAN I WAS EXPECTING....
WE COULDN'T GET HOLD OF HIM, SO I SUBBED IN AT THE LAST MINUTE.
HOPE THE PUNK DIDN'T DITCH WORK...
RM RM
...BECAUSE HE'S SCARED OF THE TYPHOON.
SHAAA
THE RAIN'S STARTED ...
SHAA
AH, THE JUNIOR DETECTIVE LEAGUE! I'VE BEEN WAITING FOR YOU!
HOW DO YOU LIKE THE JACKETS I MADE FOR YOU?
OH!
YOU MADE THESE?
I THOUGHT THE MODERN-DAY DETECTIVE BOYS OUGHT TO HAVE A UNIFORM!
THANK YOU!
I LOVE IT!!

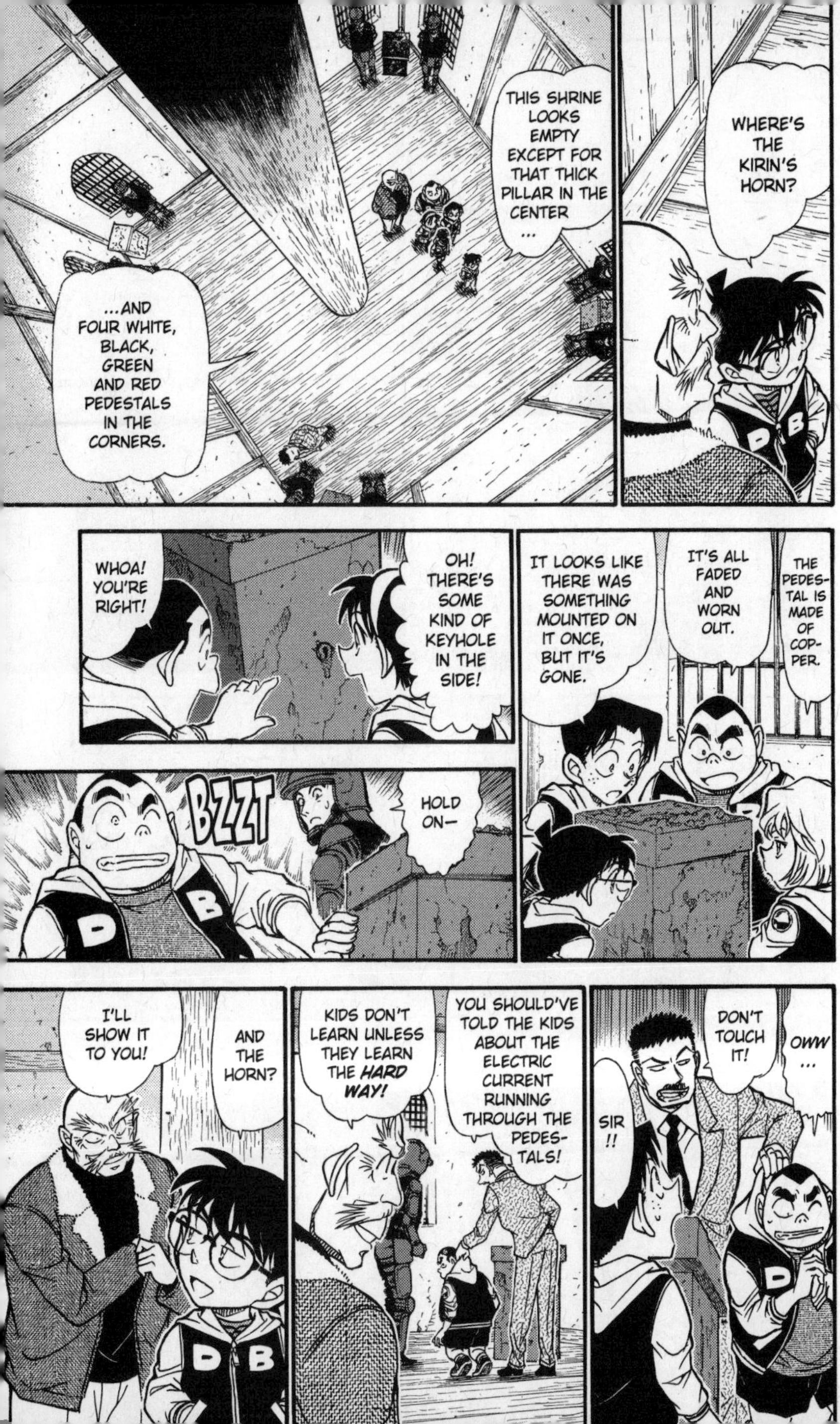
WHERE'S THE KIRIN'S HORN?
THIS SHRINE LOOKS EMPTY EXCEPT FOR THAT THICK PILLAR IN THE CENTER ...
...AND FOUR WHITE, BLACK, GREEN AND RED PEDESTALS IN THE CORNERS.
THE PEDESTAL IS MADE OF COPPER.
IT'S ALL FADED AND WORN OUT.
IT LOOKS LIKE THERE WAS SOMETHING MOUNTED ON IT ONCE, BUT IT'S GONE.
OH! THERE'S SOME KIND OF KEYHOLE IN THE SIDE!
WHOA! YOU'RE RIGHT!
HOLD ON—
BZZT
OWW ...
DON'T TOUCH IT!
SIR !!
YOU SHOULD'VE TOLD THE KIDS ABOUT THE ELECTRIC CURRENT RUNNING THROUGH THE PEDESTALS!
KIDS DON'T LEARN UNLESS THEY LEARN THE *HARD WAY!*
AND THE HORN?
I'LL SHOW IT TO YOU!

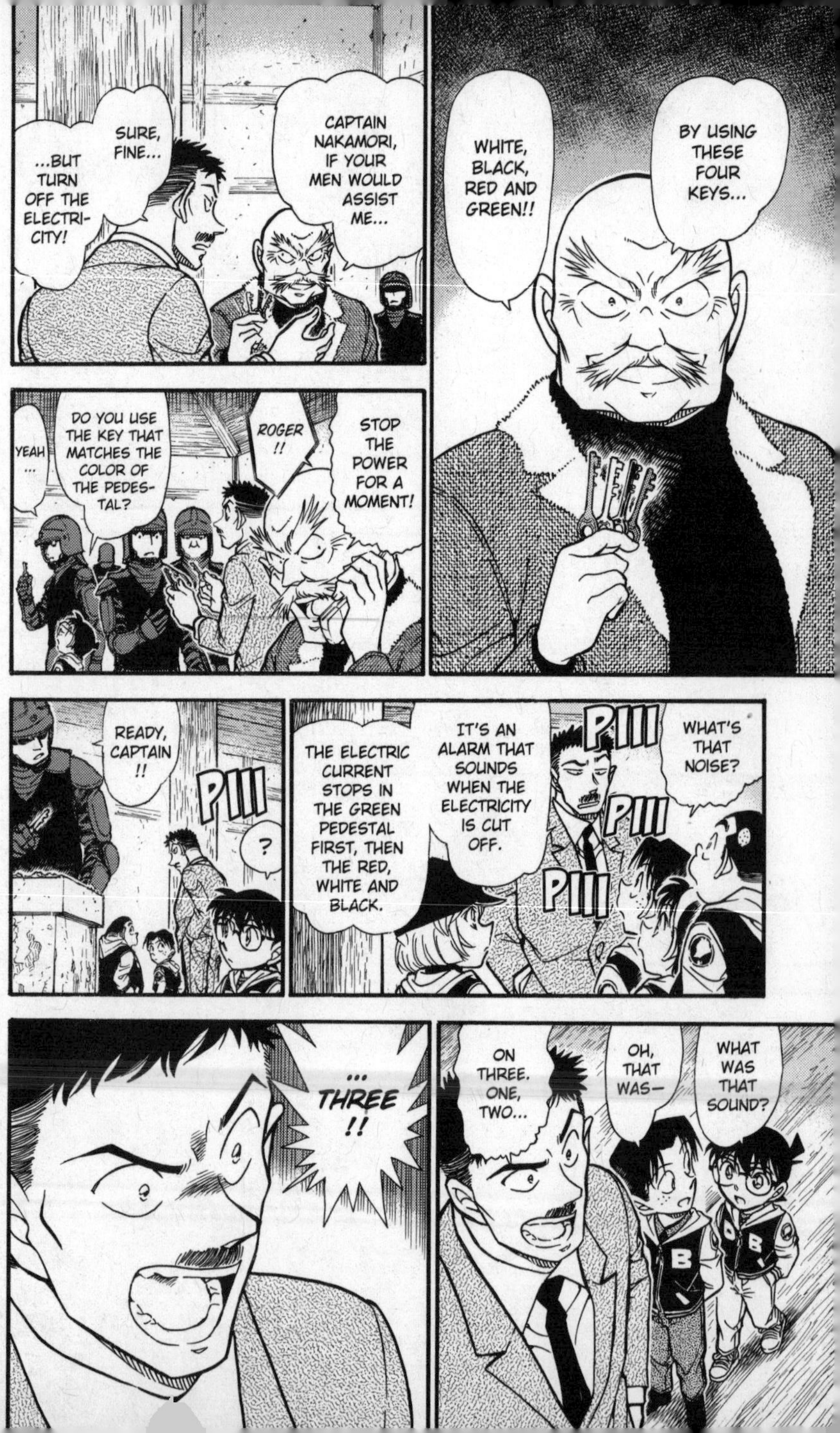
BY USING THESE FOUR KEYS...
WHITE, BLACK, RED AND GREEN!!
CAPTAIN NAKAMORI, IF YOUR MEN WOULD ASSIST ME...
SURE, FINE...
...BUT TURN OFF THE ELECTRICITY!
STOP THE POWER FOR A MOMENT!
ROGER!!
DO YOU USE THE KEY THAT MATCHES THE COLOR OF THE PEDESTAL?
YEAH...
WHAT'S THAT NOISE?
PIII
PIII
PIII
IT'S AN ALARM THAT SOUNDS WHEN THE ELECTRICITY IS CUT OFF.
THE ELECTRIC CURRENT STOPS IN THE GREEN PEDESTAL FIRST, THEN THE RED, WHITE AND BLACK.
READY, CAPTAIN!!
PIII
?
WHAT WAS THAT SOUND?
OH, THAT WAS—
ON THREE. ONE, TWO...
...THREE!!

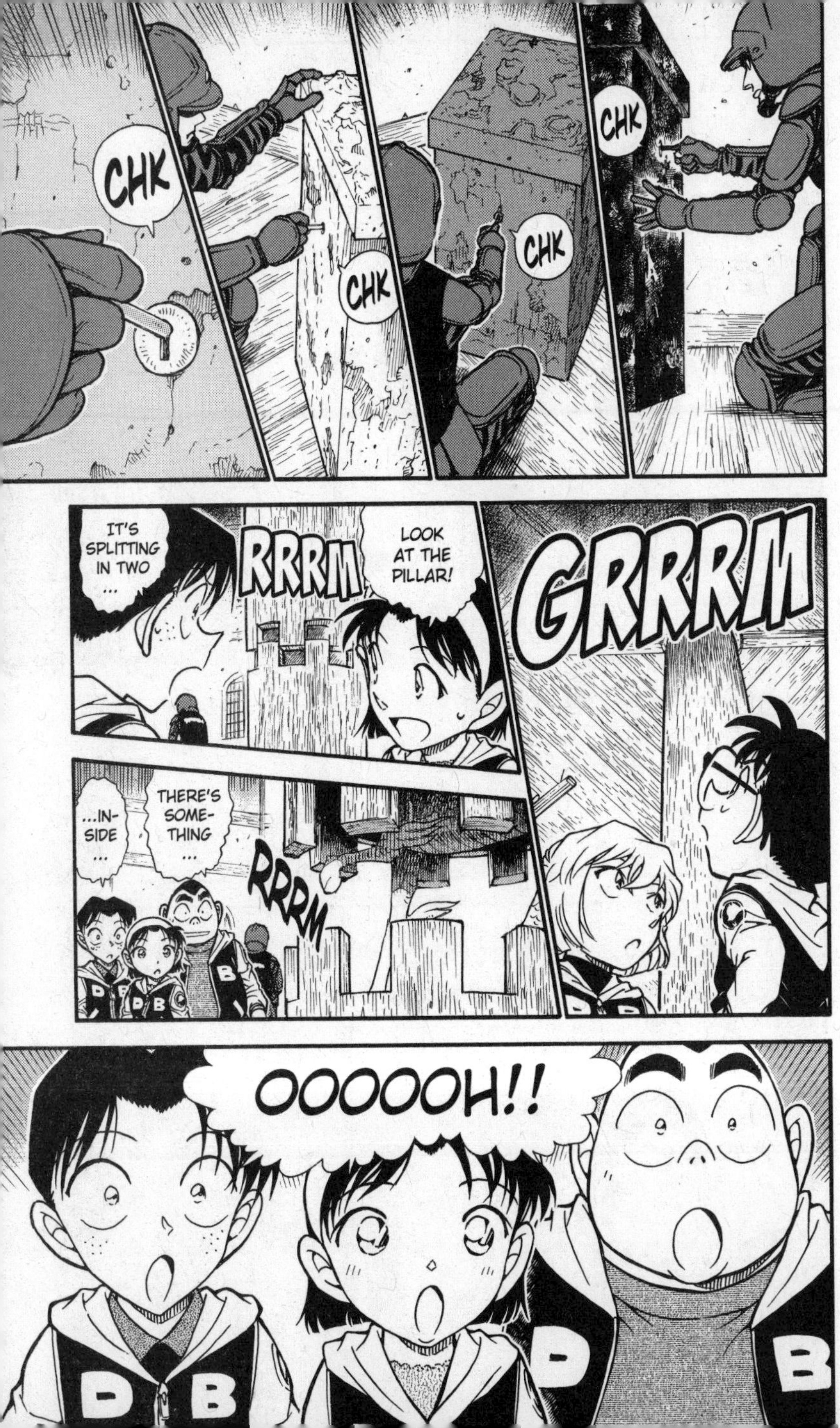
CHK
CHK
CHK
CHK
GRRRM
LOOK AT THE PILLAR!
RRRM
IT'S SPLITTING IN TWO...
RRRM
THERE'S SOMETHING...
...INSIDE...
OOOOOH!!

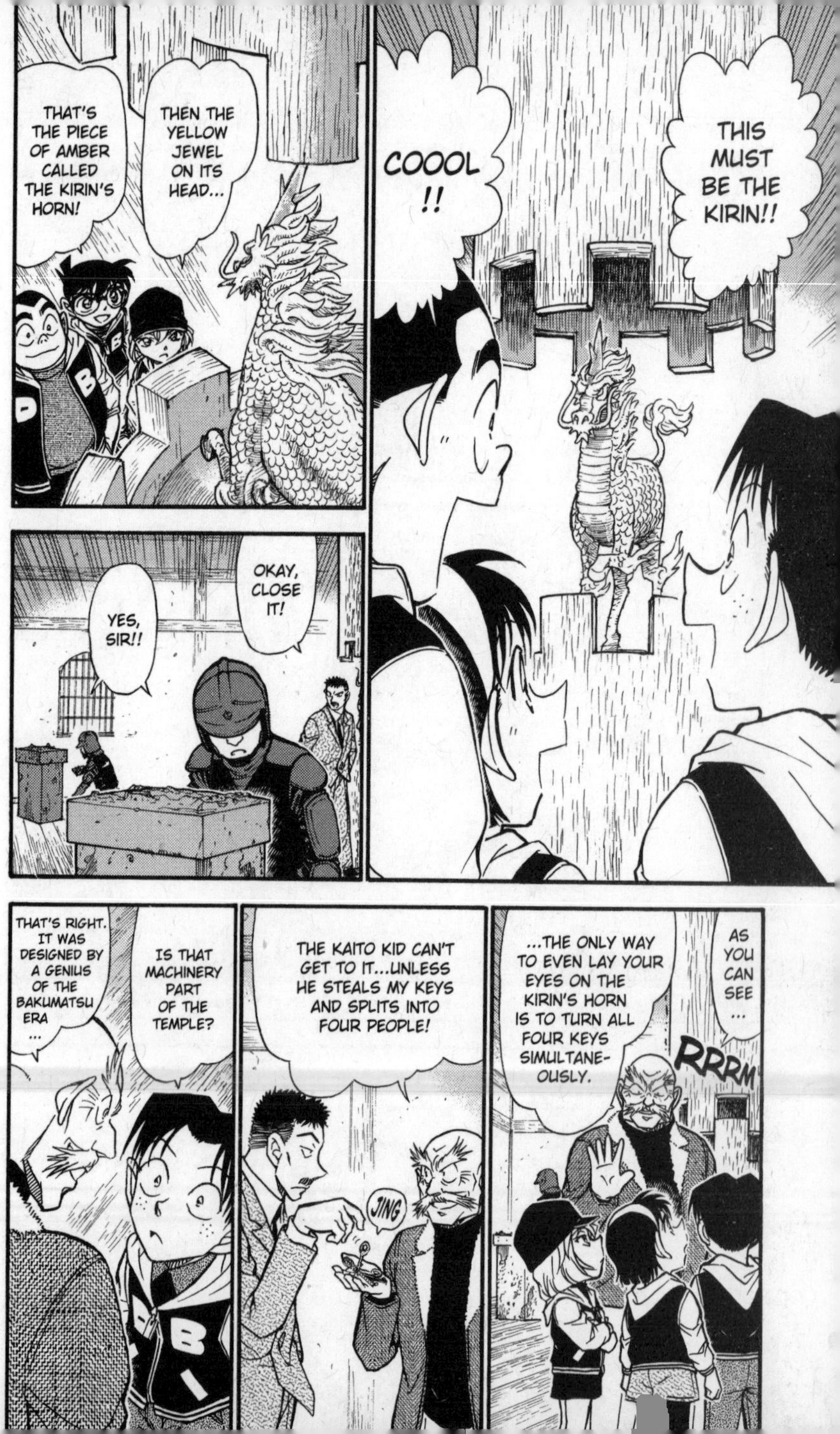
THIS MUST BE THE KIRIN!!
COOOL!!
THEN THE YELLOW JEWEL ON ITS HEAD...
THAT'S THE PIECE OF AMBER CALLED THE KIRIN'S HORN!
OKAY, CLOSE IT!
YES, SIR!!
AS YOU CAN SEE...
...THE ONLY WAY TO EVEN LAY YOUR EYES ON THE KIRIN'S HORN IS TO TURN ALL FOUR KEYS SIMULTANE-OUSLY.
RRRM
THE KAITO KID CAN'T GET TO IT...UNLESS HE STEALS MY KEYS AND SPLITS INTO FOUR PEOPLE!
JING
IS THAT MACHINERY PART OF THE TEMPLE?
THAT'S RIGHT. IT WAS DESIGNED BY A GENIUS OF THE BAKUMATSU ERA...

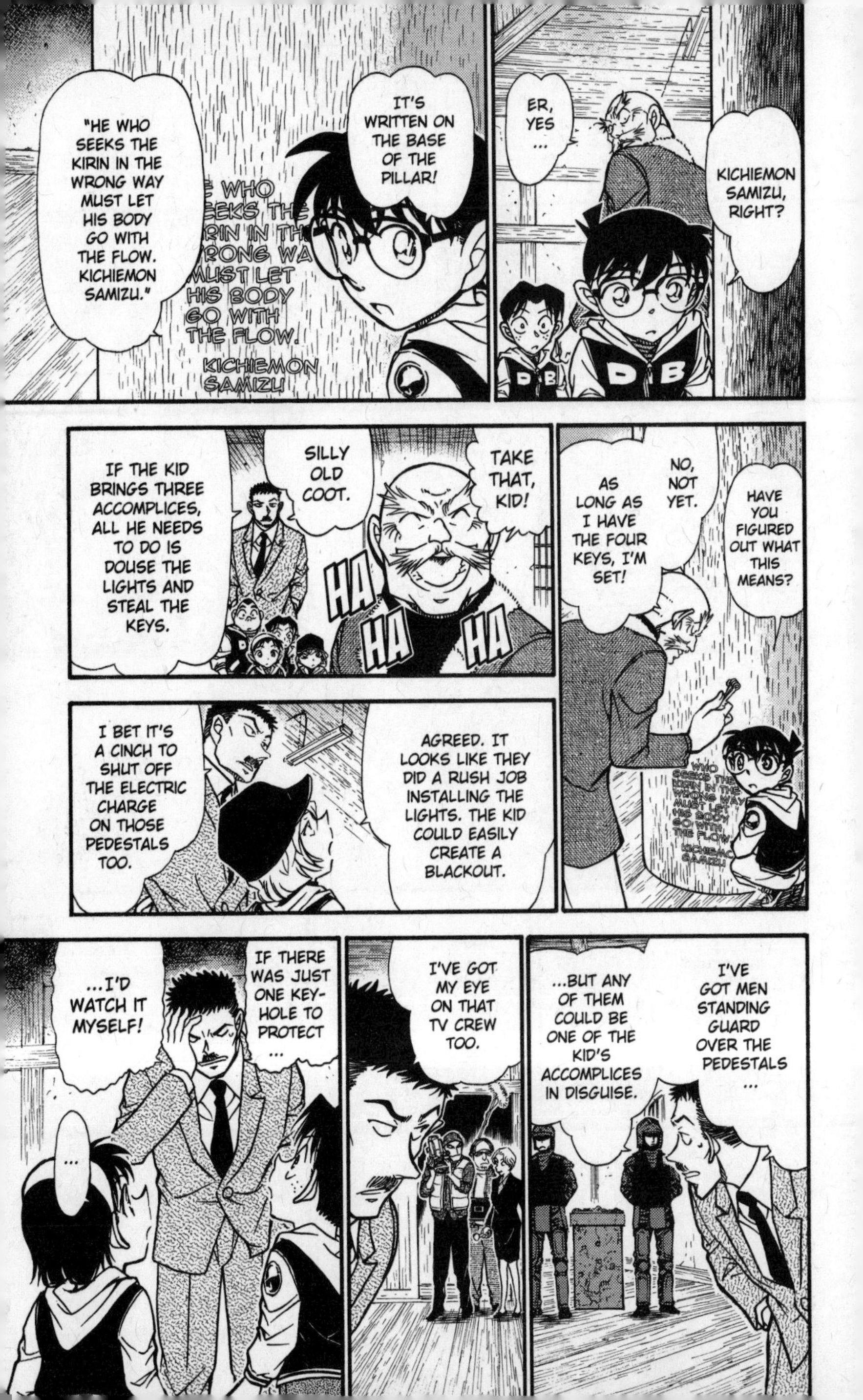
KICHIEMON SAMIZU, RIGHT?
ER, YES ...
IT'S WRITTEN ON THE BASE OF THE PILLAR!
"HE WHO SEEKS THE KIRIN IN THE WRONG WAY MUST LET HIS BODY GO WITH THE FLOW. KICHIEMON SAMIZU."
HAVE YOU FIGURED OUT WHAT THIS MEANS?
NO, NOT YET.
AS LONG AS I HAVE THE FOUR KEYS, I'M SET!
TAKE THAT, KID!
HA HA HA
SILLY OLD COOT.
IF THE KID BRINGS THREE ACCOMPLICES, ALL HE NEEDS TO DO IS DOUSE THE LIGHTS AND STEAL THE KEYS.
I BET IT'S A CINCH TO SHUT OFF THE ELECTRIC CHARGE ON THOSE PEDESTALS TOO.
AGREED. IT LOOKS LIKE THEY DID A RUSH JOB INSTALLING THE LIGHTS. THE KID COULD EASILY CREATE A BLACKOUT.
I'VE GOT MEN STANDING GUARD OVER THE PEDESTALS ...
...BUT ANY OF THEM COULD BE ONE OF THE KID'S ACCOMPLICES IN DISGUISE.
I'VE GOT MY EYE ON THAT TV CREW TOO.
IF THERE WAS JUST ONE KEY-HOLE TO PROTECT ...
...I'D WATCH IT MYSELF!
...

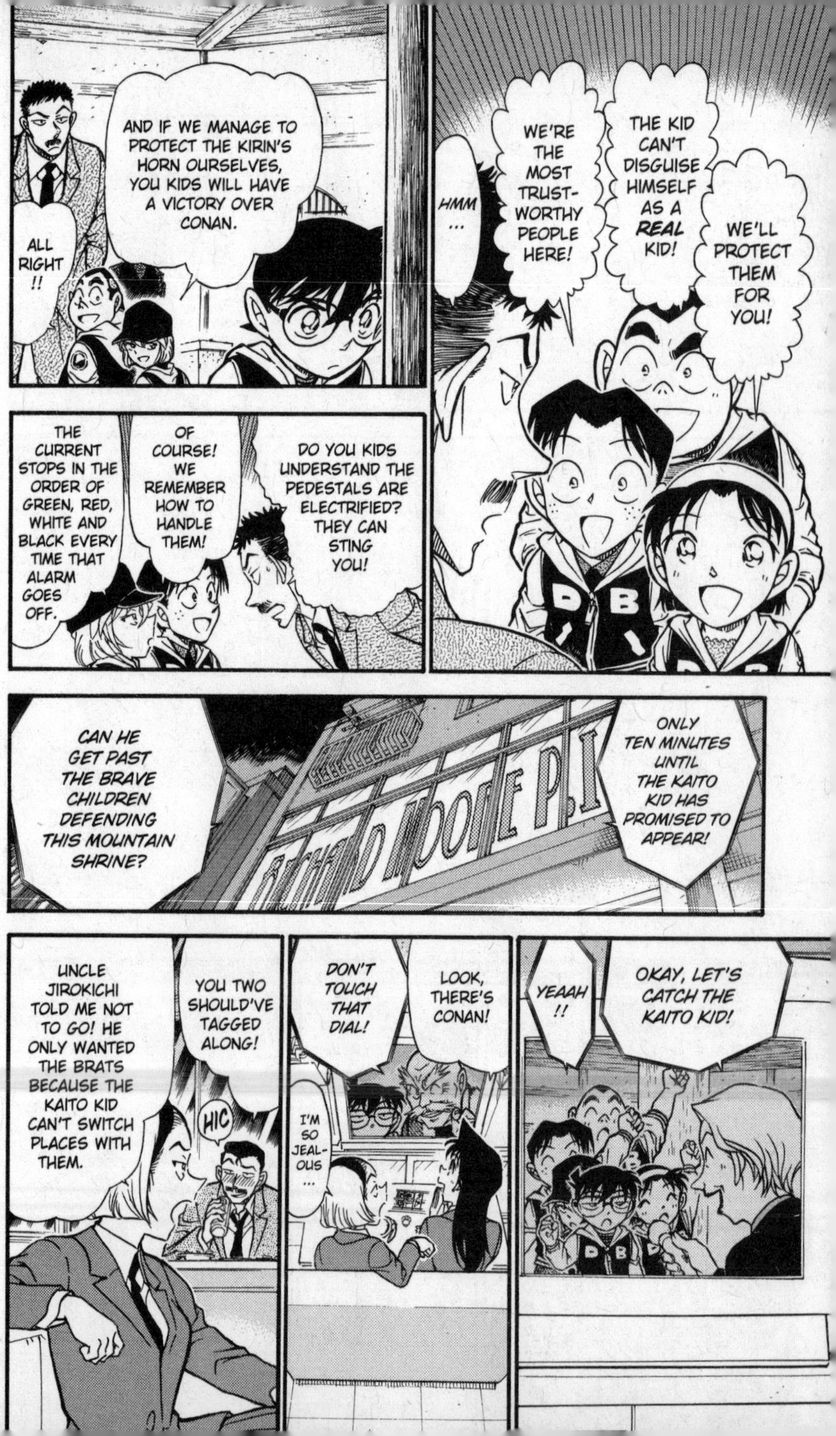
WE'LL PROTECT THEM FOR YOU!
THE KID CAN'T DISGUISE HIMSELF AS A REAL KID!
WE'RE THE MOST TRUST-WORTHY PEOPLE HERE!
HMM...
AND IF WE MANAGE TO PROTECT THE KIRIN'S HORN OURSELVES, YOU KIDS WILL HAVE A VICTORY OVER CONAN.
ALL RIGHT!!
DO YOU KIDS UNDERSTAND THE PEDESTALS ARE ELECTRIFIED? THEY CAN STING YOU!
OF COURSE! WE REMEMBER HOW TO HANDLE THEM!
THE CURRENT STOPS IN THE ORDER OF GREEN, RED, WHITE AND BLACK EVERY TIME THAT ALARM GOES OFF.
ONLY TEN MINUTES UNTIL THE KAITO KID HAS PROMISED TO APPEAR!
CAN HE GET PAST THE BRAVE CHILDREN DEFENDING THIS MOUNTAIN SHRINE?
OKAY, LET'S CATCH THE KAITO KID!
YEAAH!!
LOOK, THERE'S CONAN!
DON'T TOUCH THAT DIAL!
I'M SO JEAL-OUS...
YOU TWO SHOULD'VE TAGGED ALONG!
HIC
UNCLE JIROKICHI TOLD ME NOT TO GO! HE ONLY WANTED THE BRATS BECAUSE THE KAITO KID CAN'T SWITCH PLACES WITH THEM.

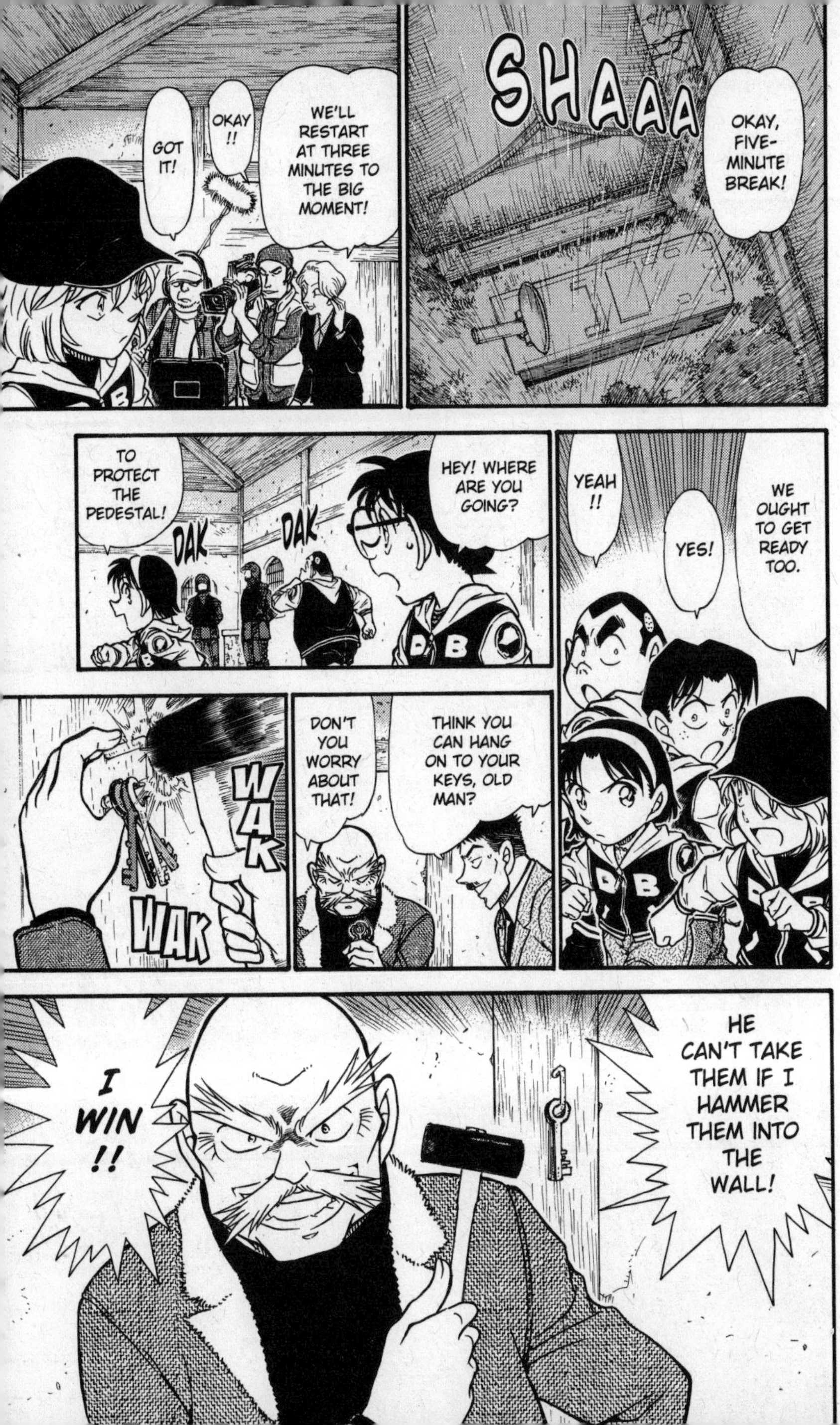
SHAAA
OKAY, FIVE-MINUTE BREAK!
WE'LL RESTART AT THREE MINUTES TO THE BIG MOMENT!
OKAY !!
GOT IT!
WE OUGHT TO GET READY TOO.
YES!
YEAH !!
HEY! WHERE ARE YOU GOING?
DAK
DAK
TO PROTECT THE PEDESTAL!
THINK YOU CAN HANG ON TO YOUR KEYS, OLD MAN?
DON'T YOU WORRY ABOUT THAT!
WAK
WAK
HE CAN'T TAKE THEM IF I HAMMER THEM INTO THE WALL!
I WIN !!

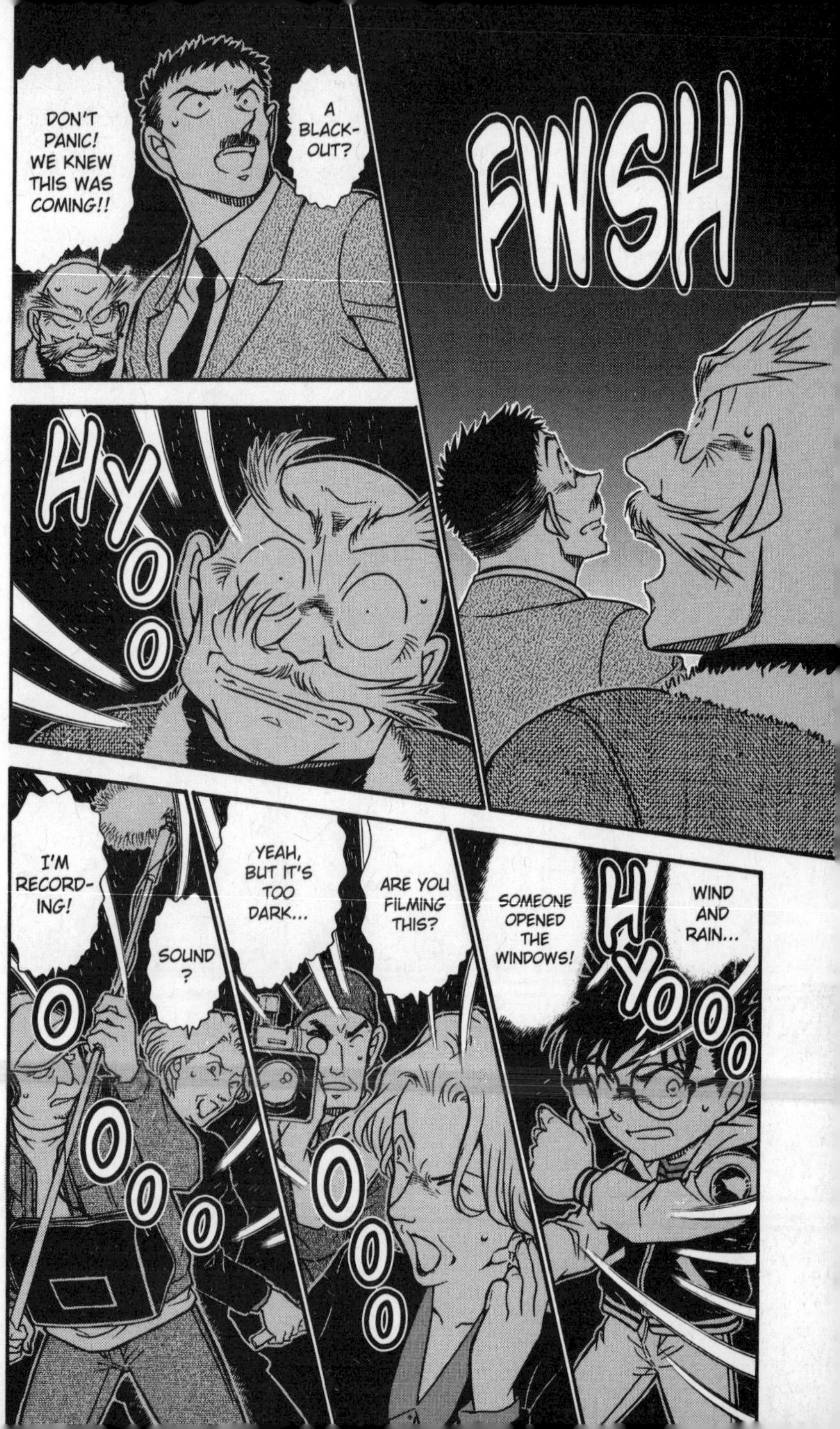
FWSH
A BLACK-OUT?
DON'T PANIC! WE KNEW THIS WAS COMING!!
HYOOO
WIND AND RAIN...
HYOOOO
SOMEONE OPENED THE WINDOWS!
ARE YOU FILMING THIS?
YEAH, BUT IT'S TOO DARK...
OOOO
SOUND?
I'M RECORDING!
OOOO

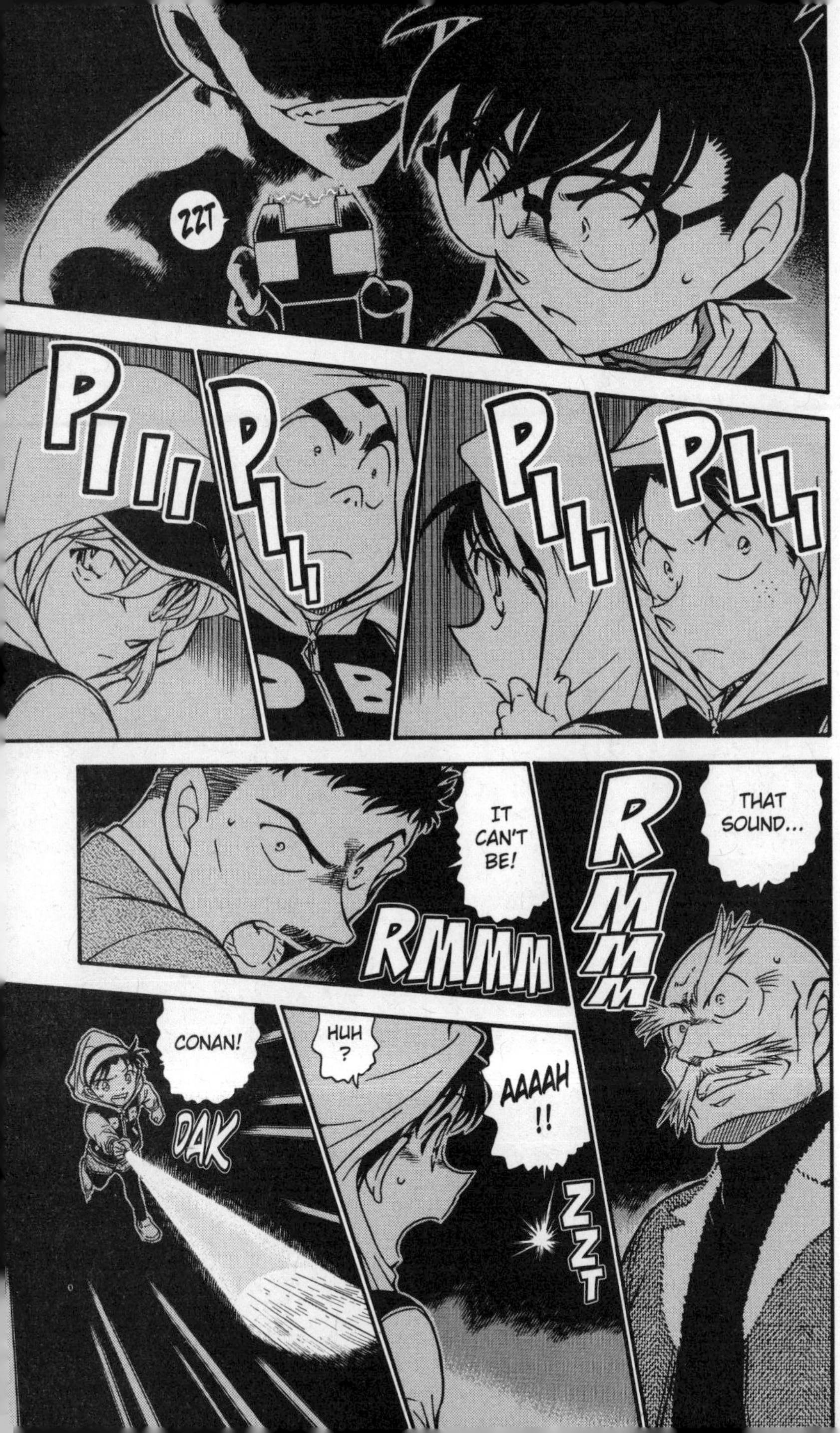
ZZT
PIII
PIII
PIII
PIII
THAT SOUND...
RMMM
IT CAN'T BE!
RMMMM
HUH?
AAAAH!!
ZZT
CONAN!
DAK

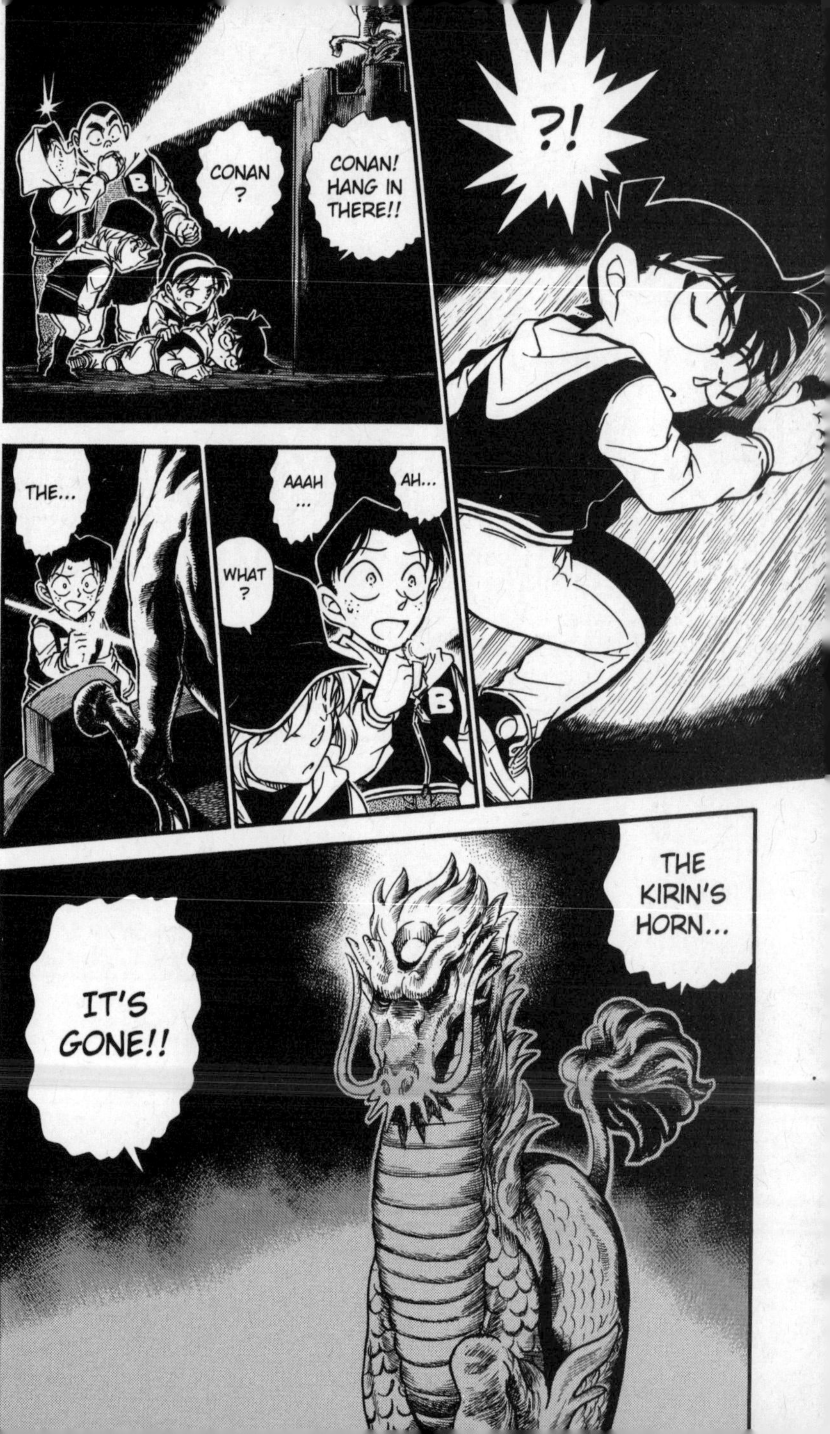
?!
CONAN! HANG IN THERE!!
CONAN ?
AH...
AAAH ...
WHAT ?
THE...
THE KIRIN'S HORN...
IT'S GONE!!

FILE 6: VERMILLION BIRD

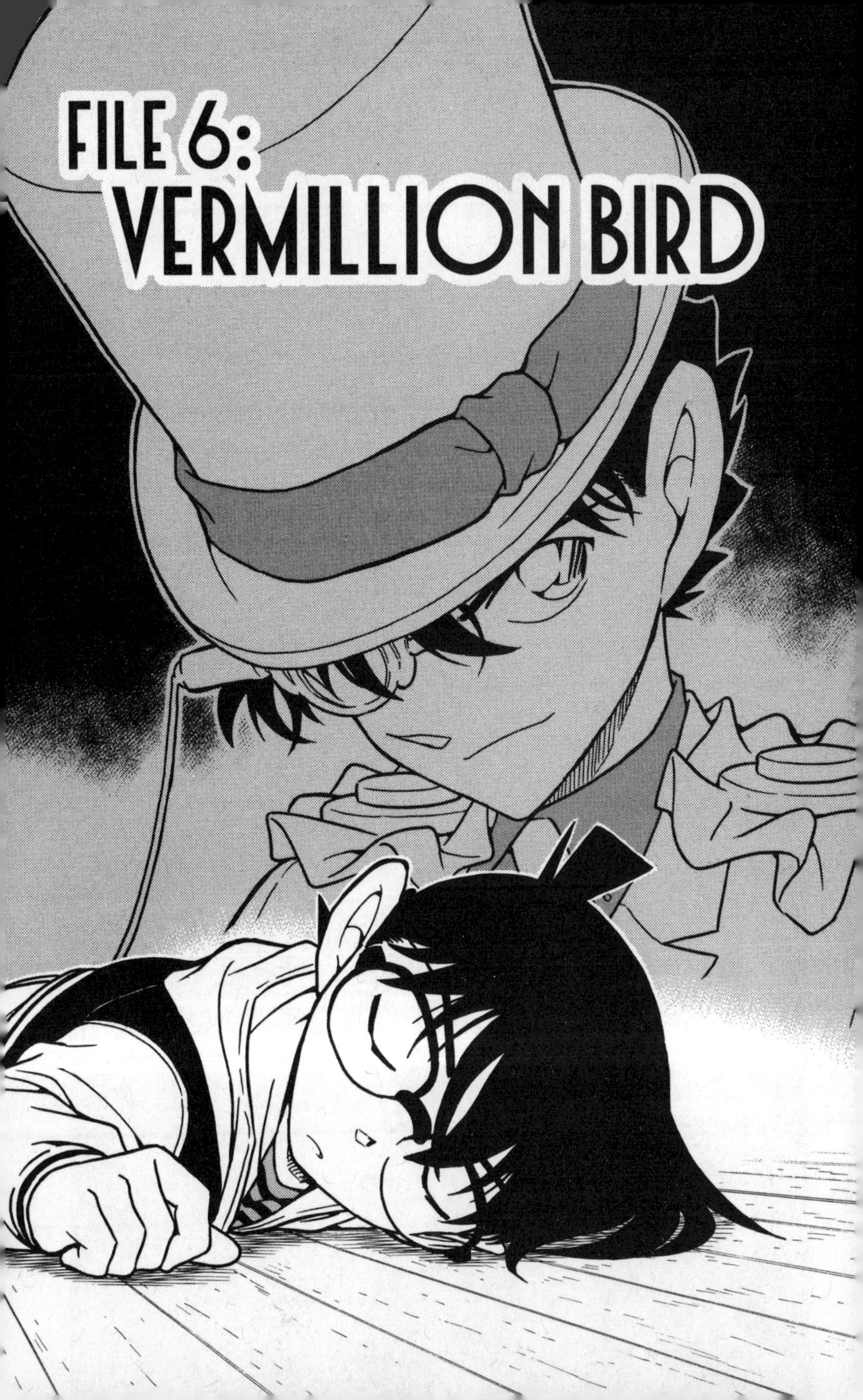

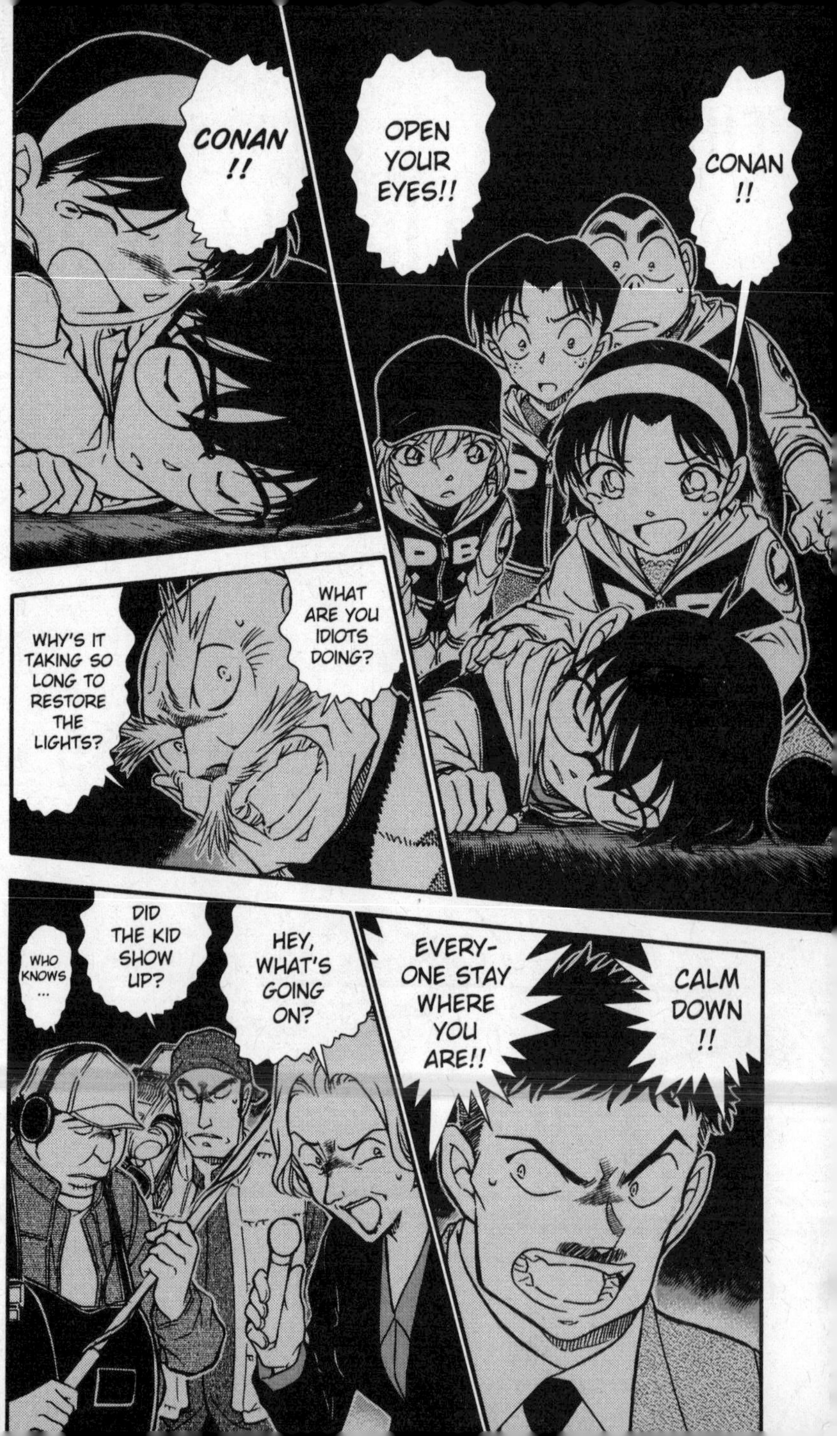
CONAN !!
OPEN YOUR EYES!!
CONAN !!
WHAT ARE YOU IDIOTS DOING?
WHY'S IT TAKING SO LONG TO RESTORE THE LIGHTS?
CALM DOWN !!
EVERY-ONE STAY WHERE YOU ARE!!
HEY, WHAT'S GOING ON?
DID THE KID SHOW UP?
WHO KNOWS ...

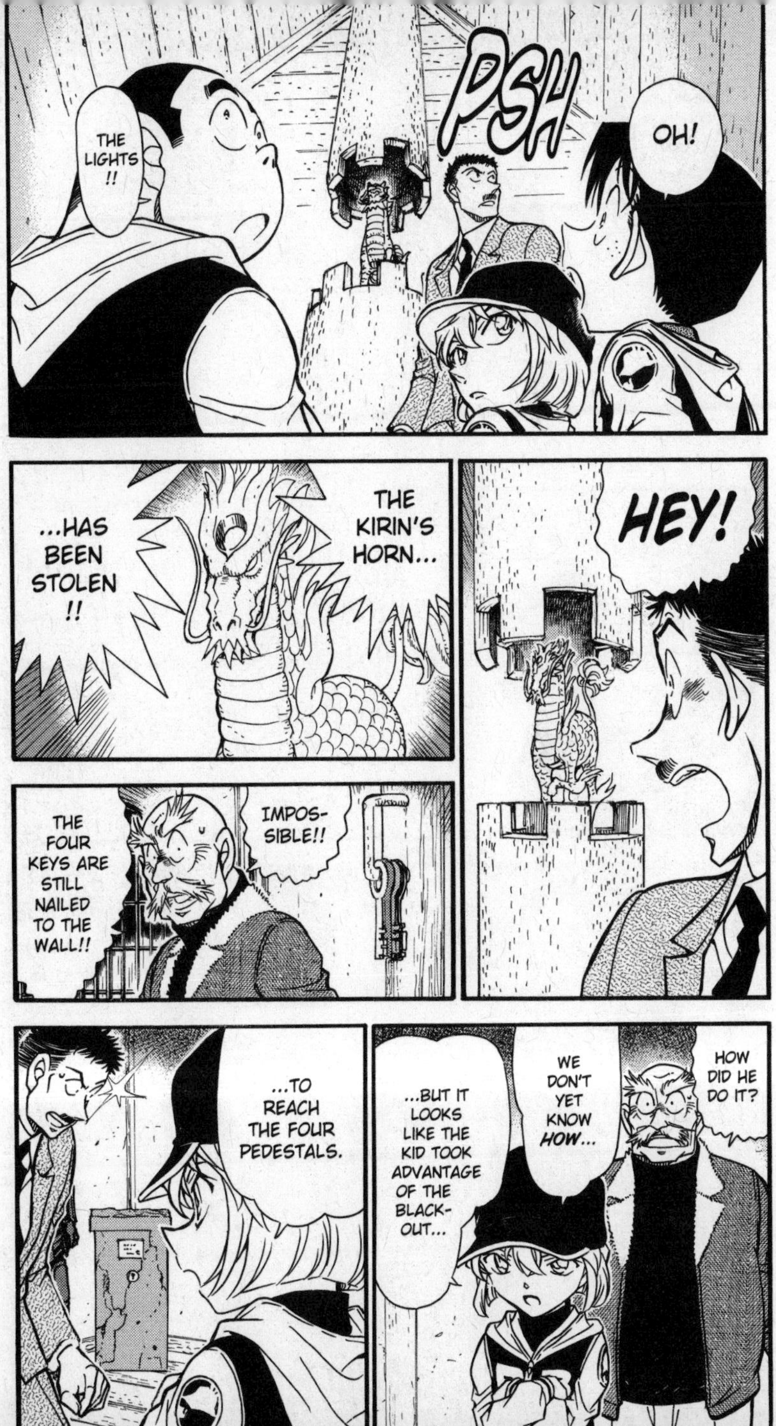
OH!
PSH
THE LIGHTS!!
HEY!
THE KIRIN'S HORN...
...HAS BEEN STOLEN!!
IMPOSSIBLE!!
THE FOUR KEYS ARE STILL NAILED TO THE WALL!!
HOW DID HE DO IT?
WE DON'T YET KNOW *HOW*...
...BUT IT LOOKS LIKE THE KID TOOK ADVANTAGE OF THE BLACKOUT...
...TO REACH THE FOUR PEDESTALS.

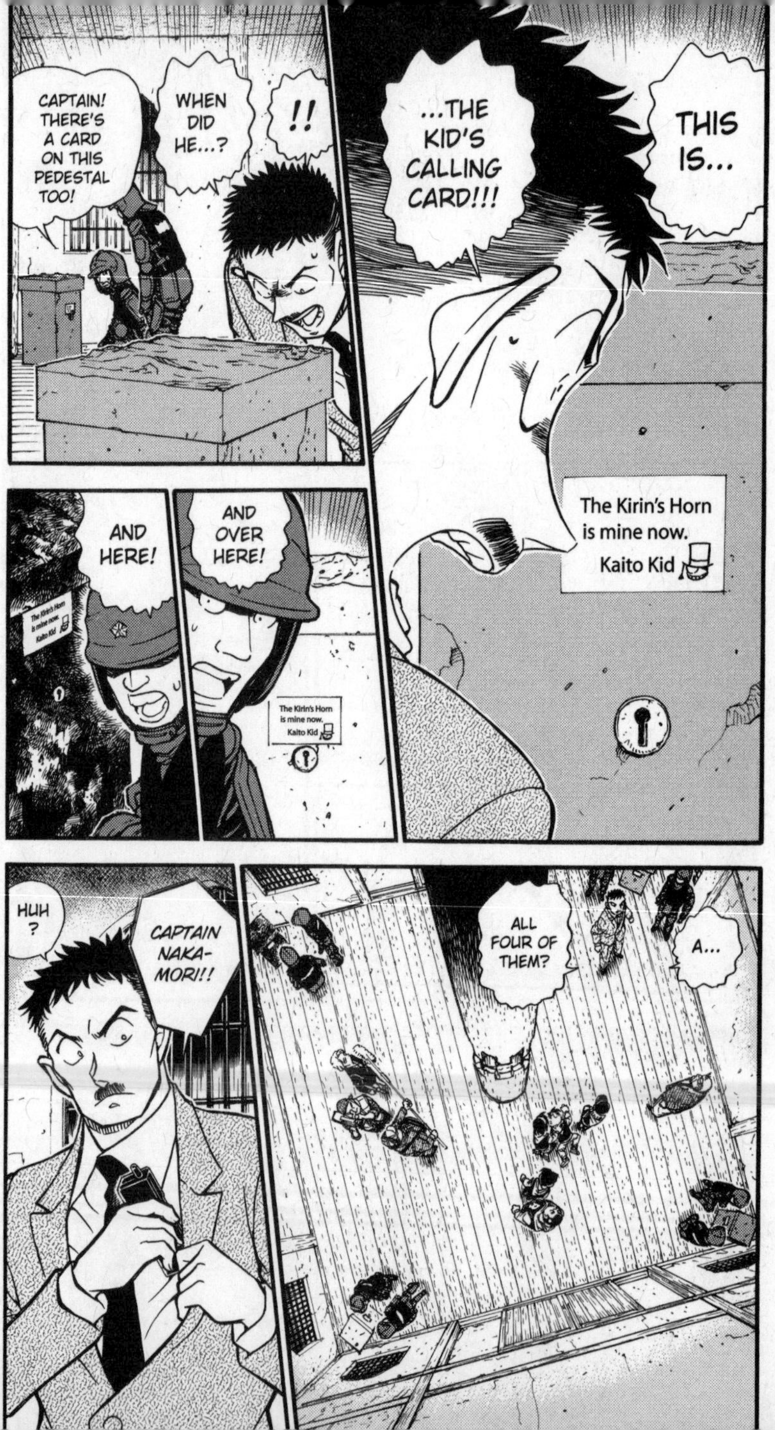
THIS IS...
...THE KID'S CALLING CARD!!!
The Kirin's Horn is mine now. Kaito Kid
!!
WHEN DID HE...?
CAPTAIN! THERE'S A CARD ON THIS PEDESTAL TOO!
AND OVER HERE!
The Kirin's Horn is mine now. Kaito Kid
AND HERE!
The Kirin's Horn is mine now. Kaito Kid
A...
ALL FOUR OF THEM?
CAPTAIN NAKAMORI!!
HUH ?

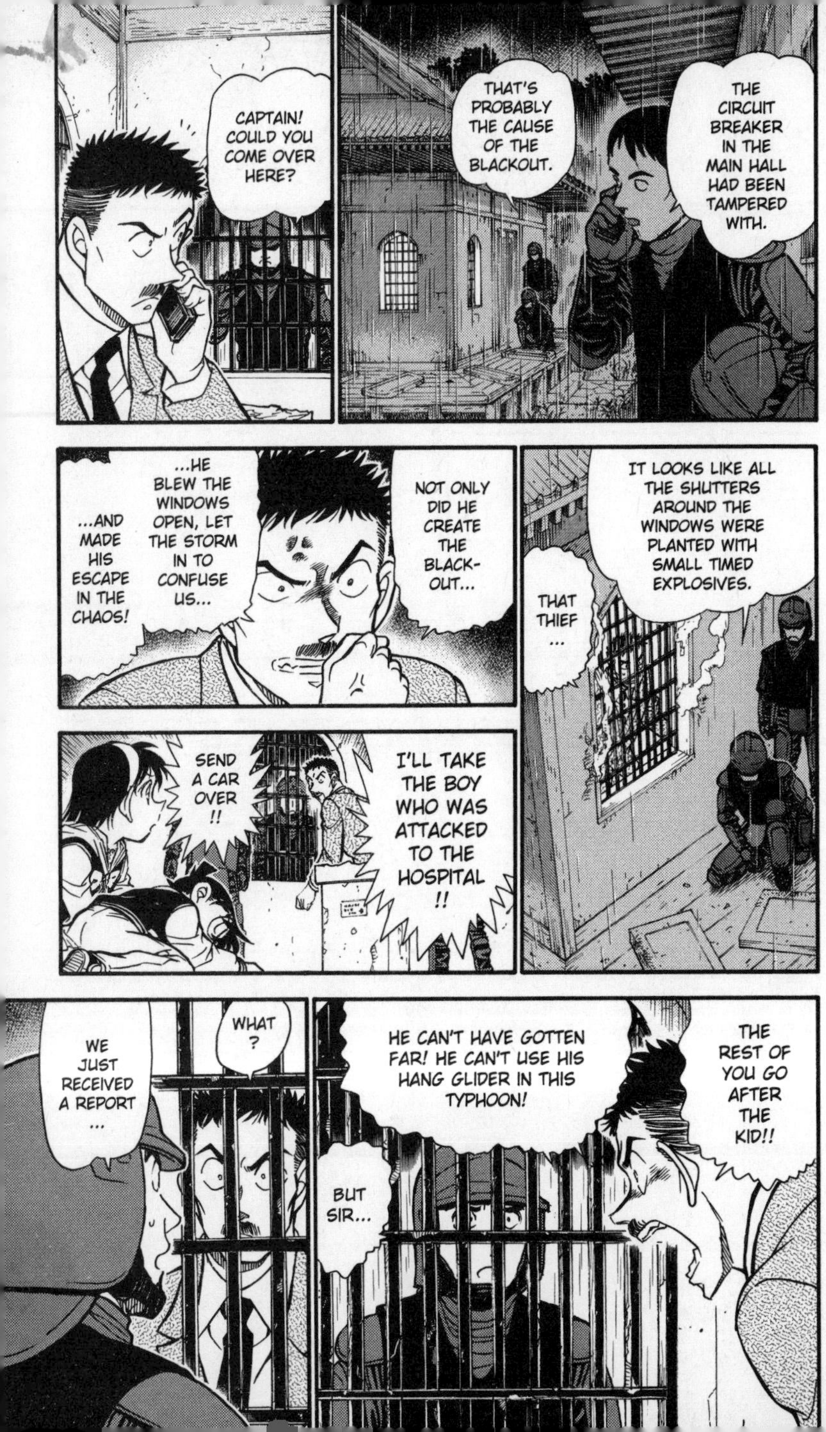
THE CIRCUIT BREAKER IN THE MAIN HALL HAD BEEN TAMPERED WITH.
THAT'S PROBABLY THE CAUSE OF THE BLACKOUT.
CAPTAIN! COULD YOU COME OVER HERE?
IT LOOKS LIKE ALL THE SHUTTERS AROUND THE WINDOWS WERE PLANTED WITH SMALL TIMED EXPLOSIVES.
THAT THIEF ...
NOT ONLY DID HE CREATE THE BLACK-OUT...
...HE BLEW THE WINDOWS OPEN, LET THE STORM IN TO CONFUSE US...
...AND MADE HIS ESCAPE IN THE CHAOS!
I'LL TAKE THE BOY WHO WAS ATTACKED TO THE HOSPITAL !!
SEND A CAR OVER !!
THE REST OF YOU GO AFTER THE KID!!
HE CAN'T HAVE GOTTEN FAR! HE CAN'T USE HIS HANG GLIDER IN THIS TYPHOON!
BUT SIR...
WHAT ?
WE JUST RECEIVED A REPORT ...

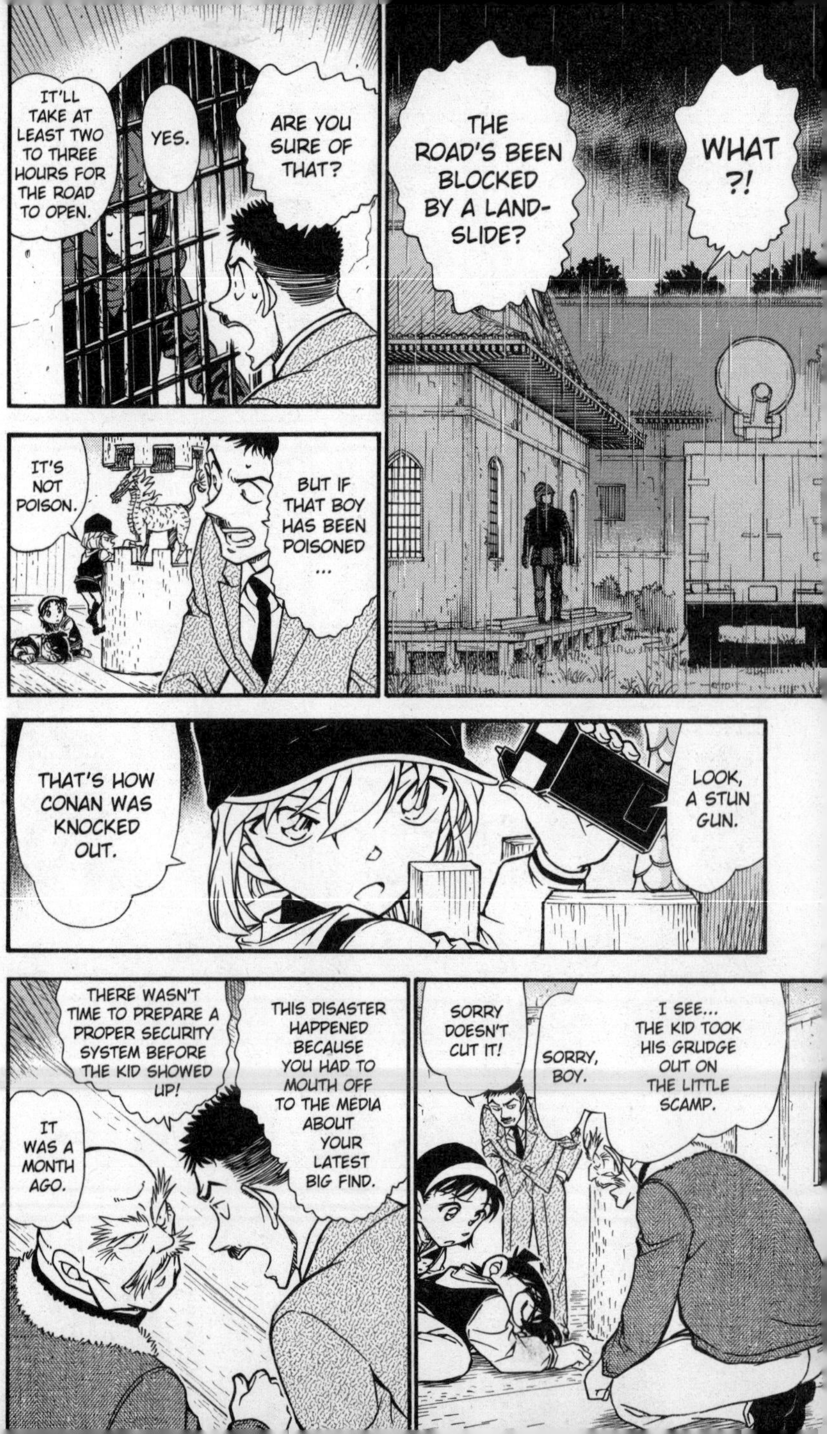
WHAT ?!
THE ROAD'S BEEN BLOCKED BY A LAND-SLIDE?
ARE YOU SURE OF THAT?
YES.
IT'LL TAKE AT LEAST TWO TO THREE HOURS FOR THE ROAD TO OPEN.
BUT IF THAT BOY HAS BEEN POISONED ...
IT'S NOT POISON.
LOOK, A STUN GUN.
THAT'S HOW CONAN WAS KNOCKED OUT.
I SEE... THE KID TOOK HIS GRUDGE OUT ON THE LITTLE SCAMP.
SORRY, BOY.
SORRY DOESN'T CUT IT!
THIS DISASTER HAPPENED BECAUSE YOU HAD TO MOUTH OFF TO THE MEDIA ABOUT YOUR LATEST BIG FIND.
THERE WASN'T TIME TO PREPARE A PROPER SECURITY SYSTEM BEFORE THE KID SHOWED UP!
IT WAS A MONTH AGO.

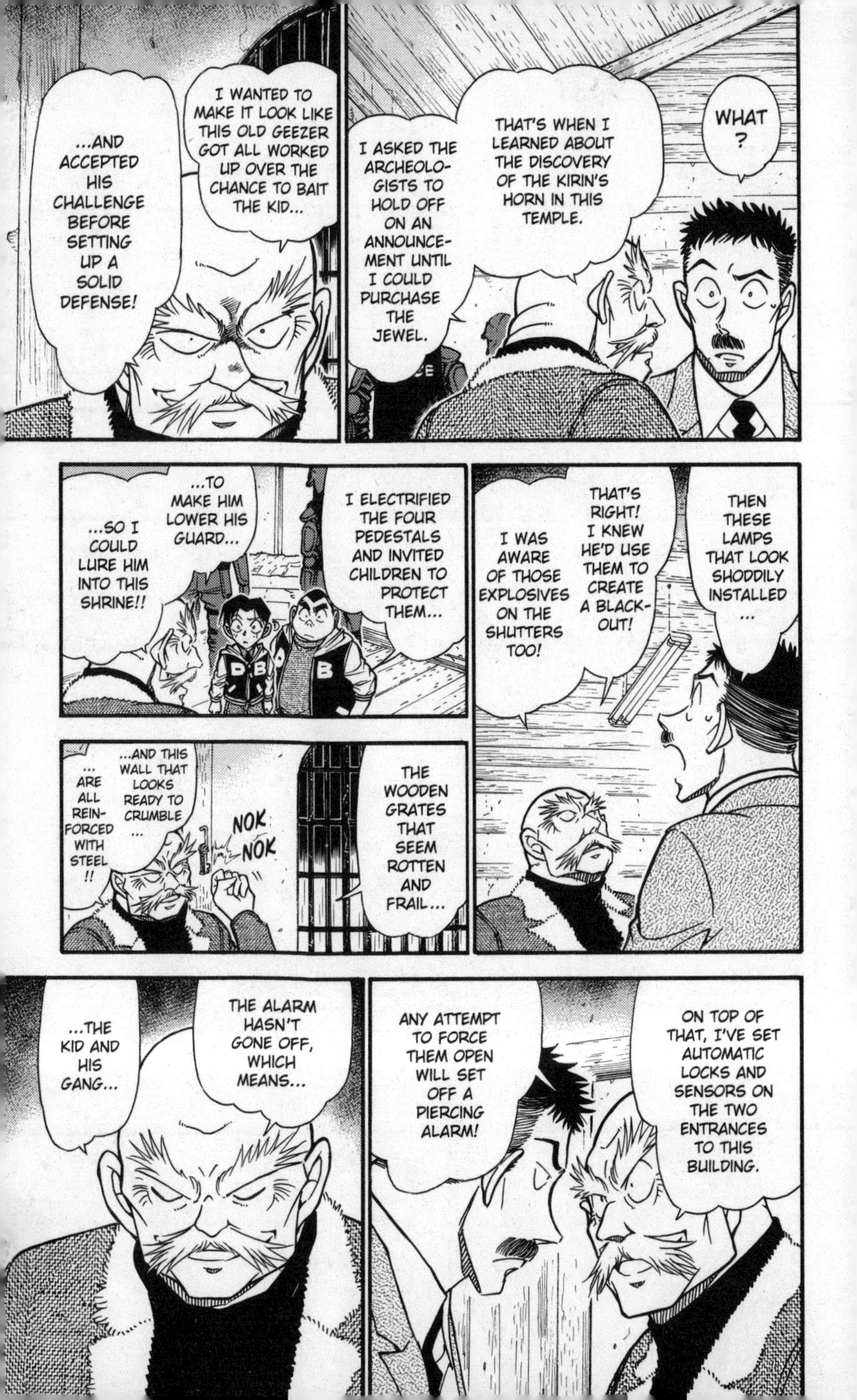
WHAT ?
THAT'S WHEN I LEARNED ABOUT THE DISCOVERY OF THE KIRIN'S HORN IN THIS TEMPLE.
I ASKED THE ARCHEOLO-GISTS TO HOLD OFF ON AN ANNOUNCE-MENT UNTIL I COULD PURCHASE THE JEWEL.
I WANTED TO MAKE IT LOOK LIKE THIS OLD GEEZER GOT ALL WORKED UP OVER THE CHANCE TO BAIT THE KID...
...AND ACCEPTED HIS CHALLENGE BEFORE SETTING UP A SOLID DEFENSE!
THEN THESE LAMPS THAT LOOK SHODDILY INSTALLED ...
THAT'S RIGHT! I KNEW HE'D USE THEM TO CREATE A BLACK-OUT!
I WAS AWARE OF THOSE EXPLOSIVES ON THE SHUTTERS TOO!
I ELECTRIFIED THE FOUR PEDESTALS AND INVITED CHILDREN TO PROTECT THEM...
...TO MAKE HIM LOWER HIS GUARD...
...SO I COULD LURE HIM INTO THIS SHRINE!!
THE WOODEN GRATES THAT SEEM ROTTEN AND FRAIL...
NOK NOK
...AND THIS WALL THAT LOOKS READY TO CRUMBLE ...
... ARE ALL REIN-FORCED WITH STEEL !!
ON TOP OF THAT, I'VE SET AUTOMATIC LOCKS AND SENSORS ON THE TWO ENTRANCES TO THIS BUILDING.
ANY ATTEMPT TO FORCE THEM OPEN WILL SET OFF A PIERCING ALARM!
THE ALARM HASN'T GONE OFF, WHICH MEANS...
...THE KID AND HIS GANG...

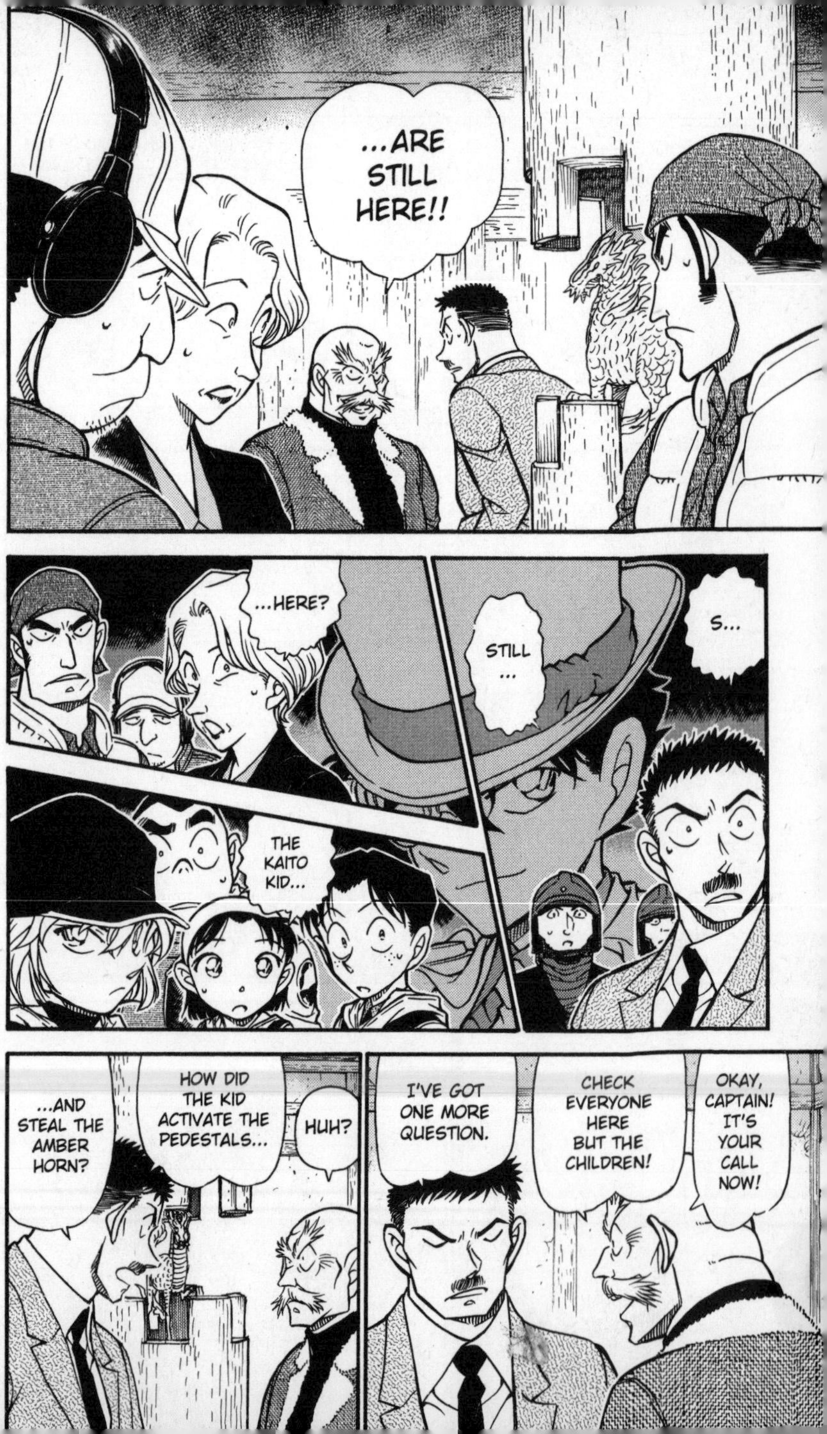
...ARE STILL HERE!!
S...
STILL ...
...HERE?
THE KAITO KID...
OKAY, CAPTAIN! IT'S YOUR CALL NOW!
CHECK EVERYONE HERE BUT THE CHILDREN!
I'VE GOT ONE MORE QUESTION.
HUH?
HOW DID THE KID ACTIVATE THE PEDESTALS...
...AND STEAL THE AMBER HORN?

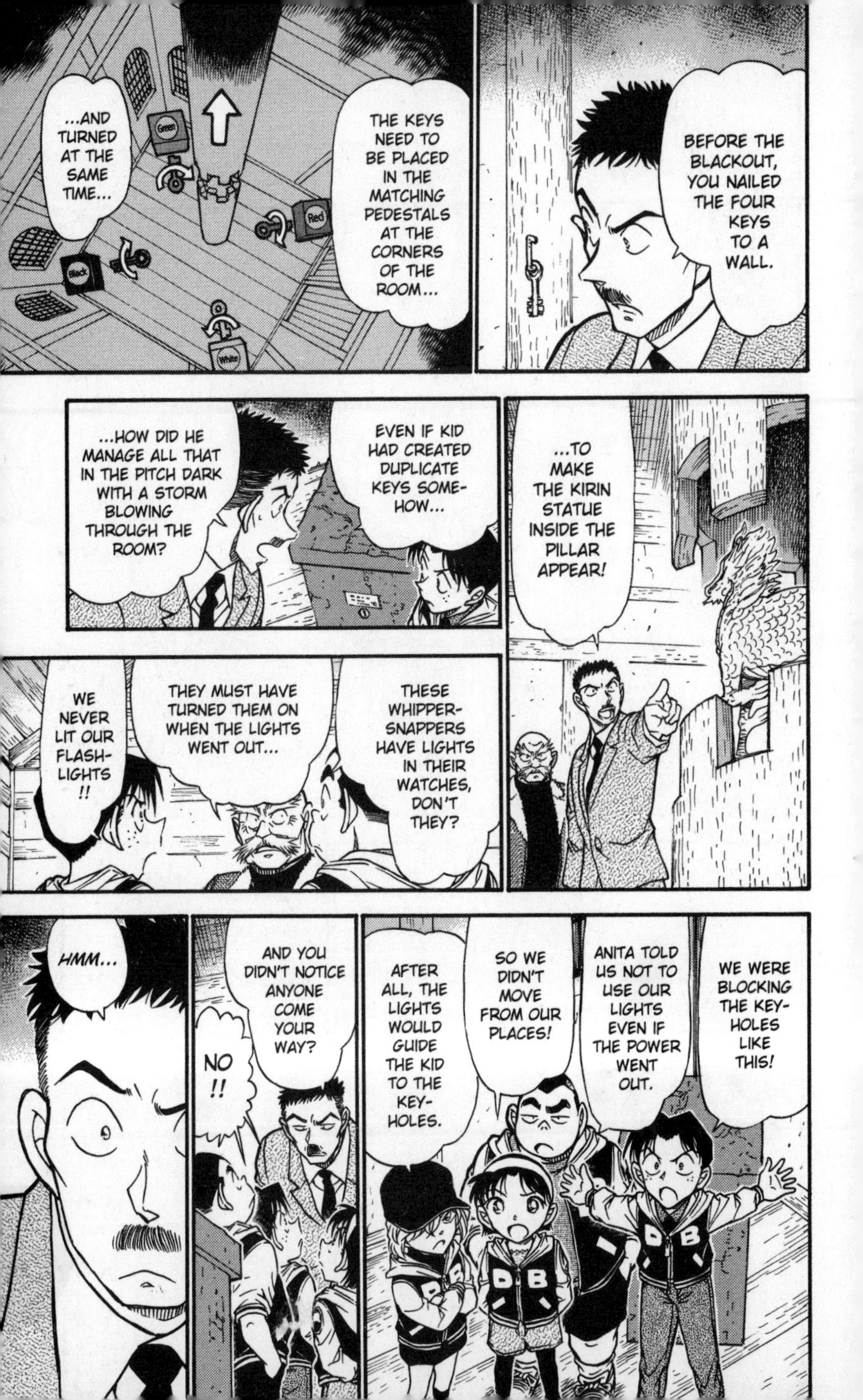
BEFORE THE BLACKOUT, YOU NAILED THE FOUR KEYS TO A WALL.
THE KEYS NEED TO BE PLACED IN THE MATCHING PEDESTALS AT THE CORNERS OF THE ROOM...
Green
Red
Black
White
...AND TURNED AT THE SAME TIME...
...TO MAKE THE KIRIN STATUE INSIDE THE PILLAR APPEAR!
EVEN IF KID HAD CREATED DUPLICATE KEYS SOMEHOW...
...HOW DID HE MANAGE ALL THAT IN THE PITCH DARK WITH A STORM BLOWING THROUGH THE ROOM?
THESE WHIPPERSNAPPERS HAVE LIGHTS IN THEIR WATCHES, DON'T THEY?
THEY MUST HAVE TURNED THEM ON WHEN THE LIGHTS WENT OUT...
WE NEVER LIT OUR FLASHLIGHTS !!
WE WERE BLOCKING THE KEYHOLES LIKE THIS!
ANITA TOLD US NOT TO USE OUR LIGHTS EVEN IF THE POWER WENT OUT.
SO WE DIDN'T MOVE FROM OUR PLACES!
AFTER ALL, THE LIGHTS WOULD GUIDE THE KID TO THE KEYHOLES.
AND YOU DIDN'T NOTICE ANYONE COME YOUR WAY?
NO !!
HMM...

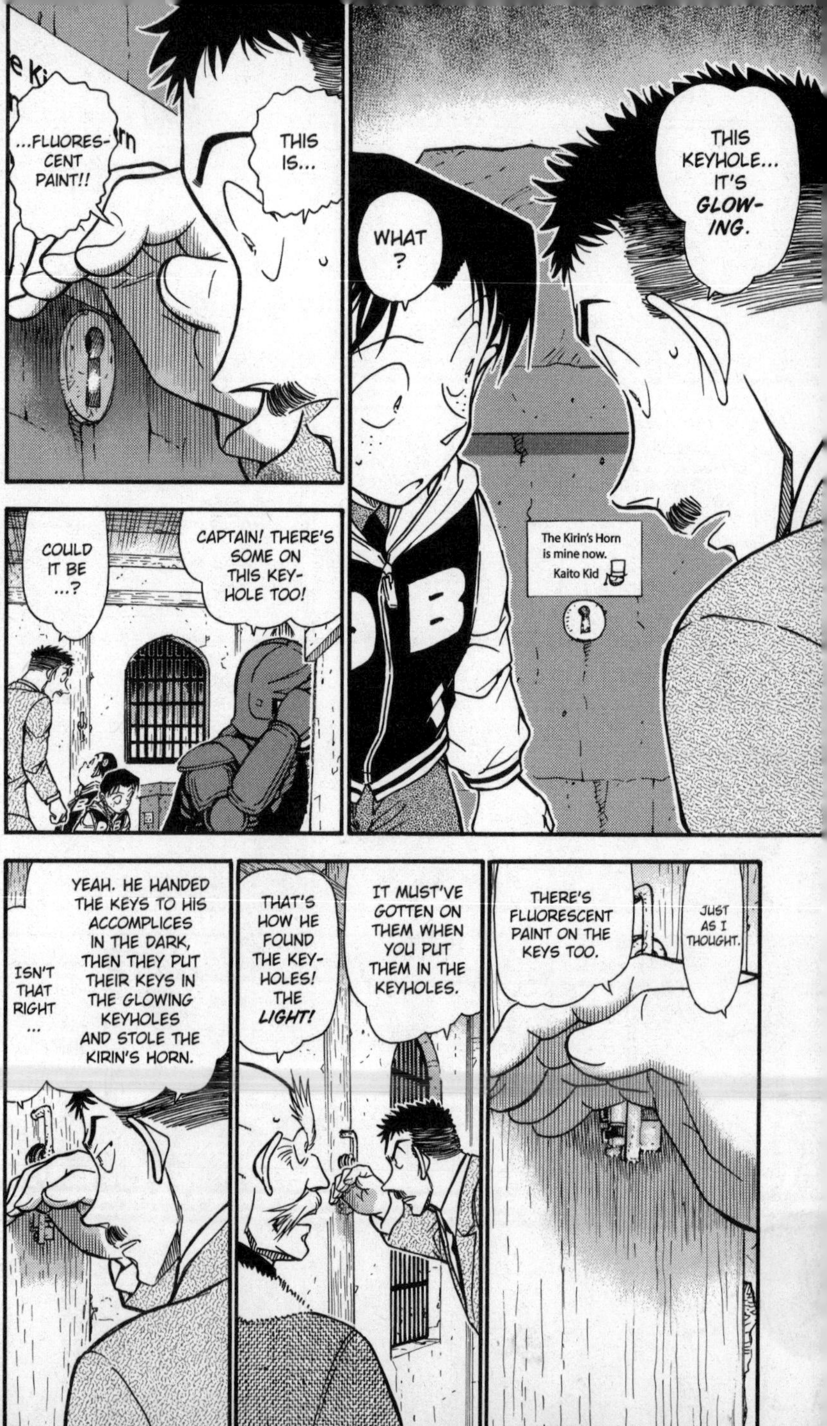
THIS KEYHOLE... IT'S GLOWING.
WHAT?
The Kirin's Horn is mine now.
Kaito Kid
THIS IS...
...FLUORESCENT PAINT!!
CAPTAIN! THERE'S SOME ON THIS KEYHOLE TOO!
COULD IT BE...?
JUST AS I THOUGHT.
THERE'S FLUORESCENT PAINT ON THE KEYS TOO.
IT MUST'VE GOTTEN ON THEM WHEN YOU PUT THEM IN THE KEYHOLES.
THAT'S HOW HE FOUND THE KEYHOLES! THE LIGHT!
YEAH. HE HANDED THE KEYS TO HIS ACCOMPLICES IN THE DARK, THEN THEY PUT THEIR KEYS IN THE GLOWING KEYHOLES AND STOLE THE KIRIN'S HORN.
ISN'T THAT RIGHT...

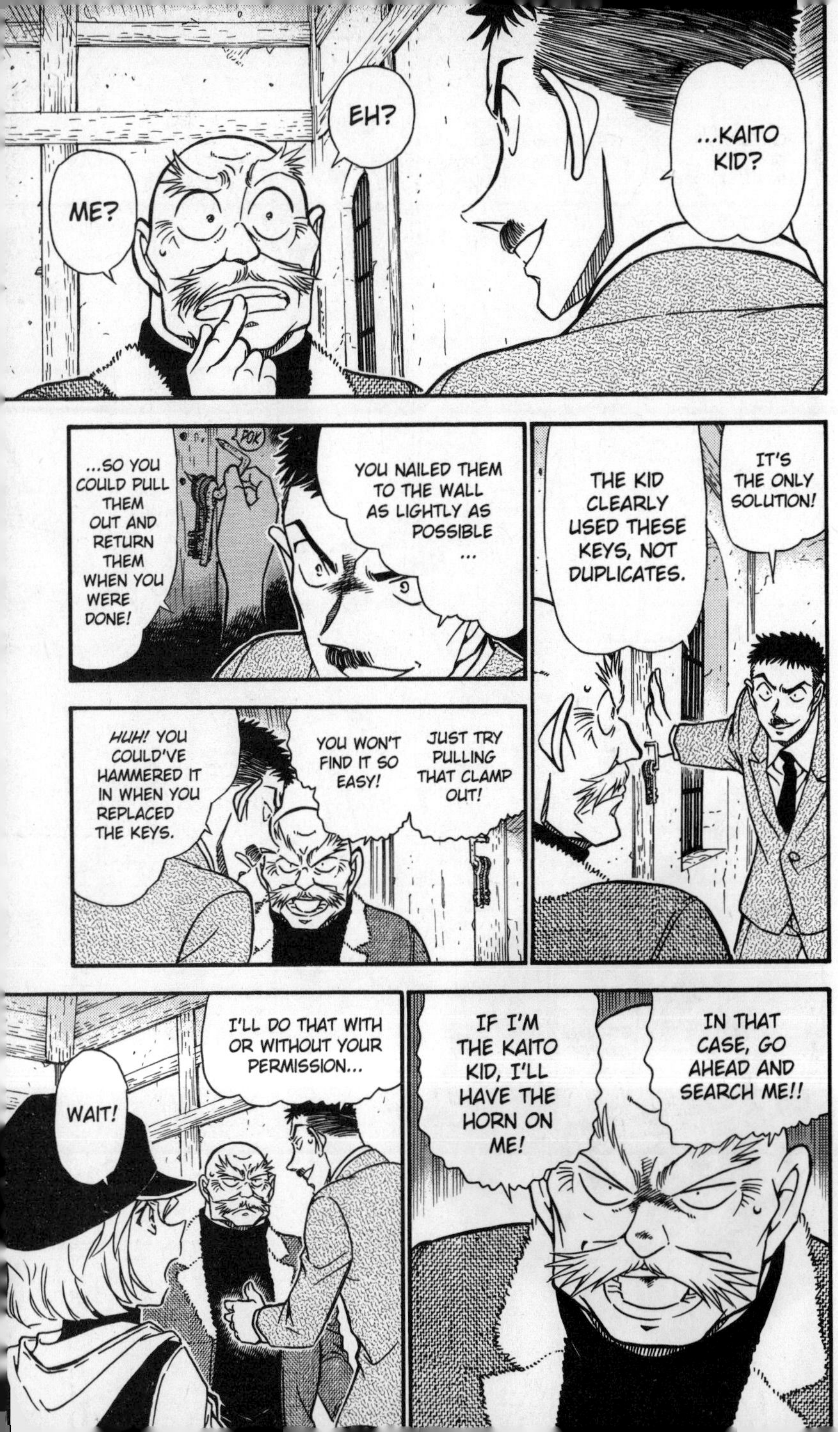
...KAITO KID?
EH?
ME?
IT'S THE ONLY SOLUTION!
THE KID CLEARLY USED THESE KEYS, NOT DUPLICATES.
YOU NAILED THEM TO THE WALL AS LIGHTLY AS POSSIBLE ...
...SO YOU COULD PULL THEM OUT AND RETURN THEM WHEN YOU WERE DONE!
POK
JUST TRY PULLING THAT CLAMP OUT!
YOU WON'T FIND IT SO EASY!
HUH! YOU COULD'VE HAMMERED IT IN WHEN YOU REPLACED THE KEYS.
IN THAT CASE, GO AHEAD AND SEARCH ME!!
IF I'M THE KAITO KID, I'LL HAVE THE HORN ON ME!
I'LL DO THAT WITH OR WITHOUT YOUR PERMISSION...
WAIT!

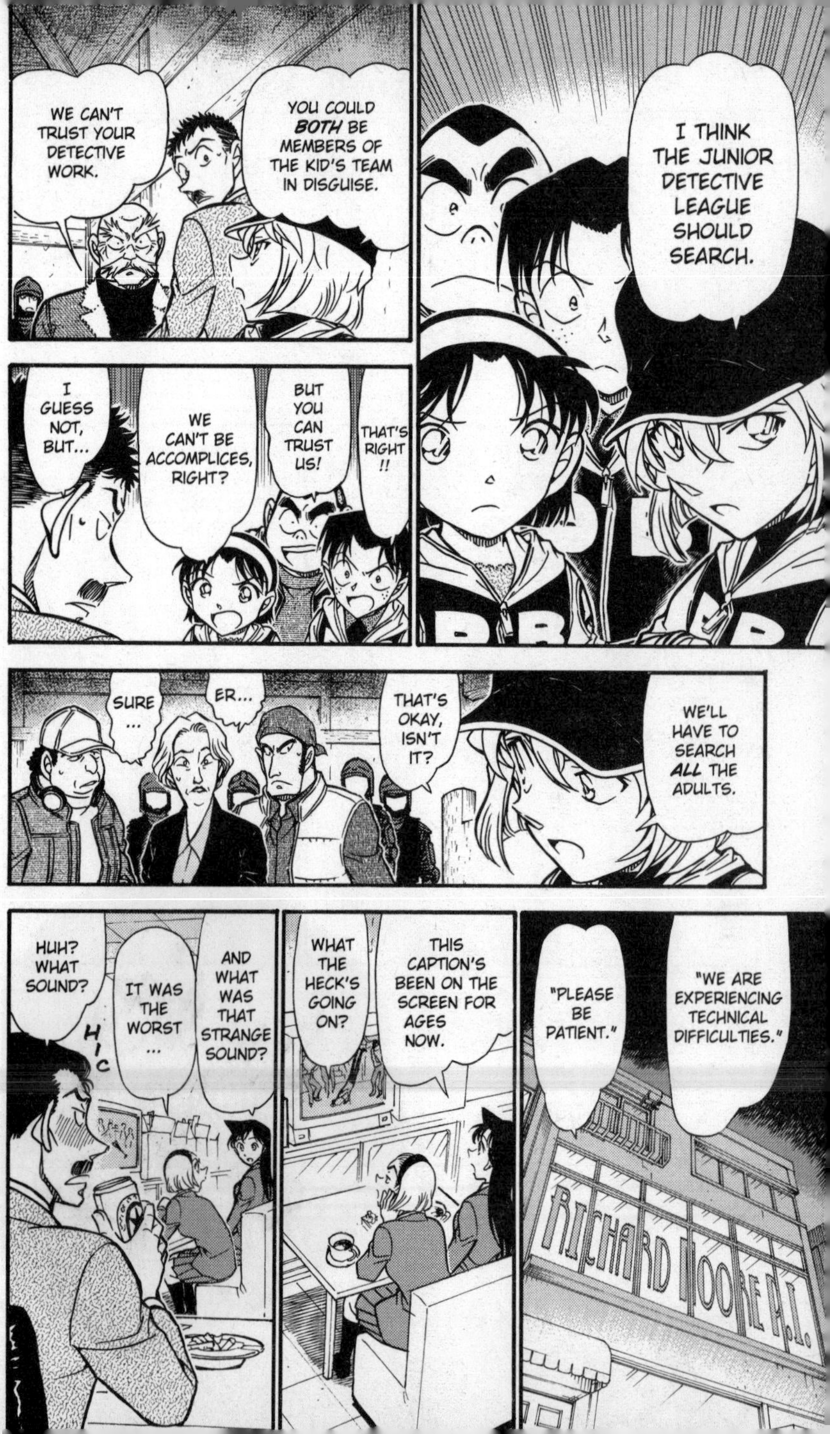
I THINK THE JUNIOR DETECTIVE LEAGUE SHOULD SEARCH.
YOU COULD BOTH BE MEMBERS OF THE KID'S TEAM IN DISGUISE.
WE CAN'T TRUST YOUR DETECTIVE WORK.
THAT'S RIGHT !!
BUT YOU CAN TRUST US!
WE CAN'T BE ACCOMPLICES, RIGHT?
I GUESS NOT, BUT...
WE'LL HAVE TO SEARCH ALL THE ADULTS.
THAT'S OKAY, ISN'T IT?
ER...
SURE ...
"WE ARE EXPERIENCING TECHNICAL DIFFICULTIES."
"PLEASE BE PATIENT."
RICHARD MOORE P.I.
THIS CAPTION'S BEEN ON THE SCREEN FOR AGES NOW.
WHAT THE HECK'S GOING ON?
AND WHAT WAS THAT STRANGE SOUND?
IT WAS THE WORST ...
HUH? WHAT SOUND?
HIC

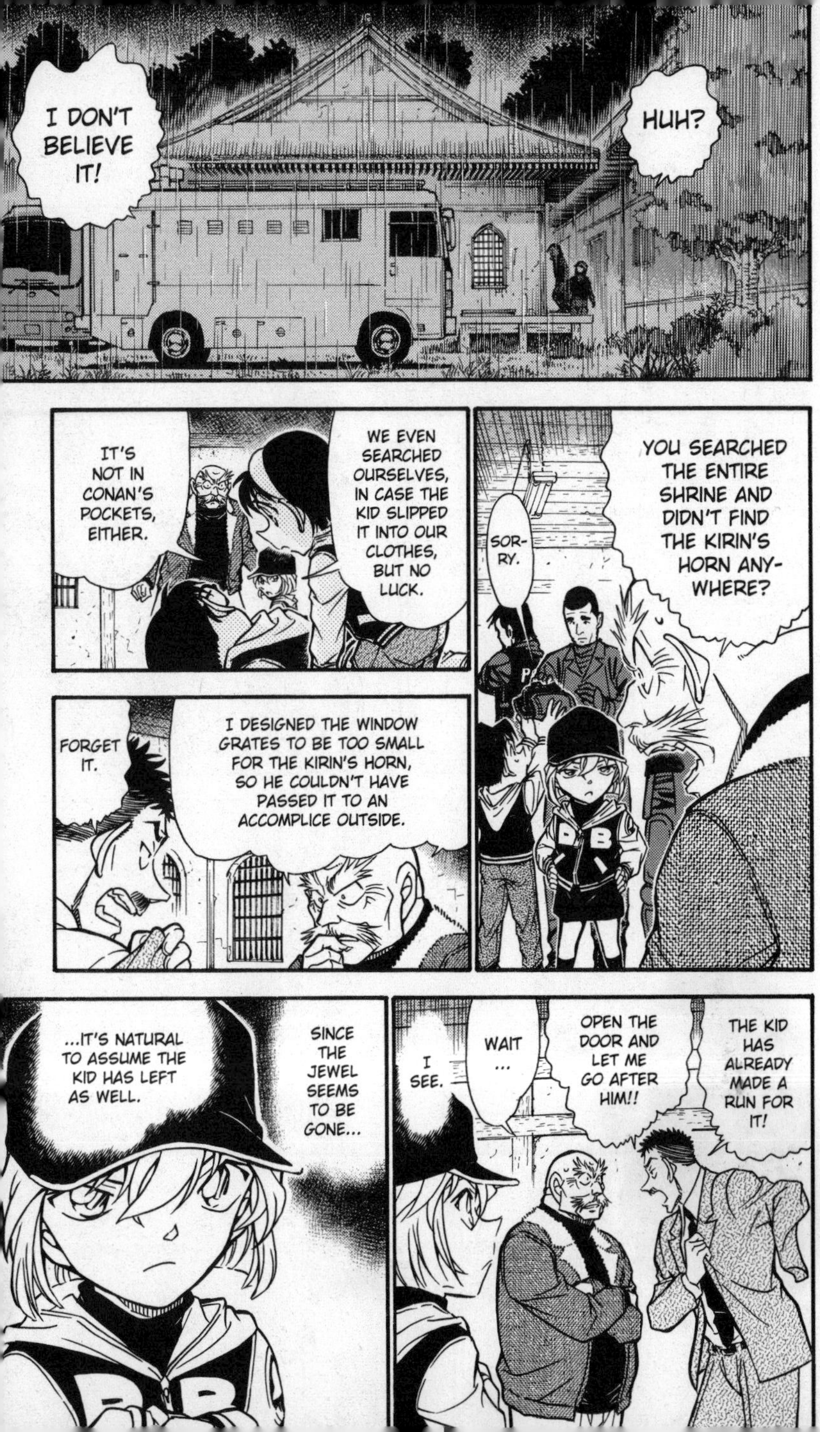
HUH?
I DON'T BELIEVE IT!
YOU SEARCHED THE ENTIRE SHRINE AND DIDN'T FIND THE KIRIN'S HORN ANYWHERE?
SORRY.
WE EVEN SEARCHED OURSELVES, IN CASE THE KID SLIPPED IT INTO OUR CLOTHES, BUT NO LUCK.
IT'S NOT IN CONAN'S POCKETS, EITHER.
I DESIGNED THE WINDOW GRATES TO BE TOO SMALL FOR THE KIRIN'S HORN, SO HE COULDN'T HAVE PASSED IT TO AN ACCOMPLICE OUTSIDE.
FORGET IT.
THE KID HAS ALREADY MADE A RUN FOR IT!
OPEN THE DOOR AND LET ME GO AFTER HIM!!
WAIT...
I SEE.
SINCE THE JEWEL SEEMS TO BE GONE...
...IT'S NATURAL TO ASSUME THE KID HAS LEFT AS WELL.

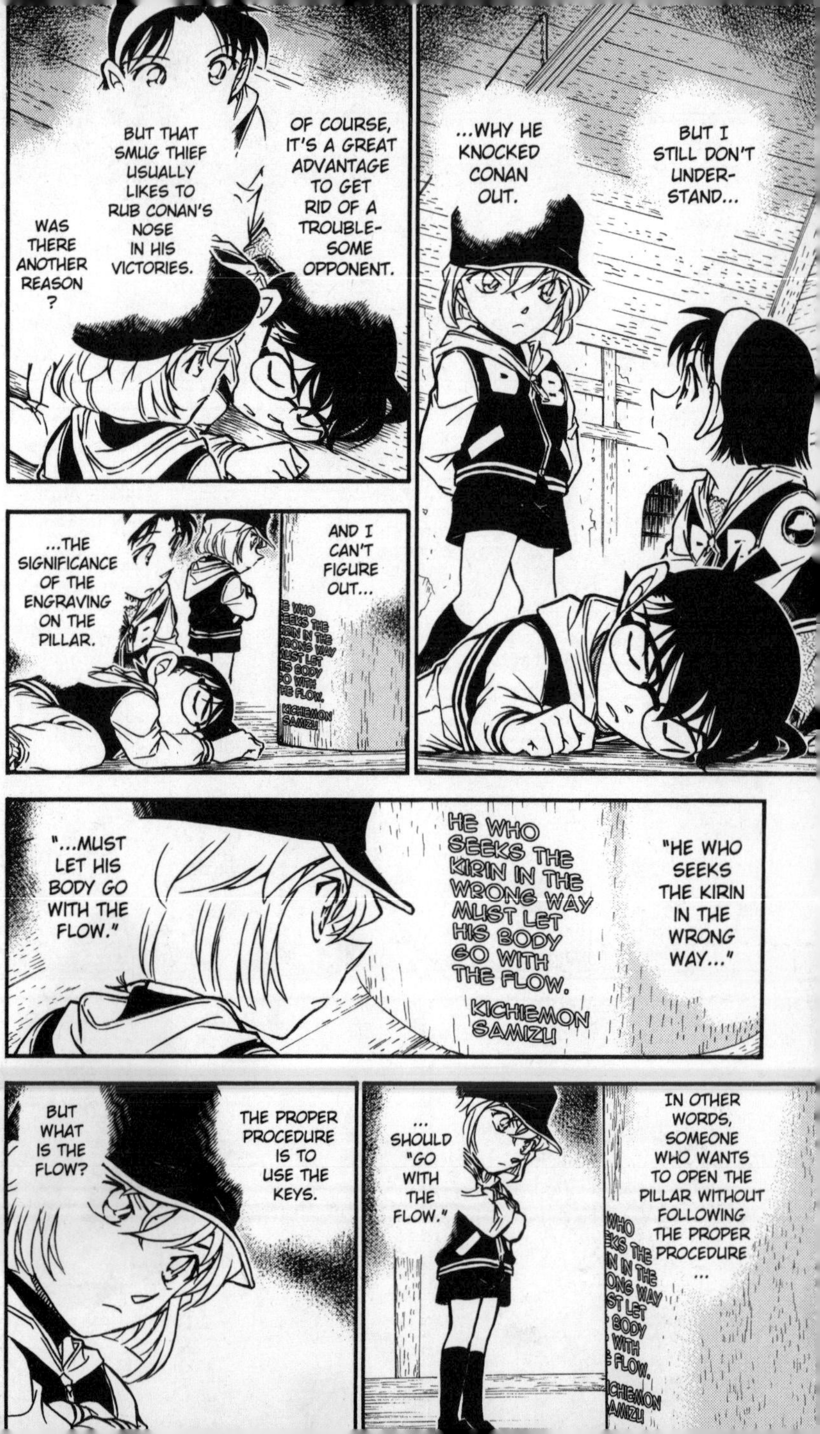
BUT I STILL DON'T UNDER-STAND...
...WHY HE KNOCKED CONAN OUT.
OF COURSE, IT'S A GREAT ADVANTAGE TO GET RID OF A TROUBLE-SOME OPPONENT.
BUT THAT SMUG THIEF USUALLY LIKES TO RUB CONAN'S NOSE IN HIS VICTORIES.
WAS THERE ANOTHER REASON?
AND I CAN'T FIGURE OUT...
...THE SIGNIFICANCE OF THE ENGRAVING ON THE PILLAR.
"HE WHO SEEKS THE KIRIN IN THE WRONG WAY..."
HE WHO SEEKS THE KIRIN IN THE WRONG WAY MUST LET HIS BODY GO WITH THE FLOW.
KICHIEMON SAMIZU
"...MUST LET HIS BODY GO WITH THE FLOW."
IN OTHER WORDS, SOMEONE WHO WANTS TO OPEN THE PILLAR WITHOUT FOLLOWING THE PROPER PROCEDURE ...
...SHOULD "GO WITH THE FLOW."
THE PROPER PROCEDURE IS TO USE THE KEYS.
BUT WHAT IS THE FLOW?

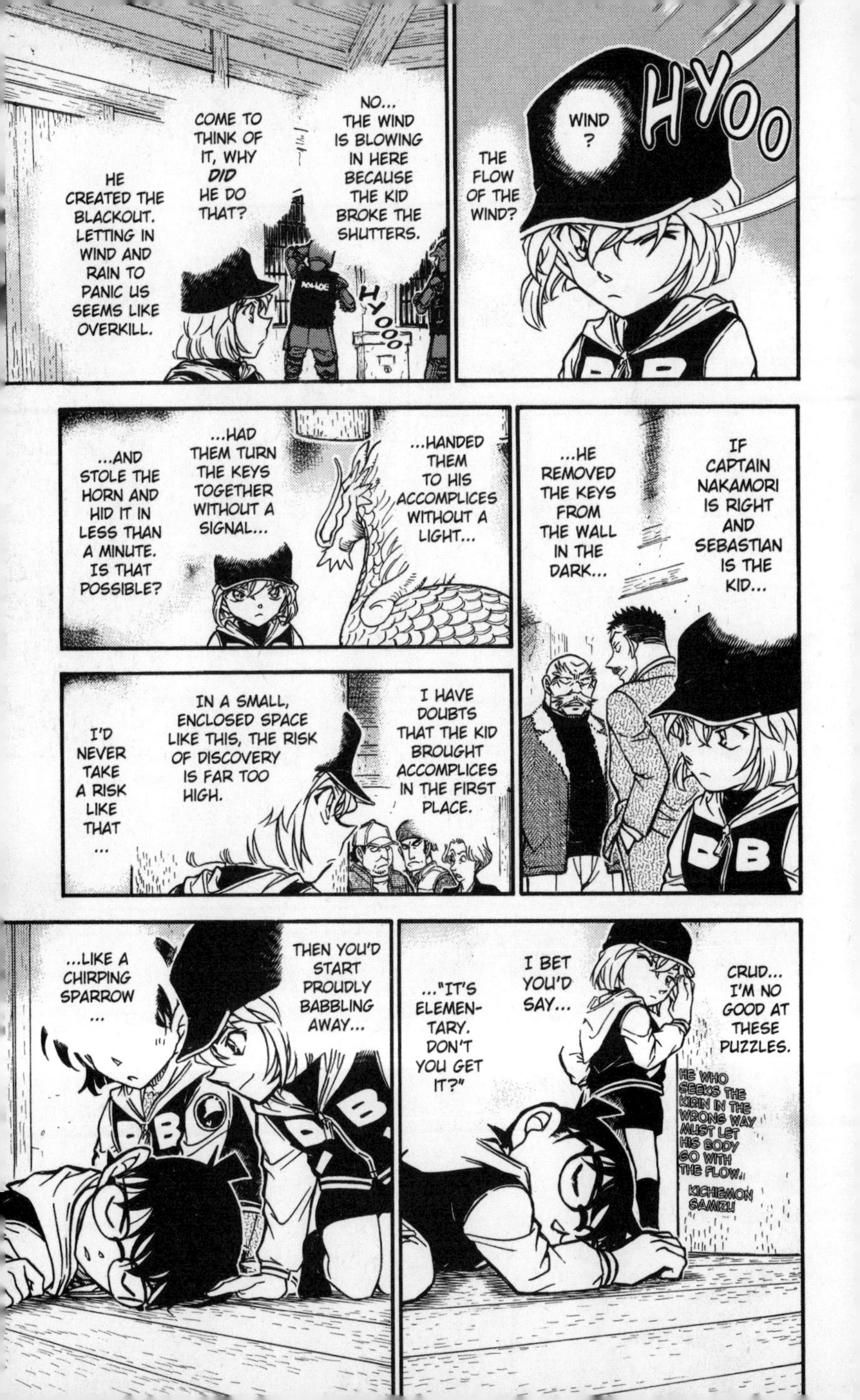
HYOO
WIND ?
THE FLOW OF THE WIND?
NO... THE WIND IS BLOWING IN HERE BECAUSE THE KID BROKE THE SHUTTERS.
HYOOO
COME TO THINK OF IT, WHY DID HE DO THAT?
HE CREATED THE BLACKOUT. LETTING IN WIND AND RAIN TO PANIC US SEEMS LIKE OVERKILL.
IF CAPTAIN NAKAMORI IS RIGHT AND SEBASTIAN IS THE KID...
...HE REMOVED THE KEYS FROM THE WALL IN THE DARK...
...HANDED THEM TO HIS ACCOMPLICES WITHOUT A LIGHT...
...HAD THEM TURN THE KEYS TOGETHER WITHOUT A SIGNAL...
...AND STOLE THE HORN AND HID IT IN LESS THAN A MINUTE. IS THAT POSSIBLE?
I HAVE DOUBTS THAT THE KID BROUGHT ACCOMPLICES IN THE FIRST PLACE.
IN A SMALL, ENCLOSED SPACE LIKE THIS, THE RISK OF DISCOVERY IS FAR TOO HIGH.
I'D NEVER TAKE A RISK LIKE THAT ...
CRUD... I'M NO GOOD AT THESE PUZZLES.
HE WHO SEEKS THE KIRIN IN THE WRONG WAY MUST LET HIS BODY GO WITH THE FLOW.
KICHIEMON SAMIZU
I BET YOU'D SAY...
..."IT'S ELEMENTARY. DON'T YOU GET IT?"
THEN YOU'D START PROUDLY BABBLING AWAY...
...LIKE A CHIRPING SPARROW ...

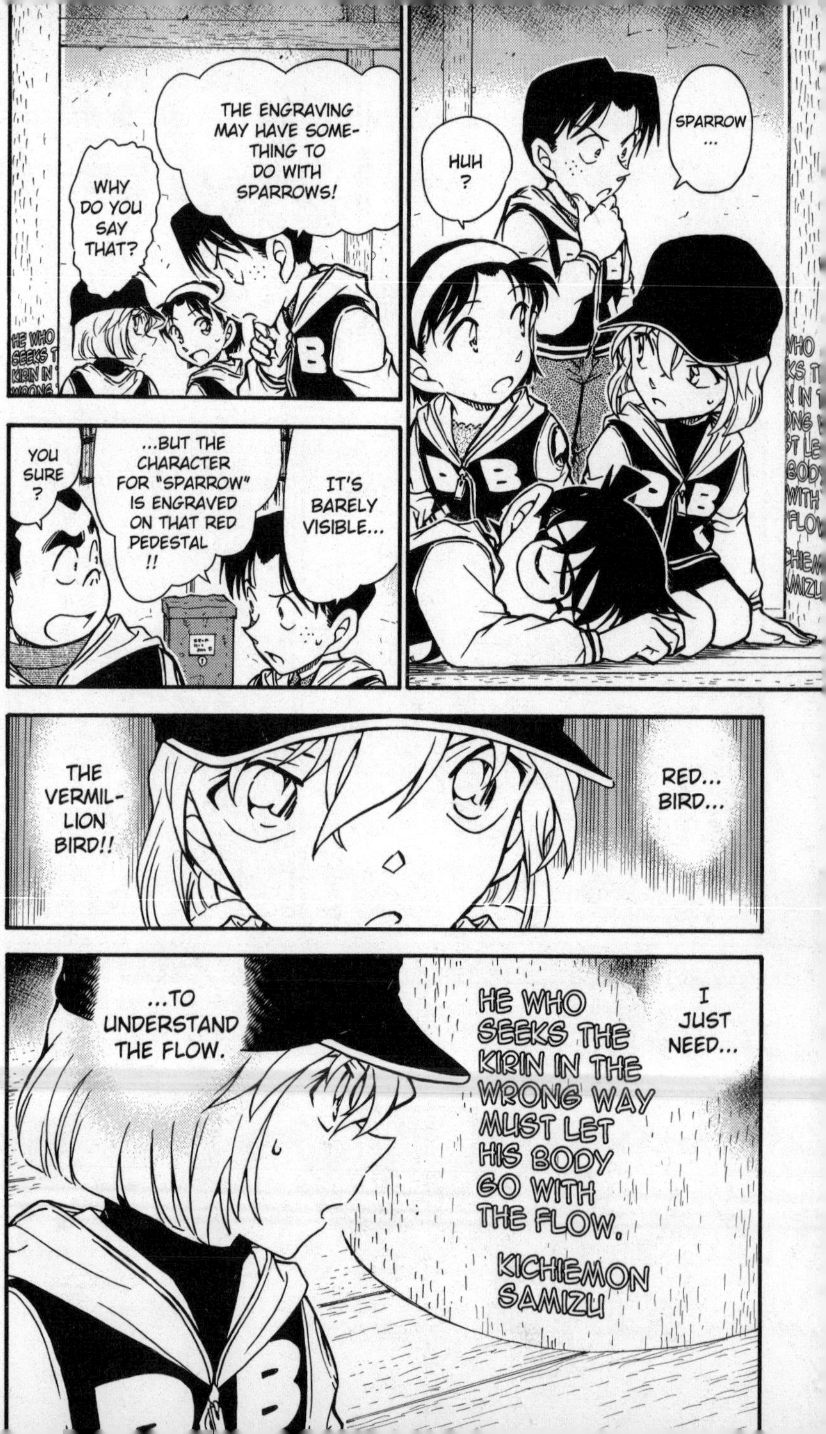
SPARROW ...
HUH ?
THE ENGRAVING MAY HAVE SOME-THING TO DO WITH SPARROWS!
WHY DO YOU SAY THAT?
IT'S BARELY VISIBLE...
...BUT THE CHARACTER FOR "SPARROW" IS ENGRAVED ON THAT RED PEDESTAL !!
YOU SURE ?
RED... BIRD...
THE VERMIL-LION BIRD!!
I JUST NEED...
HE WHO SEEKS THE KIRIN IN THE WRONG WAY MUST LET HIS BODY GO WITH THE FLOW.
KICHIEMON SAMIZU
...TO UNDERSTAND THE FLOW.

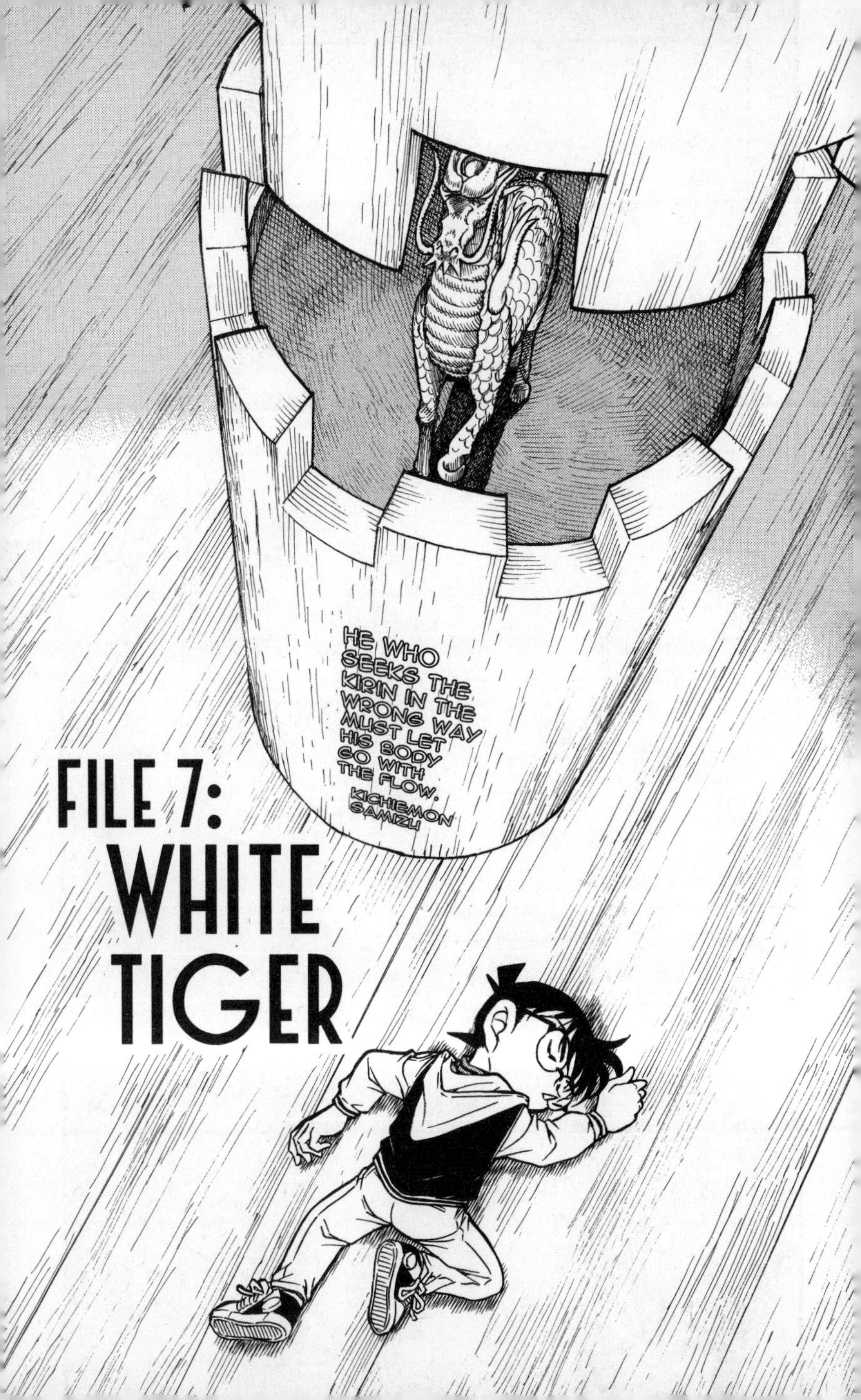
HE WHO
SEEKS THE
KIRIN IN THE
WRONG WAY
MUST LET
HIS BODY
GO WITH
THE FLOW.
KICHIEMON
SAMIZU

FILE 7: WHITE TIGER

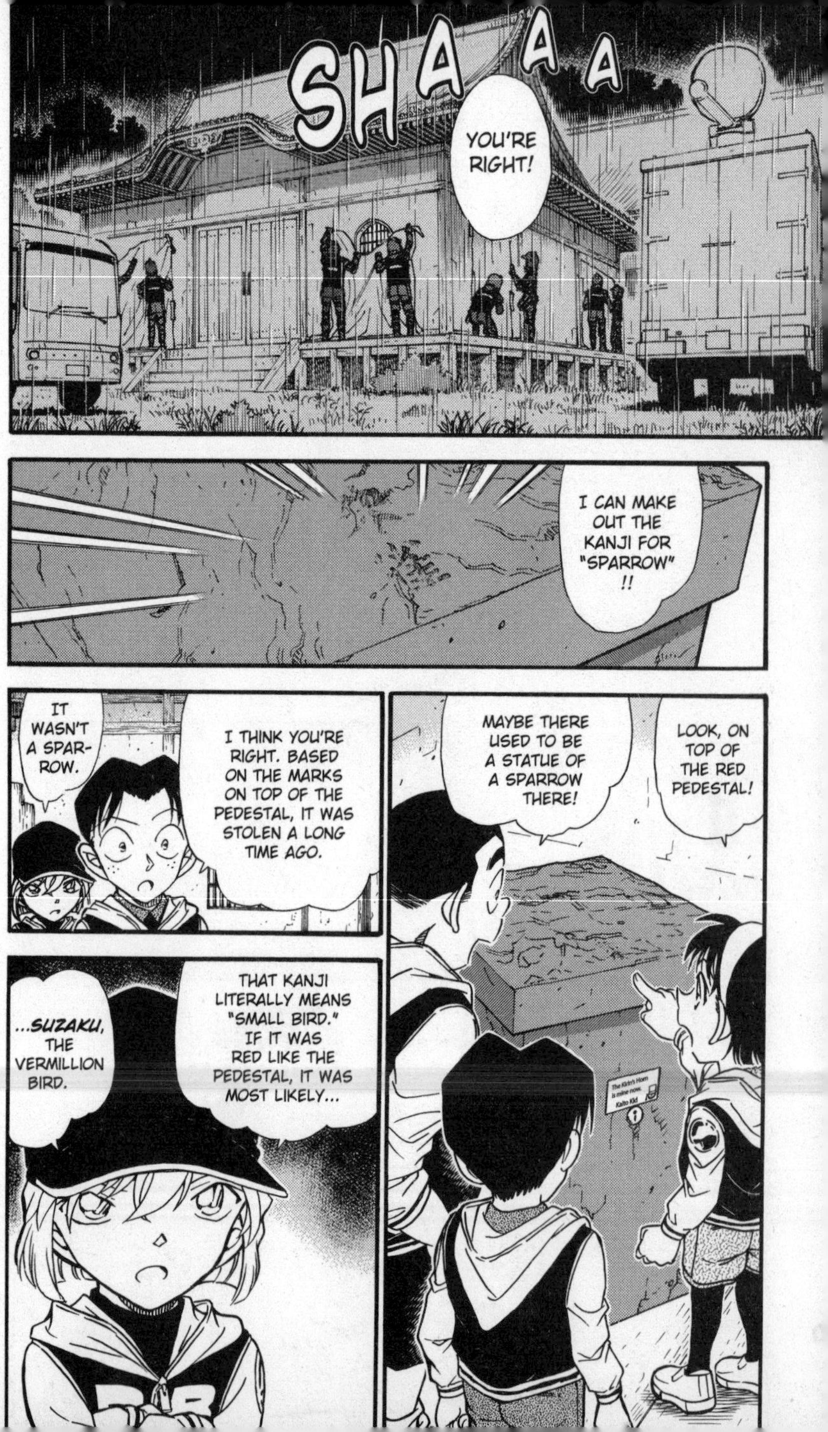
SHAAA
YOU'RE RIGHT!
I CAN MAKE OUT THE KANJI FOR "SPARROW" !!
LOOK, ON TOP OF THE RED PEDESTAL!
MAYBE THERE USED TO BE A STATUE OF A SPARROW THERE!
The Kirin's Horn is mine now. Kaito Kid
I THINK YOU'RE RIGHT. BASED ON THE MARKS ON TOP OF THE PEDESTAL, IT WAS STOLEN A LONG TIME AGO.
IT WASN'T A SPARROW.
THAT KANJI LITERALLY MEANS "SMALL BIRD." IF IT WAS RED LIKE THE PEDESTAL, IT WAS MOST LIKELY...
...SUZAKU, THE VERMILLION BIRD.

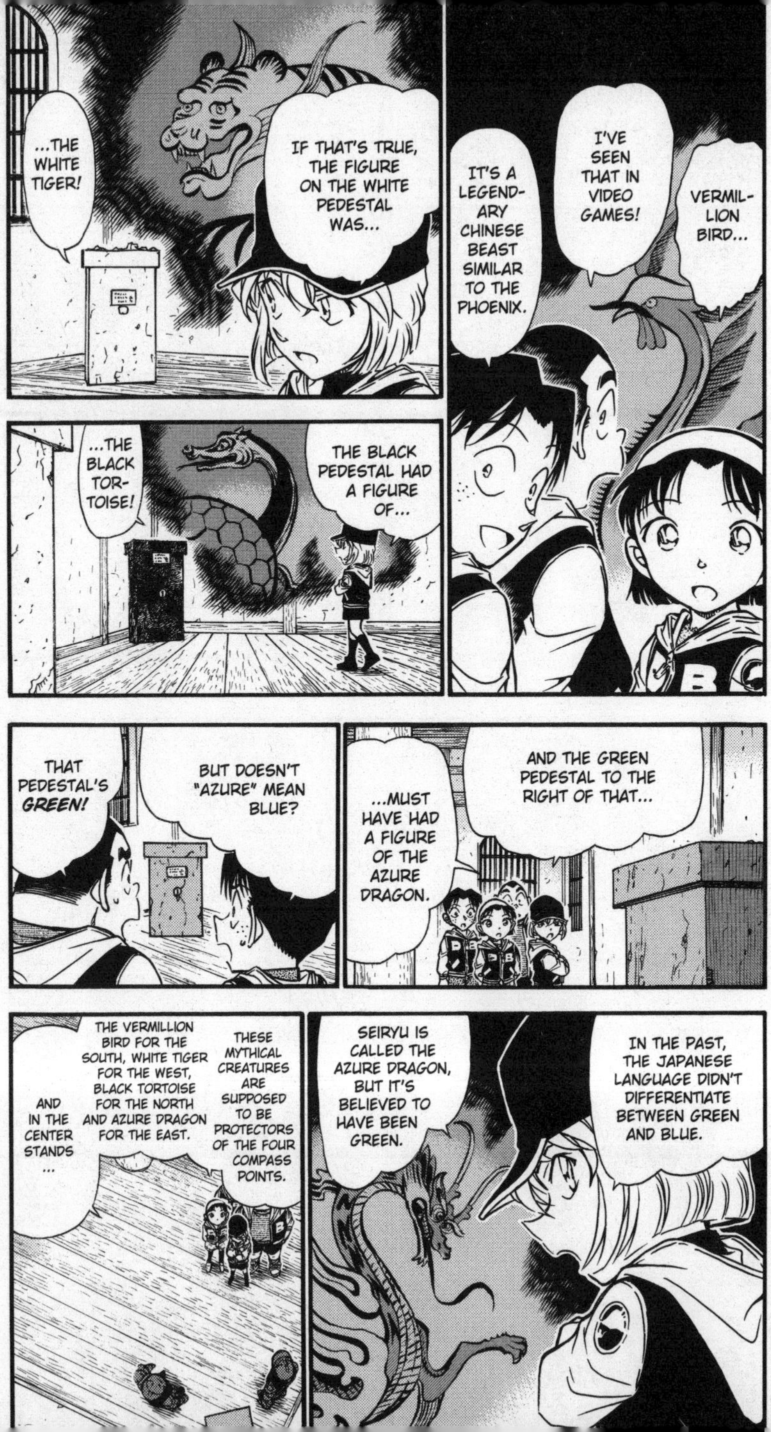
VERMIL-LION BIRD...
I'VE SEEN THAT IN VIDEO GAMES!
IT'S A LEGEND-ARY CHINESE BEAST SIMILAR TO THE PHOENIX.
IF THAT'S TRUE, THE FIGURE ON THE WHITE PEDESTAL WAS...
...THE WHITE TIGER!
THE BLACK PEDESTAL HAD A FIGURE OF...
...THE BLACK TOR-TOISE!
AND THE GREEN PEDESTAL TO THE RIGHT OF THAT...
...MUST HAVE HAD A FIGURE OF THE AZURE DRAGON.
BUT DOESN'T "AZURE" MEAN BLUE?
THAT PEDESTAL'S *GREEN!*
IN THE PAST, THE JAPANESE LANGUAGE DIDN'T DIFFERENTIATE BETWEEN GREEN AND BLUE.
SEIRYU IS CALLED THE AZURE DRAGON, BUT IT'S BELIEVED TO HAVE BEEN GREEN.
THESE MYTHICAL CREATURES ARE SUPPOSED TO BE PROTECTORS OF THE FOUR COMPASS POINTS.
THE VERMILLION BIRD FOR THE SOUTH, WHITE TIGER FOR THE WEST, BLACK TORTOISE FOR THE NORTH AND AZURE DRAGON FOR THE EAST.
AND IN THE CENTER STANDS ...

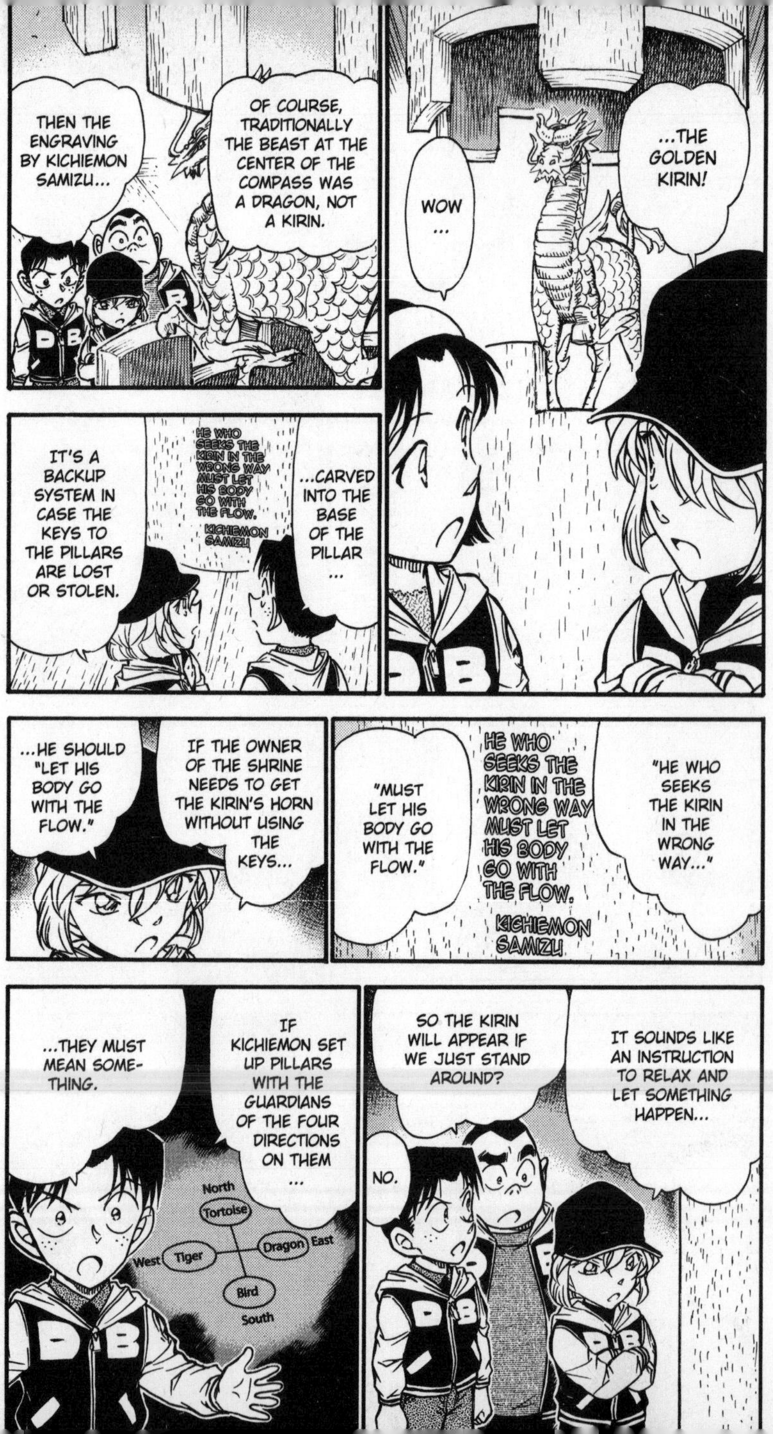
...THE GOLDEN KIRIN!
WOW...
OF COURSE, TRADITIONALLY THE BEAST AT THE CENTER OF THE COMPASS WAS A DRAGON, NOT A KIRIN.
THEN THE ENGRAVING BY KICHIEMON SAMIZU...
...CARVED INTO THE BASE OF THE PILLAR...
HE WHO SEEKS THE KIRIN IN THE WRONG WAY MUST LET HIS BODY GO WITH THE FLOW.
KICHIEMON SAMIZU
IT'S A BACKUP SYSTEM IN CASE THE KEYS TO THE PILLARS ARE LOST OR STOLEN.
"HE WHO SEEKS THE KIRIN IN THE WRONG WAY..."
HE WHO SEEKS THE KIRIN IN THE WRONG WAY MUST LET HIS BODY GO WITH THE FLOW.
KICHIEMON SAMIZU
"MUST LET HIS BODY GO WITH THE FLOW."
IF THE OWNER OF THE SHRINE NEEDS TO GET THE KIRIN'S HORN WITHOUT USING THE KEYS...
...HE SHOULD "LET HIS BODY GO WITH THE FLOW."
IT SOUNDS LIKE AN INSTRUCTION TO RELAX AND LET SOMETHING HAPPEN...
SO THE KIRIN WILL APPEAR IF WE JUST STAND AROUND?
NO.
IF KICHIEMON SET UP PILLARS WITH THE GUARDIANS OF THE FOUR DIRECTIONS ON THEM...
North
Tortoise
East
Dragon
Tiger
West
Bird
South
...THEY MUST MEAN SOME-THING.

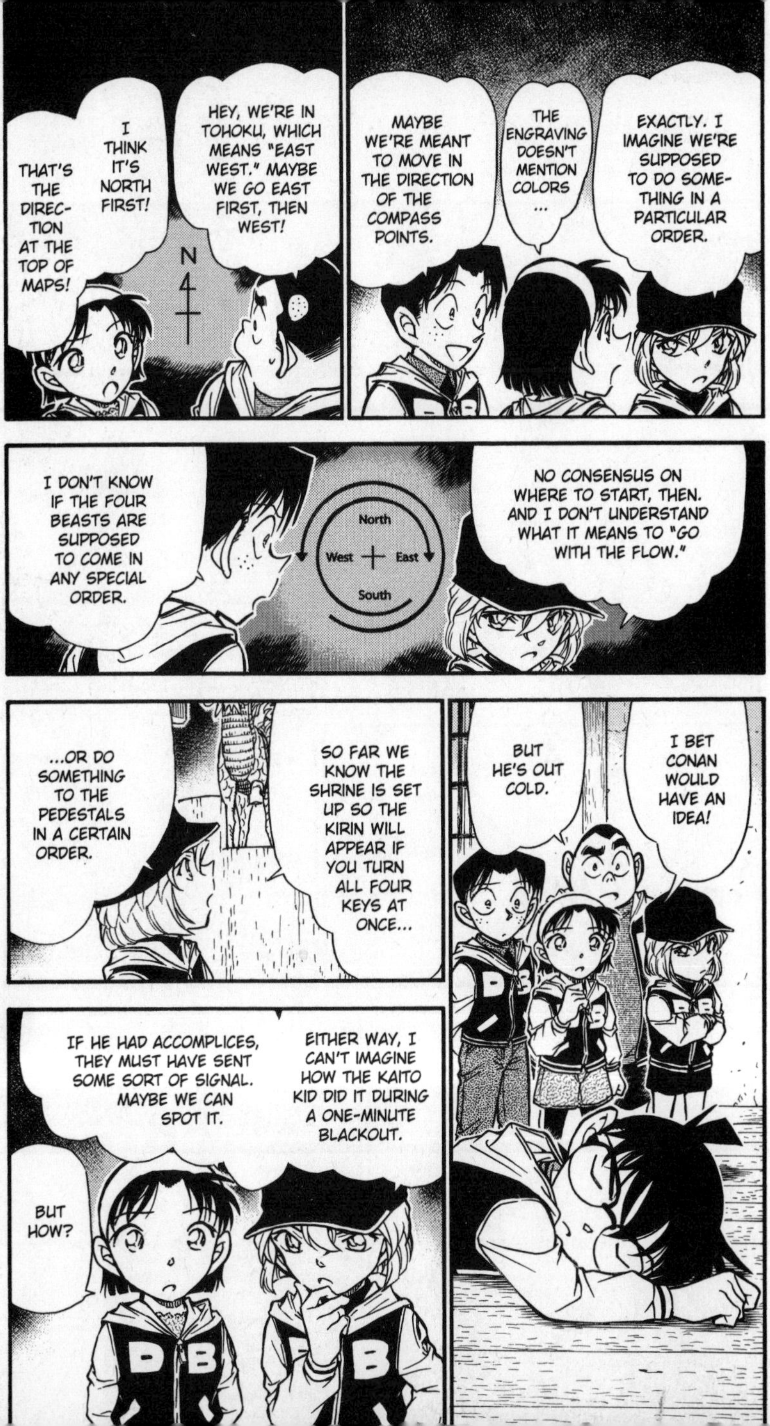
EXACTLY. I IMAGINE WE'RE SUPPOSED TO DO SOME-THING IN A PARTICULAR ORDER.
THE ENGRAVING DOESN'T MENTION COLORS ...
MAYBE WE'RE MEANT TO MOVE IN THE DIRECTION OF THE COMPASS POINTS.
HEY, WE'RE IN TOHOKU, WHICH MEANS "EAST WEST." MAYBE WE GO EAST FIRST, THEN WEST!
I THINK IT'S NORTH FIRST!
N
THAT'S THE DIREC-TION AT THE TOP OF MAPS!
NO CONSENSUS ON WHERE TO START, THEN. AND I DON'T UNDERSTAND WHAT IT MEANS TO "GO WITH THE FLOW."
North
West
East
South
I DON'T KNOW IF THE FOUR BEASTS ARE SUPPOSED TO COME IN ANY SPECIAL ORDER.
I BET CONAN WOULD HAVE AN IDEA!
BUT HE'S OUT COLD.
SO FAR WE KNOW THE SHRINE IS SET UP SO THE KIRIN WILL APPEAR IF YOU TURN ALL FOUR KEYS AT ONCE...
...OR DO SOMETHING TO THE PEDESTALS IN A CERTAIN ORDER.
EITHER WAY, I CAN'T IMAGINE HOW THE KAITO KID DID IT DURING A ONE-MINUTE BLACKOUT.
IF HE HAD ACCOMPLICES, THEY MUST HAVE SENT SOME SORT OF SIGNAL. MAYBE WE CAN SPOT IT.
BUT HOW?

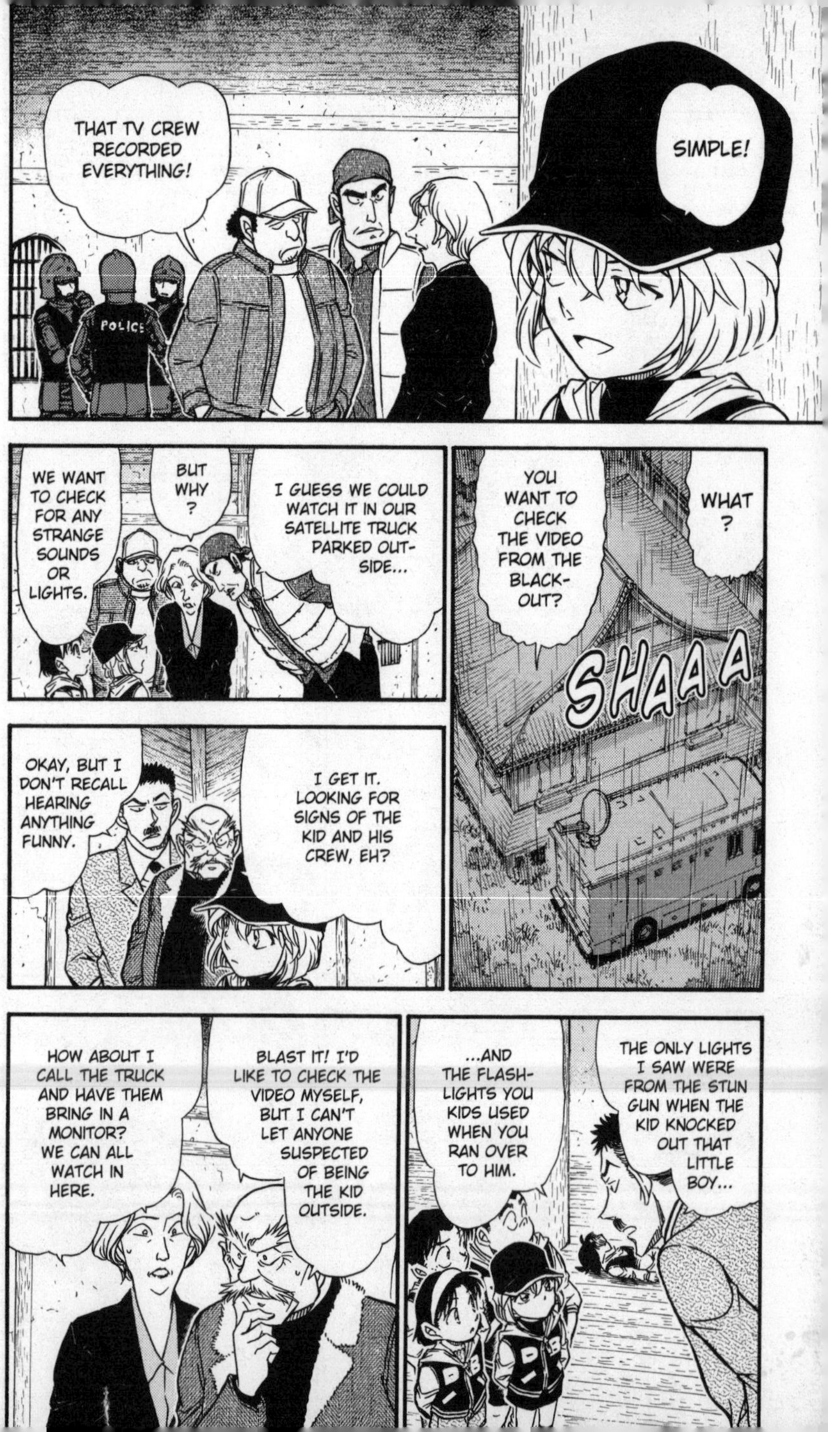
SIMPLE!
THAT TV CREW RECORDED EVERYTHING!
POLICE
WHAT?
YOU WANT TO CHECK THE VIDEO FROM THE BLACK-OUT?
SHAAA
I GUESS WE COULD WATCH IT IN OUR SATELLITE TRUCK PARKED OUT-SIDE...
BUT WHY?
WE WANT TO CHECK FOR ANY STRANGE SOUNDS OR LIGHTS.
I GET IT. LOOKING FOR SIGNS OF THE KID AND HIS CREW, EH?
OKAY, BUT I DON'T RECALL HEARING ANYTHING FUNNY.
THE ONLY LIGHTS I SAW WERE FROM THE STUN GUN WHEN THE KID KNOCKED OUT THAT LITTLE BOY...
...AND THE FLASH-LIGHTS YOU KIDS USED WHEN YOU RAN OVER TO HIM.
BLAST IT! I'D LIKE TO CHECK THE VIDEO MYSELF, BUT I CAN'T LET ANYONE SUSPECTED OF BEING THE KID OUTSIDE.
HOW ABOUT I CALL THE TRUCK AND HAVE THEM BRING IN A MONITOR? WE CAN ALL WATCH IN HERE.

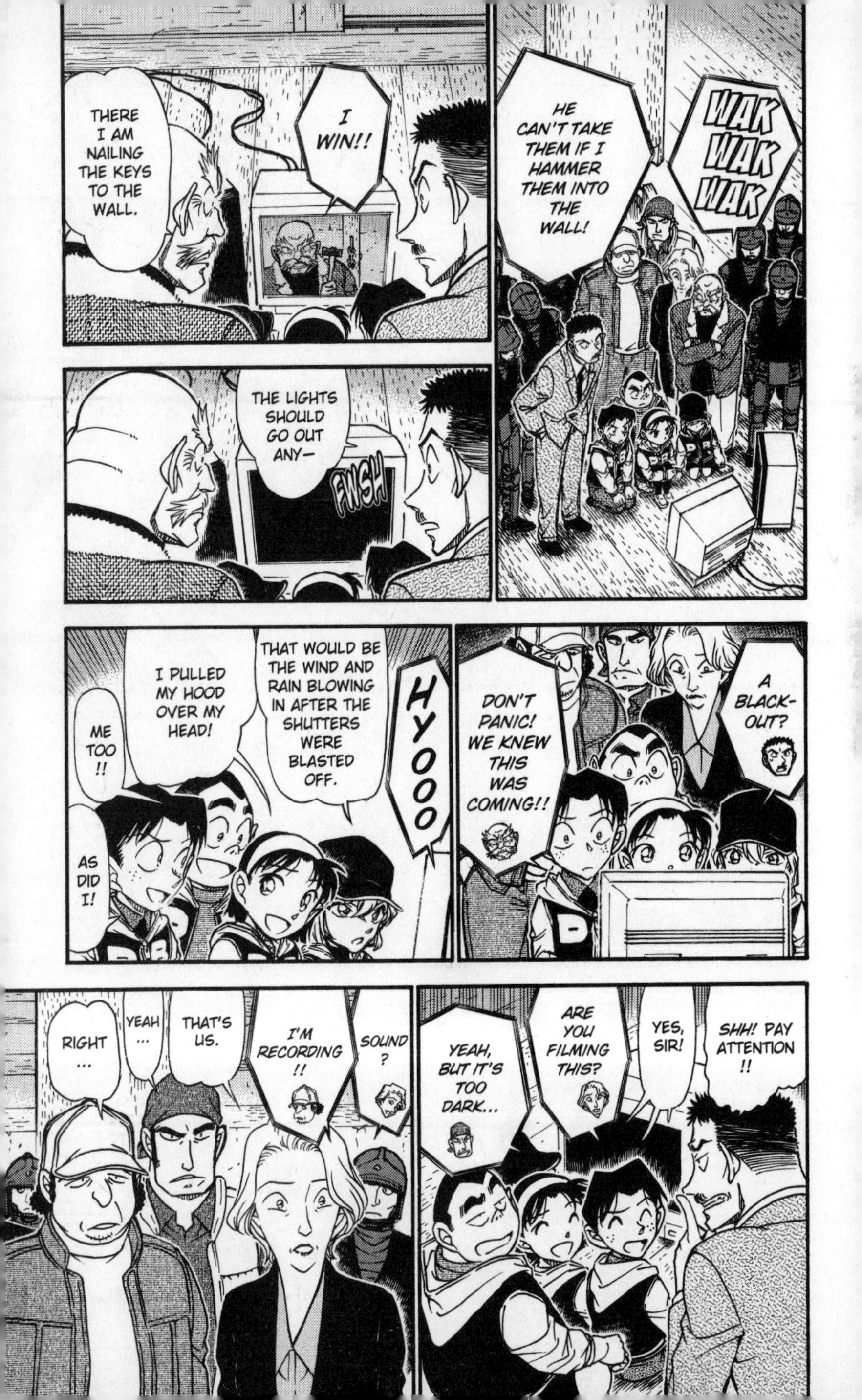
WAK WAK WAK
HE CAN'T TAKE THEM IF I HAMMER THEM INTO THE WALL!
I WIN!!
THERE I AM NAILING THE KEYS TO THE WALL.
FWSH
THE LIGHTS SHOULD GO OUT ANY—
A BLACK-OUT?
DON'T PANIC! WE KNEW THIS WAS COMING!!
HYOOO
THAT WOULD BE THE WIND AND RAIN BLOWING IN AFTER THE SHUTTERS WERE BLASTED OFF.
I PULLED MY HOOD OVER MY HEAD!
ME TOO!!
AS DID I!
SHH! PAY ATTENTION!!
YES, SIR!
ARE YOU FILMING THIS?
YEAH, BUT IT'S TOO DARK...
SOUND?
I'M RECORDING!!
THAT'S US.
YEAH...
RIGHT...

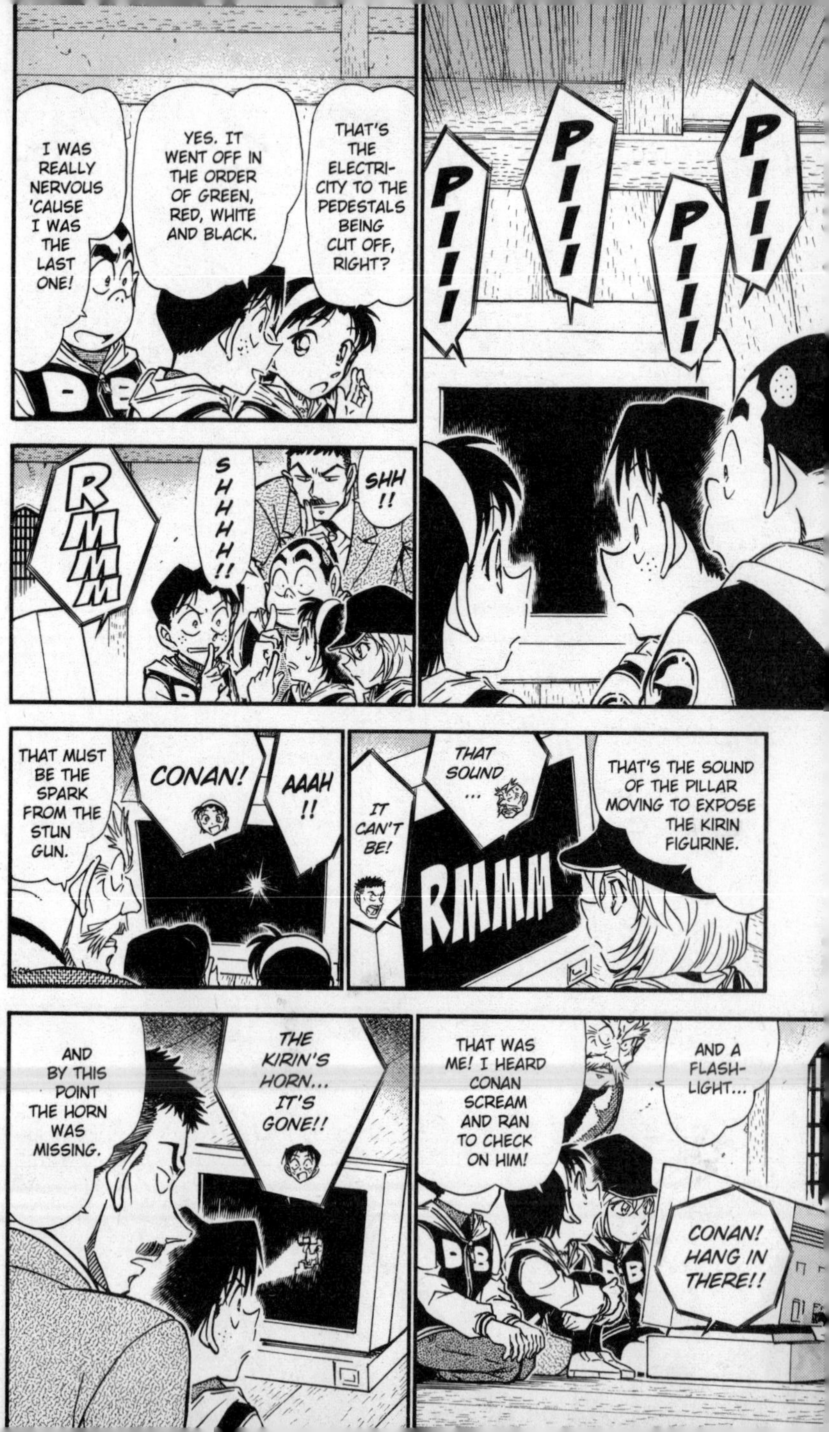
PIII
PIII
PIII
PIII
THAT'S THE ELECTRICITY TO THE PEDESTALS BEING CUT OFF, RIGHT?
YES. IT WENT OFF IN THE ORDER OF GREEN, RED, WHITE AND BLACK.
I WAS REALLY NERVOUS 'CAUSE I WAS THE LAST ONE!
SHH!!
SHHHHH!!
RMMM
THAT'S THE SOUND OF THE PILLAR MOVING TO EXPOSE THE KIRIN FIGURINE.
THAT SOUND...
IT CAN'T BE!
RMMM
AAAH!!
CONAN!
THAT MUST BE THE SPARK FROM THE STUN GUN.
AND A FLASHLIGHT...
THAT WAS ME! I HEARD CONAN SCREAM AND RAN TO CHECK ON HIM!
CONAN! HANG IN THERE!!
THE KIRIN'S HORN... IT'S GONE!!
AND BY THIS POINT THE HORN WAS MISSING.

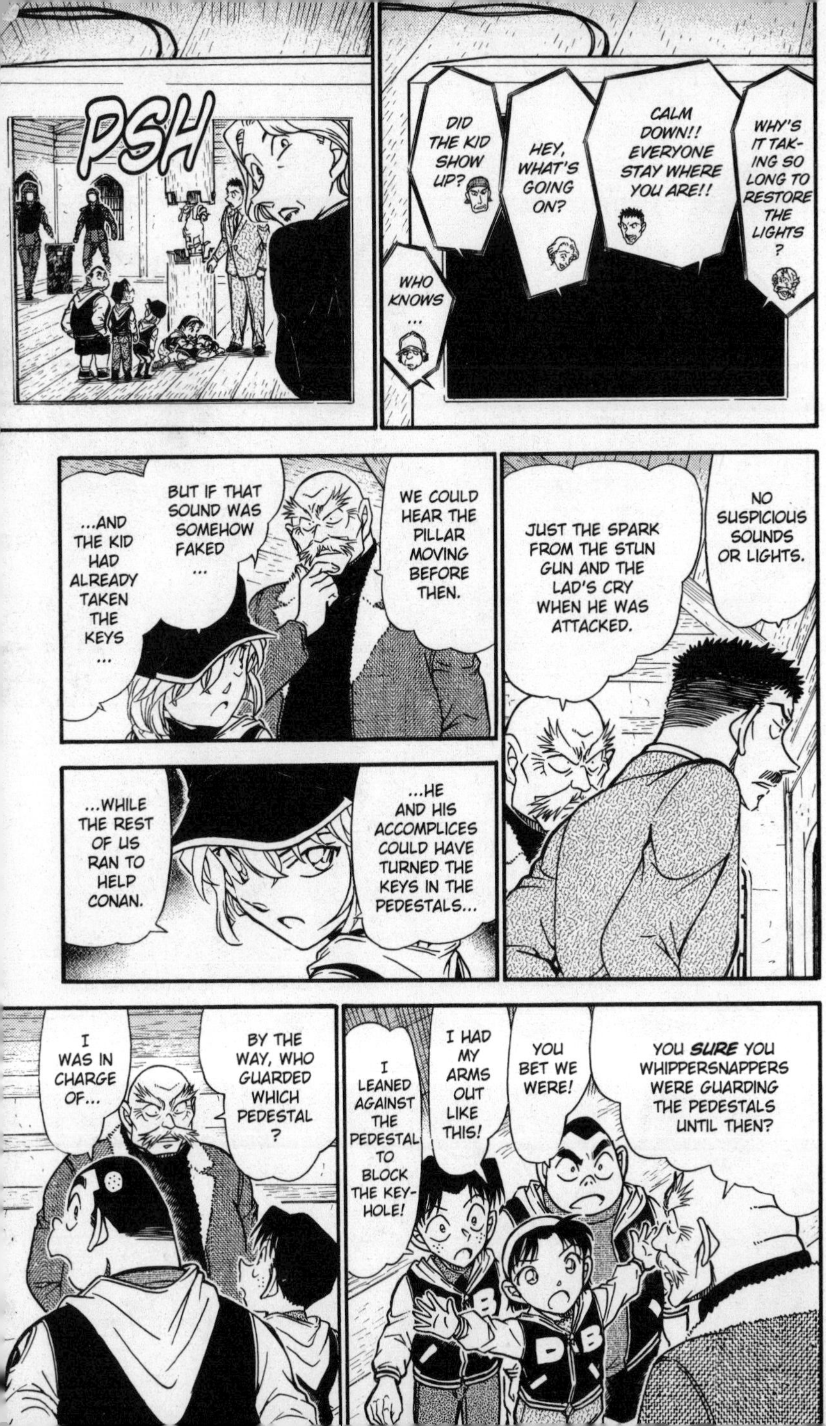
WHY'S IT TAKING SO LONG TO RESTORE THE LIGHTS?
CALM DOWN!! EVERYONE STAY WHERE YOU ARE!!
HEY, WHAT'S GOING ON?
DID THE KID SHOW UP?
WHO KNOWS...
PSH
NO SUSPICIOUS SOUNDS OR LIGHTS.
JUST THE SPARK FROM THE STUN GUN AND THE LAD'S CRY WHEN HE WAS ATTACKED.
WE COULD HEAR THE PILLAR MOVING BEFORE THEN.
BUT IF THAT SOUND WAS SOMEHOW FAKED...
...AND THE KID HAD ALREADY TAKEN THE KEYS...
...HE AND HIS ACCOMPLICES COULD HAVE TURNED THE KEYS IN THE PEDESTALS...
...WHILE THE REST OF US RAN TO HELP CONAN.
YOU *SURE* YOU WHIPPERSNAPPERS WERE GUARDING THE PEDESTALS UNTIL THEN?
YOU BET WE WERE!
I HAD MY ARMS OUT LIKE THIS!
I LEANED AGAINST THE PEDESTAL TO BLOCK THE KEY-HOLE!
BY THE WAY, WHO GUARDED WHICH PEDESTAL?
I WAS IN CHARGE OF...

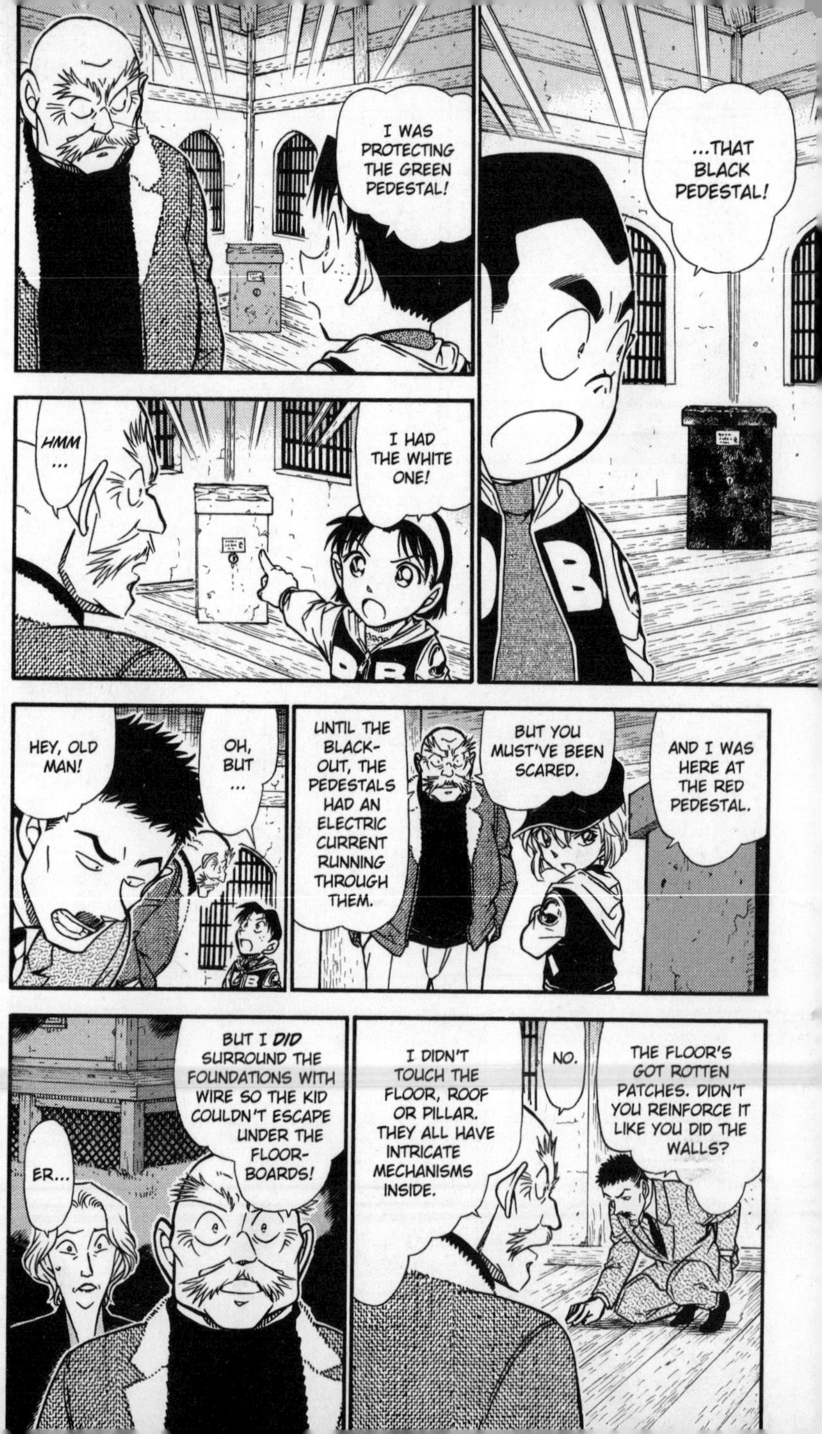
...THAT BLACK PEDESTAL!
I WAS PROTECTING THE GREEN PEDESTAL!
I HAD THE WHITE ONE!
HMM ...
AND I WAS HERE AT THE RED PEDESTAL.
BUT YOU MUST'VE BEEN SCARED.
UNTIL THE BLACK-OUT, THE PEDESTALS HAD AN ELECTRIC CURRENT RUNNING THROUGH THEM.
OH, BUT ...
HEY, OLD MAN!
THE FLOOR'S GOT ROTTEN PATCHES. DIDN'T YOU REINFORCE IT LIKE YOU DID THE WALLS?
NO.
I DIDN'T TOUCH THE FLOOR, ROOF OR PILLAR. THEY ALL HAVE INTRICATE MECHANISMS INSIDE.
BUT I *DID* SURROUND THE FOUNDATIONS WITH WIRE SO THE KID COULDN'T ESCAPE UNDER THE FLOOR-BOARDS!
ER...

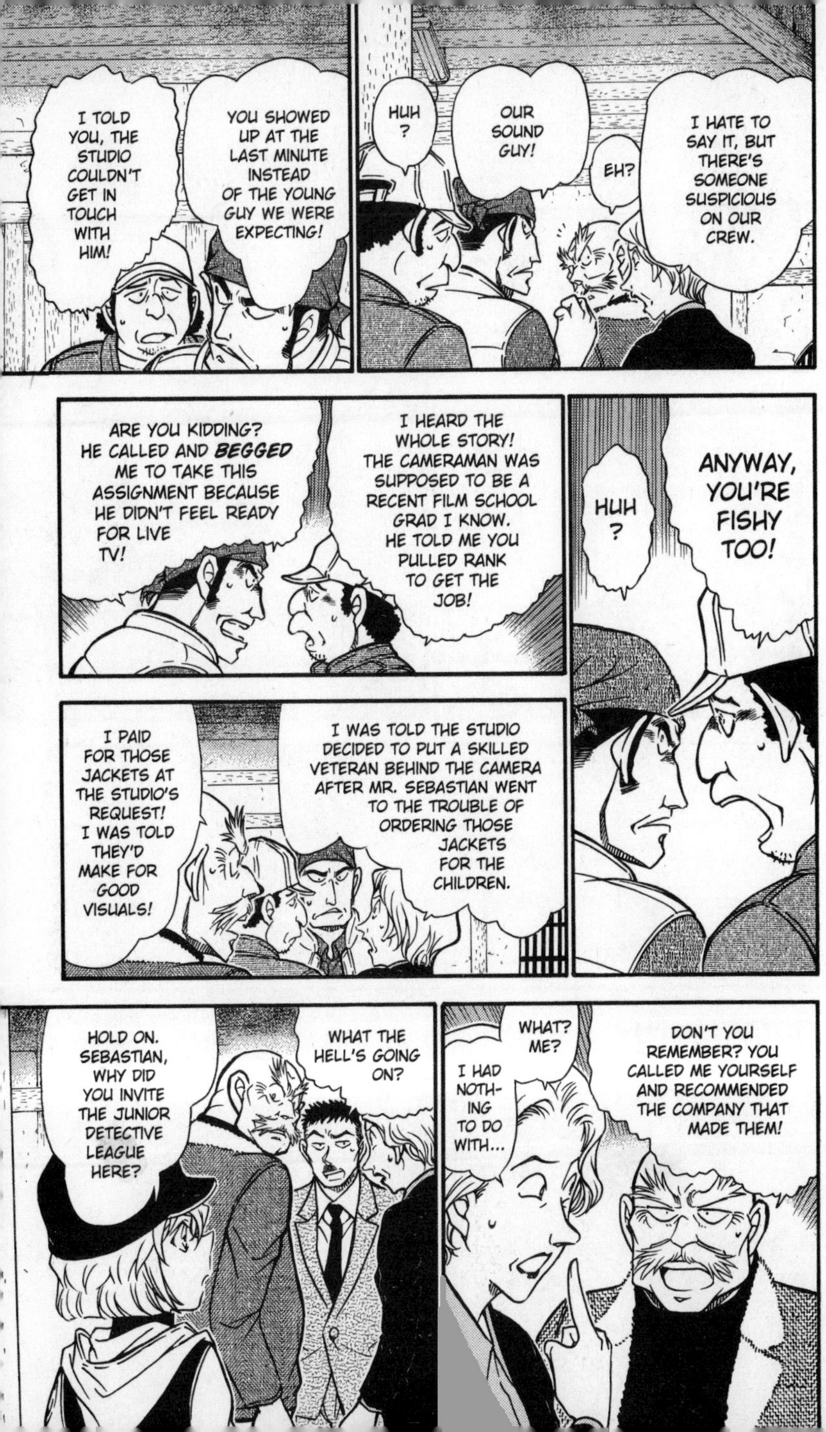
I HATE TO SAY IT, BUT THERE'S SOMEONE SUSPICIOUS ON OUR CREW.
EH?
OUR SOUND GUY!
HUH?
YOU SHOWED UP AT THE LAST MINUTE INSTEAD OF THE YOUNG GUY WE WERE EXPECTING!
I TOLD YOU, THE STUDIO COULDN'T GET IN TOUCH WITH HIM!
ANYWAY, YOU'RE FISHY TOO!
HUH?
I HEARD THE WHOLE STORY! THE CAMERAMAN WAS SUPPOSED TO BE A RECENT FILM SCHOOL GRAD I KNOW. HE TOLD ME YOU PULLED RANK TO GET THE JOB!
ARE YOU KIDDING? HE CALLED AND BEGGED ME TO TAKE THIS ASSIGNMENT BECAUSE HE DIDN'T FEEL READY FOR LIVE TV!
I WAS TOLD THE STUDIO DECIDED TO PUT A SKILLED VETERAN BEHIND THE CAMERA AFTER MR. SEBASTIAN WENT TO THE TROUBLE OF ORDERING THOSE JACKETS FOR THE CHILDREN.
I PAID FOR THOSE JACKETS AT THE STUDIO'S REQUEST! I WAS TOLD THEY'D MAKE FOR GOOD VISUALS!
DON'T YOU REMEMBER? YOU CALLED ME YOURSELF AND RECOMMENDED THE COMPANY THAT MADE THEM!
WHAT? ME?
I HAD NOTHING TO DO WITH...
WHAT THE HELL'S GOING ON?
HOLD ON. SEBASTIAN, WHY DID YOU INVITE THE JUNIOR DETECTIVE LEAGUE HERE?

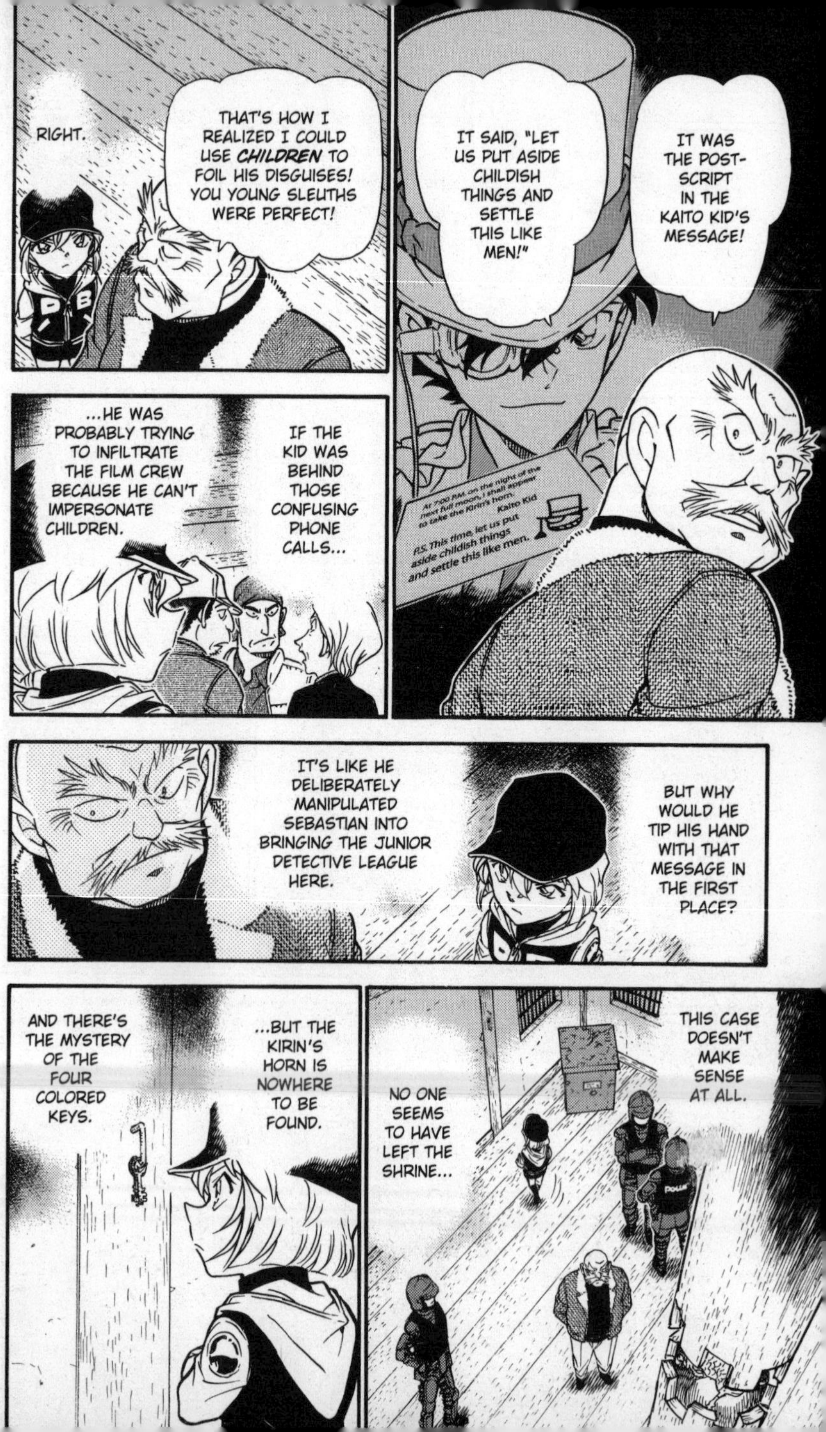
IT WAS THE POST-SCRIPT IN THE KAITO KID'S MESSAGE!
IT SAID, "LET US PUT ASIDE CHILDISH THINGS AND SETTLE THIS LIKE MEN!"
At 7:00 P.M. on the night of the next full moon, I shall appear to take the Kirin's horn.
Kaito Kid
P.S. This time, let us put aside childish things and settle this like men.
THAT'S HOW I REALIZED I COULD USE *CHILDREN* TO FOIL HIS DISGUISES! YOU YOUNG SLEUTHS WERE PERFECT!
RIGHT.
IF THE KID WAS BEHIND THOSE CONFUSING PHONE CALLS...
...HE WAS PROBABLY TRYING TO INFILTRATE THE FILM CREW BECAUSE HE CAN'T IMPERSONATE CHILDREN.
BUT WHY WOULD HE TIP HIS HAND WITH THAT MESSAGE IN THE FIRST PLACE?
IT'S LIKE HE DELIBERATELY MANIPULATED SEBASTIAN INTO BRINGING THE JUNIOR DETECTIVE LEAGUE HERE.
THIS CASE DOESN'T MAKE SENSE AT ALL.
NO ONE SEEMS TO HAVE LEFT THE SHRINE...
...BUT THE KIRIN'S HORN IS NOWHERE TO BE FOUND.
AND THERE'S THE MYSTERY OF THE FOUR COLORED KEYS.

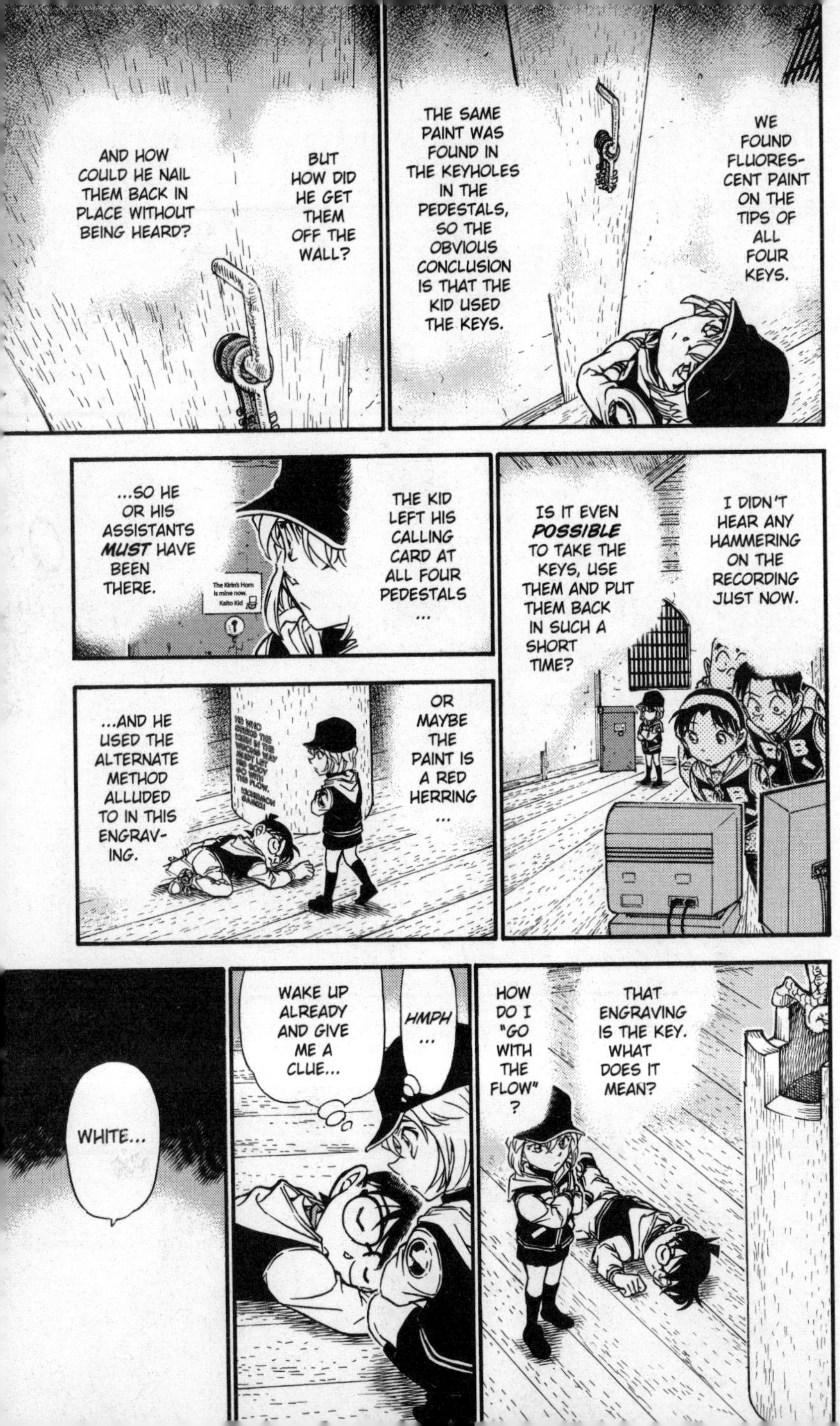
WE FOUND FLUORES-CENT PAINT ON THE TIPS OF ALL FOUR KEYS.
THE SAME PAINT WAS FOUND IN THE KEYHOLES IN THE PEDESTALS, SO THE OBVIOUS CONCLUSION IS THAT THE KID USED THE KEYS.
BUT HOW DID HE GET THEM OFF THE WALL?
AND HOW COULD HE NAIL THEM BACK IN PLACE WITHOUT BEING HEARD?
I DIDN'T HEAR ANY HAMMERING ON THE RECORDING JUST NOW.
IS IT EVEN *POSSIBLE* TO TAKE THE KEYS, USE THEM AND PUT THEM BACK IN SUCH A SHORT TIME?
THE KID LEFT HIS CALLING CARD AT ALL FOUR PEDESTALS...
The Kirin's Horn is mine now. Kaito Kid
...SO HE OR HIS ASSISTANTS *MUST* HAVE BEEN THERE.
OR MAYBE THE PAINT IS A RED HERRING...
...AND HE USED THE ALTERNATE METHOD ALLUDED TO IN THIS ENGRAV-ING.
THAT ENGRAVING IS THE KEY. WHAT DOES IT MEAN?
HOW DO I "GO WITH THE FLOW"?
HMPH...
WAKE UP ALREADY AND GIVE ME A CLUE...
WHITE...

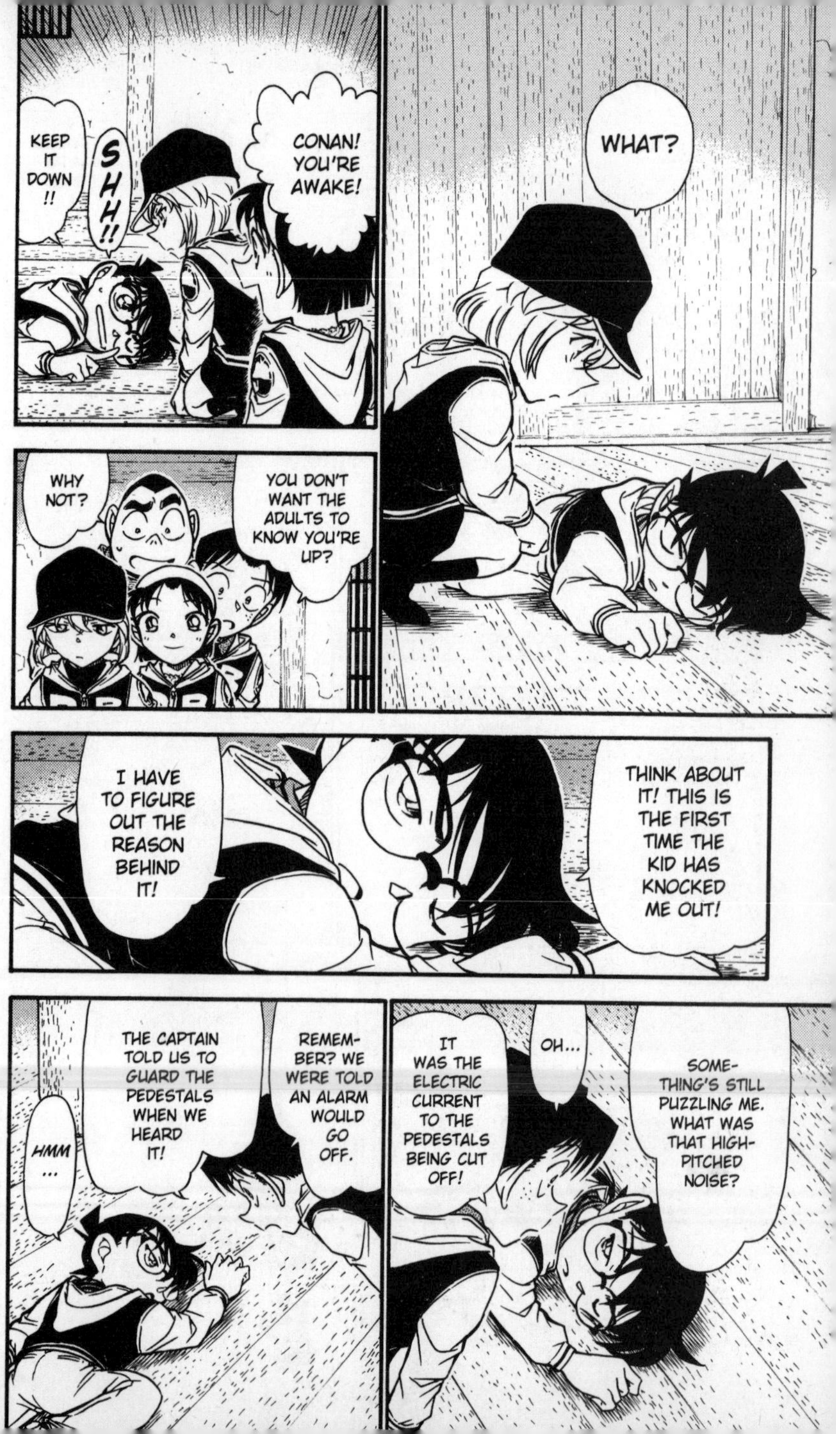
WHAT?
CONAN! YOU'RE AWAKE!
SHH!!
KEEP IT DOWN!!
YOU DON'T WANT THE ADULTS TO KNOW YOU'RE UP?
WHY NOT?
THINK ABOUT IT! THIS IS THE FIRST TIME THE KID HAS KNOCKED ME OUT!
I HAVE TO FIGURE OUT THE REASON BEHIND IT!
SOME-THING'S STILL PUZZLING ME. WHAT WAS THAT HIGH-PITCHED NOISE?
OH...
IT WAS THE ELECTRIC CURRENT TO THE PEDESTALS BEING CUT OFF!
REMEM-BER? WE WERE TOLD AN ALARM WOULD GO OFF.
THE CAPTAIN TOLD US TO GUARD THE PEDESTALS WHEN WE HEARD IT!
HMM...

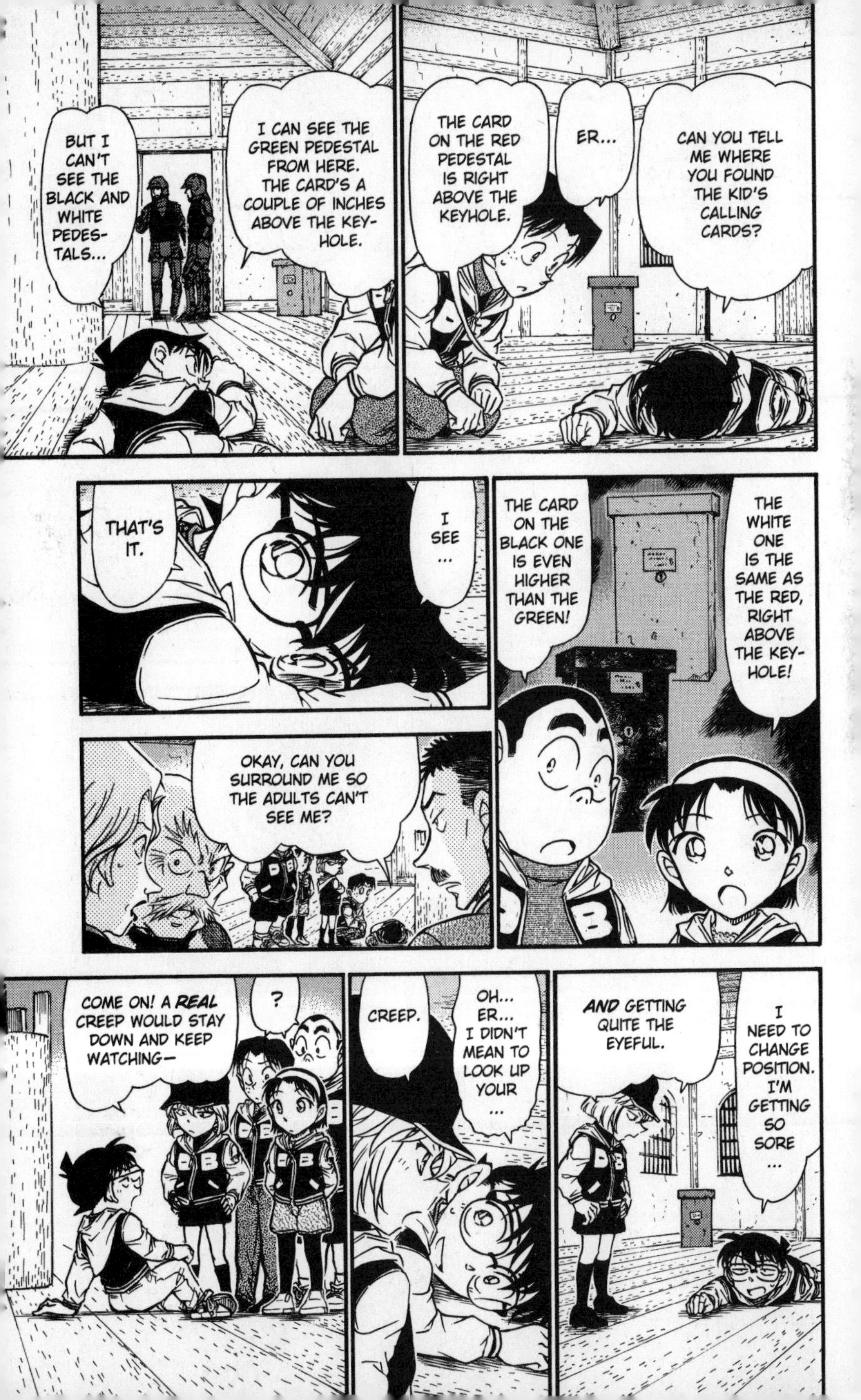
CAN YOU TELL ME WHERE YOU FOUND THE KID'S CALLING CARDS?
ER...
THE CARD ON THE RED PEDESTAL IS RIGHT ABOVE THE KEYHOLE.
I CAN SEE THE GREEN PEDESTAL FROM HERE. THE CARD'S A COUPLE OF INCHES ABOVE THE KEY-HOLE.
BUT I CAN'T SEE THE BLACK AND WHITE PEDES-TALS...
THE WHITE ONE IS THE SAME AS THE RED, RIGHT ABOVE THE KEY-HOLE!
THE CARD ON THE BLACK ONE IS EVEN HIGHER THAN THE GREEN!
I SEE...
THAT'S IT.
OKAY, CAN YOU SURROUND ME SO THE ADULTS CAN'T SEE ME?
I NEED TO CHANGE POSITION. I'M GETTING SO SORE...
AND GETTING QUITE THE EYEFUL.
OH... ER... I DIDN'T MEAN TO LOOK UP YOUR...
CREEP.
?
COME ON! A *REAL* CREEP WOULD STAY DOWN AND KEEP WATCHING—

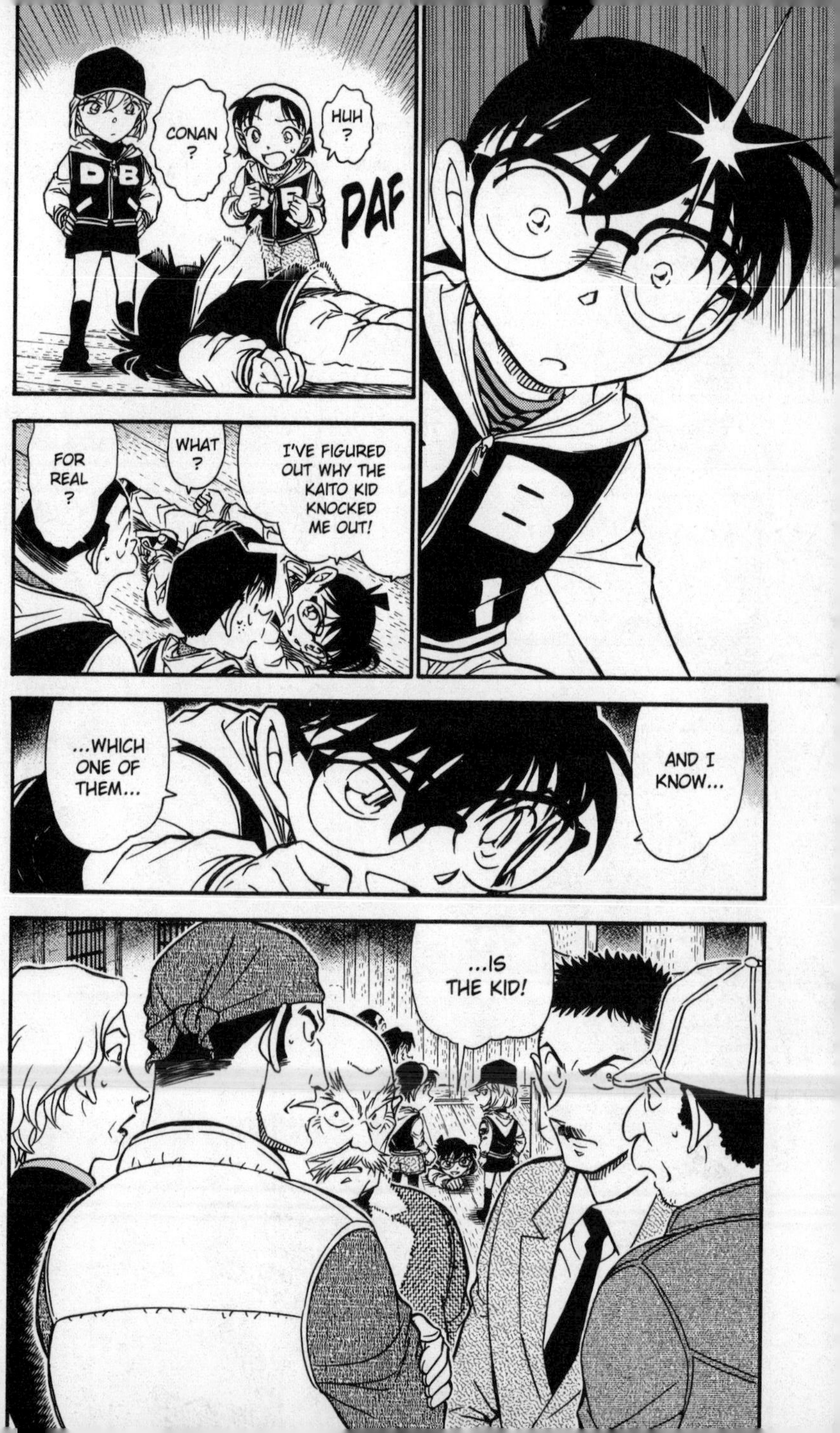
HUH ?
CONAN ?
PAF
I'VE FIGURED OUT WHY THE KAITO KID KNOCKED ME OUT!
WHAT ?
FOR REAL ?
AND I KNOW...
...WHICH ONE OF THEM...
...IS THE KID!

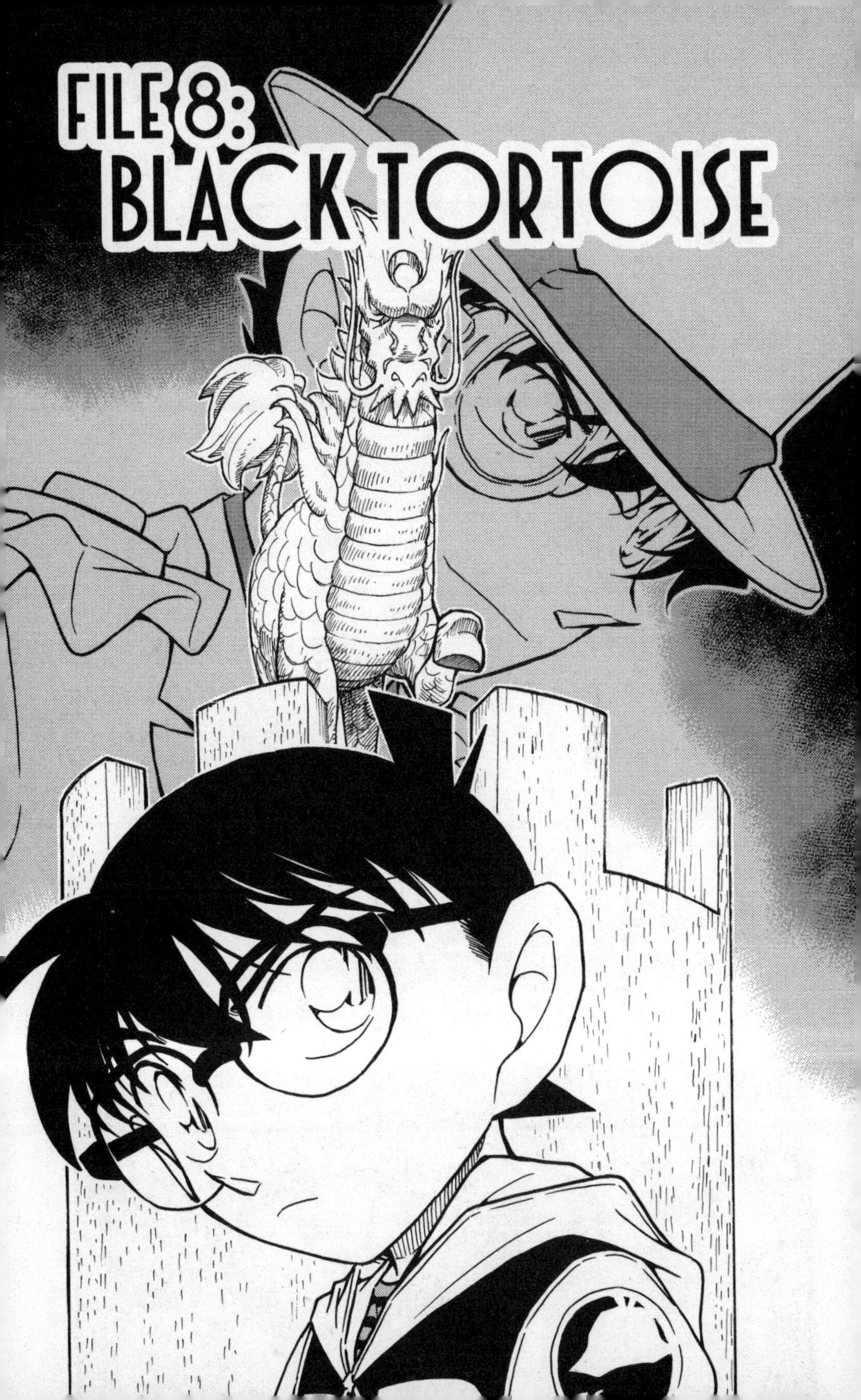
FILE 8:
BLACK TORTOISE

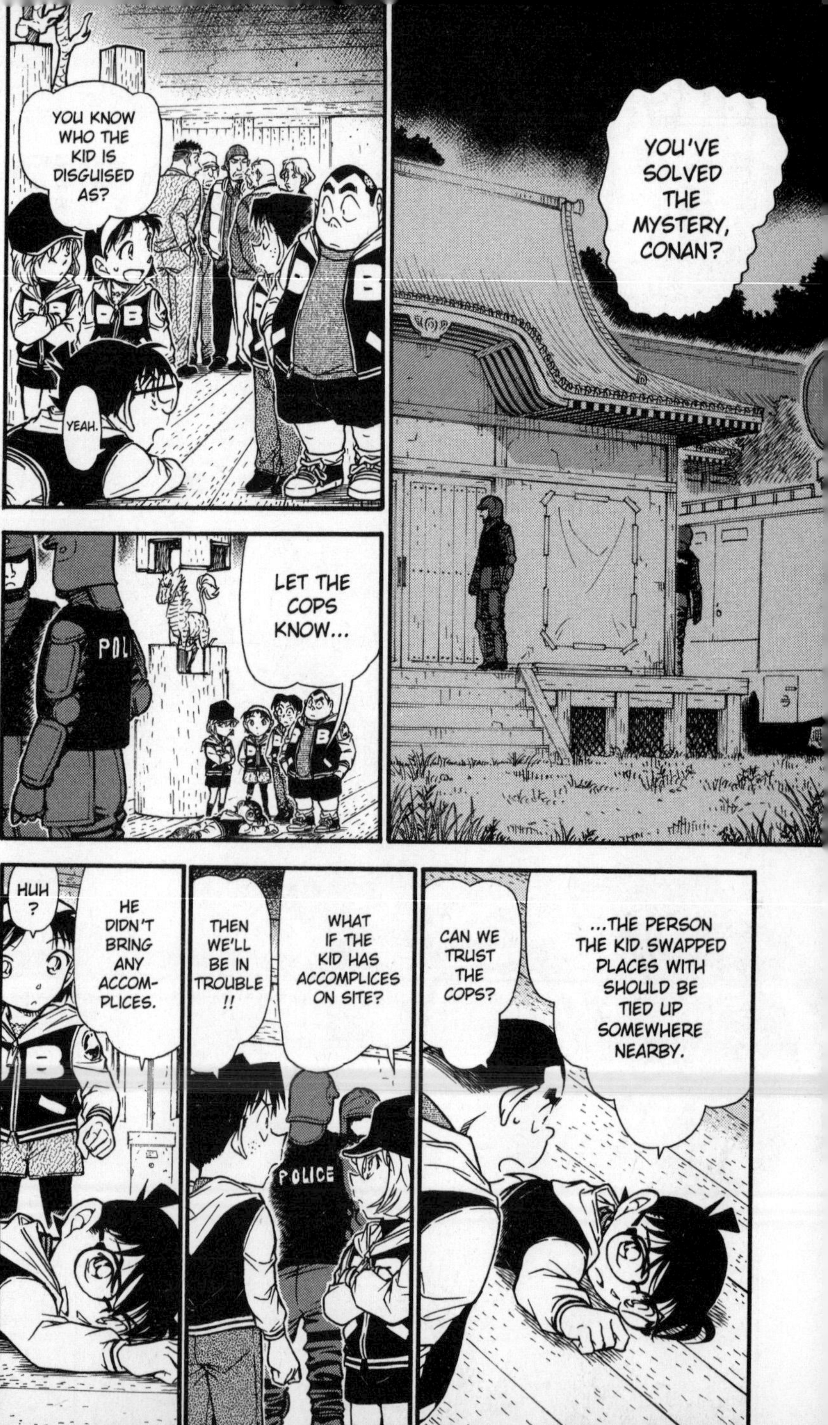
YOU'VE SOLVED THE MYSTERY, CONAN?
YOU KNOW WHO THE KID IS DISGUISED AS?
YEAH.
LET THE COPS KNOW...
...THE PERSON THE KID SWAPPED PLACES WITH SHOULD BE TIED UP SOMEWHERE NEARBY.
CAN WE TRUST THE COPS?
WHAT IF THE KID HAS ACCOMPLICES ON SITE?
THEN WE'LL BE IN TROUBLE !!
HE DIDN'T BRING ANY ACCOM-PLICES.
HUH ?

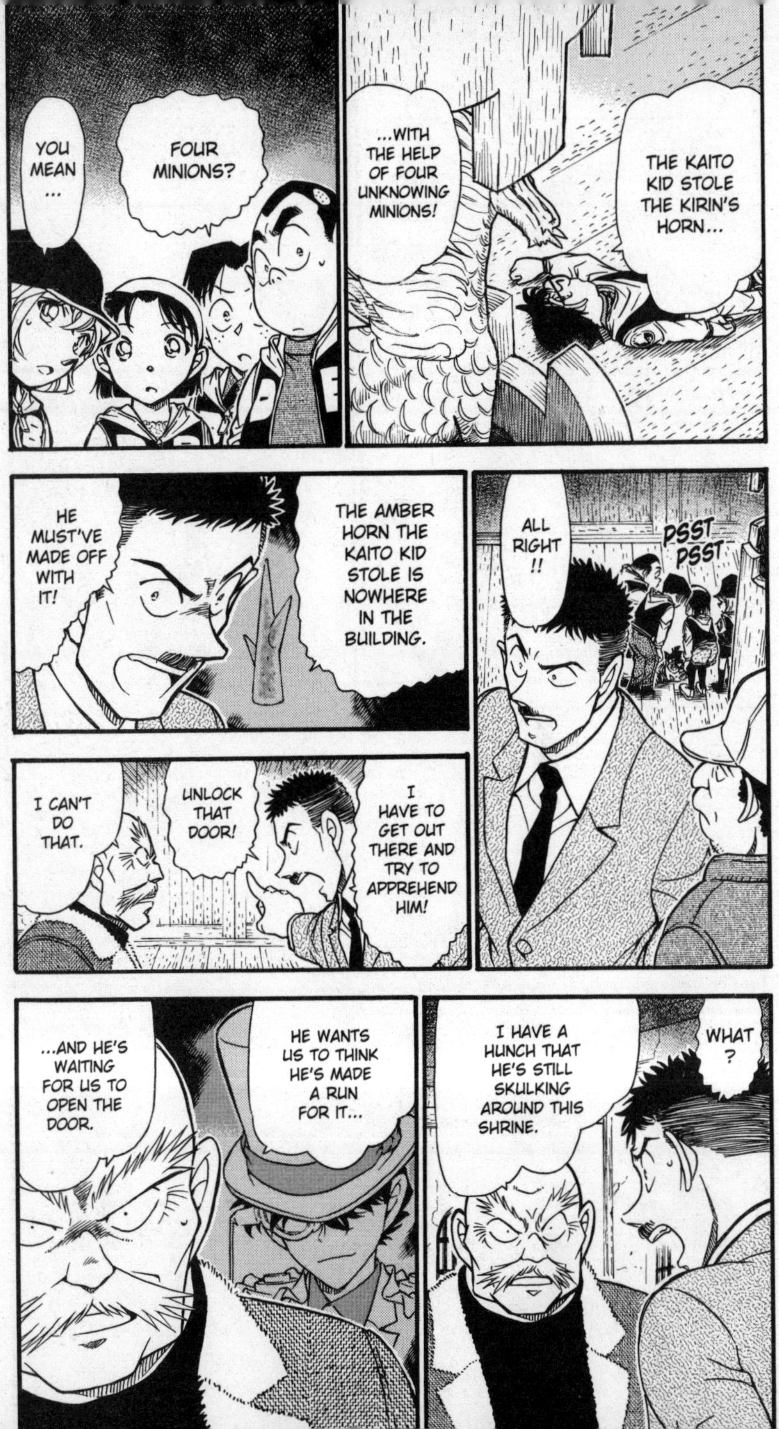
THE KAITO KID STOLE THE KIRIN'S HORN...
...WITH THE HELP OF FOUR UNKNOWING MINIONS!
FOUR MINIONS?
YOU MEAN ...
ALL RIGHT !!
PSST PSST
THE AMBER HORN THE KAITO KID STOLE IS NOWHERE IN THE BUILDING.
HE MUST'VE MADE OFF WITH IT!
I HAVE TO GET OUT THERE AND TRY TO APPREHEND HIM!
UNLOCK THAT DOOR!
I CAN'T DO THAT.
WHAT ?
I HAVE A HUNCH THAT HE'S STILL SKULKING AROUND THIS SHRINE.
HE WANTS US TO THINK HE'S MADE A RUN FOR IT...
...AND HE'S WAITING FOR US TO OPEN THE DOOR.

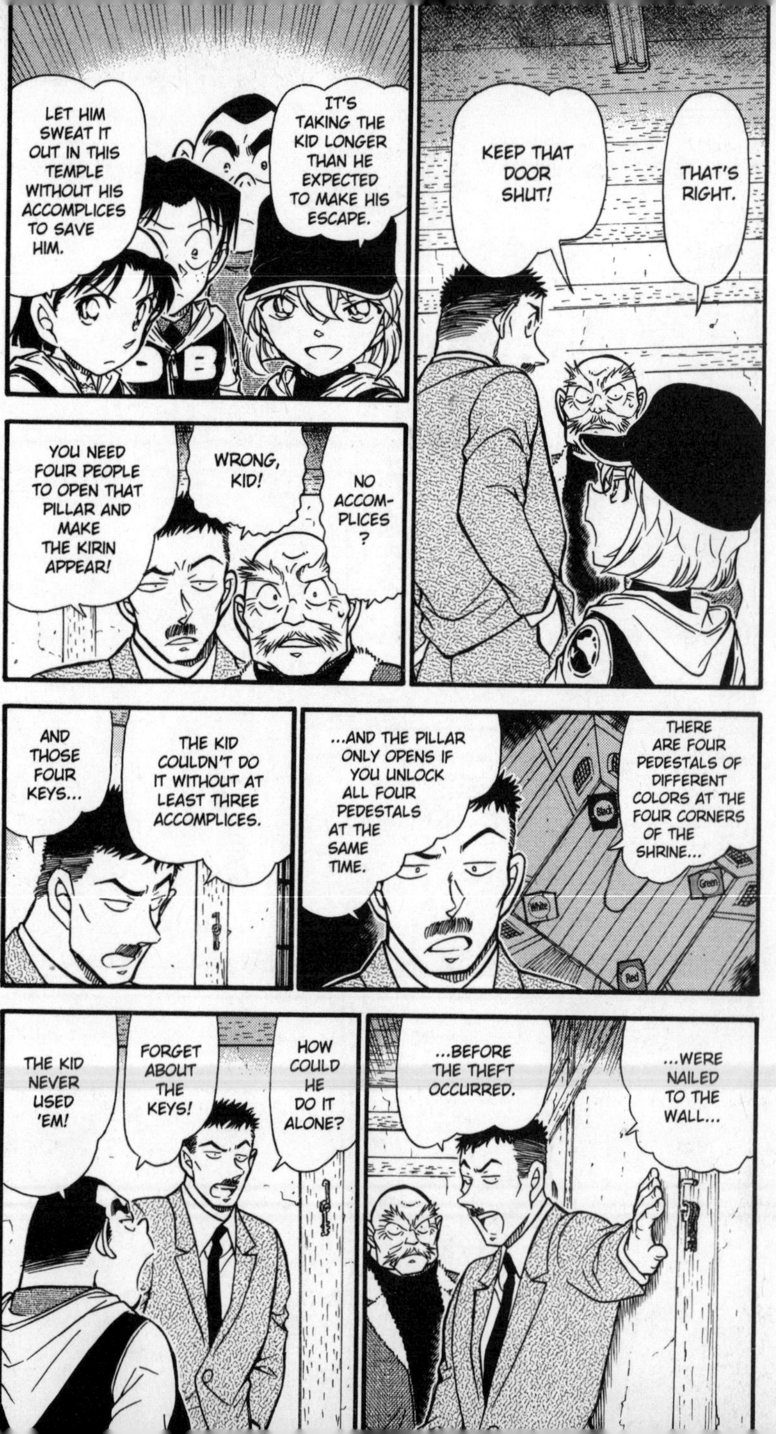
THAT'S RIGHT.
KEEP THAT DOOR SHUT!
IT'S TAKING THE KID LONGER THAN HE EXPECTED TO MAKE HIS ESCAPE.
LET HIM SWEAT IT OUT IN THIS TEMPLE WITHOUT HIS ACCOMPLICES TO SAVE HIM.
NO ACCOMPLICES?
WRONG, KID!
YOU NEED FOUR PEOPLE TO OPEN THAT PILLAR AND MAKE THE KIRIN APPEAR!
THERE ARE FOUR PEDESTALS OF DIFFERENT COLORS AT THE FOUR CORNERS OF THE SHRINE...
Black
Green
White
Red
...AND THE PILLAR ONLY OPENS IF YOU UNLOCK ALL FOUR PEDESTALS AT THE SAME TIME.
THE KID COULDN'T DO IT WITHOUT AT LEAST THREE ACCOMPLICES.
AND THOSE FOUR KEYS...
...WERE NAILED TO THE WALL...
...BEFORE THE THEFT OCCURRED.
HOW COULD HE DO IT ALONE?
FORGET ABOUT THE KEYS!
THE KID NEVER USED 'EM!

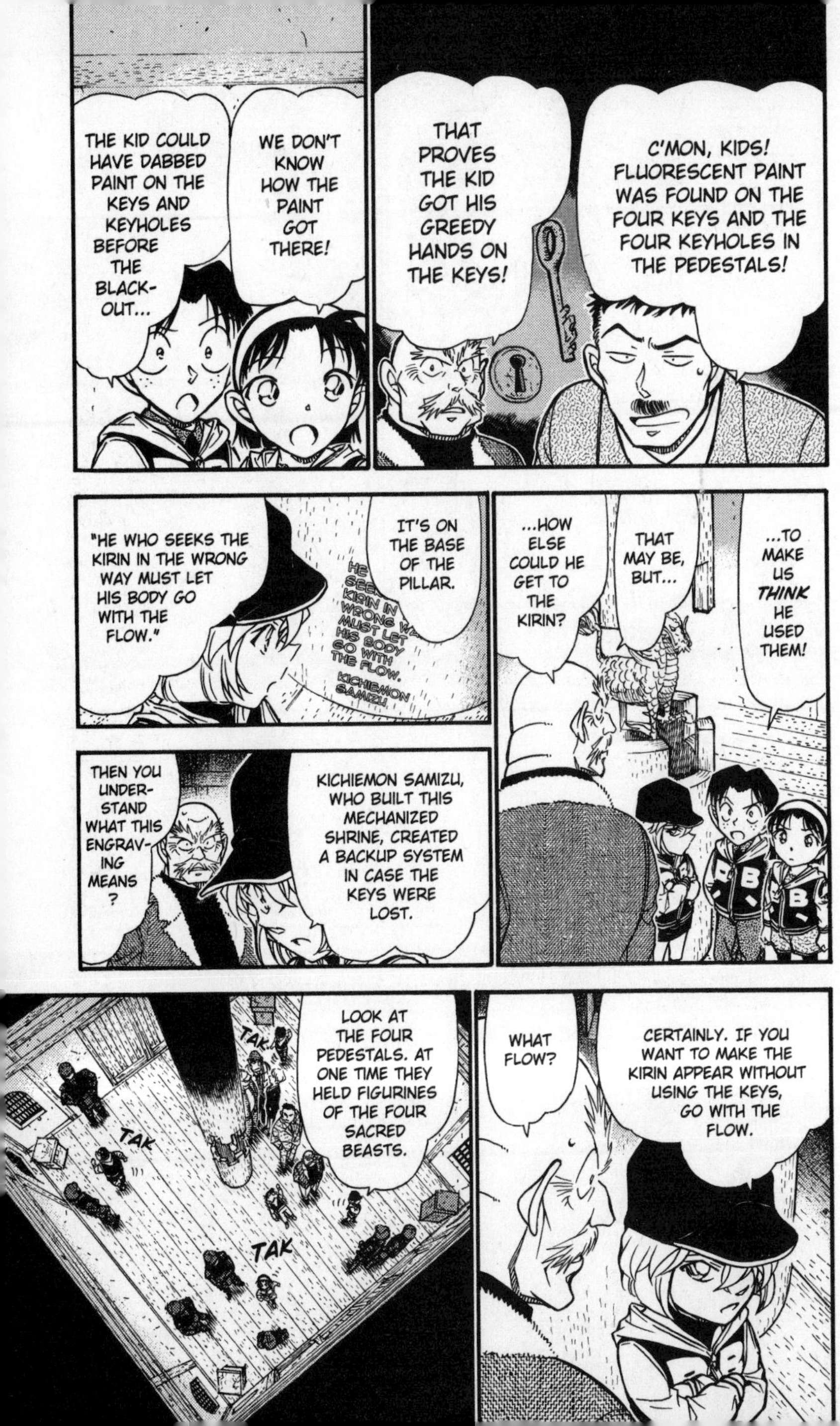
C'MON, KIDS! FLUORESCENT PAINT WAS FOUND ON THE FOUR KEYS AND THE FOUR KEYHOLES IN THE PEDESTALS!
THAT PROVES THE KID GOT HIS GREEDY HANDS ON THE KEYS!
WE DON'T KNOW HOW THE PAINT GOT THERE!
THE KID COULD HAVE DABBED PAINT ON THE KEYS AND KEYHOLES BEFORE THE BLACK-OUT...
...TO MAKE US THINK HE USED THEM!
THAT MAY BE, BUT...
...HOW ELSE COULD HE GET TO THE KIRIN?
IT'S ON THE BASE OF THE PILLAR.
"HE WHO SEEKS THE KIRIN IN THE WRONG WAY MUST LET HIS BODY GO WITH THE FLOW."
MUST LET HIS BODY GO WITH THE FLOW. KICHIEMON SAMIZU
KICHIEMON SAMIZU, WHO BUILT THIS MECHANIZED SHRINE, CREATED A BACKUP SYSTEM IN CASE THE KEYS WERE LOST.
THEN YOU UNDERSTAND WHAT THIS ENGRAVING MEANS?
CERTAINLY. IF YOU WANT TO MAKE THE KIRIN APPEAR WITHOUT USING THE KEYS, GO WITH THE FLOW.
WHAT FLOW?
LOOK AT THE FOUR PEDESTALS. AT ONE TIME THEY HELD FIGURINES OF THE FOUR SACRED BEASTS.
TAK
TAK
TAK

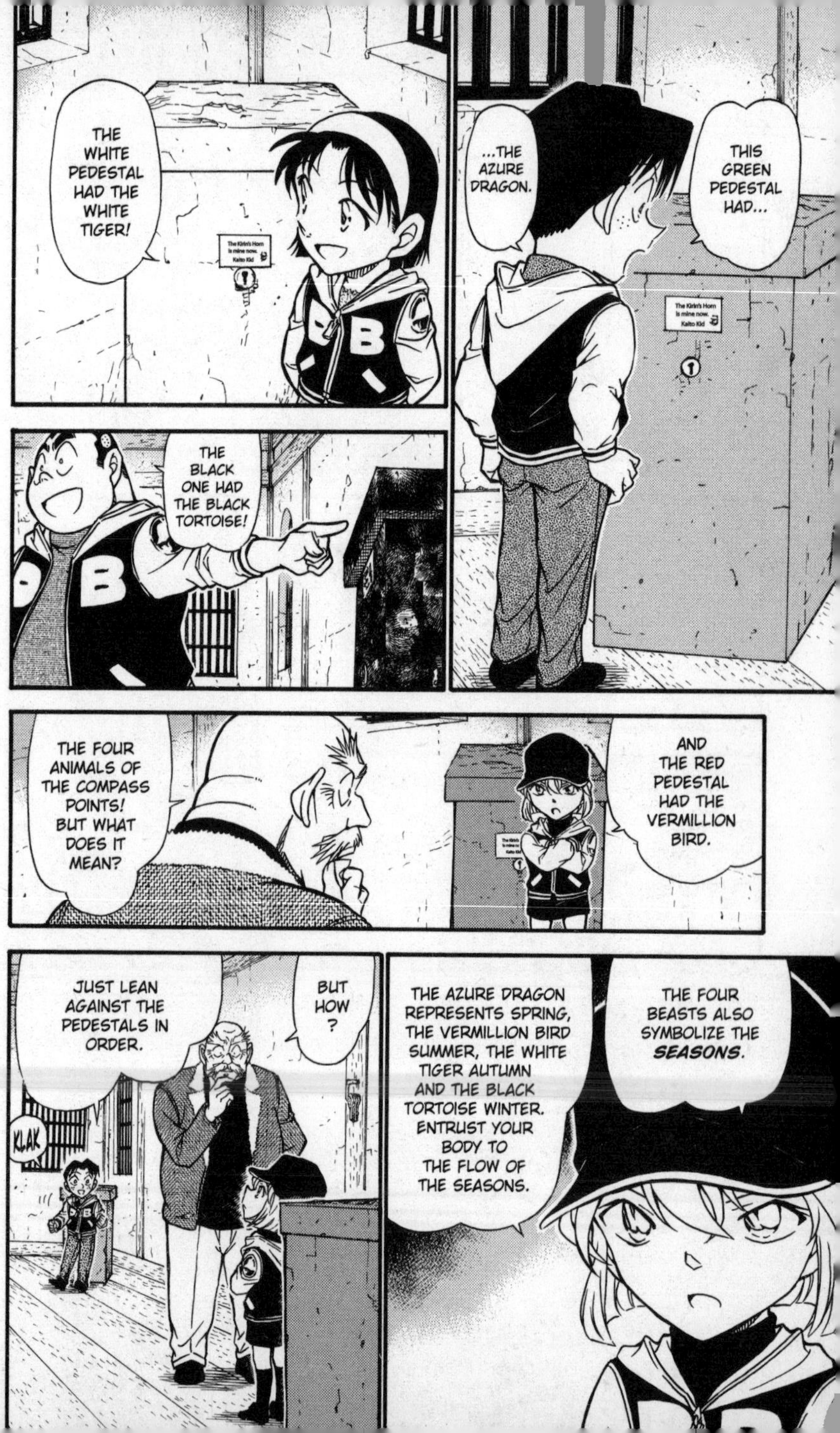
THIS GREEN PEDESTAL HAD...
...THE AZURE DRAGON.
The Kirin's Horn is mine now. Kaito Kid
THE WHITE PEDESTAL HAD THE WHITE TIGER!
The Kirin's Horn is mine now. Kaito Kid
THE BLACK ONE HAD THE BLACK TORTOISE!
AND THE RED PEDESTAL HAD THE VERMILLION BIRD.
THE FOUR ANIMALS OF THE COMPASS POINTS! BUT WHAT DOES IT MEAN?
THE FOUR BEASTS ALSO SYMBOLIZE THE *SEASONS*.
THE AZURE DRAGON REPRESENTS SPRING, THE VERMILLION BIRD SUMMER, THE WHITE TIGER AUTUMN AND THE BLACK TORTOISE WINTER. ENTRUST YOUR BODY TO THE FLOW OF THE SEASONS.
BUT HOW ?
JUST LEAN AGAINST THE PEDESTALS IN ORDER.
KLAK

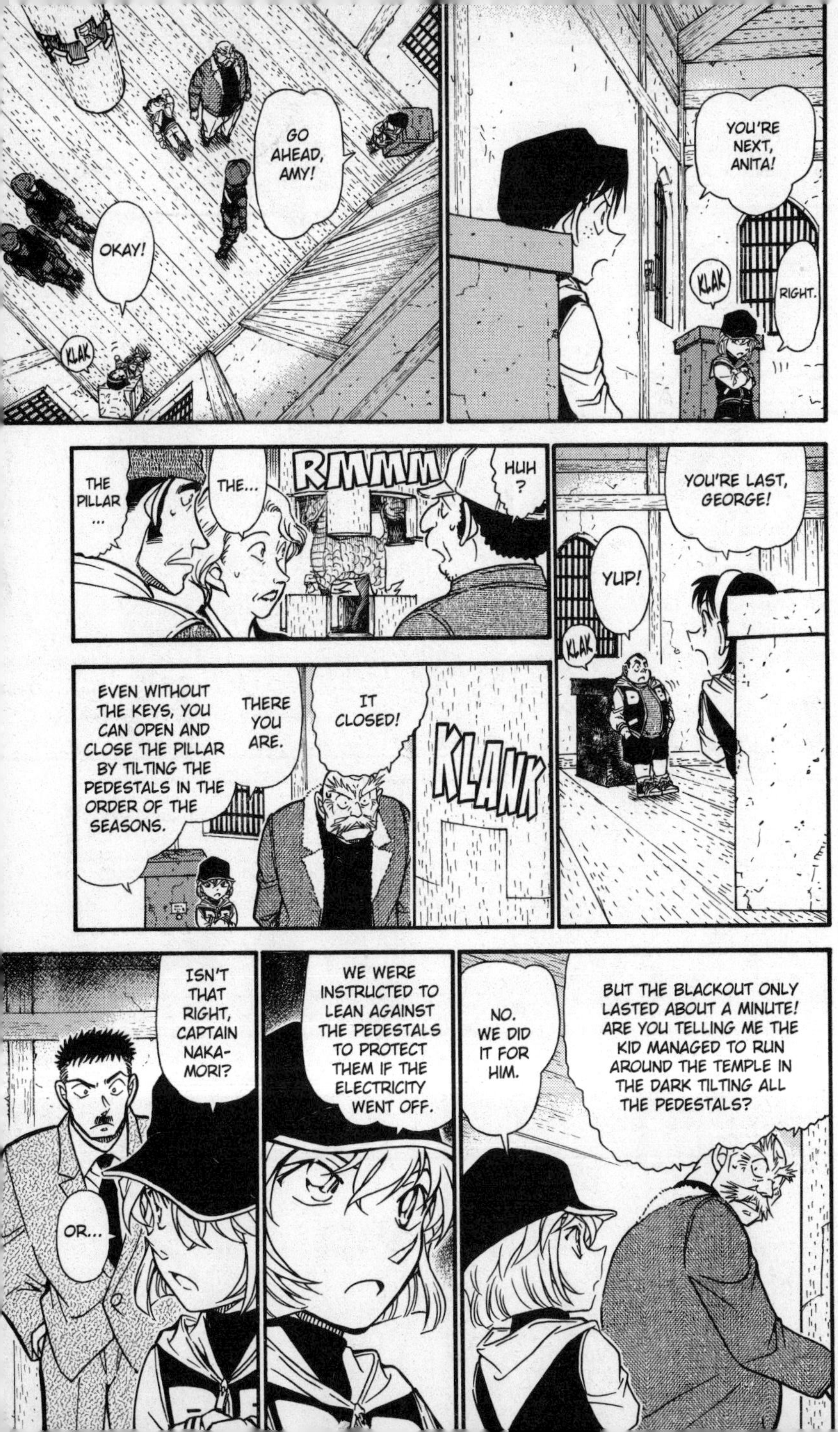
YOU'RE NEXT, ANITA!
KLAK
RIGHT.
GO AHEAD, AMY!
OKAY!
KLAK
YOU'RE LAST, GEORGE!
YUP!
KLAK
RMMMM
HUH?
THE...
THE PILLAR...
KLANK
IT CLOSED!
THERE YOU ARE.
EVEN WITHOUT THE KEYS, YOU CAN OPEN AND CLOSE THE PILLAR BY TILTING THE PEDESTALS IN THE ORDER OF THE SEASONS.
BUT THE BLACKOUT ONLY LASTED ABOUT A MINUTE! ARE YOU TELLING ME THE KID MANAGED TO RUN AROUND THE TEMPLE IN THE DARK TILTING ALL THE PEDESTALS?
NO. WE DID IT FOR HIM.
WE WERE INSTRUCTED TO LEAN AGAINST THE PEDESTALS TO PROTECT THEM IF THE ELECTRICITY WENT OFF.
ISN'T THAT RIGHT, CAPTAIN NAKA-MORI?
OR...

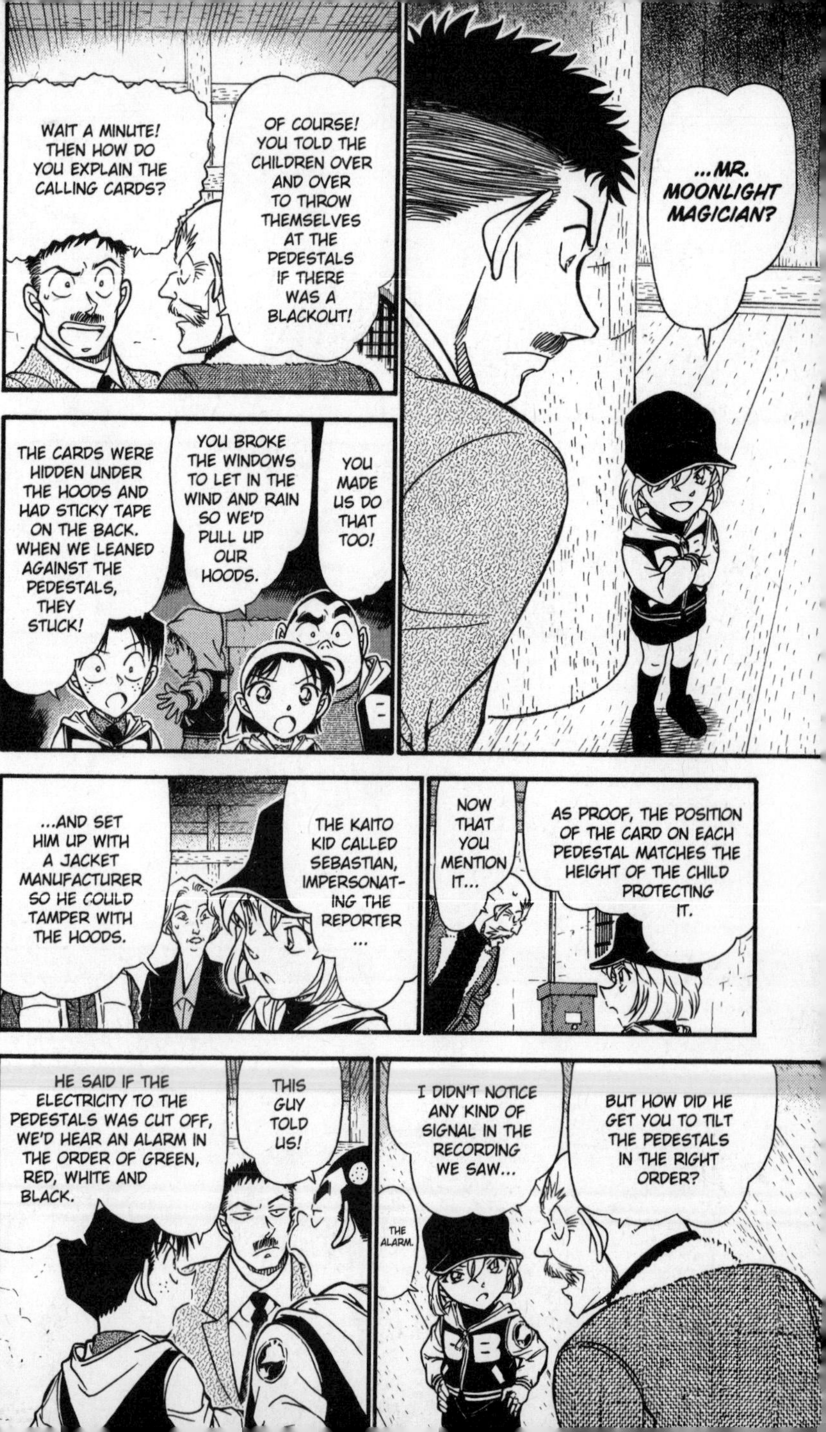
...MR. MOONLIGHT MAGICIAN?
OF COURSE! YOU TOLD THE CHILDREN OVER AND OVER TO THROW THEMSELVES AT THE PEDESTALS IF THERE WAS A BLACKOUT!
WAIT A MINUTE! THEN HOW DO YOU EXPLAIN THE CALLING CARDS?
YOU MADE US DO THAT TOO!
YOU BROKE THE WINDOWS TO LET IN THE WIND AND RAIN SO WE'D PULL UP OUR HOODS.
THE CARDS WERE HIDDEN UNDER THE HOODS AND HAD STICKY TAPE ON THE BACK. WHEN WE LEANED AGAINST THE PEDESTALS, THEY STUCK!
AS PROOF, THE POSITION OF THE CARD ON EACH PEDESTAL MATCHES THE HEIGHT OF THE CHILD PROTECTING IT.
NOW THAT YOU MENTION IT...
THE KAITO KID CALLED SEBASTIAN, IMPERSONATING THE REPORTER...
...AND SET HIM UP WITH A JACKET MANUFACTURER SO HE COULD TAMPER WITH THE HOODS.
BUT HOW DID HE GET YOU TO TILT THE PEDESTALS IN THE RIGHT ORDER?
I DIDN'T NOTICE ANY KIND OF SIGNAL IN THE RECORDING WE SAW...
THE ALARM.
THIS GUY TOLD US!
HE SAID IF THE ELECTRICITY TO THE PEDESTALS WAS CUT OFF, WE'D HEAR AN ALARM IN THE ORDER OF GREEN, RED, WHITE AND BLACK.

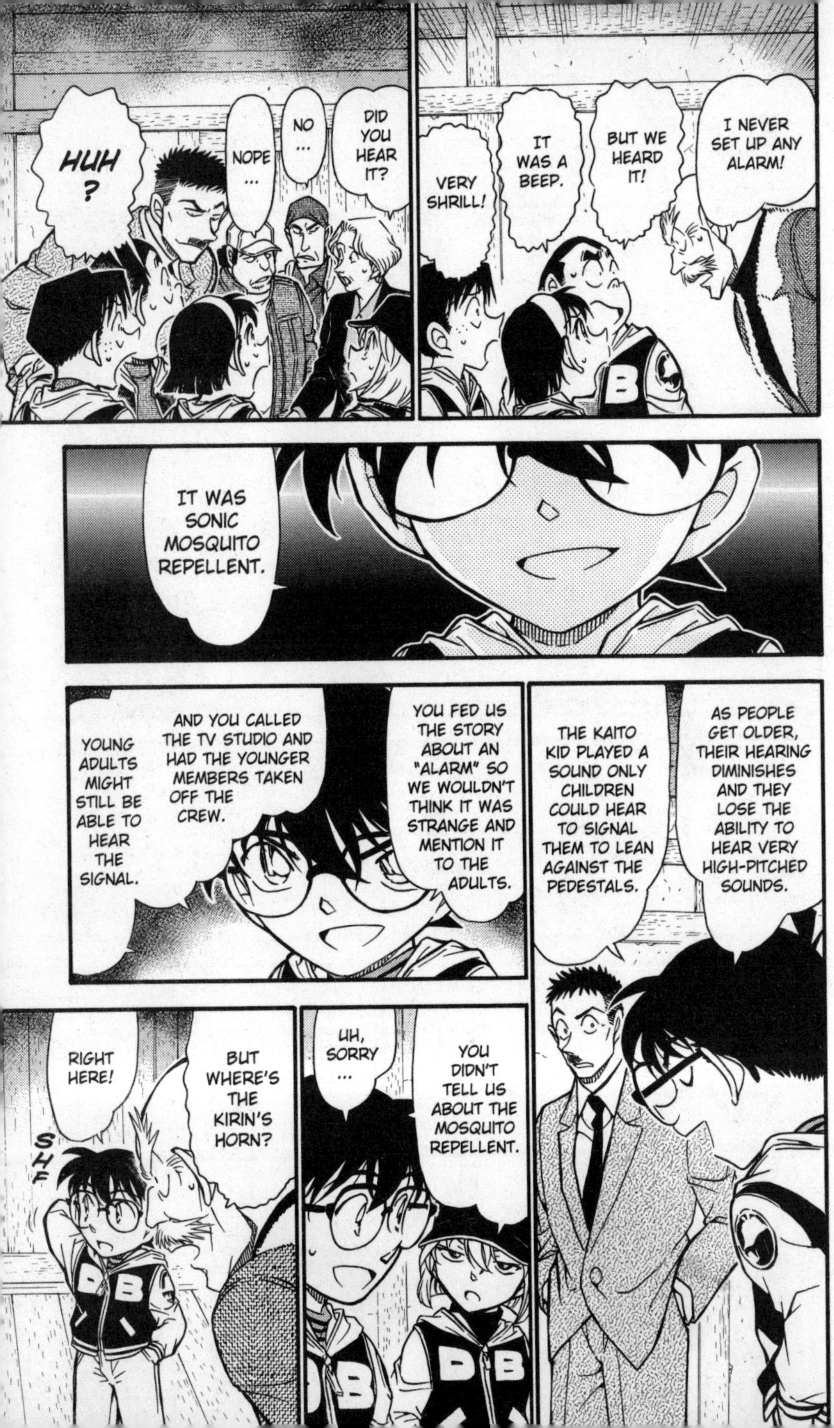
I NEVER SET UP ANY ALARM!
BUT WE HEARD IT!
IT WAS A BEEP.
VERY SHRILL!
DID YOU HEAR IT?
NO ...
NOPE ...
HUH ?
IT WAS SONIC MOSQUITO REPELLENT.
AS PEOPLE GET OLDER, THEIR HEARING DIMINISHES AND THEY LOSE THE ABILITY TO HEAR VERY HIGH-PITCHED SOUNDS.
THE KAITO KID PLAYED A SOUND ONLY CHILDREN COULD HEAR TO SIGNAL THEM TO LEAN AGAINST THE PEDESTALS.
YOU FED US THE STORY ABOUT AN "ALARM" SO WE WOULDN'T THINK IT WAS STRANGE AND MENTION IT TO THE ADULTS.
AND YOU CALLED THE TV STUDIO AND HAD THE YOUNGER MEMBERS TAKEN OFF THE CREW.
YOUNG ADULTS MIGHT STILL BE ABLE TO HEAR THE SIGNAL.
YOU DIDN'T TELL US ABOUT THE MOSQUITO REPELLENT.
UH, SORRY ...
BUT WHERE'S THE KIRIN'S HORN?
RIGHT HERE!
SHF

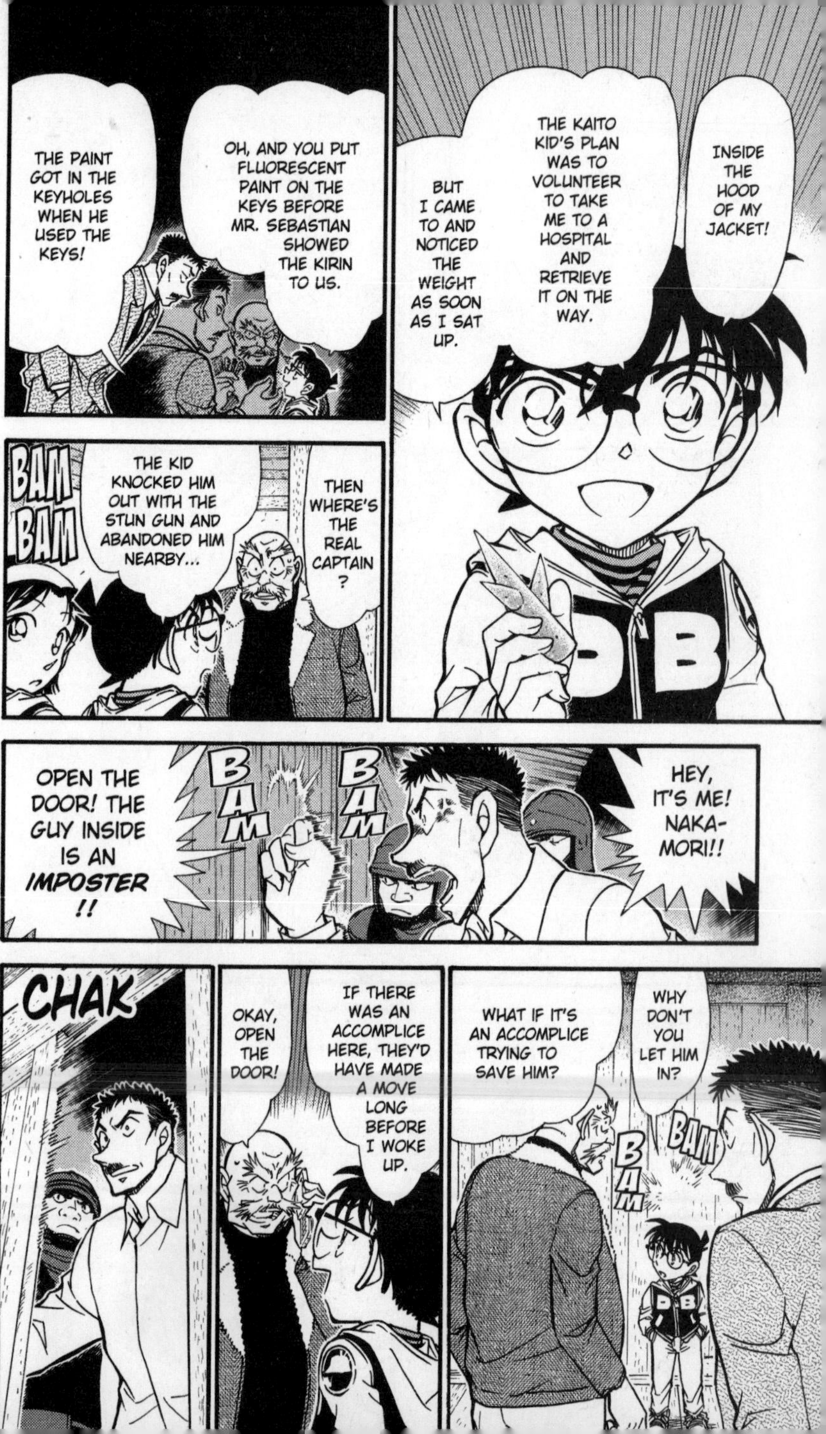
INSIDE THE HOOD OF MY JACKET!
THE KAITO KID'S PLAN WAS TO VOLUNTEER TO TAKE ME TO A HOSPITAL AND RETRIEVE IT ON THE WAY.
BUT I CAME TO AND NOTICED THE WEIGHT AS SOON AS I SAT UP.
OH, AND YOU PUT FLUORESCENT PAINT ON THE KEYS BEFORE MR. SEBASTIAN SHOWED THE KIRIN TO US.
THE PAINT GOT IN THE KEYHOLES WHEN HE USED THE KEYS!
THEN WHERE'S THE REAL CAPTAIN?
THE KID KNOCKED HIM OUT WITH THE STUN GUN AND ABANDONED HIM NEARBY...
BAM BAM
HEY, IT'S ME! NAKA-MORI!!
BAM
BAM
OPEN THE DOOR! THE GUY INSIDE IS AN *IMPOSTER* !!
WHY DON'T YOU LET HIM IN?
BAM
BAM
WHAT IF IT'S AN ACCOMPLICE TRYING TO SAVE HIM?
IF THERE WAS AN ACCOMPLICE HERE, THEY'D HAVE MADE A MOVE LONG BEFORE I WOKE UP.
OKAY, OPEN THE DOOR!
CHAK

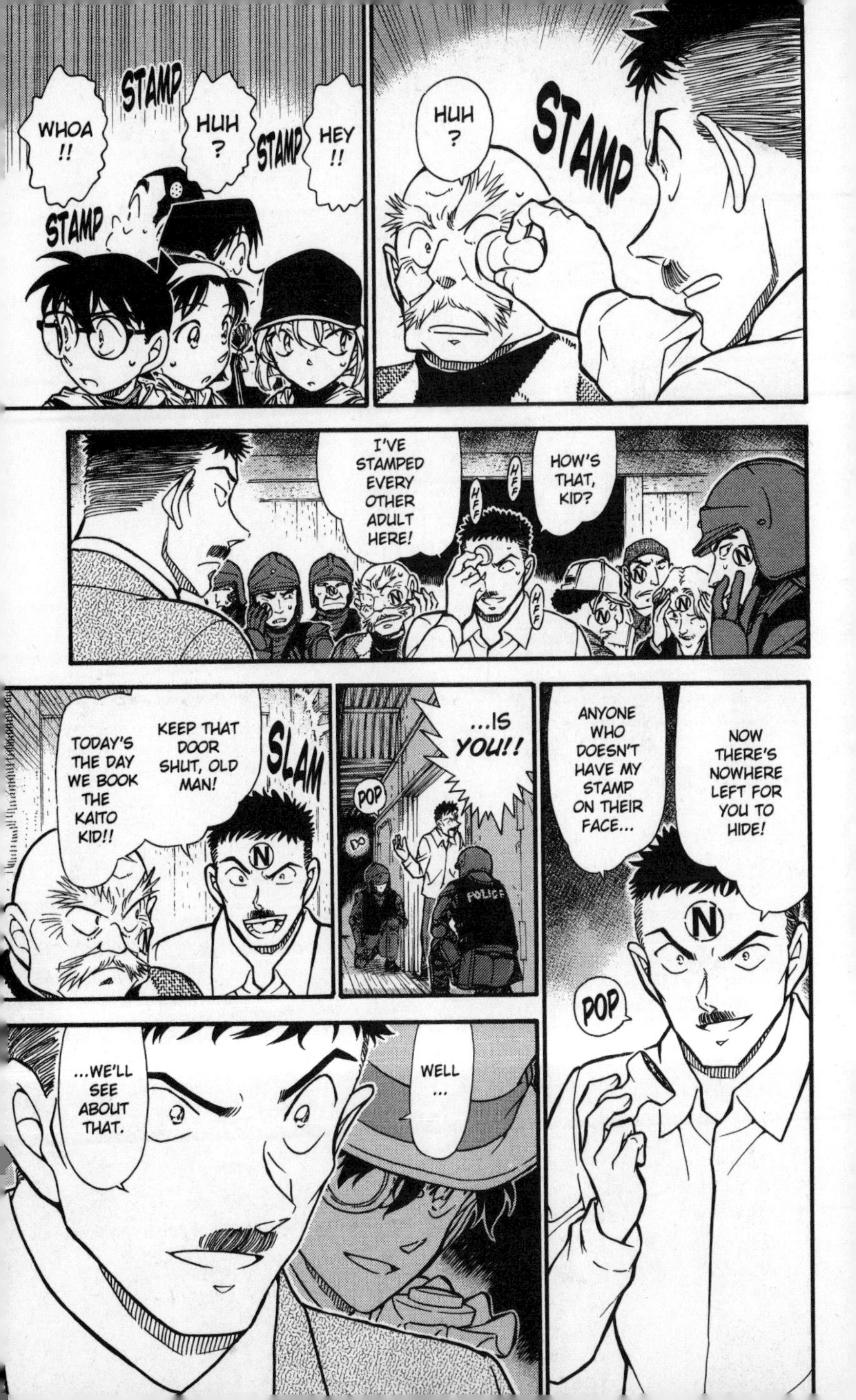
HUH ?
STAMP
HEY !!
STAMP
HUH ?
STAMP
WHOA !!
STAMP
HOW'S THAT, KID?
HFF
HFF
HFF
I'VE STAMPED EVERY OTHER ADULT HERE!
NOW THERE'S NOWHERE LEFT FOR YOU TO HIDE!
ANYONE WHO DOESN'T HAVE MY STAMP ON THEIR FACE...
POP
...IS *YOU!!*
POP
SLAM
KEEP THAT DOOR SHUT, OLD MAN!
TODAY'S THE DAY WE BOOK THE KAITO KID!!
WELL ...
...WE'LL SEE ABOUT THAT.

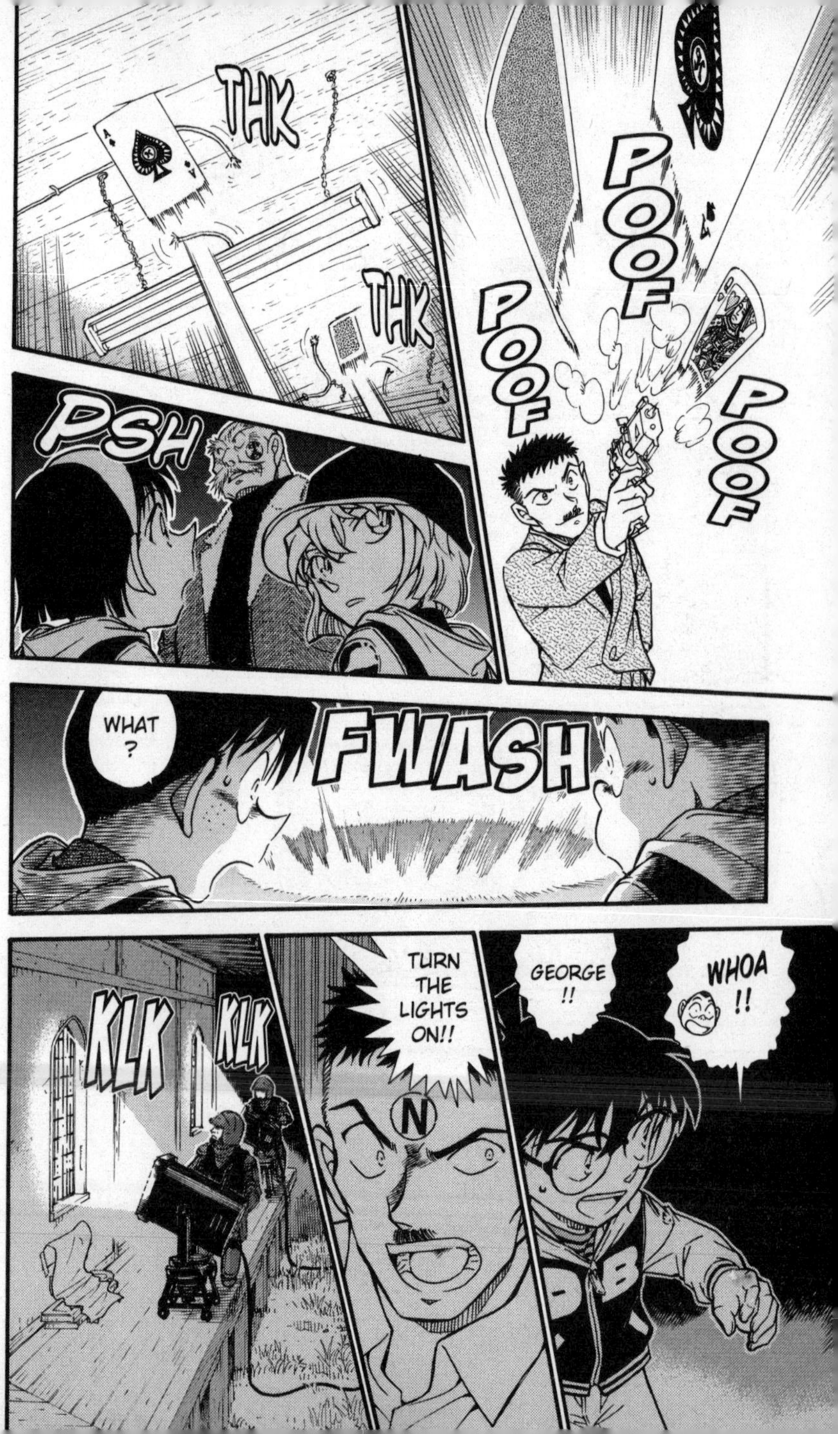
POOF
POOF
POOF
THK
THK
PSH
FWASH
WHAT?
WHOA!!
GEORGE!!
TURN THE LIGHTS ON!!
KLK
KLK

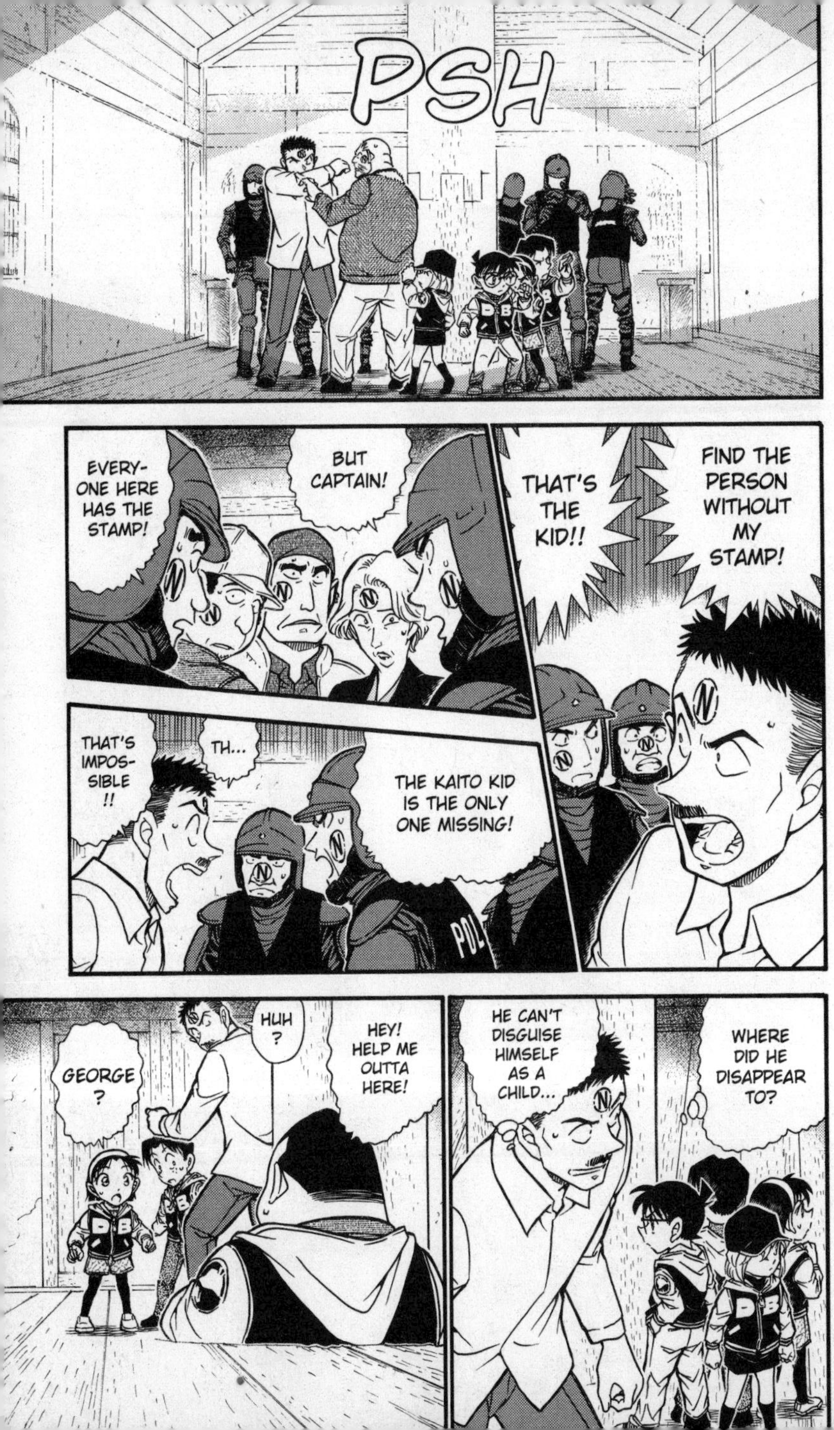
PSH
FIND THE PERSON WITHOUT MY STAMP!
THAT'S THE KID!!
BUT CAPTAIN!
EVERY-ONE HERE HAS THE STAMP!
THE KAITO KID IS THE ONLY ONE MISSING!
TH...
THAT'S IMPOS-SIBLE !!
WHERE DID HE DISAPPEAR TO?
HE CAN'T DISGUISE HIMSELF AS A CHILD...
HEY! HELP ME OUTTA HERE!
HUH ?
GEORGE ?

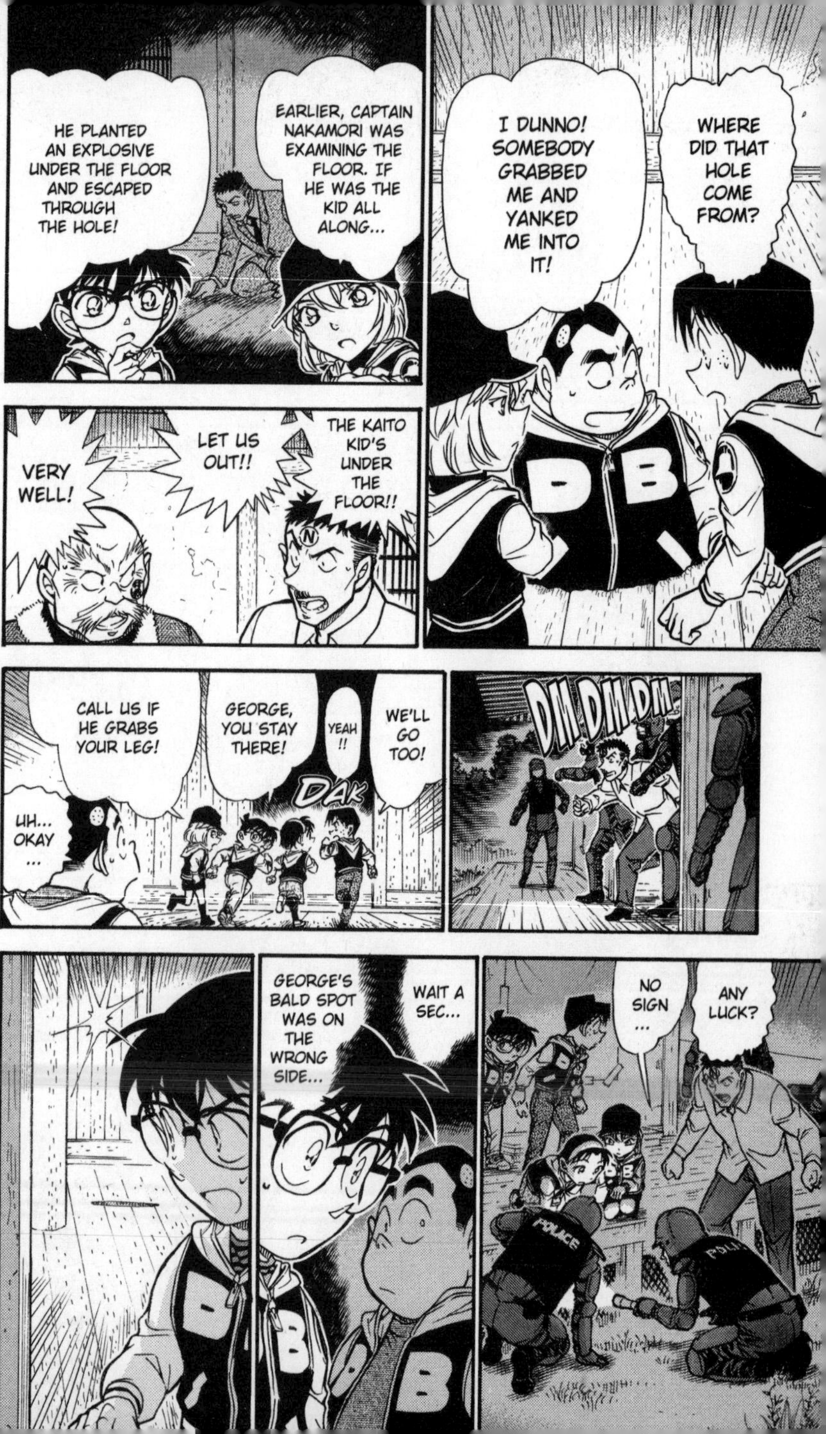
WHERE DID THAT HOLE COME FROM?
I DUNNO! SOMEBODY GRABBED ME AND YANKED ME INTO IT!
EARLIER, CAPTAIN NAKAMORI WAS EXAMINING THE FLOOR. IF HE WAS THE KID ALL ALONG...
HE PLANTED AN EXPLOSIVE UNDER THE FLOOR AND ESCAPED THROUGH THE HOLE!
THE KAITO KID'S UNDER THE FLOOR!!
LET US OUT!!
VERY WELL!
DM DM DM
WE'LL GO TOO!
YEAH !!
DAK
GEORGE, YOU STAY THERE!
CALL US IF HE GRABS YOUR LEG!
UH... OKAY ...
ANY LUCK?
NO SIGN ...
WAIT A SEC...
GEORGE'S BALD SPOT WAS ON THE WRONG SIDE...

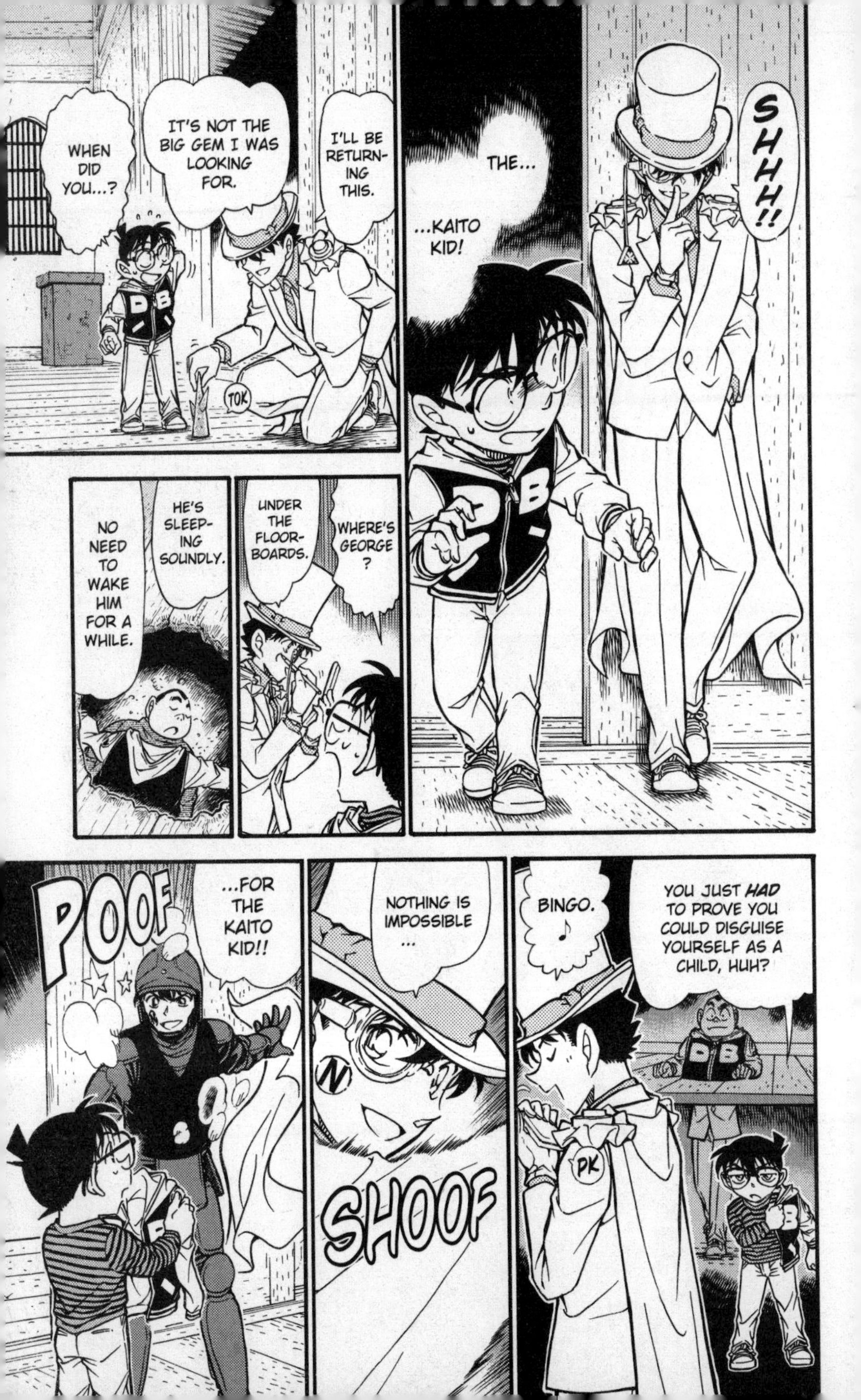
SHHHH!!
THE...
...KAITO KID!
I'LL BE RETURNING THIS.
IT'S NOT THE BIG GEM I WAS LOOKING FOR.
WHEN DID YOU...?
TOK
WHERE'S GEORGE?
UNDER THE FLOORBOARDS.
HE'S SLEEPING SOUNDLY.
NO NEED TO WAKE HIM FOR A WHILE.
YOU JUST HAD TO PROVE YOU COULD DISGUISE YOURSELF AS A CHILD, HUH?
BINGO. ♪
NOTHING IS IMPOSSIBLE ...
SHOOF
...FOR THE KAITO KID!!
POOF

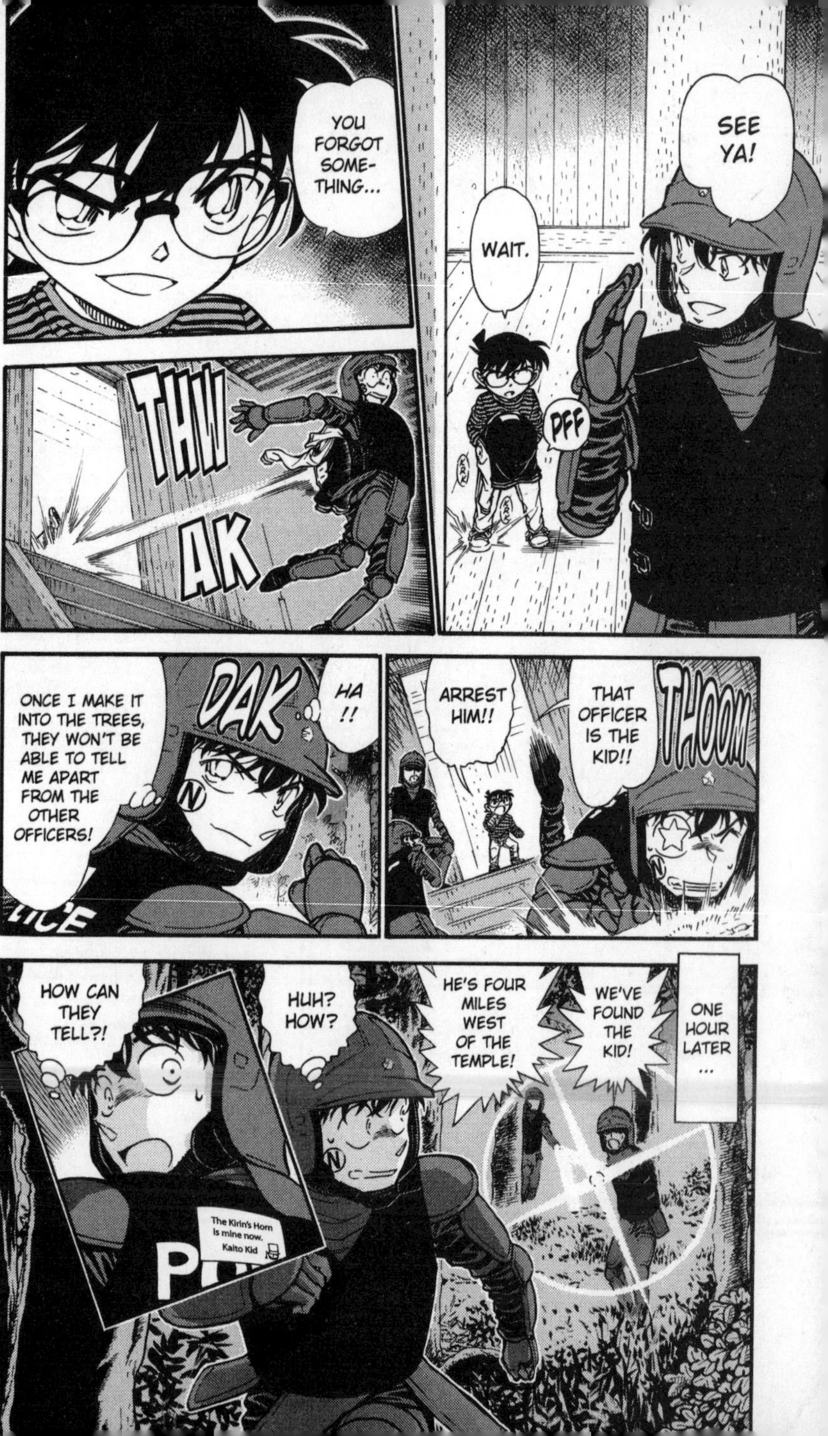
SEE YA!
WAIT.
PFF
KRK
KRK
YOU FORGOT SOME-THING...
THWAK
THOOM
THAT OFFICER IS THE KID!!
ARREST HIM!!
HA!!
DAK
ONCE I MAKE IT INTO THE TREES, THEY WON'T BE ABLE TO TELL ME APART FROM THE OTHER OFFICERS!
ONE HOUR LATER...
WE'VE FOUND THE KID!
HE'S FOUR MILES WEST OF THE TEMPLE!
HUH? HOW?
HOW CAN THEY TELL?!
The Kirin's Horn is mine now.
Kaito Kid

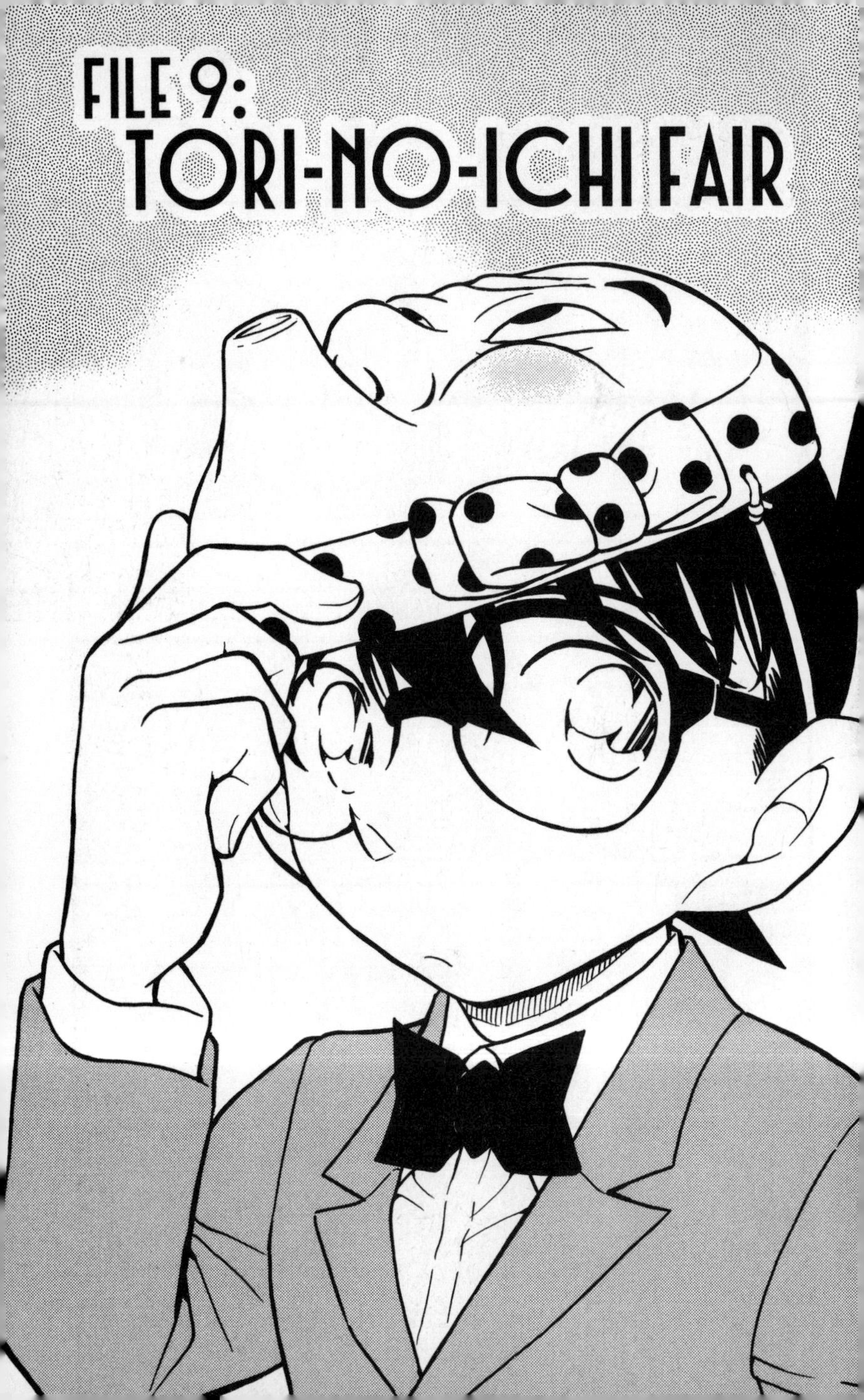
FILE 9:
TORI-NO-ICHI FAIR

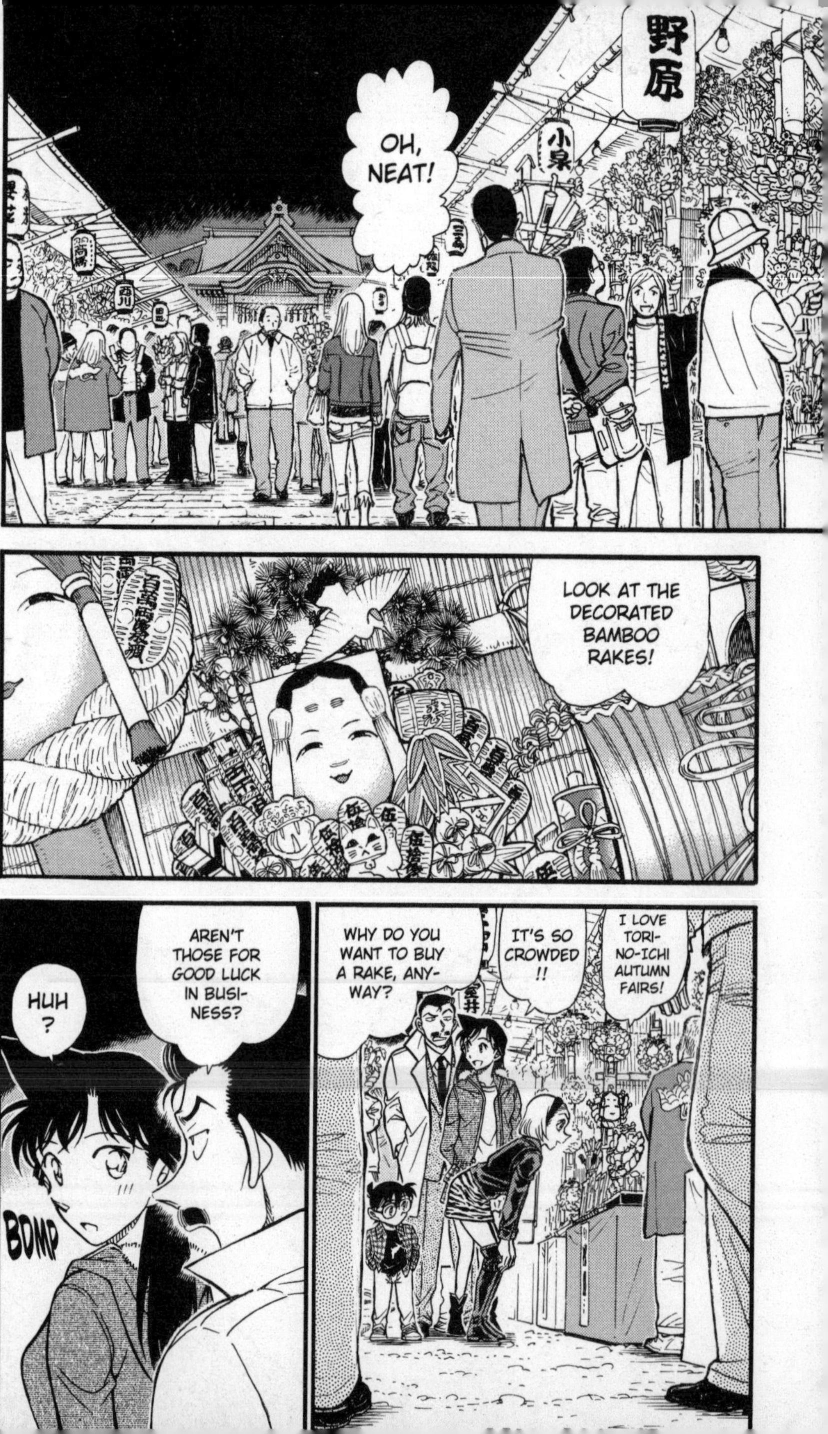
野原
小泉
OH, NEAT!
LOOK AT THE DECORATED BAMBOO RAKES!
I LOVE TORI-NO-ICHI AUTUMN FAIRS!
IT'S SO CROWDED!!
WHY DO YOU WANT TO BUY A RAKE, ANYWAY?
AREN'T THOSE FOR GOOD LUCK IN BUSINESS?
HUH?
BDMP

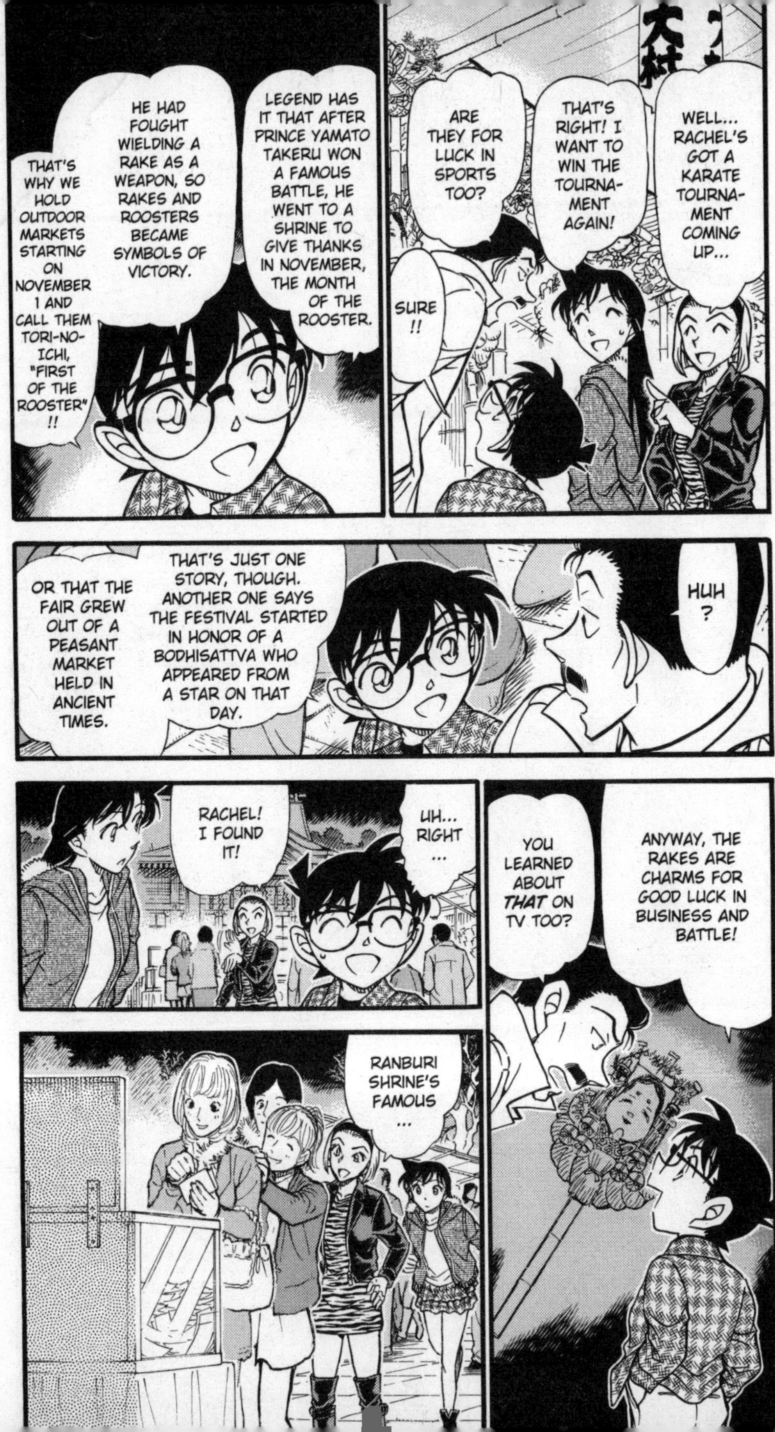
WELL... RACHEL'S GOT A KARATE TOURNAMENT COMING UP...
THAT'S RIGHT! I WANT TO WIN THE TOURNAMENT AGAIN!
ARE THEY FOR LUCK IN SPORTS TOO?
SURE!!
LEGEND HAS IT THAT AFTER PRINCE YAMATO TAKERU WON A FAMOUS BATTLE, HE WENT TO A SHRINE TO GIVE THANKS IN NOVEMBER, THE MONTH OF THE ROOSTER.
HE HAD FOUGHT WIELDING A RAKE AS A WEAPON, SO RAKES AND ROOSTERS BECAME SYMBOLS OF VICTORY.
THAT'S WHY WE HOLD OUTDOOR MARKETS STARTING ON NOVEMBER 1 AND CALL THEM TORI-NO-ICHI, "FIRST OF THE ROOSTER"!!
HUH?
THAT'S JUST ONE STORY, THOUGH. ANOTHER ONE SAYS THE FESTIVAL STARTED IN HONOR OF A BODHISATTVA WHO APPEARED FROM A STAR ON THAT DAY.
OR THAT THE FAIR GREW OUT OF A PEASANT MARKET HELD IN ANCIENT TIMES.
ANYWAY, THE RAKES ARE CHARMS FOR GOOD LUCK IN BUSINESS AND BATTLE!
YOU LEARNED ABOUT *THAT* ON TV TOO?
UH... RIGHT...
RACHEL! I FOUND IT!
RANBURI SHRINE'S FAMOUS...

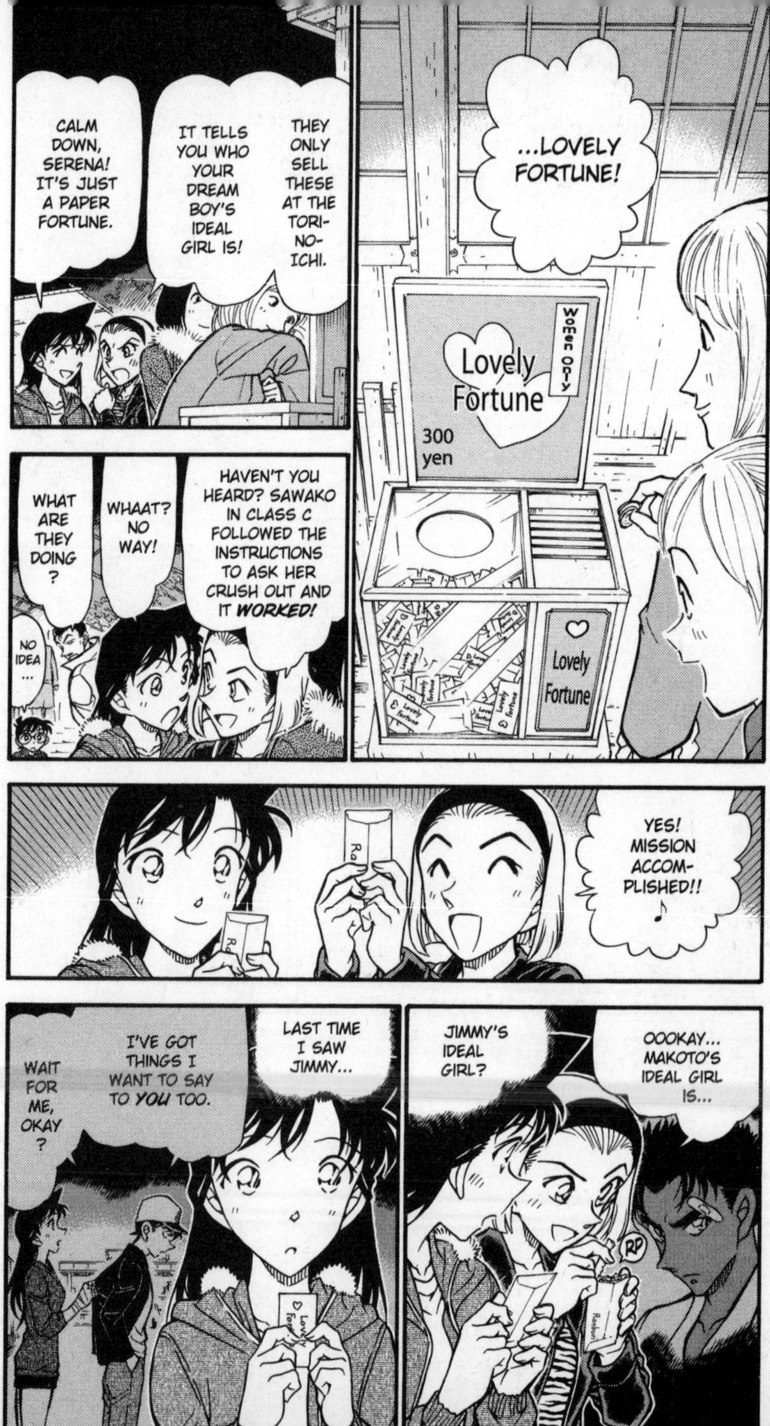
...LOVELY FORTUNE!
Lovely Fortune
Women Only
300 yen
Lovely Fortune
THEY ONLY SELL THESE AT THE TORI-NO-ICHI.
IT TELLS YOU WHO YOUR DREAM BOY'S IDEAL GIRL IS!
CALM DOWN, SERENA! IT'S JUST A PAPER FORTUNE.
HAVEN'T YOU HEARD? SAWAKO IN CLASS C FOLLOWED THE INSTRUCTIONS TO ASK HER CRUSH OUT AND IT *WORKED!*
WHAAT? NO WAY!
WHAT ARE THEY DOING?
NO IDEA...
YES! MISSION ACCOMPLISHED!! ♪
OOOKAY... MAKOTO'S IDEAL GIRL IS...
JIMMY'S IDEAL GIRL?
RIP
LAST TIME I SAW JIMMY...
I'VE GOT THINGS I WANT TO SAY TO *YOU* TOO.
WAIT FOR ME, OKAY?

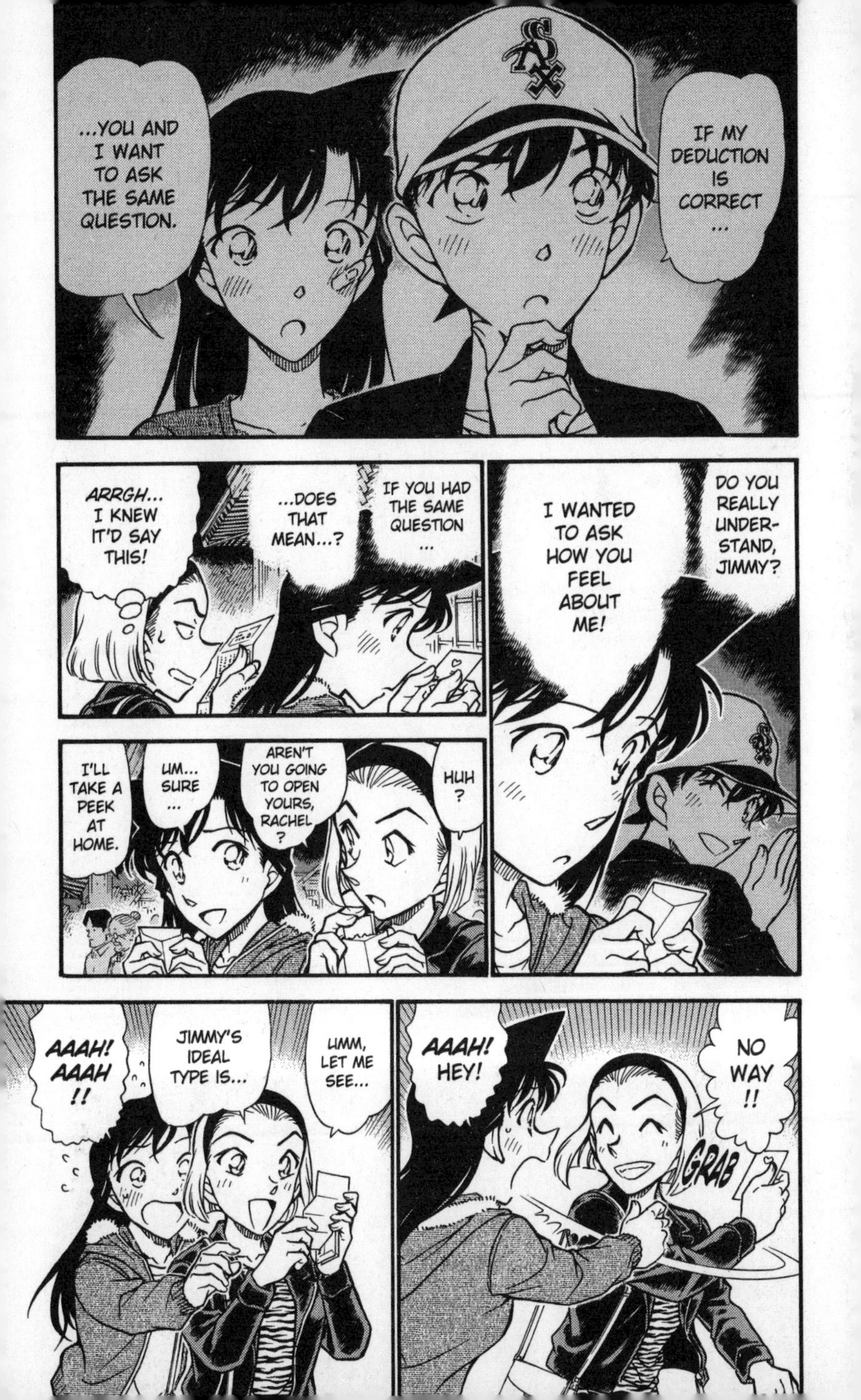
IF MY DEDUCTION IS CORRECT ...
...YOU AND I WANT TO ASK THE SAME QUESTION.
DO YOU REALLY UNDER-STAND, JIMMY?
I WANTED TO ASK HOW YOU FEEL ABOUT ME!
IF YOU HAD THE SAME QUESTION ...
...DOES THAT MEAN...?
ARRGH... I KNEW IT'D SAY THIS!
HUH ?
AREN'T YOU GOING TO OPEN YOURS, RACHEL ?
UM... SURE ...
I'LL TAKE A PEEK AT HOME.
NO WAY !!
GRAB
AAAH! HEY!
UMM, LET ME SEE...
JIMMY'S IDEAL TYPE IS...
AAAH! AAAH !!

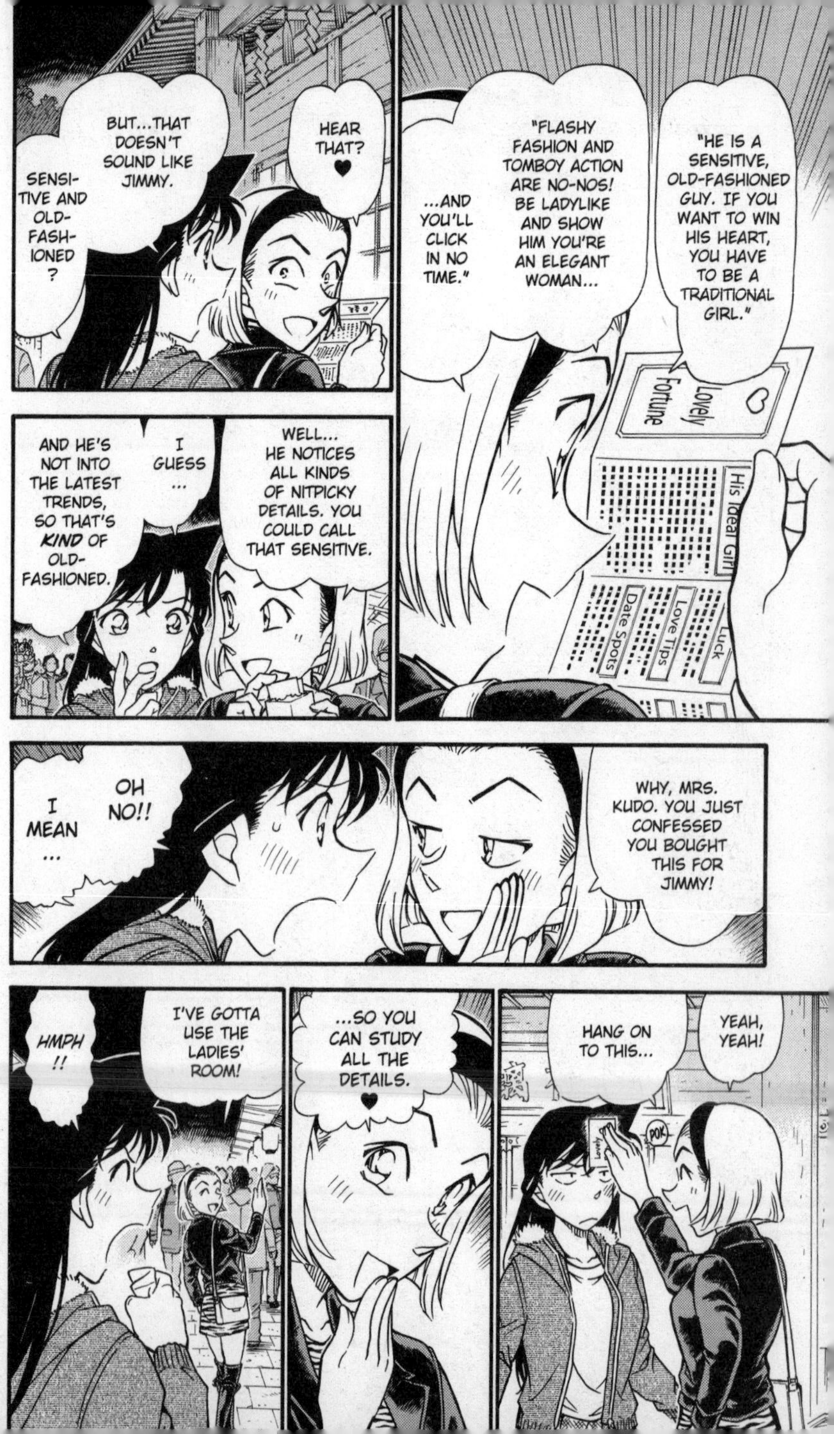
"HE IS A SENSITIVE, OLD-FASHIONED GUY. IF YOU WANT TO WIN HIS HEART, YOU HAVE TO BE A TRADITIONAL GIRL."
"FLASHY FASHION AND TOMBOY ACTION ARE NO-NOS! BE LADYLIKE AND SHOW HIM YOU'RE AN ELEGANT WOMAN...
...AND YOU'LL CLICK IN NO TIME."
Lovely Fortune
His Ideal Girl
Luck
Love Tips
Date Spots
HEAR THAT? ♥
BUT...THAT DOESN'T SOUND LIKE JIMMY.
SENSI-TIVE AND OLD-FASH-IONED?
WELL... HE NOTICES ALL KINDS OF NITPICKY DETAILS. YOU COULD CALL THAT SENSITIVE.
I GUESS...
AND HE'S NOT INTO THE LATEST TRENDS, SO THAT'S *KIND* OF OLD-FASHIONED.
WHY, MRS. KUDO. YOU JUST CONFESSED YOU BOUGHT THIS FOR JIMMY!
OH NO!!
I MEAN...
YEAH, YEAH!
HANG ON TO THIS...
POK
Lovely
...SO YOU CAN STUDY ALL THE DETAILS. ♥
I'VE GOTTA USE THE LADIES' ROOM!
HMPH!!

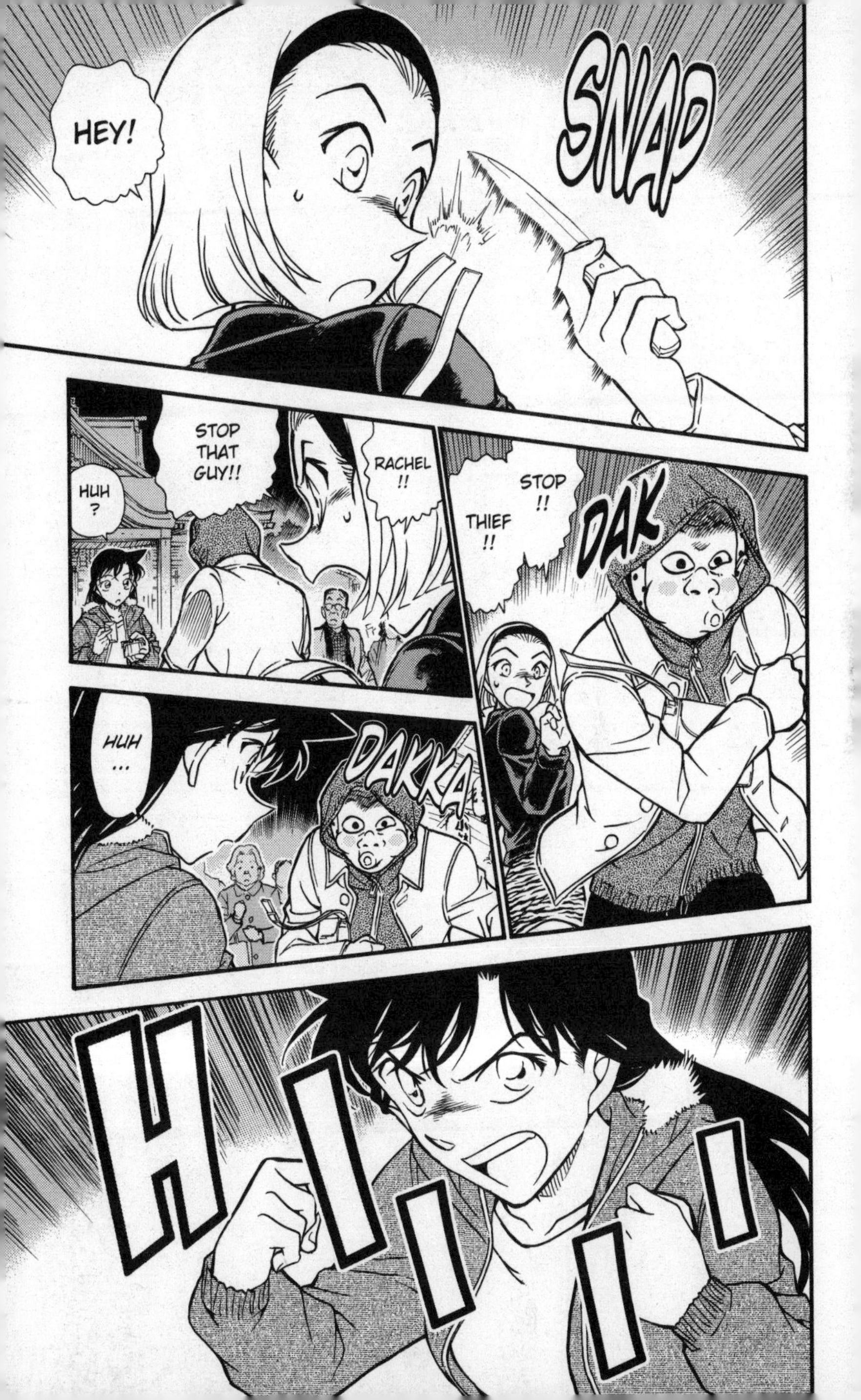
SNAP
HEY!
STOP !!
THIEF !!
DAK
RACHEL !!
STOP THAT GUY!!
HUH ?
DAKKA
HUH ...
HIIIII

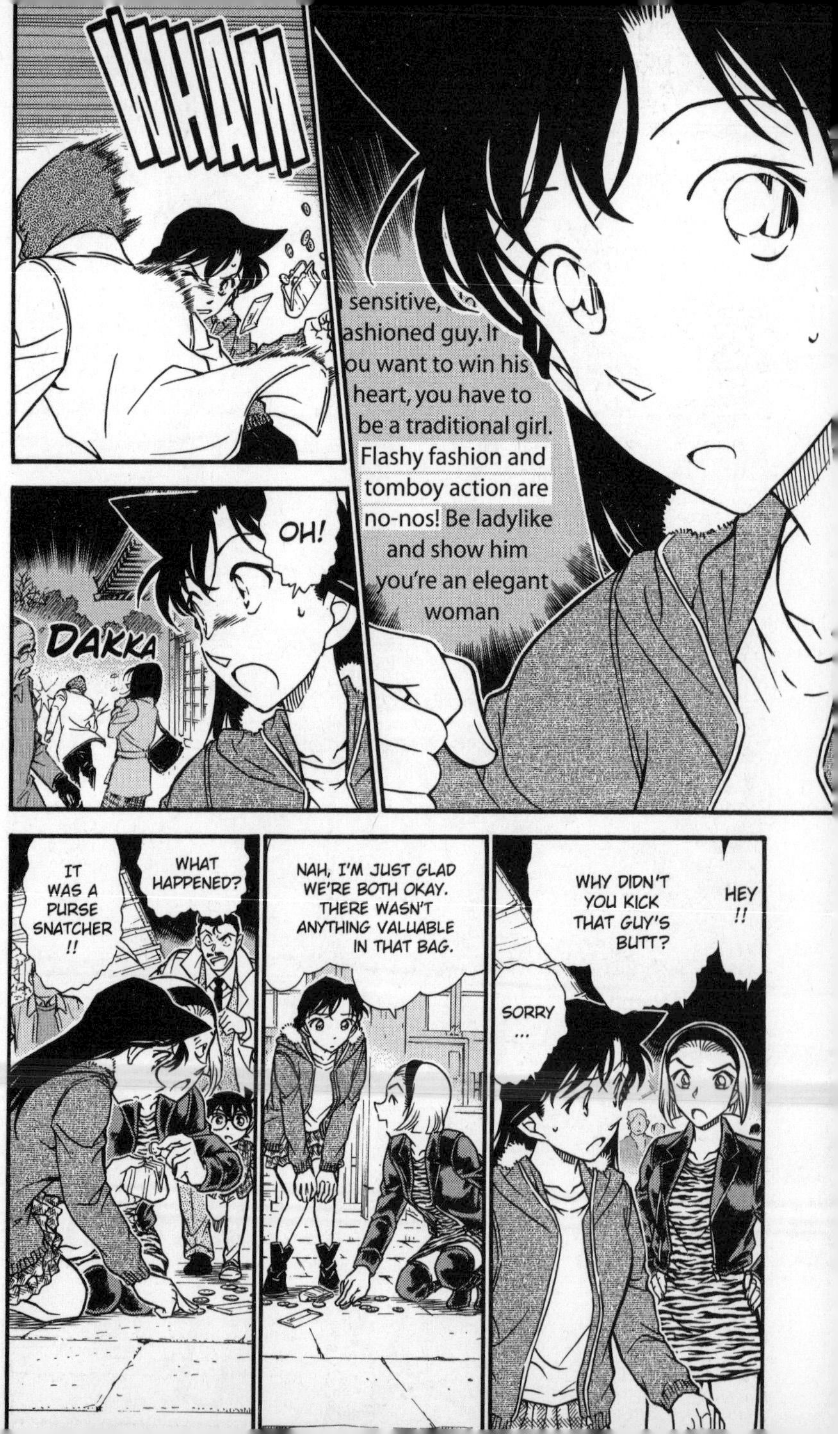

sensitive,
ashioned guy. If
ou want to win his
heart, you have to
be a traditional girl.
Flashy fashion and
tomboy action are
no-nos! Be ladylike
and show him
you're an elegant
woman
WHAM
OH!
DAKKA
HEY!!
WHY DIDN'T YOU KICK THAT GUY'S BUTT?
SORRY...
NAH, I'M JUST GLAD WE'RE BOTH OKAY. THERE WASN'T ANYTHING VALUABLE IN THAT BAG.
WHAT HAPPENED?
IT WAS A PURSE SNATCHER!!

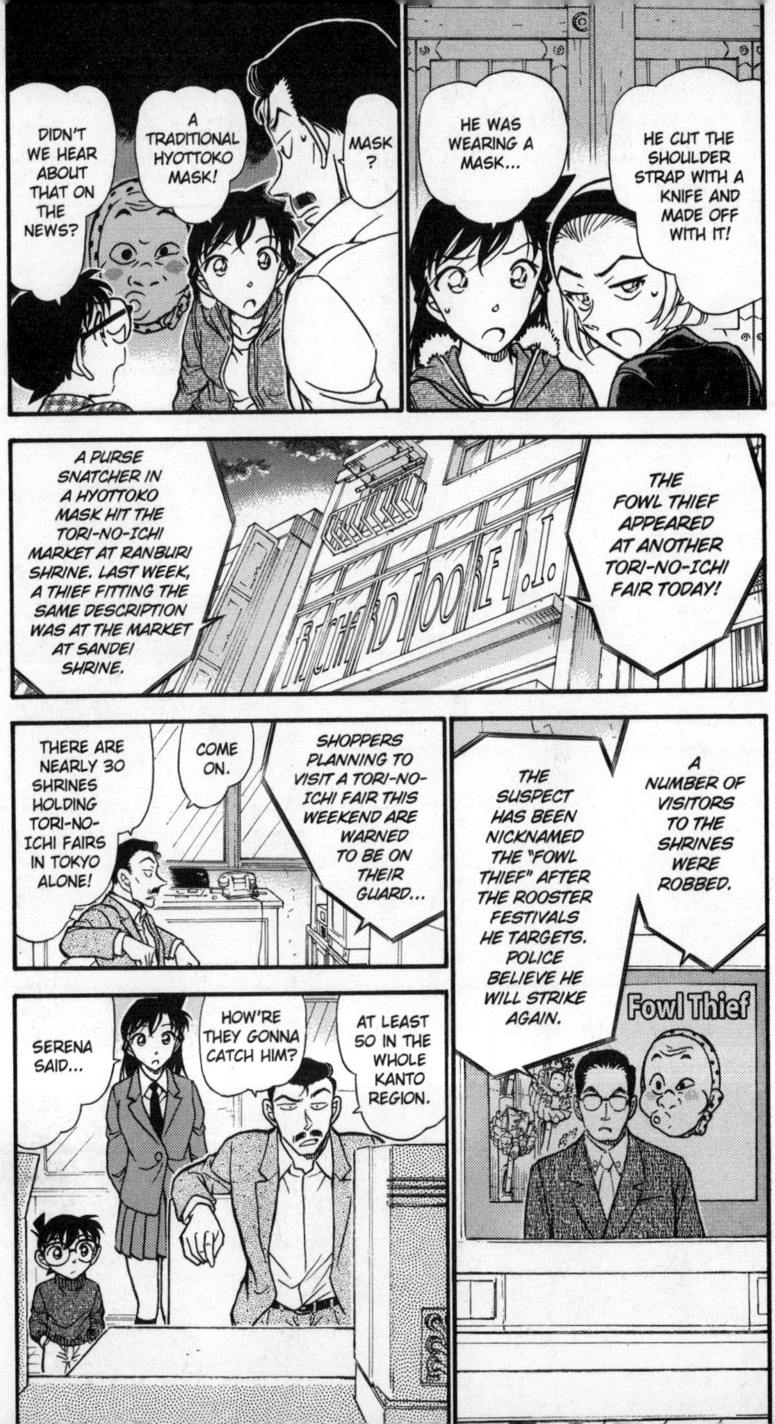
HE CUT THE SHOULDER STRAP WITH A KNIFE AND MADE OFF WITH IT!
HE WAS WEARING A MASK...
MASK?
A TRADITIONAL HYOTTOKO MASK!
DIDN'T WE HEAR ABOUT THAT ON THE NEWS?
THE FOWL THIEF APPEARED AT ANOTHER TORI-NO-ICHI FAIR TODAY!
RICHARD MOORE P.I.
A PURSE SNATCHER IN A HYOTTOKO MASK HIT THE TORI-NO-ICHI MARKET AT RANBURI SHRINE. LAST WEEK, A THIEF FITTING THE SAME DESCRIPTION WAS AT THE MARKET AT SANDEI SHRINE.
A NUMBER OF VISITORS TO THE SHRINES WERE ROBBED.
THE SUSPECT HAS BEEN NICKNAMED THE "FOWL THIEF" AFTER THE ROOSTER FESTIVALS HE TARGETS. POLICE BELIEVE HE WILL STRIKE AGAIN.
Fowl Thief
SHOPPERS PLANNING TO VISIT A TORI-NO-ICHI FAIR THIS WEEKEND ARE WARNED TO BE ON THEIR GUARD...
COME ON.
THERE ARE NEARLY 30 SHRINES HOLDING TORI-NO-ICHI FAIRS IN TOKYO ALONE!
AT LEAST 50 IN THE WHOLE KANTO REGION.
HOW'RE THEY GONNA CATCH HIM?
SERENA SAID...

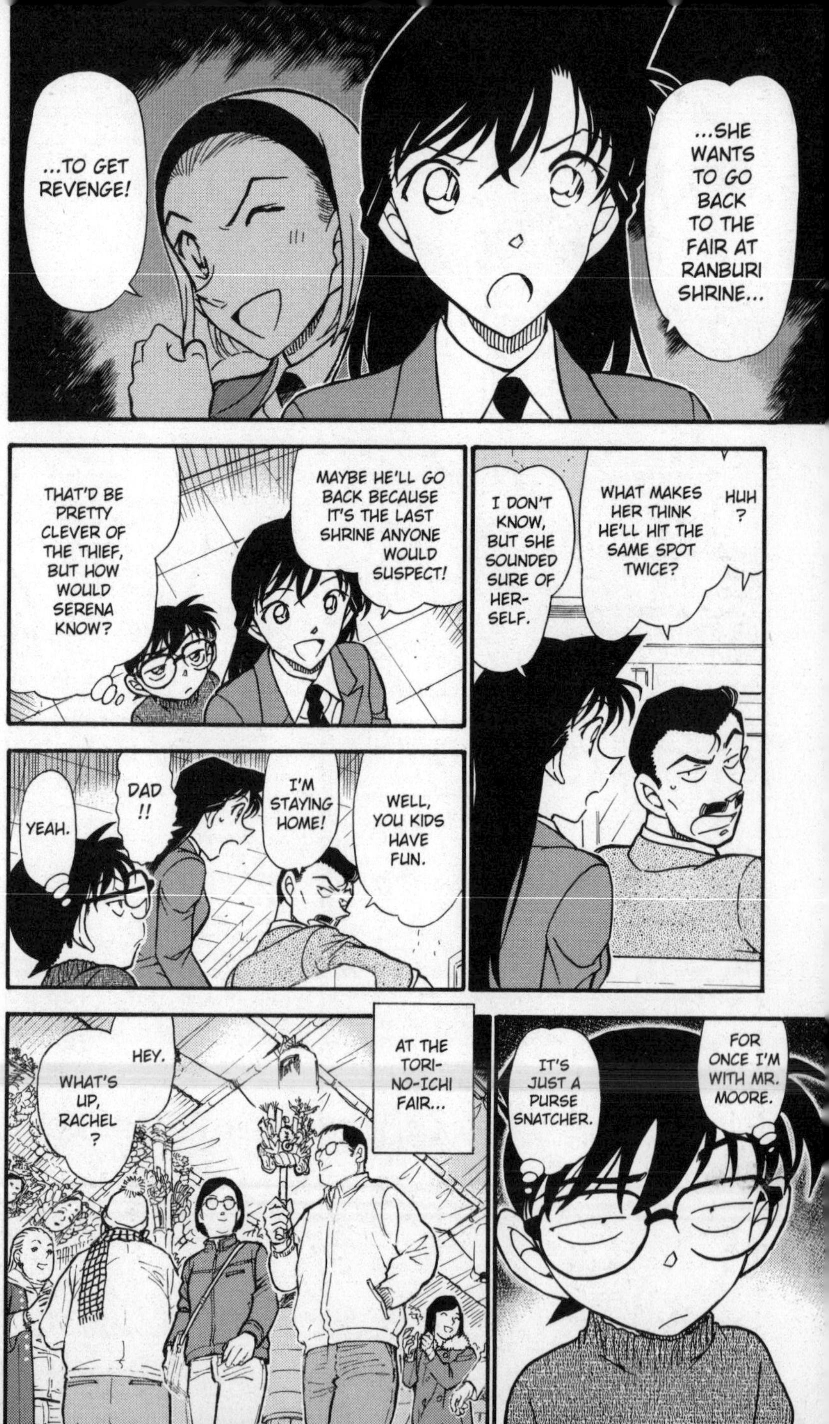
...SHE WANTS TO GO BACK TO THE FAIR AT RANBURI SHRINE...
...TO GET REVENGE!
HUH?
WHAT MAKES HER THINK HE'LL HIT THE SAME SPOT TWICE?
I DON'T KNOW, BUT SHE SOUNDED SURE OF HER-SELF.
MAYBE HE'LL GO BACK BECAUSE IT'S THE LAST SHRINE ANYONE WOULD SUSPECT!
THAT'D BE PRETTY CLEVER OF THE THIEF, BUT HOW WOULD SERENA KNOW?
WELL, YOU KIDS HAVE FUN.
I'M STAYING HOME!
DAD!!
YEAH.
FOR ONCE I'M WITH MR. MOORE.
IT'S JUST A PURSE SNATCHER.
AT THE TORI-NO-ICHI FAIR...
HEY.
WHAT'S UP, RACHEL?

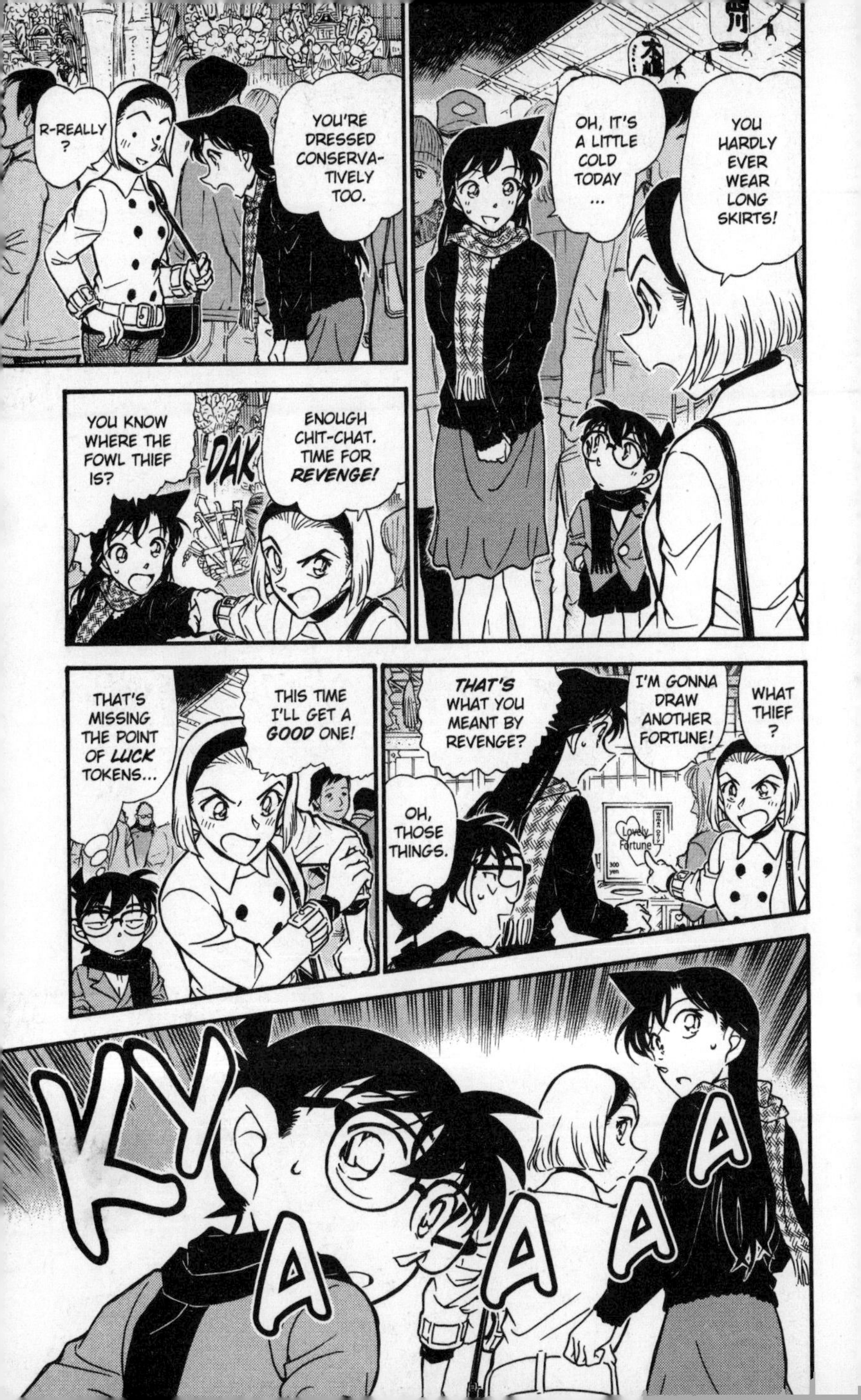
YOU HARDLY EVER WEAR LONG SKIRTS!
OH, IT'S A LITTLE COLD TODAY ...
YOU'RE DRESSED CONSERVATIVELY TOO.
R-REALLY?
ENOUGH CHIT-CHAT. TIME FOR REVENGE!
DAK
YOU KNOW WHERE THE FOWL THIEF IS?
WHAT THIEF?
I'M GONNA DRAW ANOTHER FORTUNE!
THAT'S WHAT YOU MEANT BY REVENGE?
Lovely Fortune
300 yen
OH, THOSE THINGS.
THIS TIME I'LL GET A GOOD ONE!
THAT'S MISSING THE POINT OF LUCK TOKENS...
KYAAAAA

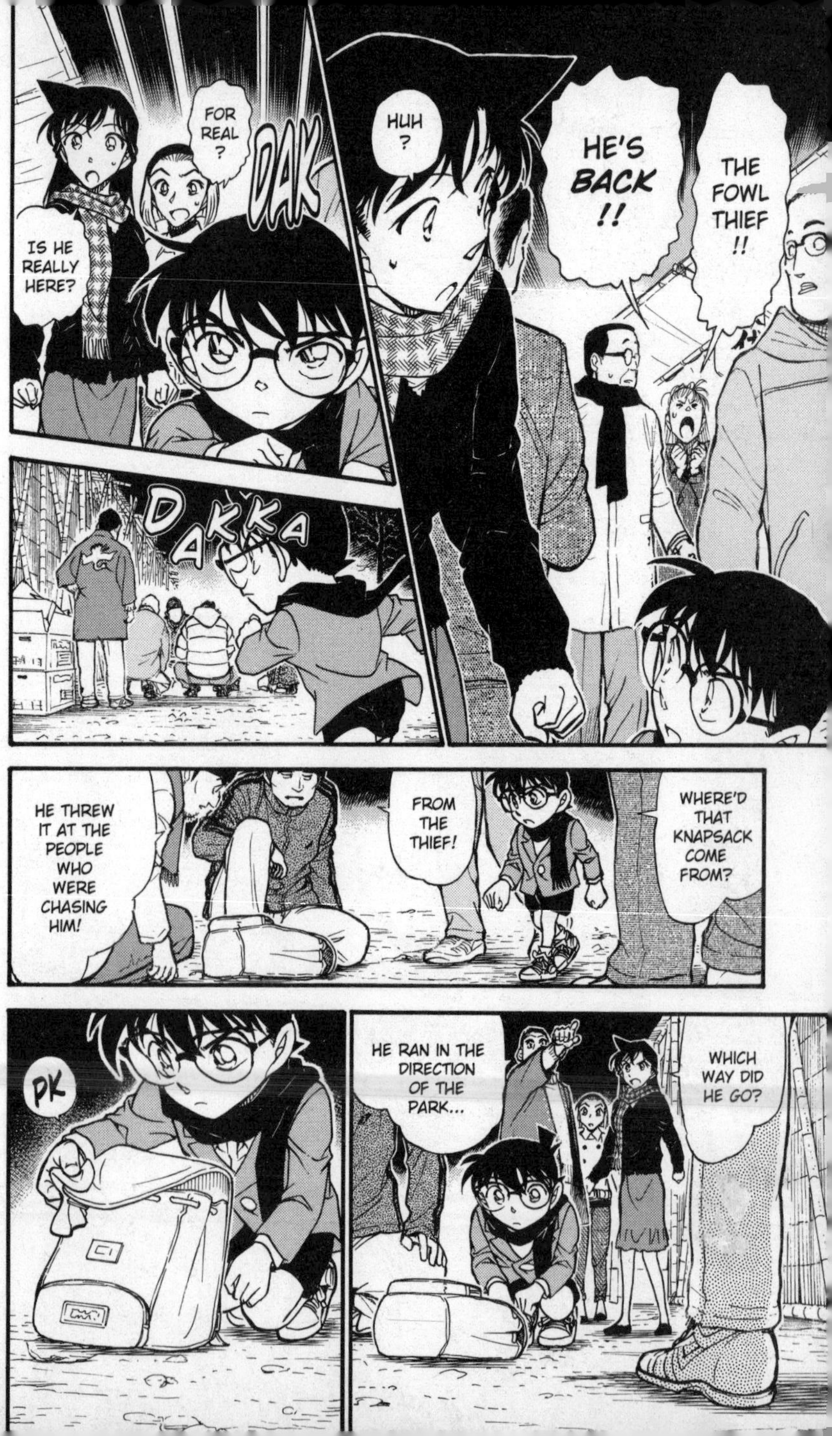
THE FOWL THIEF!!
HE'S BACK!!
HUH?
DAK
FOR REAL?
IS HE REALLY HERE?
DAKKA
WHERE'D THAT KNAPSACK COME FROM?
FROM THE THIEF!
HE THREW IT AT THE PEOPLE WHO WERE CHASING HIM!
WHICH WAY DID HE GO?
HE RAN IN THE DIRECTION OF THE PARK...
PK

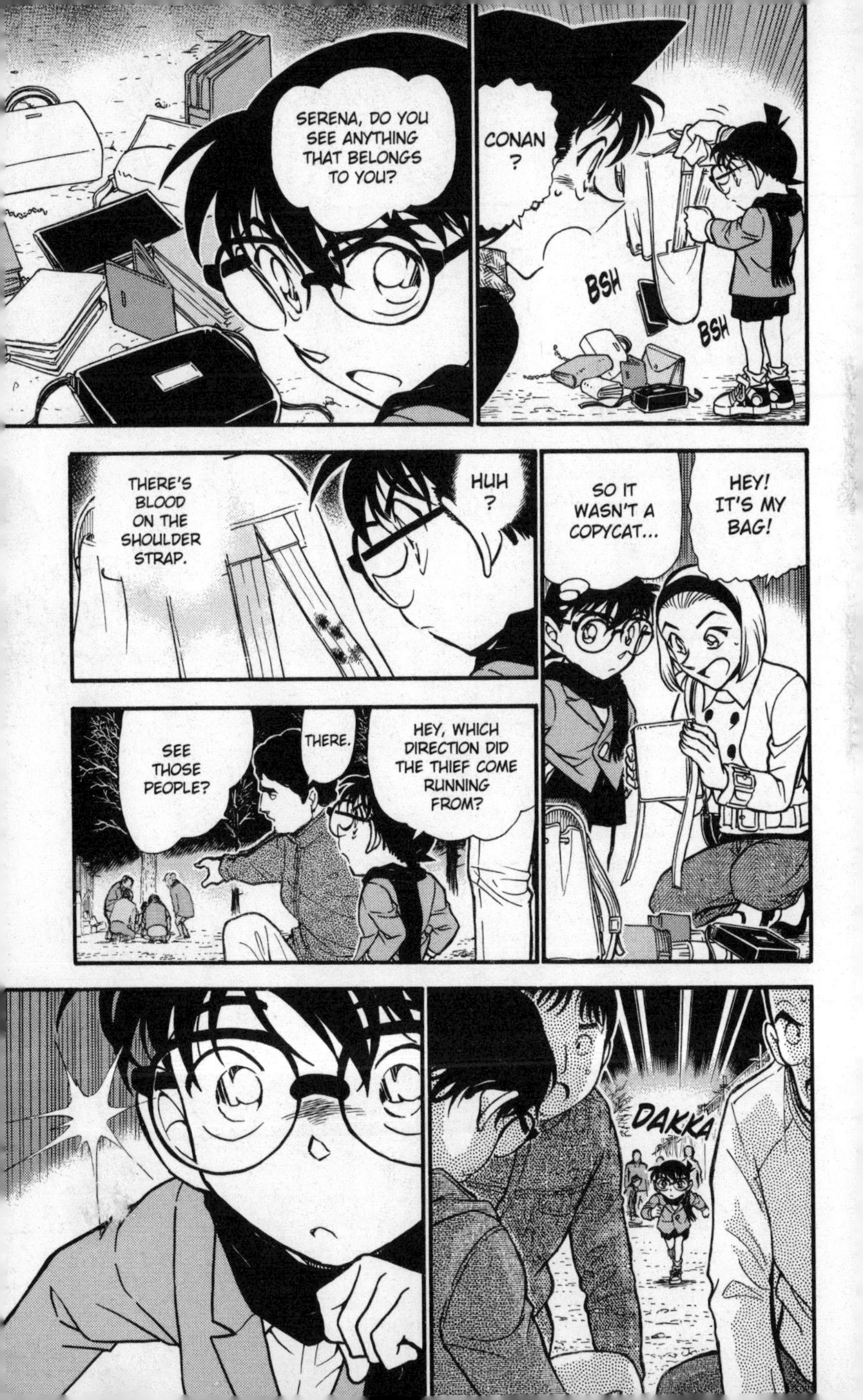
CONAN ?
BSH
BSH
SERENA, DO YOU SEE ANYTHING THAT BELONGS TO YOU?
HEY! IT'S MY BAG!
SO IT WASN'T A COPYCAT...
HUH ?
THERE'S BLOOD ON THE SHOULDER STRAP.
HEY, WHICH DIRECTION DID THE THIEF COME RUNNING FROM?
THERE.
SEE THOSE PEOPLE?
DAKKA

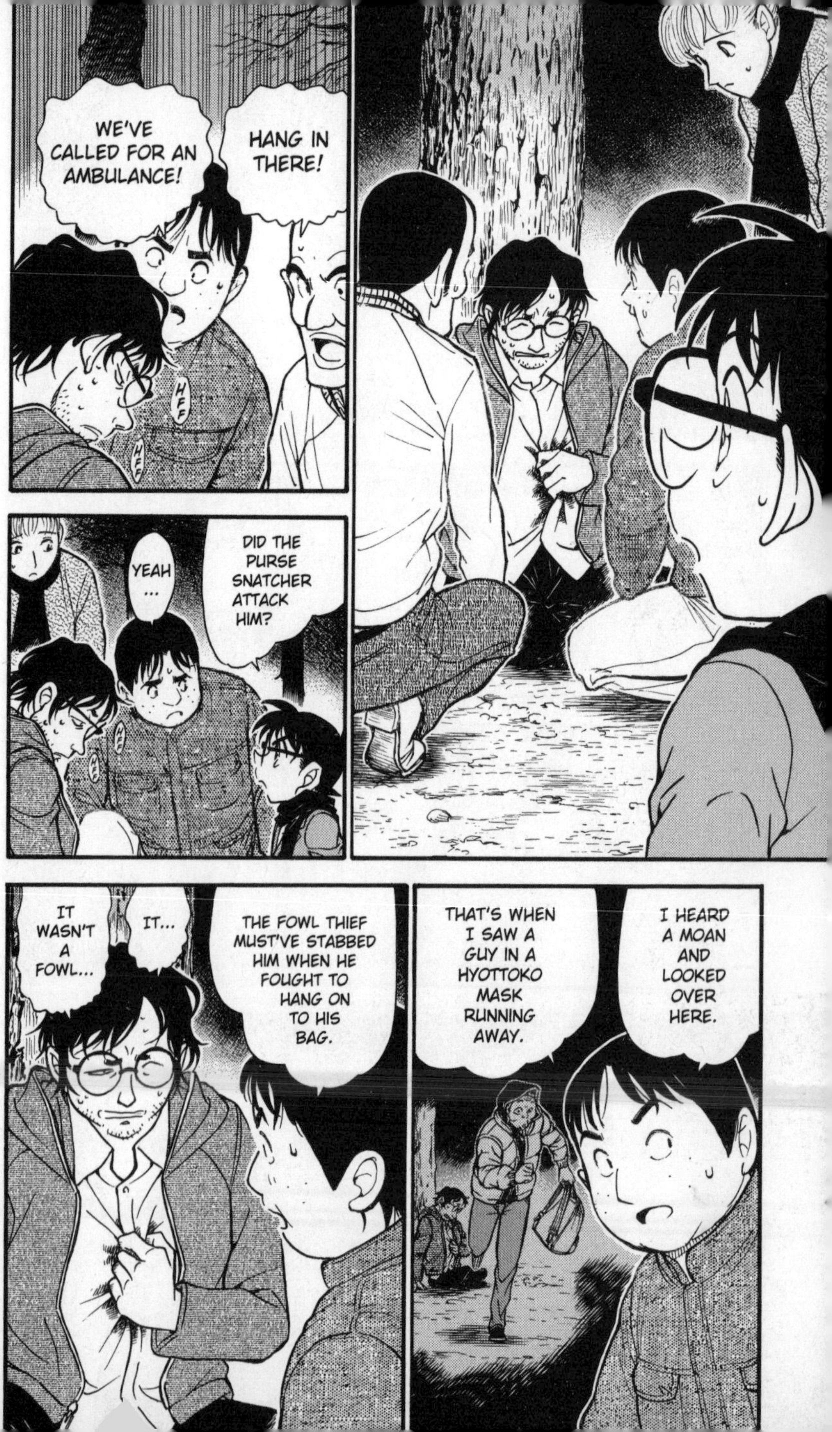
HANG IN THERE!
WE'VE CALLED FOR AN AMBULANCE!
HFF
HFF
DID THE PURSE SNATCHER ATTACK HIM?
YEAH ...
HFF
HFF
I HEARD A MOAN AND LOOKED OVER HERE.
THAT'S WHEN I SAW A GUY IN A HYOTTOKO MASK RUNNING AWAY.
THE FOWL THIEF MUST'VE STABBED HIM WHEN HE FOUGHT TO HANG ON TO HIS BAG.
IT...
IT WASN'T A FOWL...

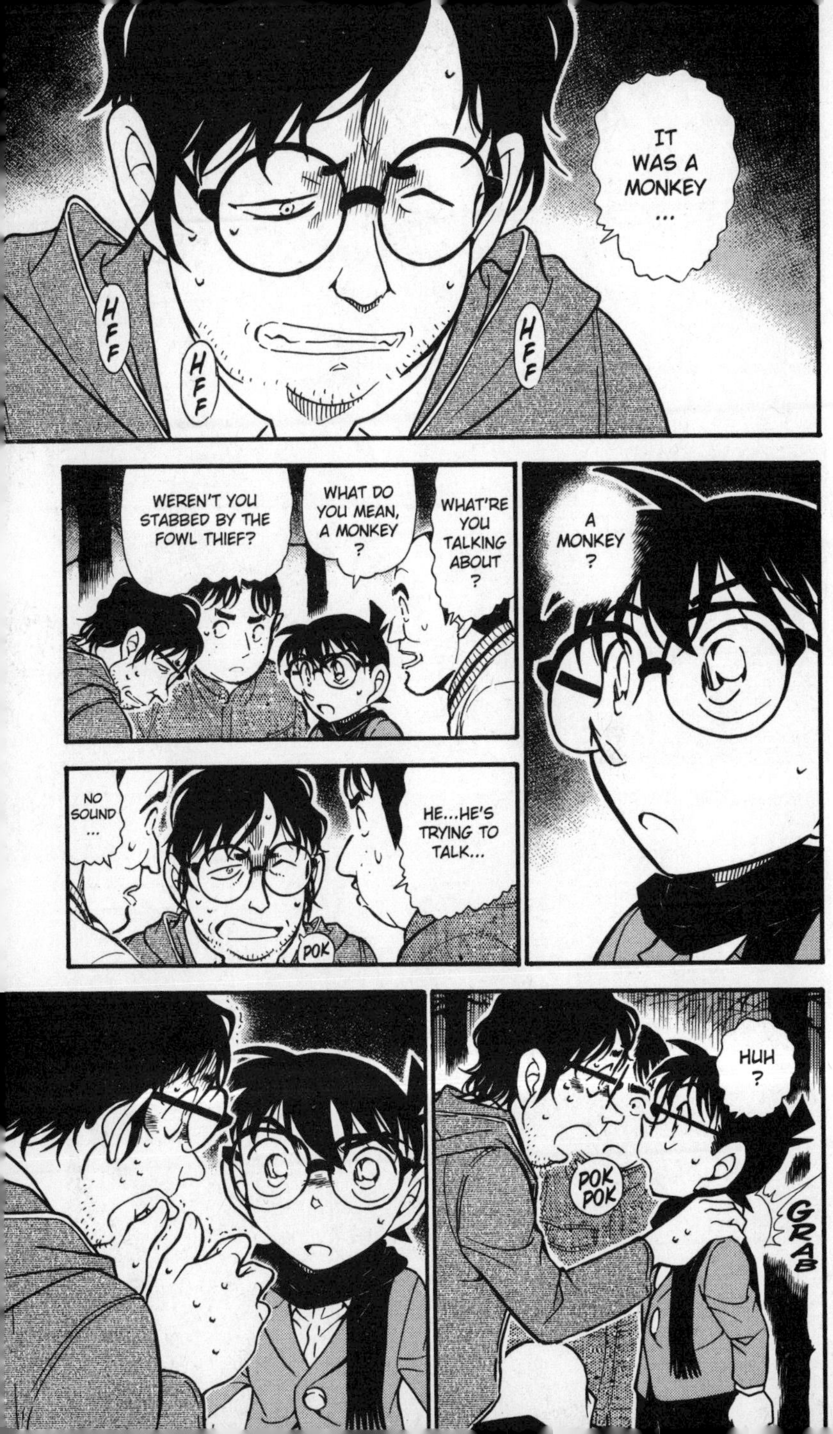
IT WAS A MONKEY ...
HFF
HFF
HFF
A MONKEY ?
WHAT'RE YOU TALKING ABOUT ?
WHAT DO YOU MEAN, A MONKEY ?
WEREN'T YOU STABBED BY THE FOWL THIEF?
HE...HE'S TRYING TO TALK...
POK
NO SOUND ...
HUH ?
GRAB
POK POK

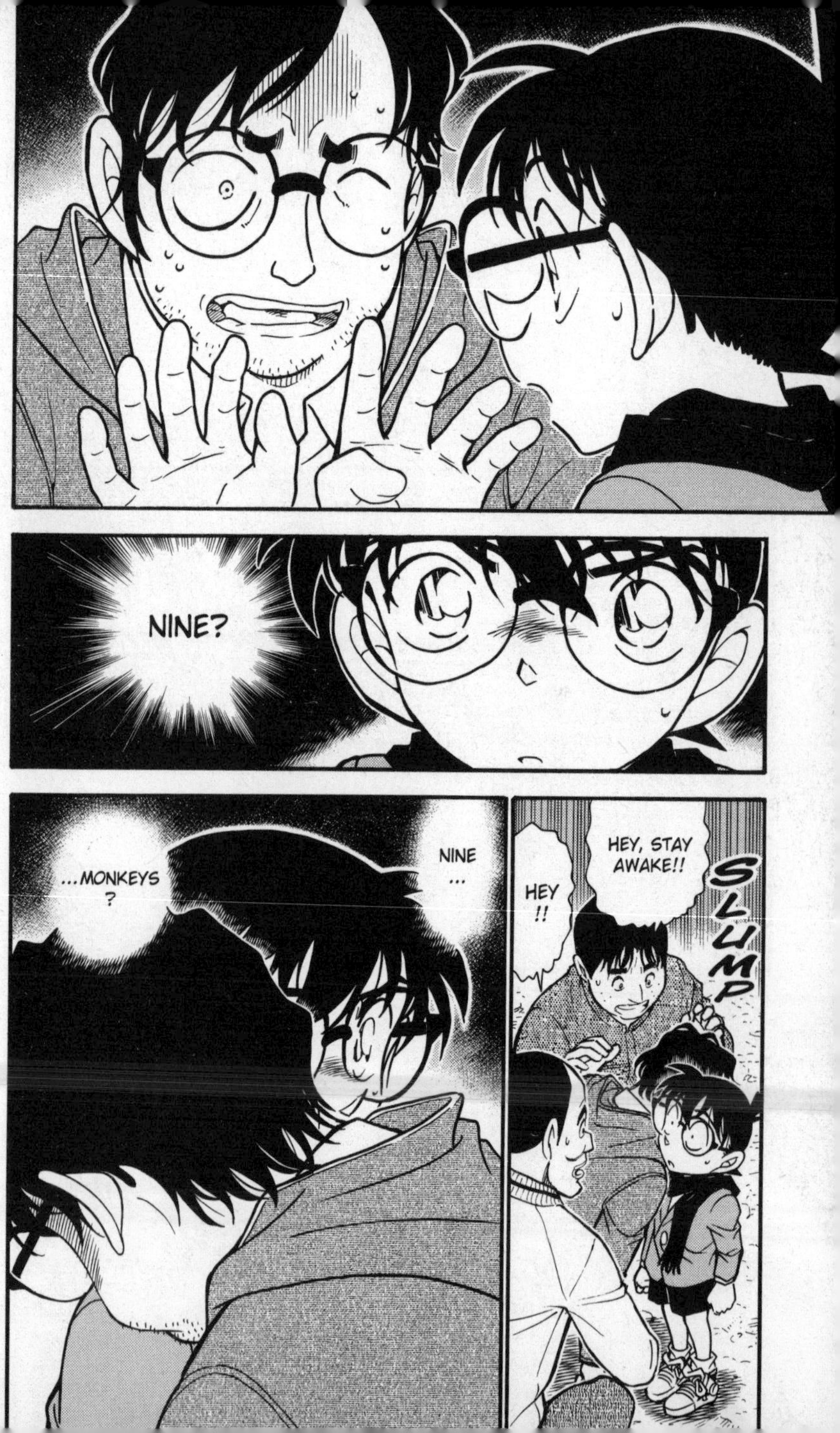
NINE?
SLUMP
HEY, STAY AWAKE!!
HEY!!
NINE...
...MONKEYS?

FILE 10: THE CLUES OF MONKEY AND NINE

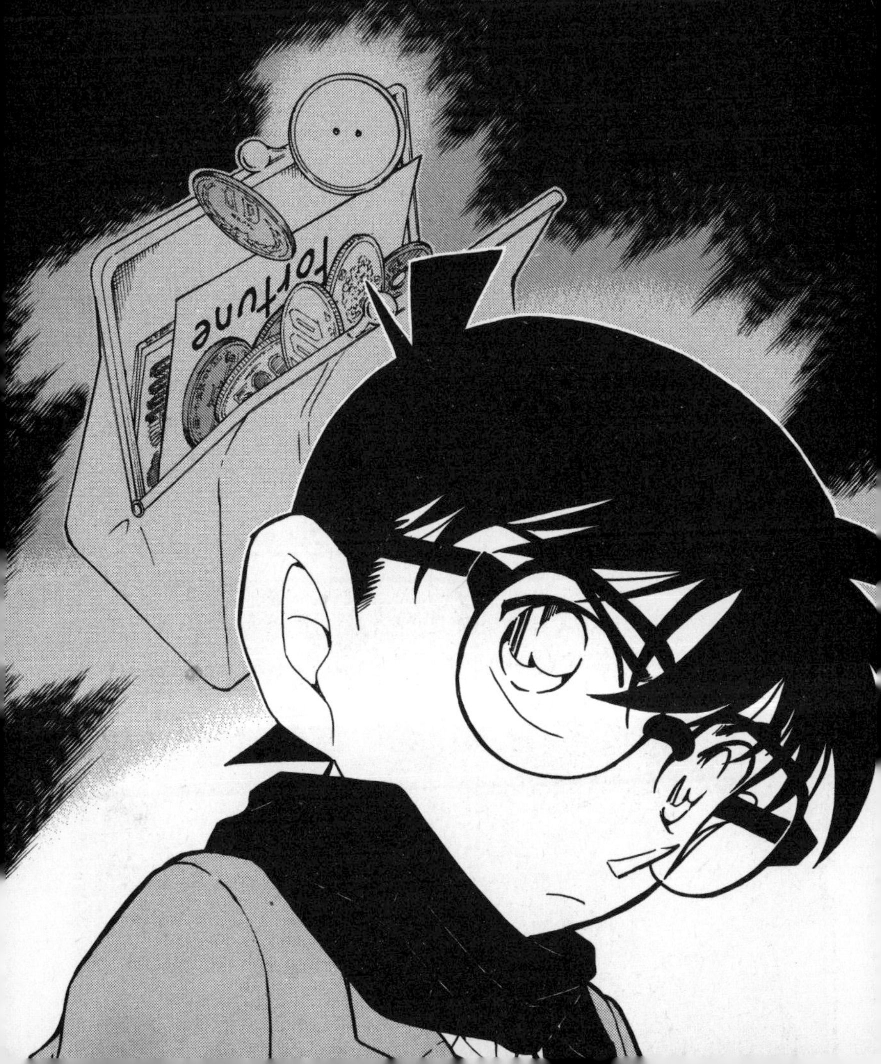

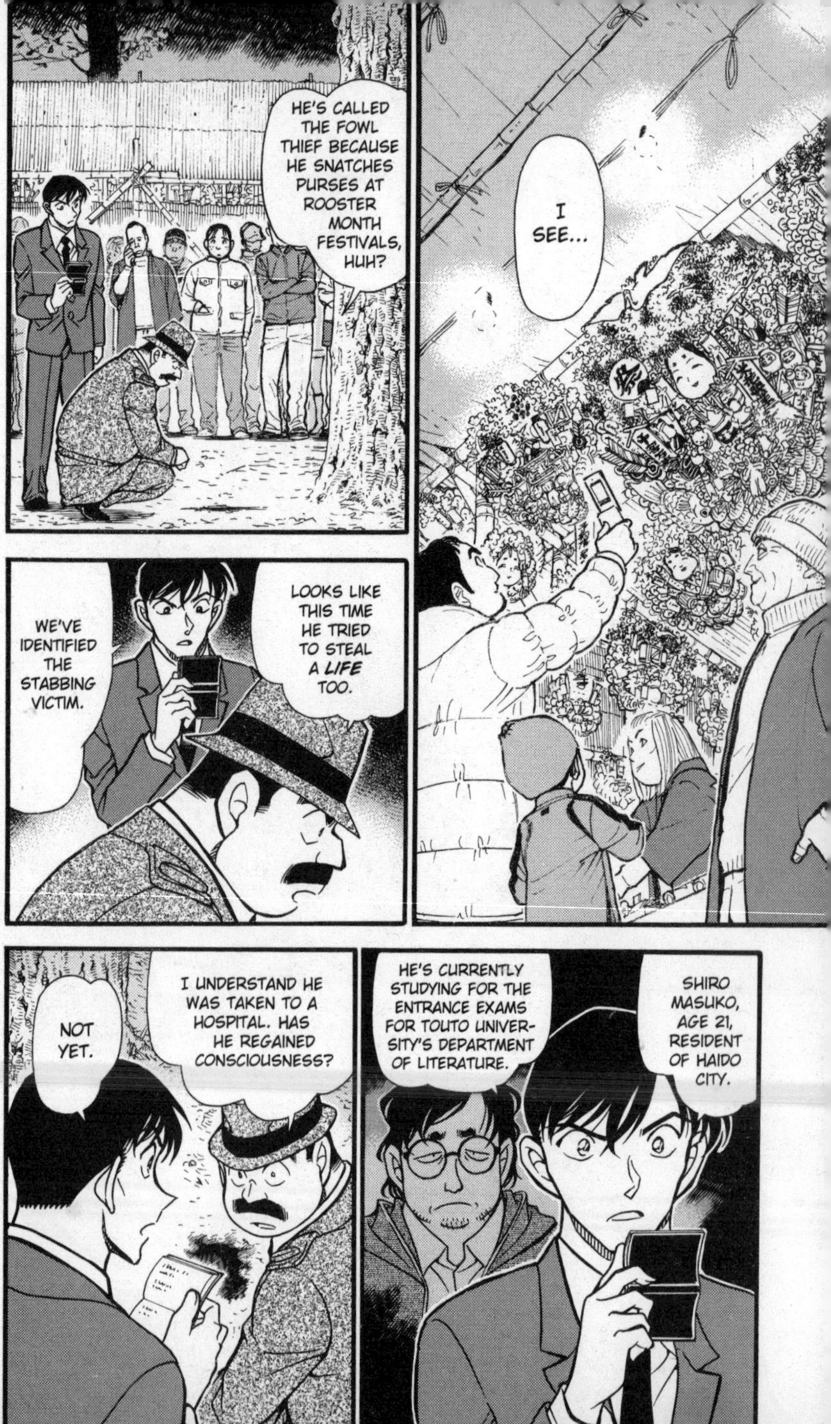
I SEE...
HE'S CALLED THE FOWL THIEF BECAUSE HE SNATCHES PURSES AT ROOSTER MONTH FESTIVALS, HUH?
LOOKS LIKE THIS TIME HE TRIED TO STEAL A *LIFE* TOO.
WE'VE IDENTIFIED THE STABBING VICTIM.
SHIRO MASUKO, AGE 21, RESIDENT OF HAIDO CITY.
HE'S CURRENTLY STUDYING FOR THE ENTRANCE EXAMS FOR TOUTO UNIVERSITY'S DEPARTMENT OF LITERATURE.
I UNDERSTAND HE WAS TAKEN TO A HOSPITAL. HAS HE REGAINED CONSCIOUSNESS?
NOT YET.

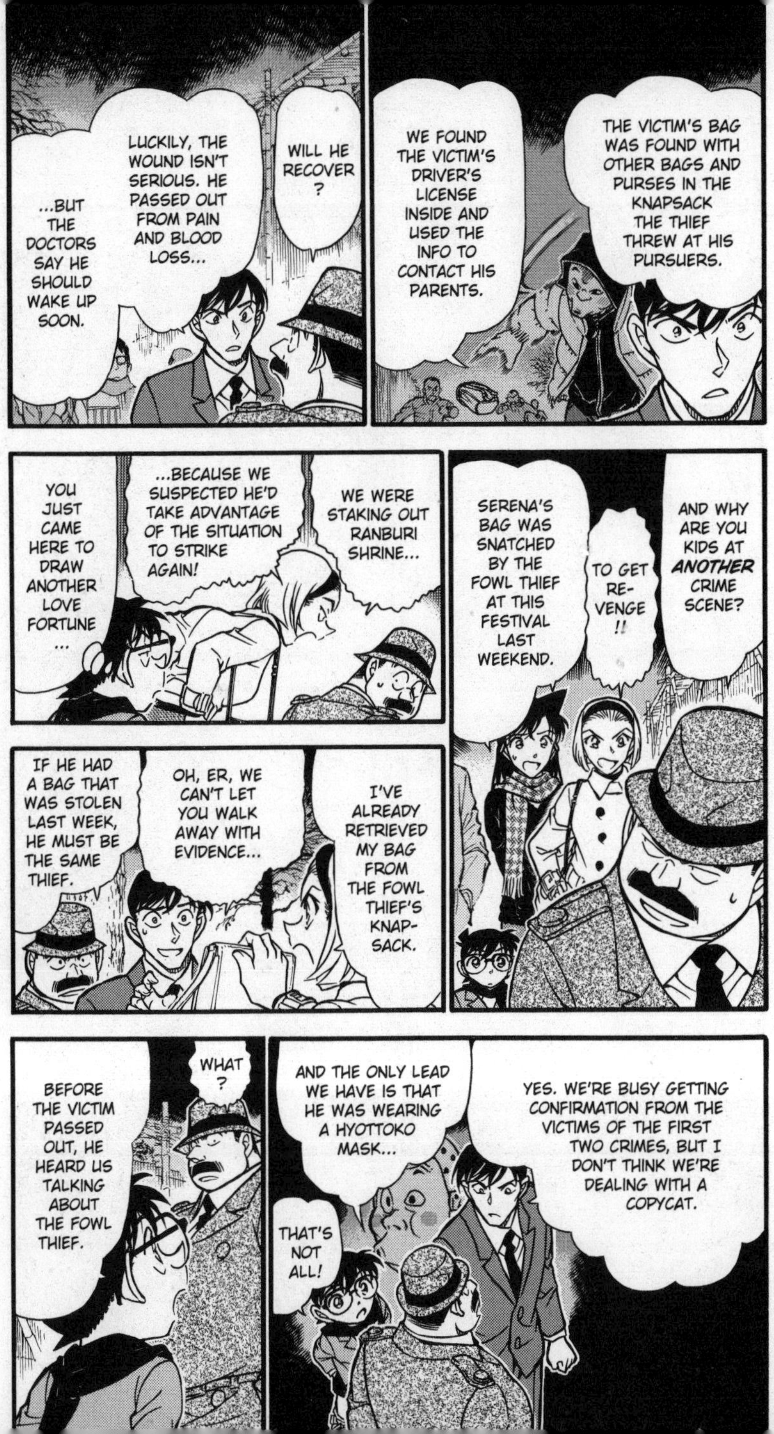
THE VICTIM'S BAG WAS FOUND WITH OTHER BAGS AND PURSES IN THE KNAPSACK THE THIEF THREW AT HIS PURSUERS.
WE FOUND THE VICTIM'S DRIVER'S LICENSE INSIDE AND USED THE INFO TO CONTACT HIS PARENTS.
WILL HE RECOVER?
LUCKILY, THE WOUND ISN'T SERIOUS. HE PASSED OUT FROM PAIN AND BLOOD LOSS...
...BUT THE DOCTORS SAY HE SHOULD WAKE UP SOON.
AND WHY ARE YOU KIDS AT *ANOTHER* CRIME SCENE?
TO GET RE-VENGE!!
SERENA'S BAG WAS SNATCHED BY THE FOWL THIEF AT THIS FESTIVAL LAST WEEKEND.
WE WERE STAKING OUT RANBURI SHRINE...
...BECAUSE WE SUSPECTED HE'D TAKE ADVANTAGE OF THE SITUATION TO STRIKE AGAIN!
YOU JUST CAME HERE TO DRAW ANOTHER LOVE FORTUNE...
I'VE ALREADY RETRIEVED MY BAG FROM THE FOWL THIEF'S KNAP-SACK.
OH, ER, WE CAN'T LET YOU WALK AWAY WITH EVIDENCE...
IF HE HAD A BAG THAT WAS STOLEN LAST WEEK, HE MUST BE THE SAME THIEF.
YES. WE'RE BUSY GETTING CONFIRMATION FROM THE VICTIMS OF THE FIRST TWO CRIMES, BUT I DON'T THINK WE'RE DEALING WITH A COPYCAT.
AND THE ONLY LEAD WE HAVE IS THAT HE WAS WEARING A HYOTTOKO MASK...
THAT'S NOT ALL!
WHAT?
BEFORE THE VICTIM PASSED OUT, HE HEARD US TALKING ABOUT THE FOWL THIEF.

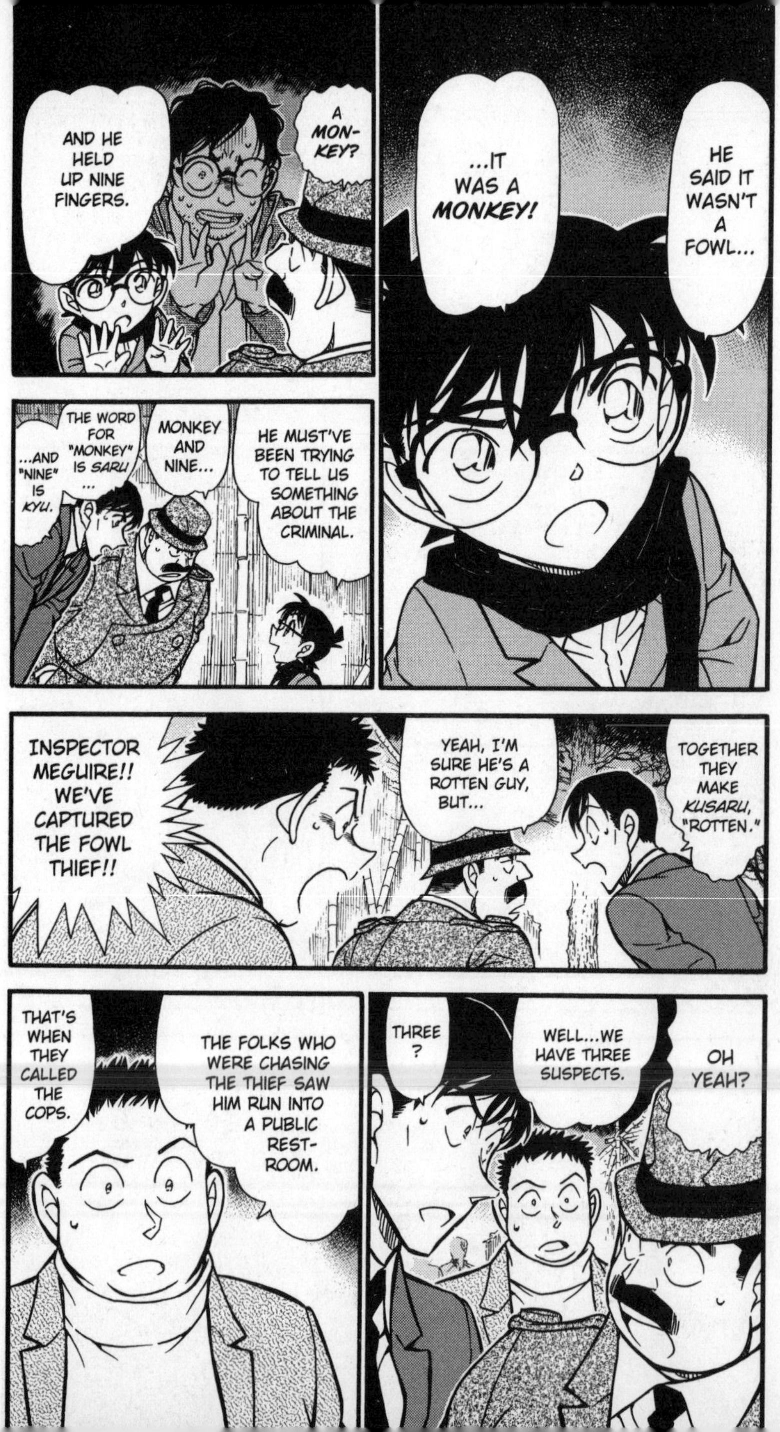
HE SAID IT WASN'T A FOWL...
...IT WAS A *MONKEY!*
A *MON-KEY?*
AND HE HELD UP NINE FINGERS.
HE MUST'VE BEEN TRYING TO TELL US SOMETHING ABOUT THE CRIMINAL.
MONKEY AND NINE...
THE WORD FOR "MONKEY" IS *SARU* ...
...AND "NINE" IS *KYU*.
TOGETHER THEY MAKE *KUSARU*, "ROTTEN."
YEAH, I'M SURE HE'S A ROTTEN GUY, BUT...
INSPECTOR MEGUIRE!! WE'VE CAPTURED THE FOWL THIEF!!
OH YEAH?
WELL...WE HAVE THREE SUSPECTS.
THREE ?
THE FOLKS WHO WERE CHASING THE THIEF SAW HIM RUN INTO A PUBLIC REST-ROOM.
THAT'S WHEN THEY CALLED THE COPS.

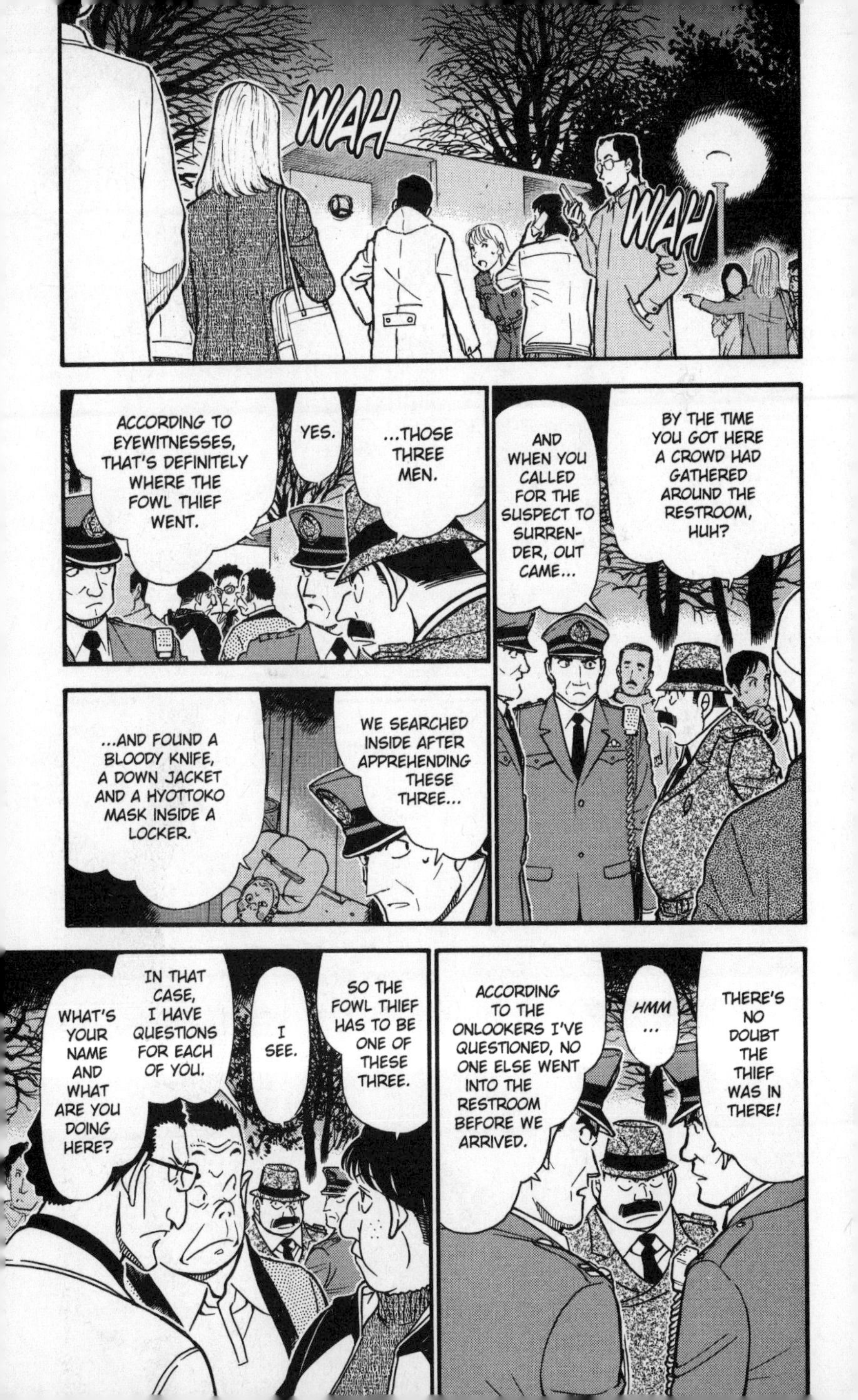
WAH
WAH
BY THE TIME YOU GOT HERE A CROWD HAD GATHERED AROUND THE RESTROOM, HUH?
AND WHEN YOU CALLED FOR THE SUSPECT TO SURREN-DER, OUT CAME...
...THOSE THREE MEN.
YES.
ACCORDING TO EYEWITNESSES, THAT'S DEFINITELY WHERE THE FOWL THIEF WENT.
WE SEARCHED INSIDE AFTER APPREHENDING THESE THREE...
...AND FOUND A BLOODY KNIFE, A DOWN JACKET AND A HYOTTOKO MASK INSIDE A LOCKER.
THERE'S NO DOUBT THE THIEF WAS IN THERE!
HMM...
ACCORDING TO THE ONLOOKERS I'VE QUESTIONED, NO ONE ELSE WENT INTO THE RESTROOM BEFORE WE ARRIVED.
SO THE FOWL THIEF HAS TO BE ONE OF THESE THREE.
I SEE.
IN THAT CASE, I HAVE QUESTIONS FOR EACH OF YOU.
WHAT'S YOUR NAME AND WHAT ARE YOU DOING HERE?

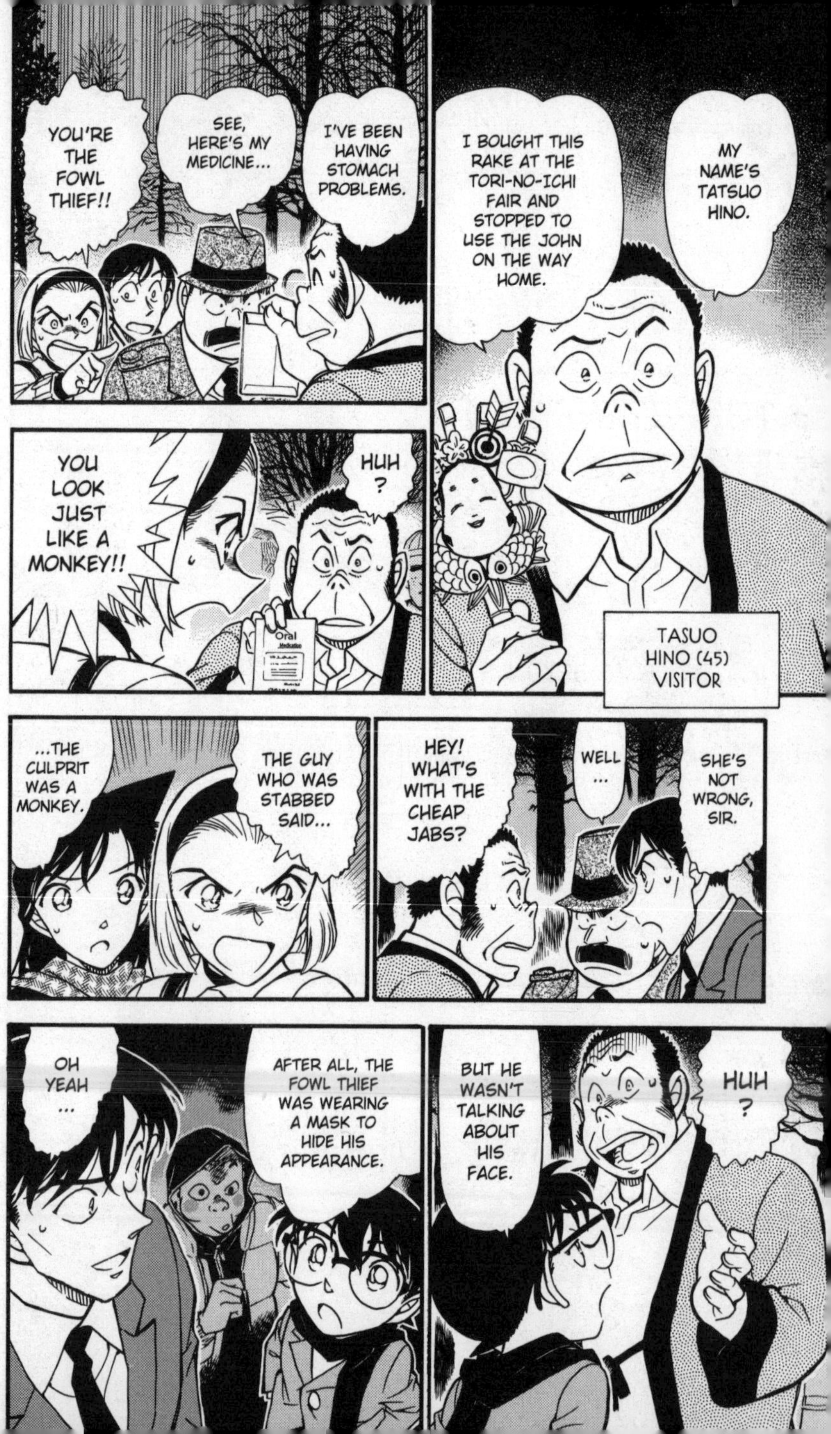
MY NAME'S TATSUO HINO.
I BOUGHT THIS RAKE AT THE TORI-NO-ICHI FAIR AND STOPPED TO USE THE JOHN ON THE WAY HOME.
TASUO HINO (45) VISITOR
I'VE BEEN HAVING STOMACH PROBLEMS.
SEE, HERE'S MY MEDICINE...
YOU'RE THE FOWL THIEF!!
HUH?
YOU LOOK JUST LIKE A MONKEY!!
Oral Medication
SHE'S NOT WRONG, SIR.
WELL...
HEY! WHAT'S WITH THE CHEAP JABS?
THE GUY WHO WAS STABBED SAID...
...THE CULPRIT WAS A MONKEY.
HUH?
BUT HE WASN'T TALKING ABOUT HIS FACE.
AFTER ALL, THE FOWL THIEF WAS WEARING A MASK TO HIDE HIS APPEARANCE.
OH YEAH...

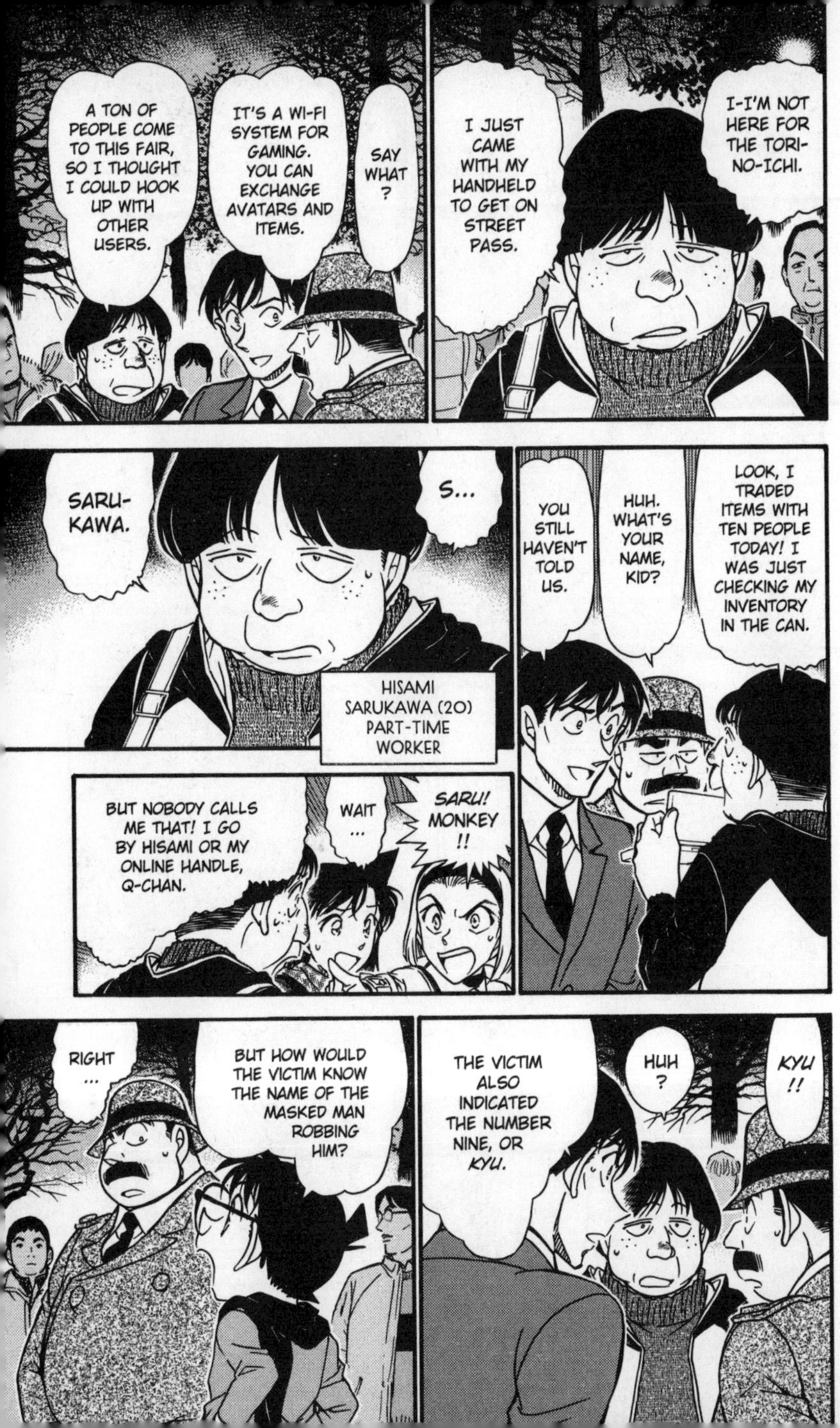
I-I'M NOT HERE FOR THE TORI-NO-ICHI.
I JUST CAME WITH MY HANDHELD TO GET ON STREET PASS.
SAY WHAT?
IT'S A WI-FI SYSTEM FOR GAMING. YOU CAN EXCHANGE AVATARS AND ITEMS.
A TON OF PEOPLE COME TO THIS FAIR, SO I THOUGHT I COULD HOOK UP WITH OTHER USERS.
LOOK, I TRADED ITEMS WITH TEN PEOPLE TODAY! I WAS JUST CHECKING MY INVENTORY IN THE CAN.
HUH. WHAT'S YOUR NAME, KID?
YOU STILL HAVEN'T TOLD US.
S...
SARU-KAWA.
HISAMI SARUKAWA (20) PART-TIME WORKER
SARU! MONKEY!!
WAIT...
BUT NOBODY CALLS ME THAT! I GO BY HISAMI OR MY ONLINE HANDLE, Q-CHAN.
KYU!!
HUH?
THE VICTIM ALSO INDICATED THE NUMBER NINE, OR KYU.
BUT HOW WOULD THE VICTIM KNOW THE NAME OF THE MASKED MAN ROBBING HIM?
RIGHT...

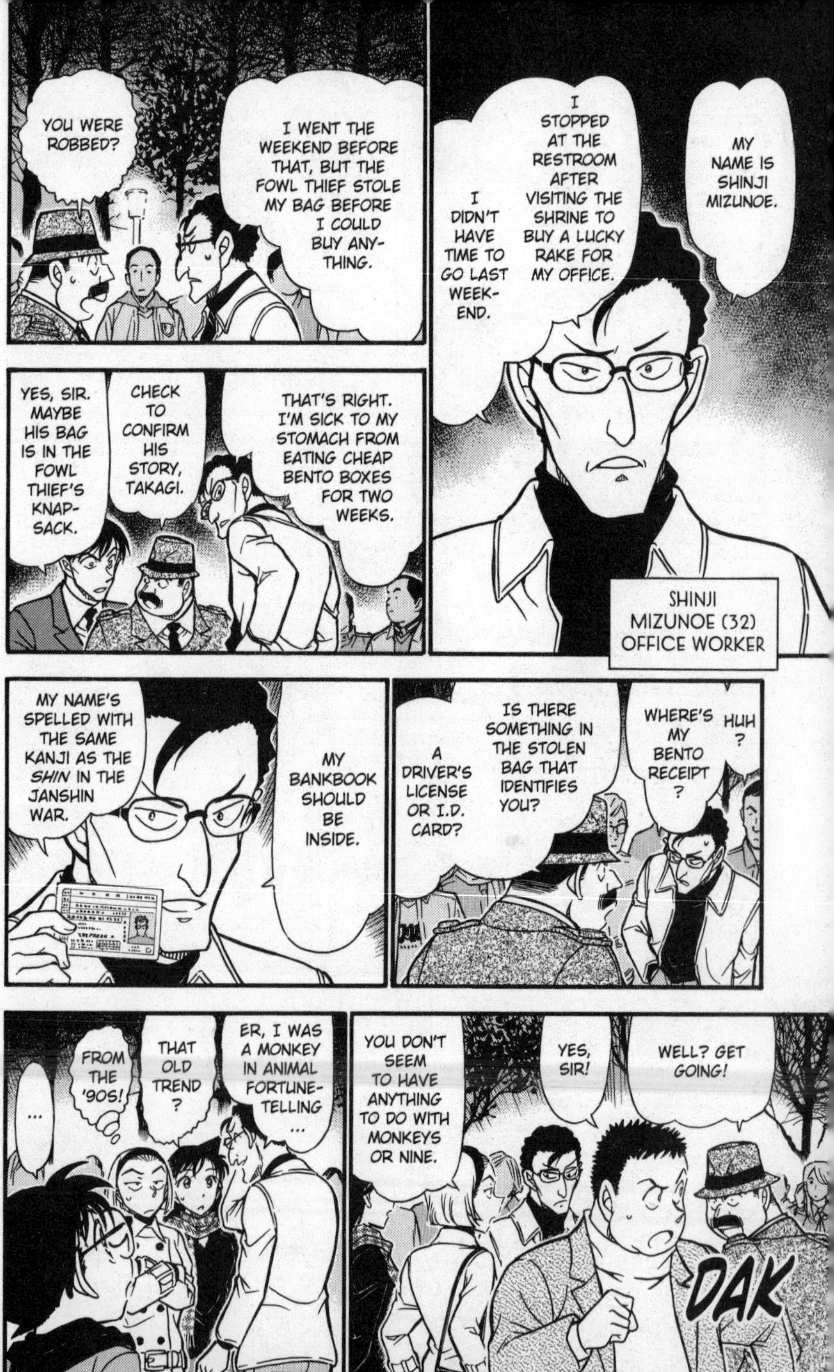
MY NAME IS SHINJI MIZUNOE.
I STOPPED AT THE RESTROOM AFTER VISITING THE SHRINE TO BUY A LUCKY RAKE FOR MY OFFICE.
I DIDN'T HAVE TIME TO GO LAST WEEKEND.
SHINJI MIZUNOE (32) OFFICE WORKER
I WENT THE WEEKEND BEFORE THAT, BUT THE FOWL THIEF STOLE MY BAG BEFORE I COULD BUY ANYTHING.
YOU WERE ROBBED?
THAT'S RIGHT. I'M SICK TO MY STOMACH FROM EATING CHEAP BENTO BOXES FOR TWO WEEKS.
CHECK TO CONFIRM HIS STORY, TAKAGI.
YES, SIR. MAYBE HIS BAG IS IN THE FOWL THIEF'S KNAPSACK.
HUH?
WHERE'S MY BENTO RECEIPT?
IS THERE SOMETHING IN THE STOLEN BAG THAT IDENTIFIES YOU?
A DRIVER'S LICENSE OR I.D. CARD?
MY BANKBOOK SHOULD BE INSIDE.
MY NAME'S SPELLED WITH THE SAME KANJI AS THE *SHIN* IN THE JANSHIN WAR.
WELL? GET GOING!
YES, SIR!
DAK
YOU DON'T SEEM TO HAVE ANYTHING TO DO WITH MONKEYS OR NINE.
ER, I WAS A MONKEY IN ANIMAL FORTUNE-TELLING...
THAT OLD TREND?
FROM THE '90S!
...

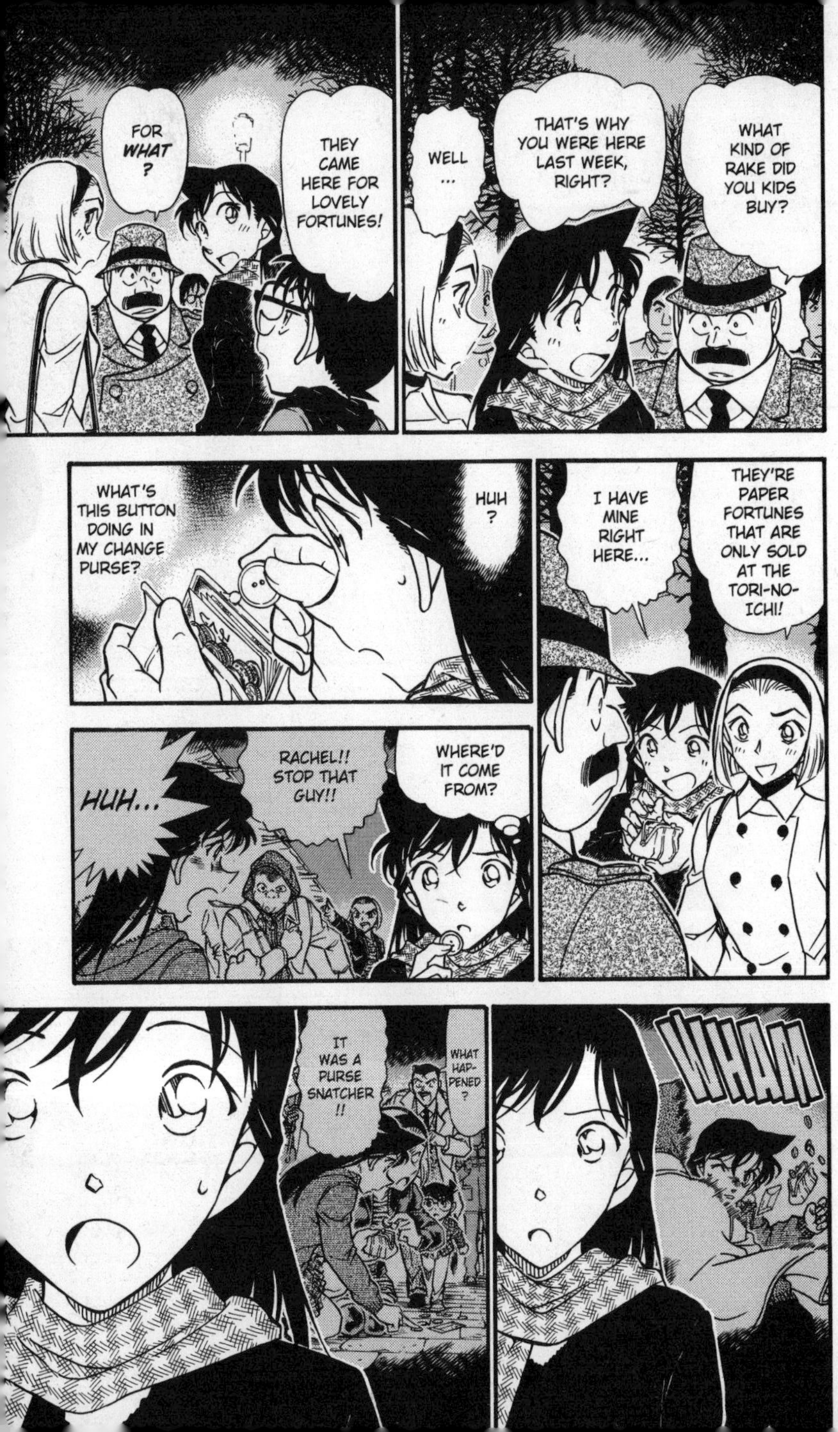
WHAT KIND OF RAKE DID YOU KIDS BUY?
THAT'S WHY YOU WERE HERE LAST WEEK, RIGHT?
WELL ...
THEY CAME HERE FOR LOVELY FORTUNES!
FOR WHAT?
THEY'RE PAPER FORTUNES THAT ARE ONLY SOLD AT THE TORI-NO-ICHI!
I HAVE MINE RIGHT HERE...
HUH?
WHAT'S THIS BUTTON DOING IN MY CHANGE PURSE?
WHERE'D IT COME FROM?
RACHEL!! STOP THAT GUY!!
HUH...
WHAM
WHAT HAP-PENED?
IT WAS A PURSE SNATCHER!!

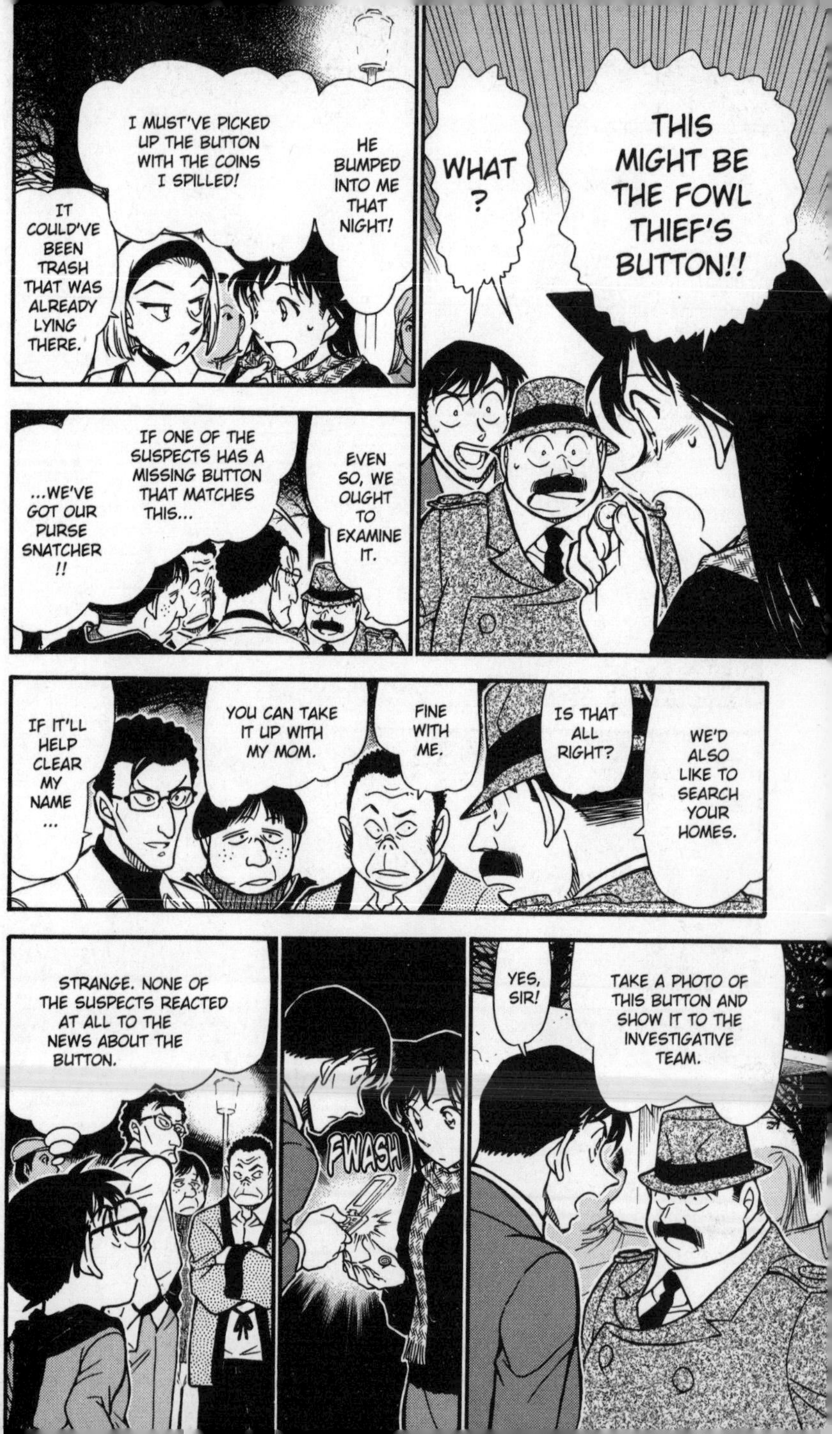
THIS MIGHT BE THE FOWL THIEF'S BUTTON!!
WHAT?
HE BUMPED INTO ME THAT NIGHT!
I MUST'VE PICKED UP THE BUTTON WITH THE COINS I SPILLED!
IT COULD'VE BEEN TRASH THAT WAS ALREADY LYING THERE.
EVEN SO, WE OUGHT TO EXAMINE IT.
IF ONE OF THE SUSPECTS HAS A MISSING BUTTON THAT MATCHES THIS...
...WE'VE GOT OUR PURSE SNATCHER!!
WE'D ALSO LIKE TO SEARCH YOUR HOMES.
IS THAT ALL RIGHT?
FINE WITH ME.
YOU CAN TAKE IT UP WITH MY MOM.
IF IT'LL HELP CLEAR MY NAME...
TAKE A PHOTO OF THIS BUTTON AND SHOW IT TO THE INVESTIGATIVE TEAM.
YES, SIR!
FWASH
STRANGE. NONE OF THE SUSPECTS REACTED AT ALL TO THE NEWS ABOUT THE BUTTON.

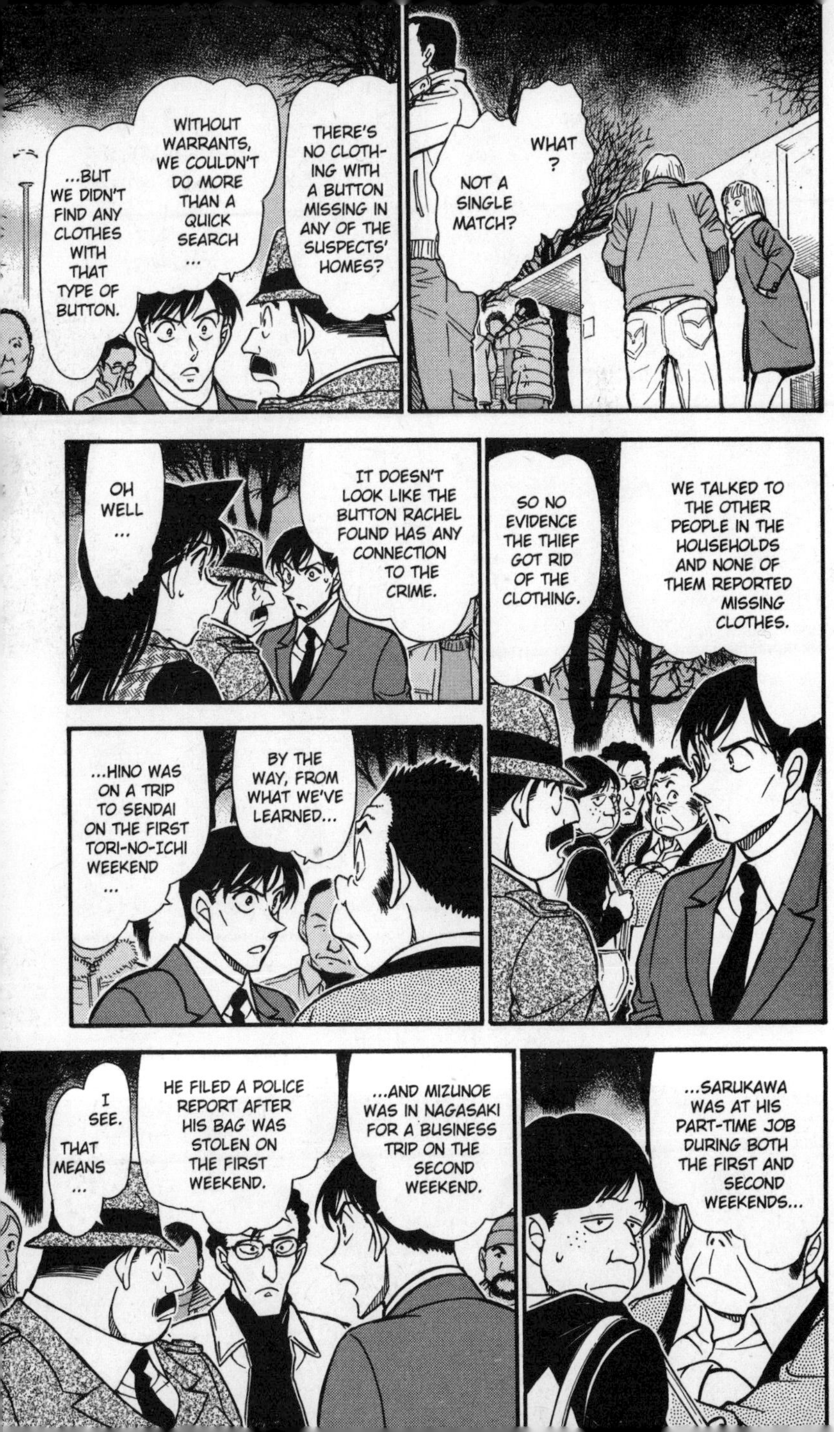
WHAT ?
NOT A SINGLE MATCH?
THERE'S NO CLOTHING WITH A BUTTON MISSING IN ANY OF THE SUSPECTS' HOMES?
WITHOUT WARRANTS, WE COULDN'T DO MORE THAN A QUICK SEARCH ...
...BUT WE DIDN'T FIND ANY CLOTHES WITH THAT TYPE OF BUTTON.
WE TALKED TO THE OTHER PEOPLE IN THE HOUSEHOLDS AND NONE OF THEM REPORTED MISSING CLOTHES.
SO NO EVIDENCE THE THIEF GOT RID OF THE CLOTHING.
IT DOESN'T LOOK LIKE THE BUTTON RACHEL FOUND HAS ANY CONNECTION TO THE CRIME.
OH WELL ...
BY THE WAY, FROM WHAT WE'VE LEARNED...
...HINO WAS ON A TRIP TO SENDAI ON THE FIRST TORI-NO-ICHI WEEKEND ...
...SARUKAWA WAS AT HIS PART-TIME JOB DURING BOTH THE FIRST AND SECOND WEEKENDS...
...AND MIZUNOE WAS IN NAGASAKI FOR A BUSINESS TRIP ON THE SECOND WEEKEND.
HE FILED A POLICE REPORT AFTER HIS BAG WAS STOLEN ON THE FIRST WEEKEND.
I SEE. THAT MEANS ...

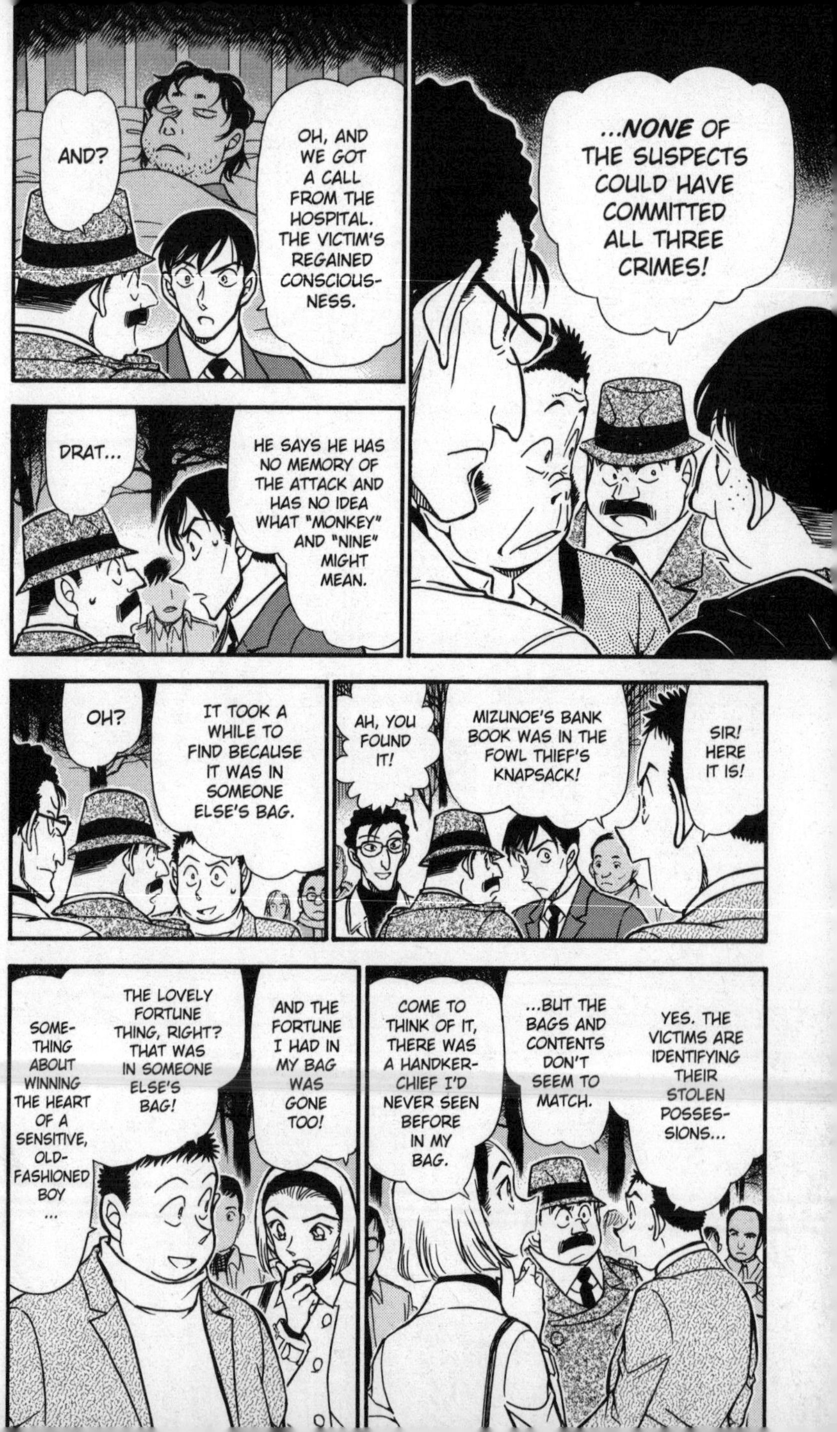
...NONE OF THE SUSPECTS COULD HAVE COMMITTED ALL THREE CRIMES!
OH, AND WE GOT A CALL FROM THE HOSPITAL. THE VICTIM'S REGAINED CONSCIOUS-NESS.
AND?
HE SAYS HE HAS NO MEMORY OF THE ATTACK AND HAS NO IDEA WHAT "MONKEY" AND "NINE" MIGHT MEAN.
DRAT...
SIR! HERE IT IS!
MIZUNOE'S BANK BOOK WAS IN THE FOWL THIEF'S KNAPSACK!
AH, YOU FOUND IT!
IT TOOK A WHILE TO FIND BECAUSE IT WAS IN SOMEONE ELSE'S BAG.
OH?
YES. THE VICTIMS ARE IDENTIFYING THEIR STOLEN POSSES-SIONS...
...BUT THE BAGS AND CONTENTS DON'T SEEM TO MATCH.
COME TO THINK OF IT, THERE WAS A HANDKER-CHIEF I'D NEVER SEEN BEFORE IN MY BAG.
AND THE FORTUNE I HAD IN MY BAG WAS GONE TOO!
THE LOVELY FORTUNE THING, RIGHT? THAT WAS IN SOMEONE ELSE'S BAG!
SOME-THING ABOUT WINNING THE HEART OF A SENSITIVE, OLD-FASHIONED BOY...

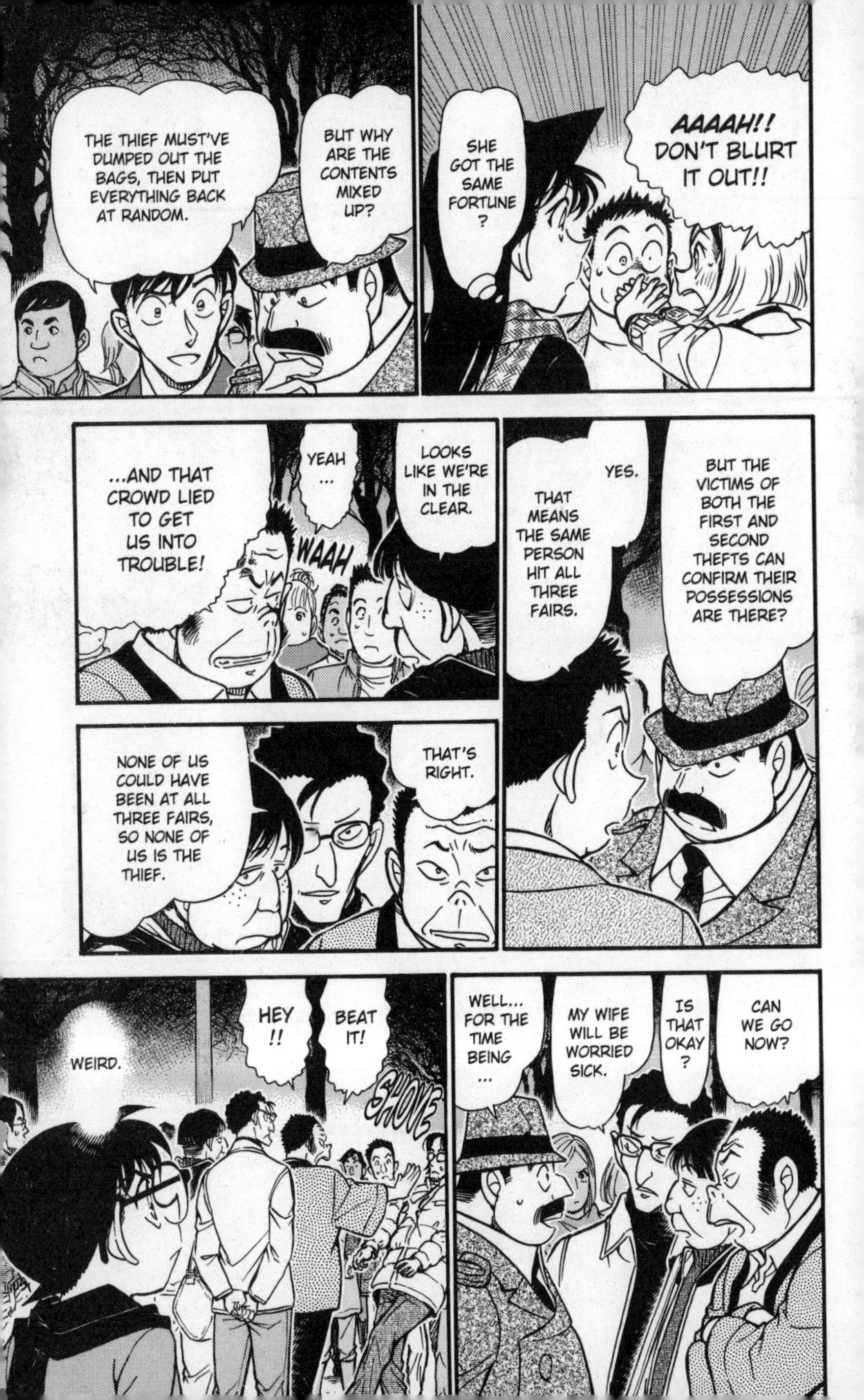
AAAAH!! DON'T BLURT IT OUT!!
SHE GOT THE SAME FORTUNE?
BUT WHY ARE THE CONTENTS MIXED UP?
THE THIEF MUST'VE DUMPED OUT THE BAGS, THEN PUT EVERYTHING BACK AT RANDOM.
BUT THE VICTIMS OF BOTH THE FIRST AND SECOND THEFTS CAN CONFIRM THEIR POSSESSIONS ARE THERE?
YES.
THAT MEANS THE SAME PERSON HIT ALL THREE FAIRS.
LOOKS LIKE WE'RE IN THE CLEAR.
YEAH...
WAAH
...AND THAT CROWD LIED TO GET US INTO TROUBLE!
THAT'S RIGHT.
NONE OF US COULD HAVE BEEN AT ALL THREE FAIRS, SO NONE OF US IS THE THIEF.
CAN WE GO NOW?
IS THAT OKAY?
MY WIFE WILL BE WORRIED SICK.
WELL... FOR THE TIME BEING...
BEAT IT!
HEY!!
SHOVE
WEIRD.

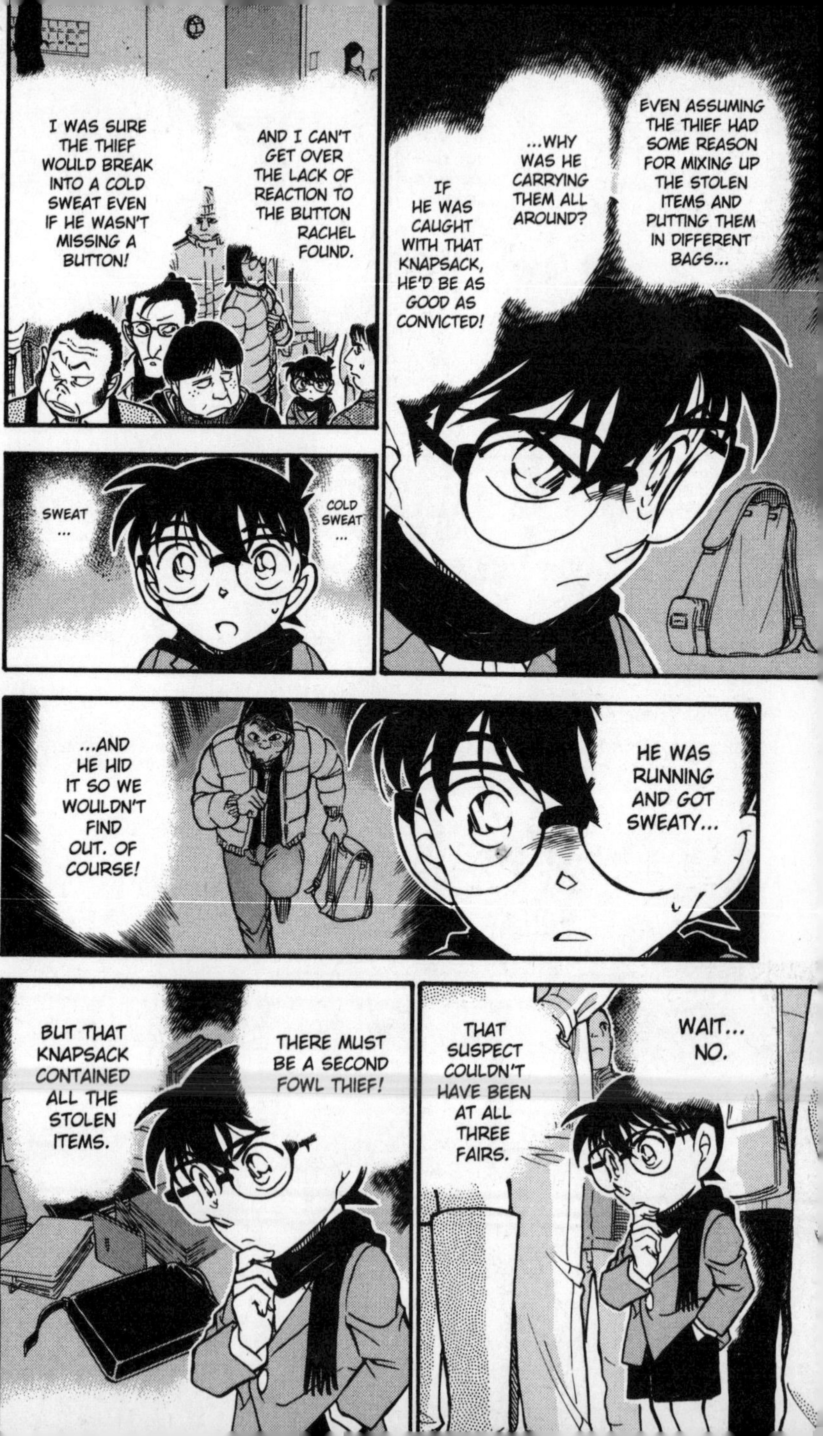
EVEN ASSUMING THE THIEF HAD SOME REASON FOR MIXING UP THE STOLEN ITEMS AND PUTTING THEM IN DIFFERENT BAGS...
...WHY WAS HE CARRYING THEM ALL AROUND?
IF HE WAS CAUGHT WITH THAT KNAPSACK, HE'D BE AS GOOD AS CONVICTED!
AND I CAN'T GET OVER THE LACK OF REACTION TO THE BUTTON RACHEL FOUND.
I WAS SURE THE THIEF WOULD BREAK INTO A COLD SWEAT EVEN IF HE WASN'T MISSING A BUTTON!
COLD SWEAT ...
SWEAT ...
HE WAS RUNNING AND GOT SWEATY...
...AND HE HID IT SO WE WOULDN'T FIND OUT. OF COURSE!
WAIT... NO.
THAT SUSPECT COULDN'T HAVE BEEN AT ALL THREE FAIRS.
THERE MUST BE A SECOND FOWL THIEF!
BUT THAT KNAPSACK CONTAINED ALL THE STOLEN ITEMS.

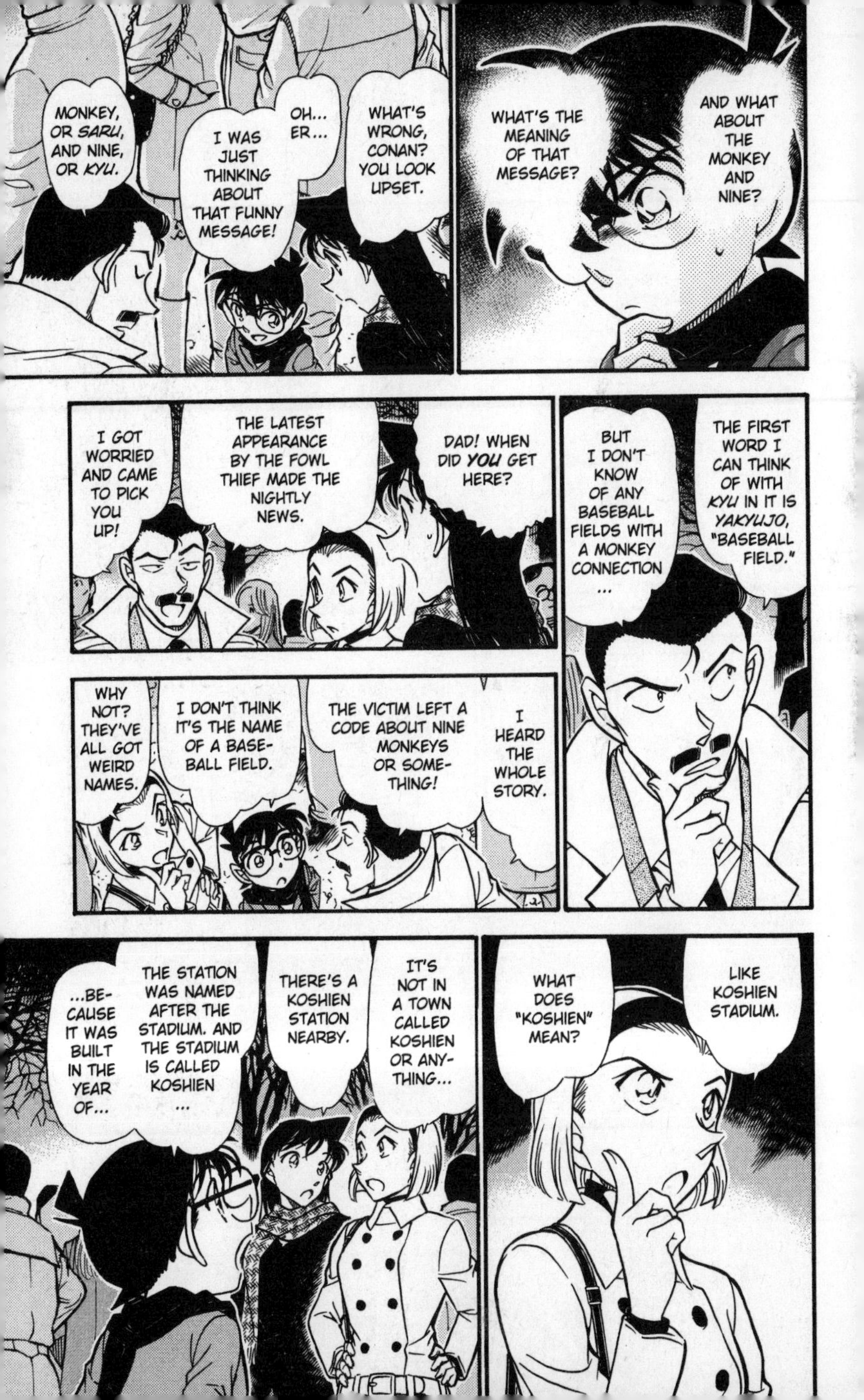
AND WHAT ABOUT THE MONKEY AND NINE?
WHAT'S THE MEANING OF THAT MESSAGE?
WHAT'S WRONG, CONAN? YOU LOOK UPSET.
OH... ER...
I WAS JUST THINKING ABOUT THAT FUNNY MESSAGE!
MONKEY, OR *SARU*, AND NINE, OR *KYU*.
THE FIRST WORD I CAN THINK OF WITH *KYU* IN IT IS *YAKYUJO*, "BASEBALL FIELD."
BUT I DON'T KNOW OF ANY BASEBALL FIELDS WITH A MONKEY CONNECTION ...
DAD! WHEN DID *YOU* GET HERE?
THE LATEST APPEARANCE BY THE FOWL THIEF MADE THE NIGHTLY NEWS.
I GOT WORRIED AND CAME TO PICK YOU UP!
I HEARD THE WHOLE STORY.
THE VICTIM LEFT A CODE ABOUT NINE MONKEYS OR SOME-THING!
I DON'T THINK IT'S THE NAME OF A BASE-BALL FIELD.
WHY NOT? THEY'VE ALL GOT WEIRD NAMES.
LIKE KOSHIEN STADIUM.
WHAT DOES "KOSHIEN" MEAN?
IT'S NOT IN A TOWN CALLED KOSHIEN OR ANY-THING...
THERE'S A KOSHIEN STATION NEARBY.
THE STATION WAS NAMED AFTER THE STADIUM. AND THE STADIUM IS CALLED KOSHIEN ...
...BE-CAUSE IT WAS BUILT IN THE YEAR OF...

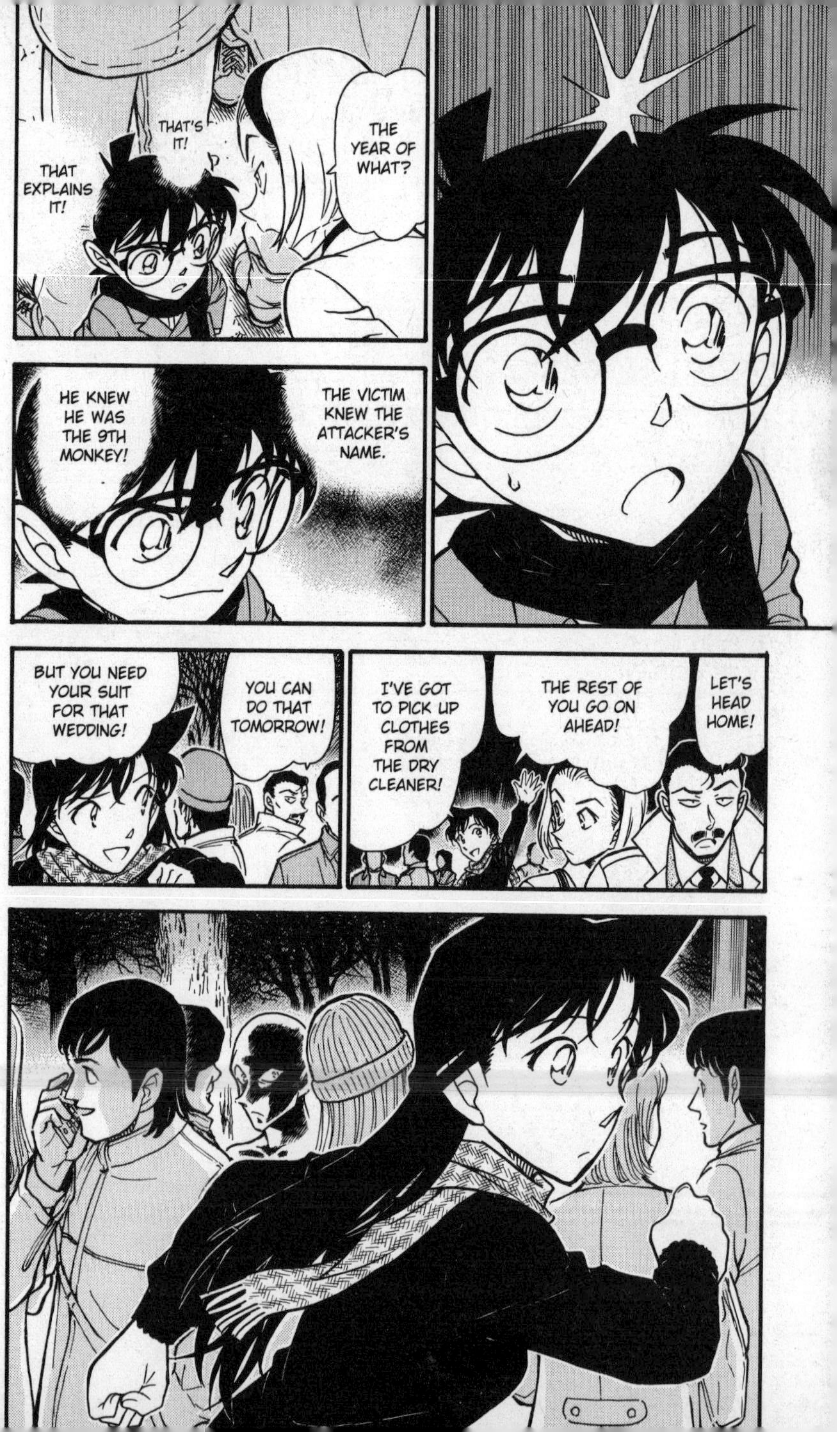
THE YEAR OF WHAT?
THAT'S IT!
THAT EXPLAINS IT!
THE VICTIM KNEW THE ATTACKER'S NAME.
HE KNEW HE WAS THE 9TH MONKEY!
LET'S HEAD HOME!
THE REST OF YOU GO ON AHEAD!
I'VE GOT TO PICK UP CLOTHES FROM THE DRY CLEANER!
YOU CAN DO THAT TOMORROW!
BUT YOU NEED YOUR SUIT FOR THAT WEDDING!

FILE 11: NAIVE AND INNOCENT

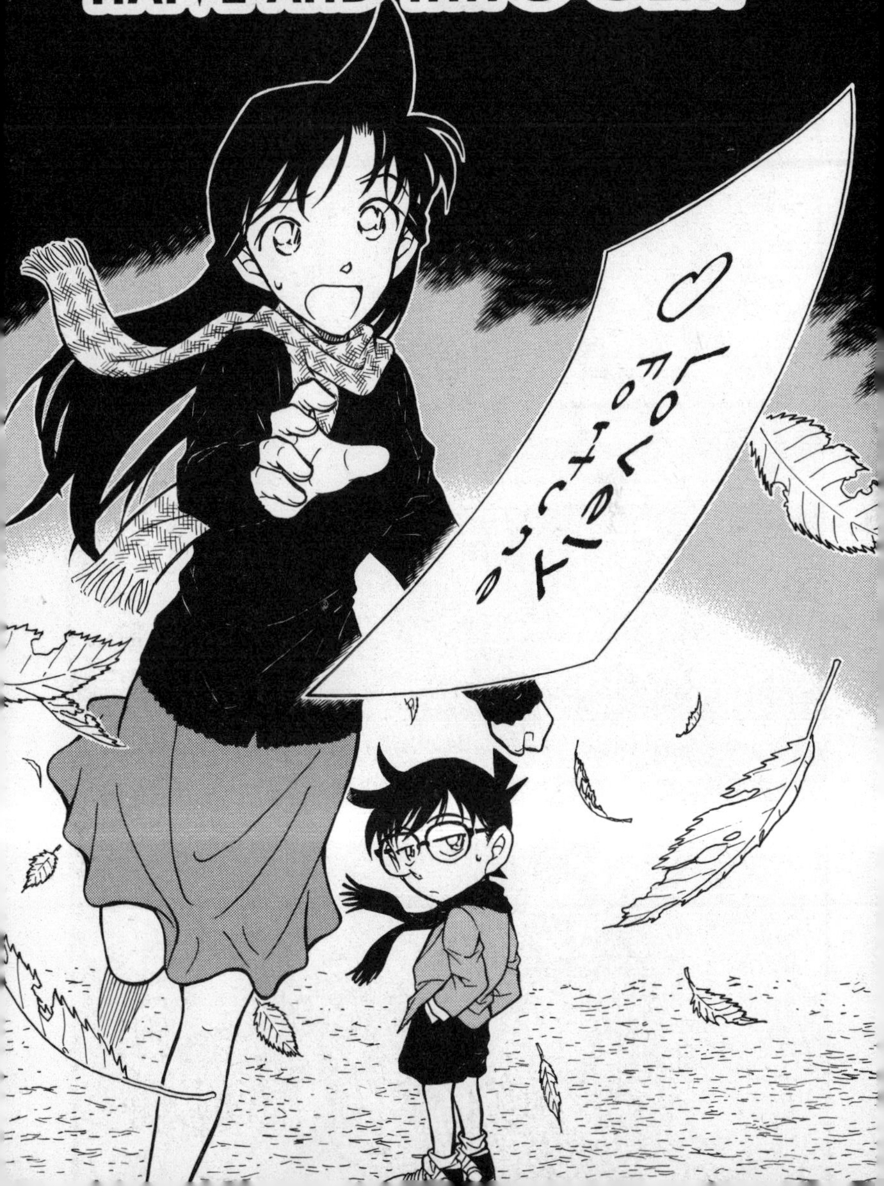
Lovely Fortune

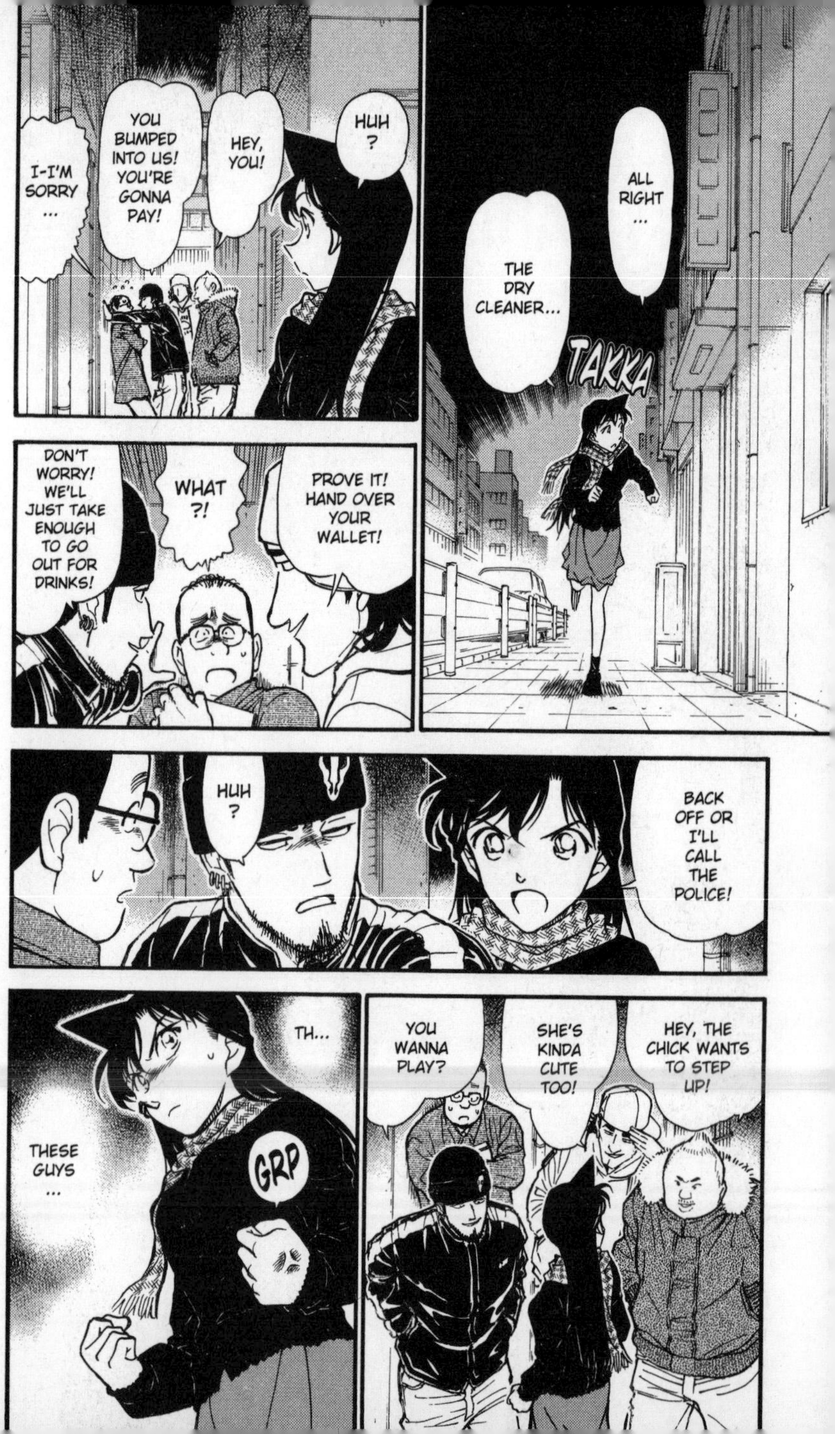
ALL RIGHT...
THE DRY CLEANER...
TAKKA
HUH?
HEY, YOU!
YOU BUMPED INTO US! YOU'RE GONNA PAY!
I-I'M SORRY...
PROVE IT! HAND OVER YOUR WALLET!
WHAT?!
DON'T WORRY! WE'LL JUST TAKE ENOUGH TO GO OUT FOR DRINKS!
BACK OFF OR I'LL CALL THE POLICE!
HUH?
HEY, THE CHICK WANTS TO STEP UP!
SHE'S KINDA CUTE TOO!
YOU WANNA PLAY?
TH...
GRP
THESE GUYS...

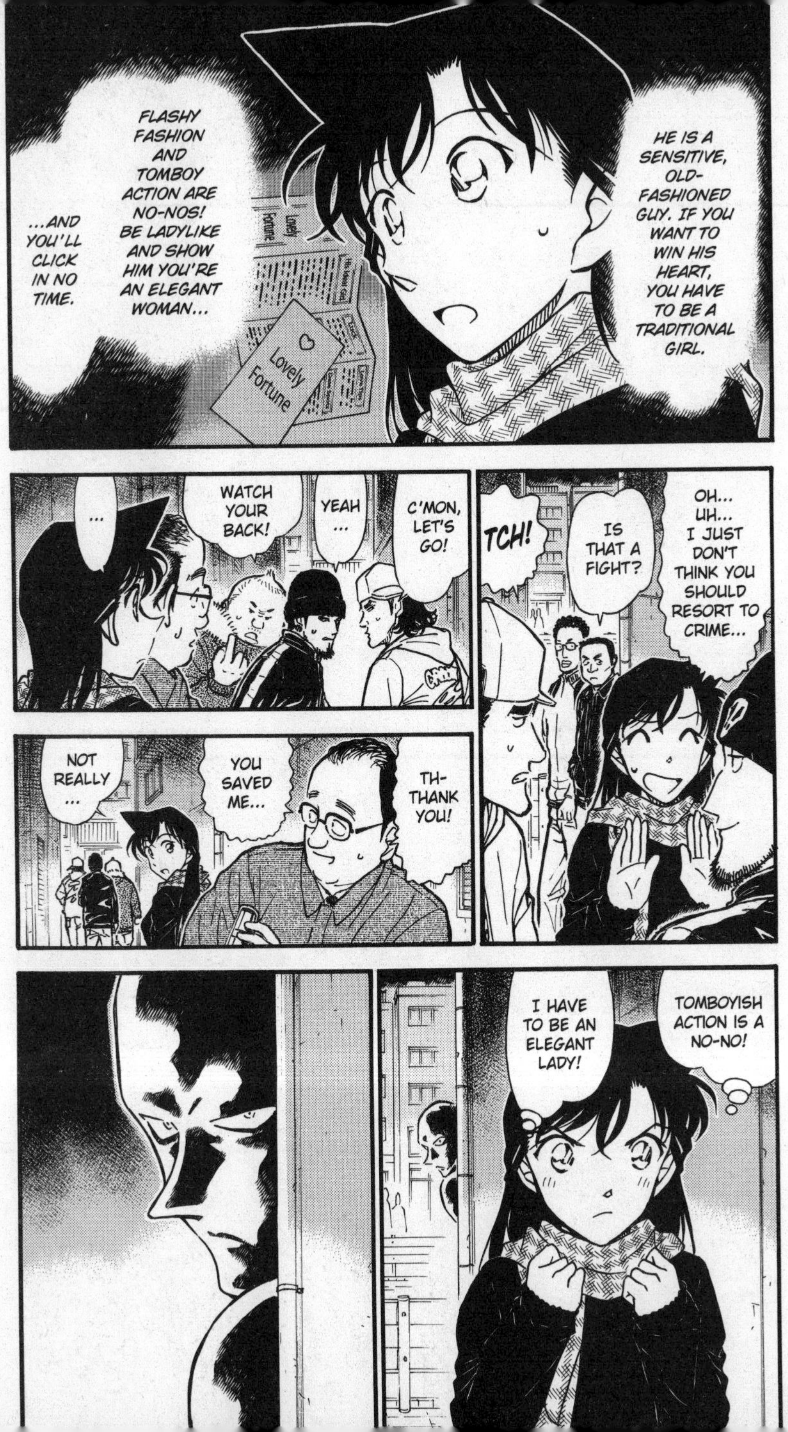
HE IS A SENSITIVE, OLD-FASHIONED GUY. IF YOU WANT TO WIN HIS HEART, YOU HAVE TO BE A TRADITIONAL GIRL.
FLASHY FASHION AND TOMBOY ACTION ARE NO-NOS! BE LADYLIKE AND SHOW HIM YOU'RE AN ELEGANT WOMAN...
...AND YOU'LL CLICK IN NO TIME.
Lovely Fortune
Lovely Fortune
OH... UH... I JUST DON'T THINK YOU SHOULD RESORT TO CRIME...
IS THAT A FIGHT?
TCH!
C'MON, LET'S GO!
YEAH ...
WATCH YOUR BACK!
...
TH-THANK YOU!
YOU SAVED ME...
NOT REALLY ...
TOMBOYISH ACTION IS A NO-NO!
I HAVE TO BE AN ELEGANT LADY!

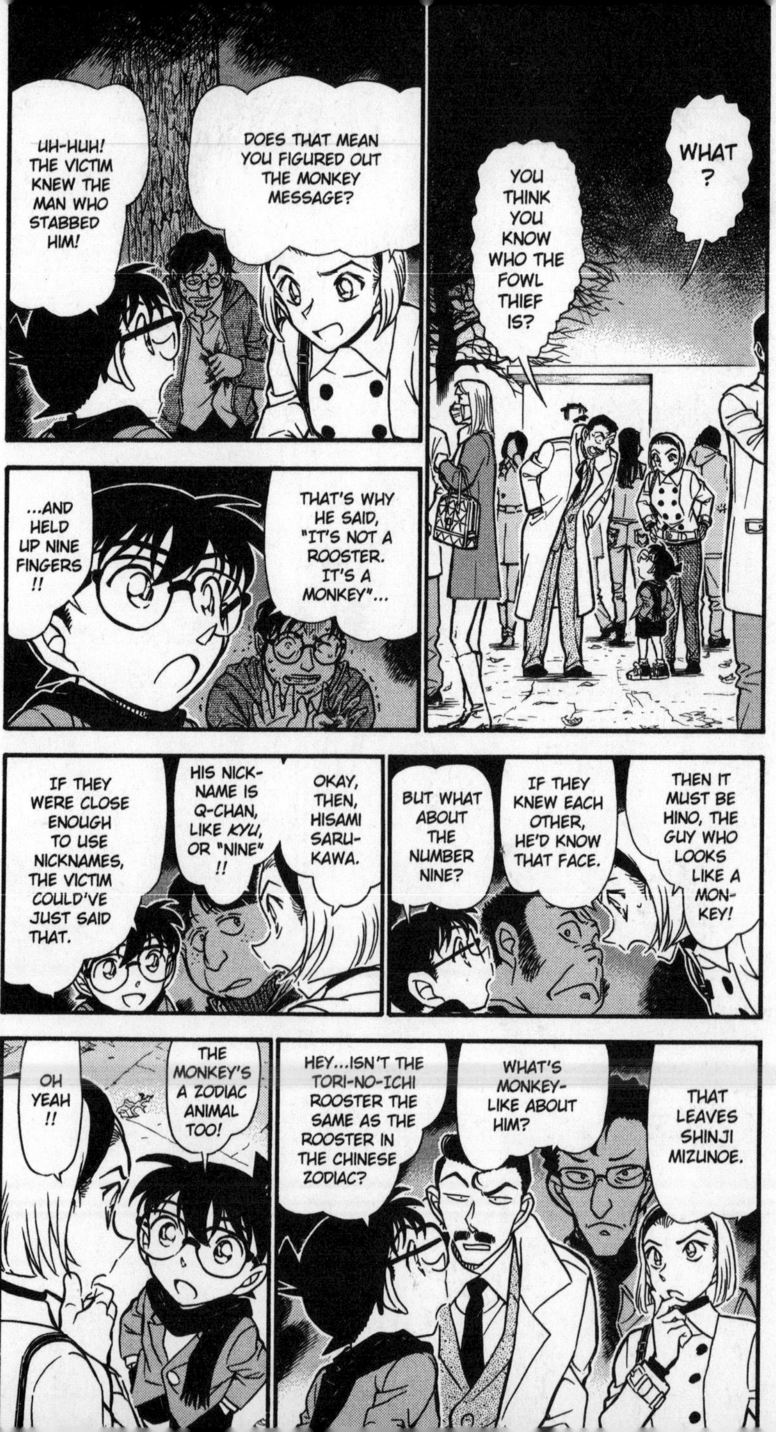
WHAT?
YOU THINK YOU KNOW WHO THE FOWL THIEF IS?
DOES THAT MEAN YOU FIGURED OUT THE MONKEY MESSAGE?
UH-HUH! THE VICTIM KNEW THE MAN WHO STABBED HIM!
THAT'S WHY HE SAID, "IT'S NOT A ROOSTER. IT'S A MONKEY"...
...AND HELD UP NINE FINGERS!!
THEN IT MUST BE HINO, THE GUY WHO LOOKS LIKE A MONKEY!
IF THEY KNEW EACH OTHER, HE'D KNOW THAT FACE.
BUT WHAT ABOUT THE NUMBER NINE?
OKAY, THEN, HISAMI SARUKAWA.
HIS NICKNAME IS Q-CHAN, LIKE *KYU*, OR "NINE"!!
IF THEY WERE CLOSE ENOUGH TO USE NICKNAMES, THE VICTIM COULD'VE JUST SAID THAT.
THAT LEAVES SHINJI MIZUNOE.
WHAT'S MONKEY-LIKE ABOUT HIM?
HEY...ISN'T THE TORI-NO-ICHI ROOSTER THE SAME AS THE ROOSTER IN THE CHINESE ZODIAC?
THE MONKEY'S A ZODIAC ANIMAL TOO!
OH YEAH!!

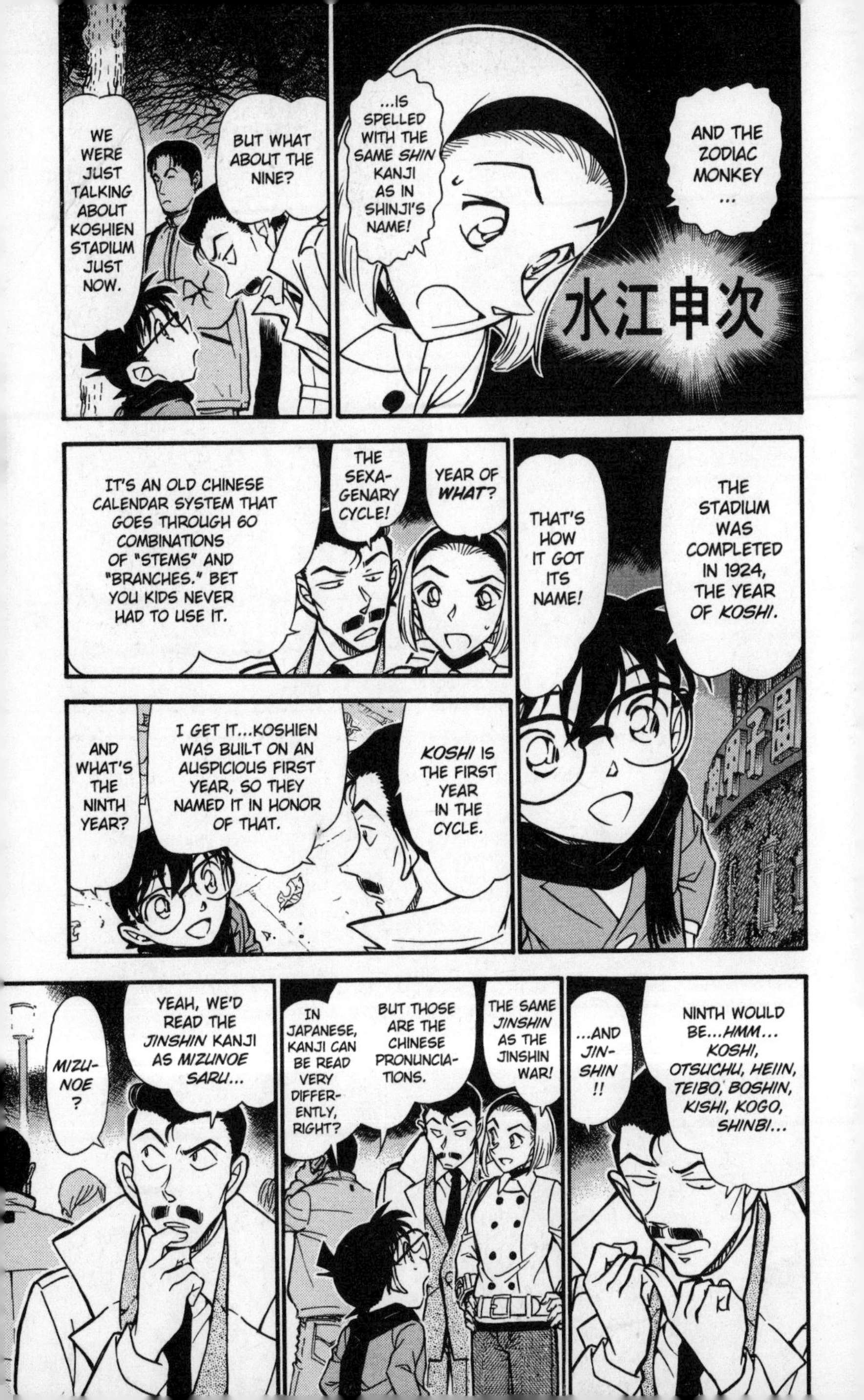
AND THE ZODIAC MONKEY ...
水江申次
...IS SPELLED WITH THE SAME *SHIN* KANJI AS IN SHINJI'S NAME!
BUT WHAT ABOUT THE NINE?
WE WERE JUST TALKING ABOUT KOSHIEN STADIUM JUST NOW.
THE STADIUM WAS COMPLETED IN 1924, THE YEAR OF *KOSHI*.
THAT'S HOW IT GOT ITS NAME!
YEAR OF *WHAT*?
THE SEXAGENARY CYCLE!
IT'S AN OLD CHINESE CALENDAR SYSTEM THAT GOES THROUGH 60 COMBINATIONS OF "STEMS" AND "BRANCHES." BET YOU KIDS NEVER HAD TO USE IT.
KOSHI IS THE FIRST YEAR IN THE CYCLE.
I GET IT...KOSHIEN WAS BUILT ON AN AUSPICIOUS FIRST YEAR, SO THEY NAMED IT IN HONOR OF THAT.
AND WHAT'S THE NINTH YEAR?
NINTH WOULD BE...*HMM... KOSHI, OTSUCHU, HEIIN, TEIBO, BOSHIN, KISHI, KOGO, SHINBI*...
...AND *JINSHIN* !!
THE SAME *JINSHIN* AS THE JINSHIN WAR!
BUT THOSE ARE THE CHINESE PRONUNCIATIONS.
IN JAPANESE, KANJI CAN BE READ VERY DIFFERENTLY, RIGHT?
YEAH, WE'D READ THE *JINSHIN* KANJI AS *MIZUNOE SARU*...
MIZUNOE ?

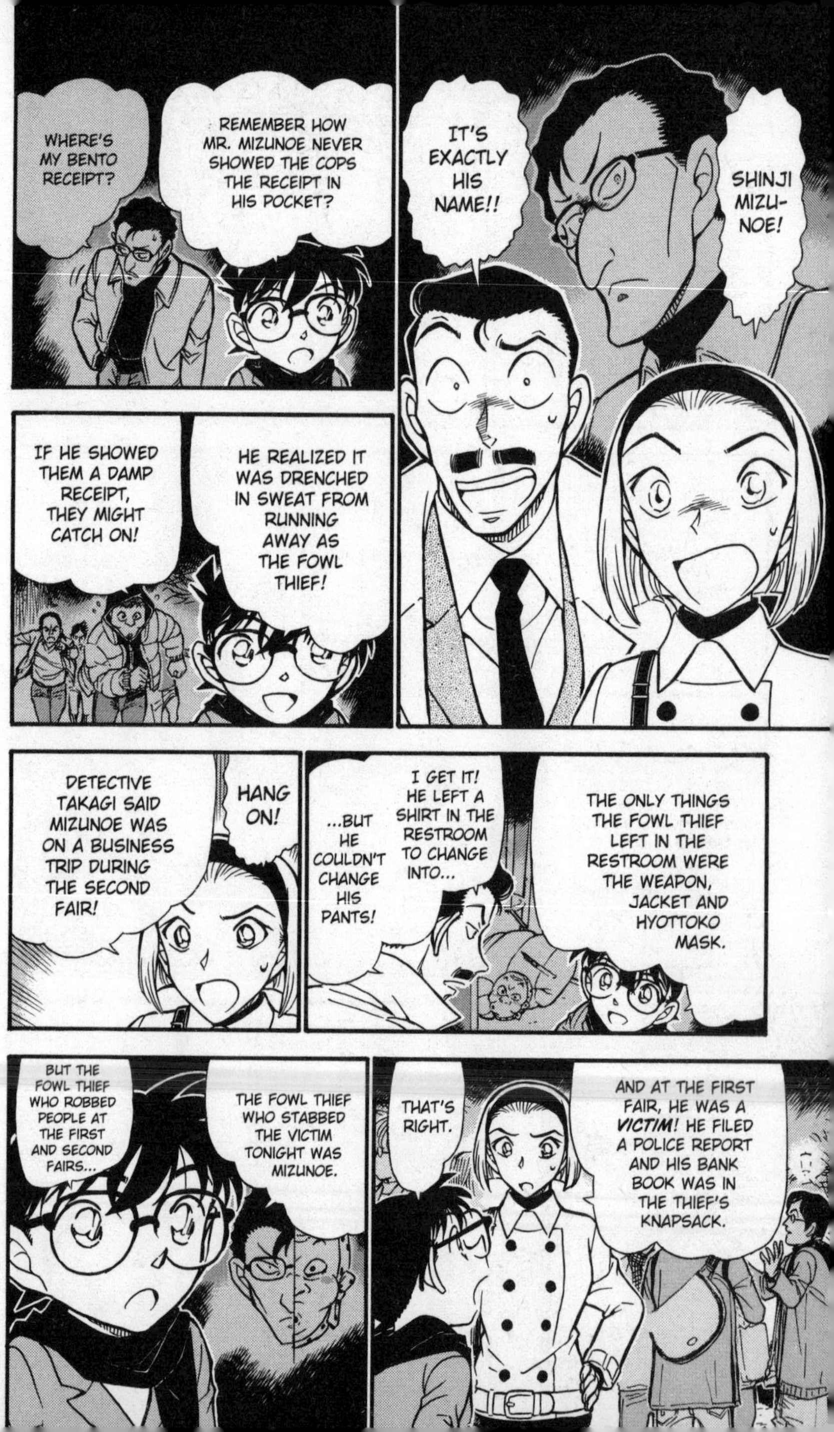
SHINJI MIZUNOE!
IT'S EXACTLY HIS NAME!!
REMEMBER HOW MR. MIZUNOE NEVER SHOWED THE COPS THE RECEIPT IN HIS POCKET?
WHERE'S MY BENTO RECEIPT?
HE REALIZED IT WAS DRENCHED IN SWEAT FROM RUNNING AWAY AS THE FOWL THIEF!
IF HE SHOWED THEM A DAMP RECEIPT, THEY MIGHT CATCH ON!
THE ONLY THINGS THE FOWL THIEF LEFT IN THE RESTROOM WERE THE WEAPON, JACKET AND HYOTTOKO MASK.
I GET IT! HE LEFT A SHIRT IN THE RESTROOM TO CHANGE INTO...
...BUT HE COULDN'T CHANGE HIS PANTS!
HANG ON!
DETECTIVE TAKAGI SAID MIZUNOE WAS ON A BUSINESS TRIP DURING THE SECOND FAIR!
AND AT THE FIRST FAIR, HE WAS A *VICTIM*! HE FILED A POLICE REPORT AND HIS BANK BOOK WAS IN THE THIEF'S KNAPSACK.
THAT'S RIGHT.
THE FOWL THIEF WHO STABBED THE VICTIM TONIGHT WAS MIZUNOE.
BUT THE FOWL THIEF WHO ROBBED PEOPLE AT THE FIRST AND SECOND FAIRS...

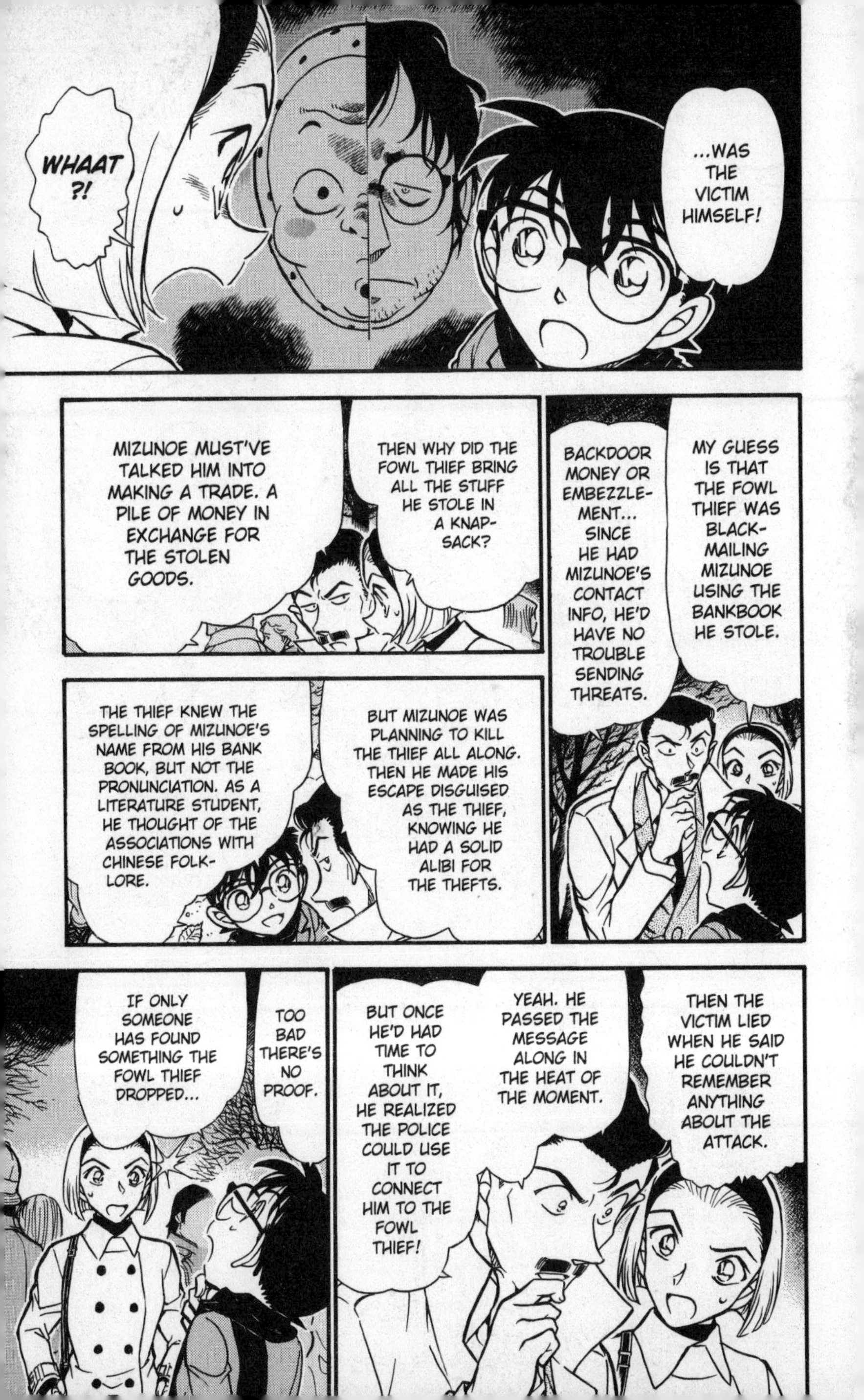
...WAS THE VICTIM HIMSELF!
WHAAT ?!
MY GUESS IS THAT THE FOWL THIEF WAS BLACK-MAILING MIZUNOE USING THE BANKBOOK HE STOLE.
BACKDOOR MONEY OR EMBEZZLE-MENT... SINCE HE HAD MIZUNOE'S CONTACT INFO, HE'D HAVE NO TROUBLE SENDING THREATS.
THEN WHY DID THE FOWL THIEF BRING ALL THE STUFF HE STOLE IN A KNAP-SACK?
MIZUNOE MUST'VE TALKED HIM INTO MAKING A TRADE. A PILE OF MONEY IN EXCHANGE FOR THE STOLEN GOODS.
BUT MIZUNOE WAS PLANNING TO KILL THE THIEF ALL ALONG. THEN HE MADE HIS ESCAPE DISGUISED AS THE THIEF, KNOWING HE HAD A SOLID ALIBI FOR THE THEFTS.
THE THIEF KNEW THE SPELLING OF MIZUNOE'S NAME FROM HIS BANK BOOK, BUT NOT THE PRONUNCIATION. AS A LITERATURE STUDENT, HE THOUGHT OF THE ASSOCIATIONS WITH CHINESE FOLK-LORE.
THEN THE VICTIM LIED WHEN HE SAID HE COULDN'T REMEMBER ANYTHING ABOUT THE ATTACK.
YEAH. HE PASSED THE MESSAGE ALONG IN THE HEAT OF THE MOMENT.
BUT ONCE HE'D HAD TIME TO THINK ABOUT IT, HE REALIZED THE POLICE COULD USE IT TO CONNECT HIM TO THE FOWL THIEF!
TOO BAD THERE'S NO PROOF.
IF ONLY SOMEONE HAS FOUND SOMETHING THE FOWL THIEF DROPPED...

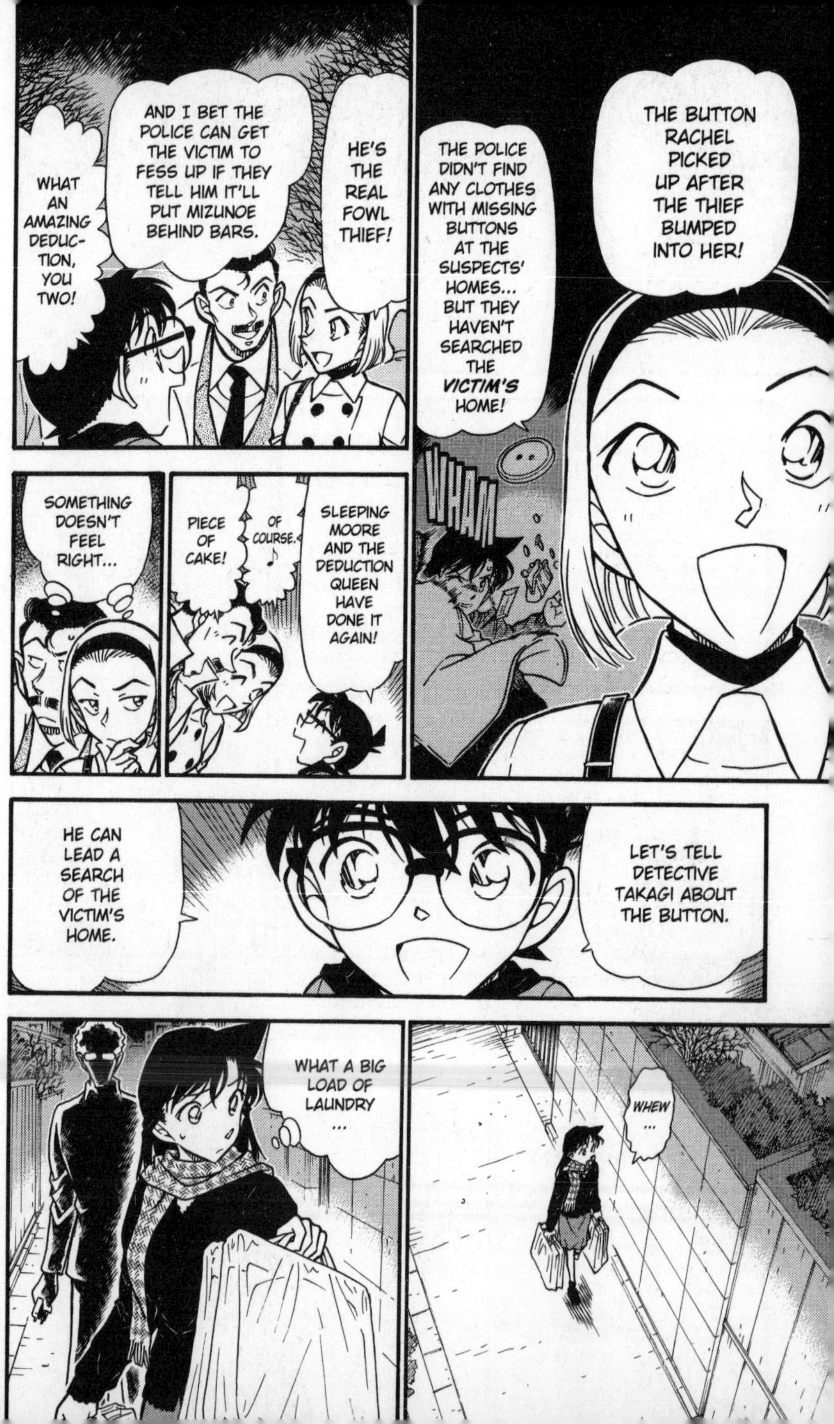
THE BUTTON RACHEL PICKED UP AFTER THE THIEF BUMPED INTO HER!
THE POLICE DIDN'T FIND ANY CLOTHES WITH MISSING BUTTONS AT THE SUSPECTS' HOMES... BUT THEY HAVEN'T SEARCHED THE *VICTIM'S* HOME!
WHAM
HE'S THE REAL FOWL THIEF!
AND I BET THE POLICE CAN GET THE VICTIM TO FESS UP IF THEY TELL HIM IT'LL PUT MIZUNOE BEHIND BARS.
WHAT AN AMAZING DEDUCTION, YOU TWO!
SLEEPING MOORE AND THE DEDUCTION QUEEN HAVE DONE IT AGAIN!
OF COURSE. ♪
PIECE OF CAKE!
SOMETHING DOESN'T FEEL RIGHT...
LET'S TELL DETECTIVE TAKAGI ABOUT THE BUTTON.
HE CAN LEAD A SEARCH OF THE VICTIM'S HOME.
WHEW ...
WHAT A BIG LOAD OF LAUNDRY ...

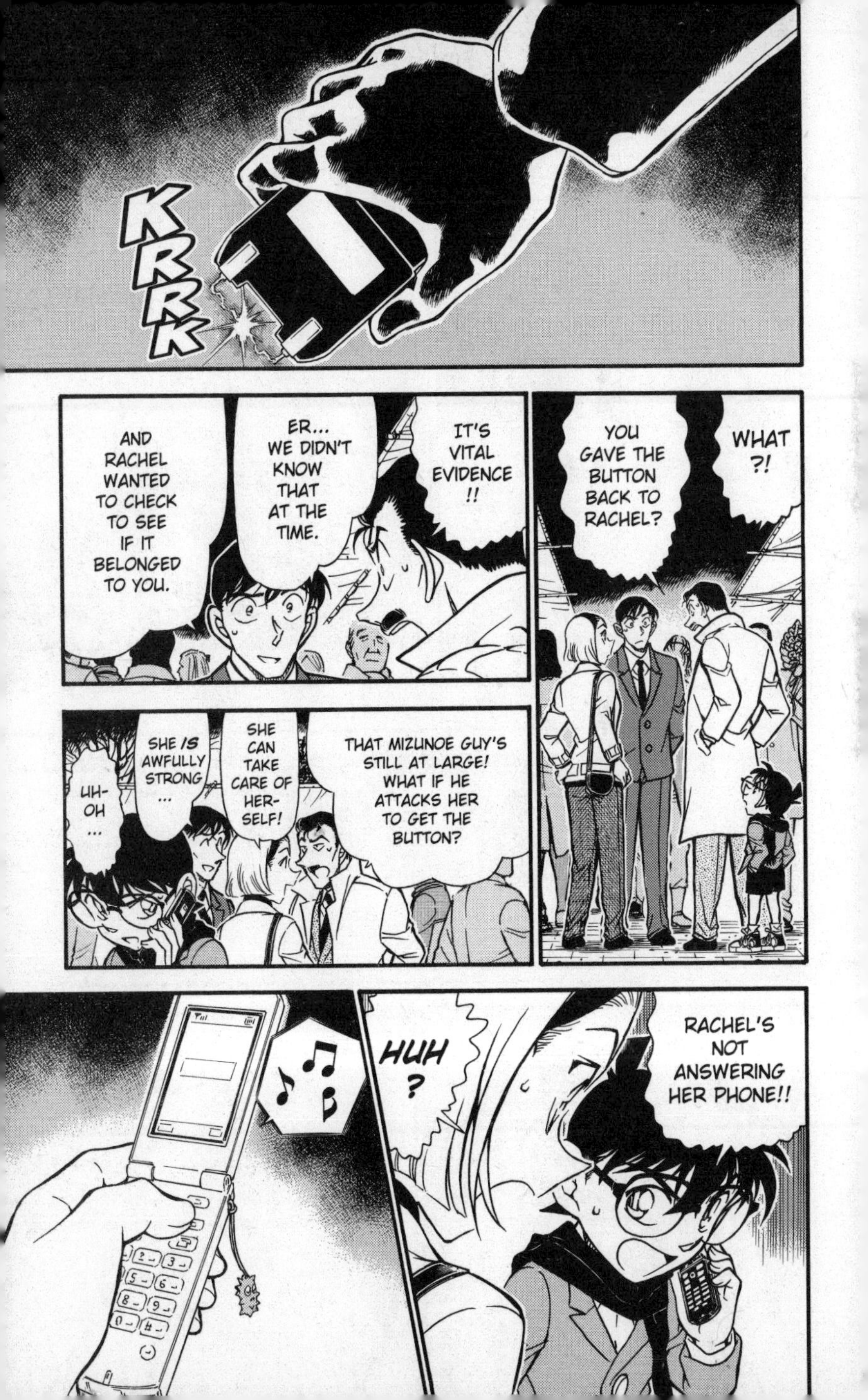
KRRK
WHAT ?!
YOU GAVE THE BUTTON BACK TO RACHEL?
IT'S VITAL EVIDENCE !!
ER... WE DIDN'T KNOW THAT AT THE TIME.
AND RACHEL WANTED TO CHECK TO SEE IF IT BELONGED TO YOU.
THAT MIZUNOE GUY'S STILL AT LARGE! WHAT IF HE ATTACKS HER TO GET THE BUTTON?
SHE CAN TAKE CARE OF HER-SELF!
SHE *IS* AWFULLY STRONG ...
UH-OH ...
RACHEL'S NOT ANSWERING HER PHONE!!
HUH ?

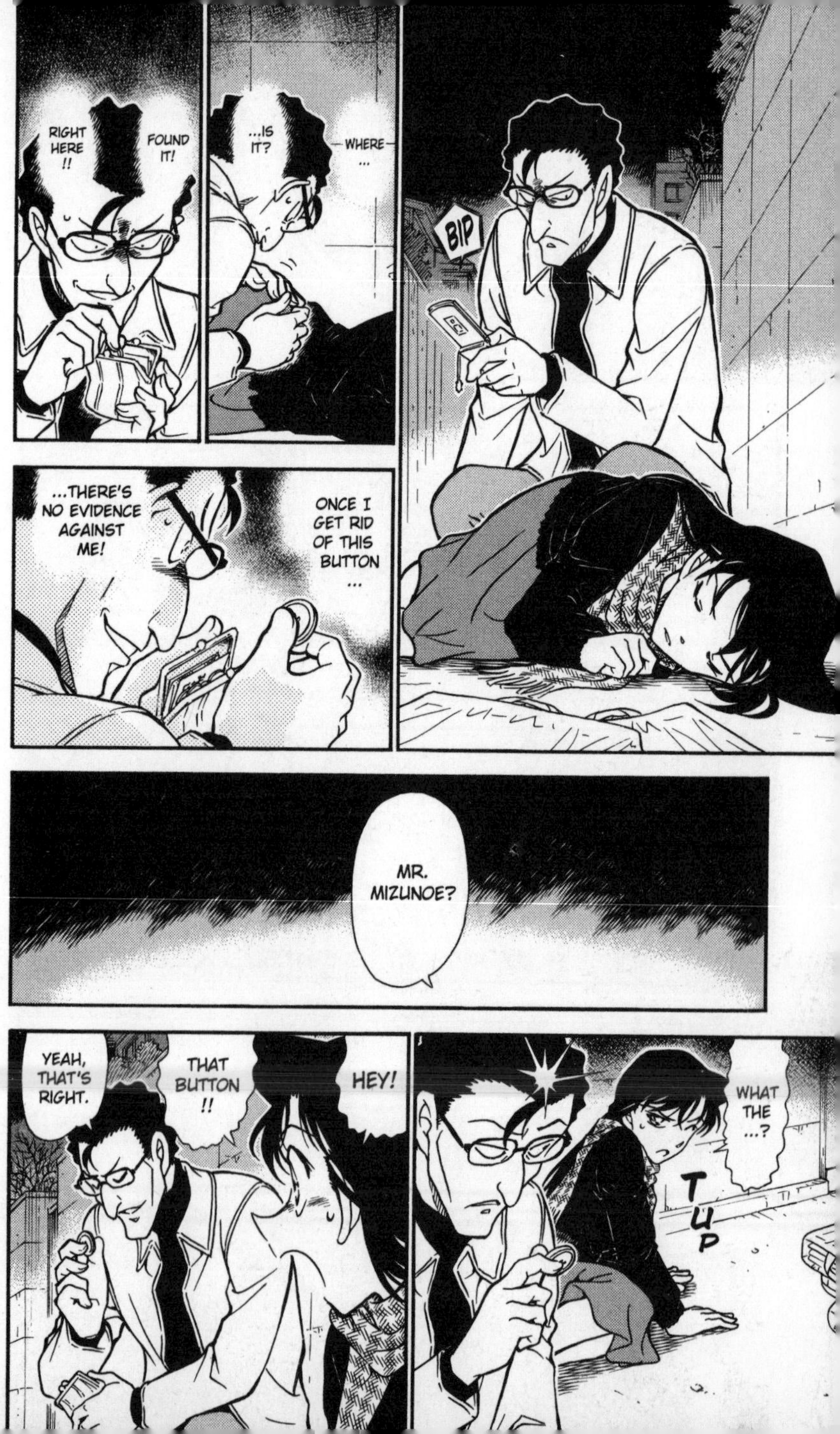
BIP
—WHERE—...
...IS IT?
FOUND IT!
RIGHT HERE!!
ONCE I GET RID OF THIS BUTTON...
...THERE'S NO EVIDENCE AGAINST ME!
MR. MIZUNOE?
WHAT THE...?
TUP
HEY!
THAT BUTTON!!
YEAH, THAT'S RIGHT.

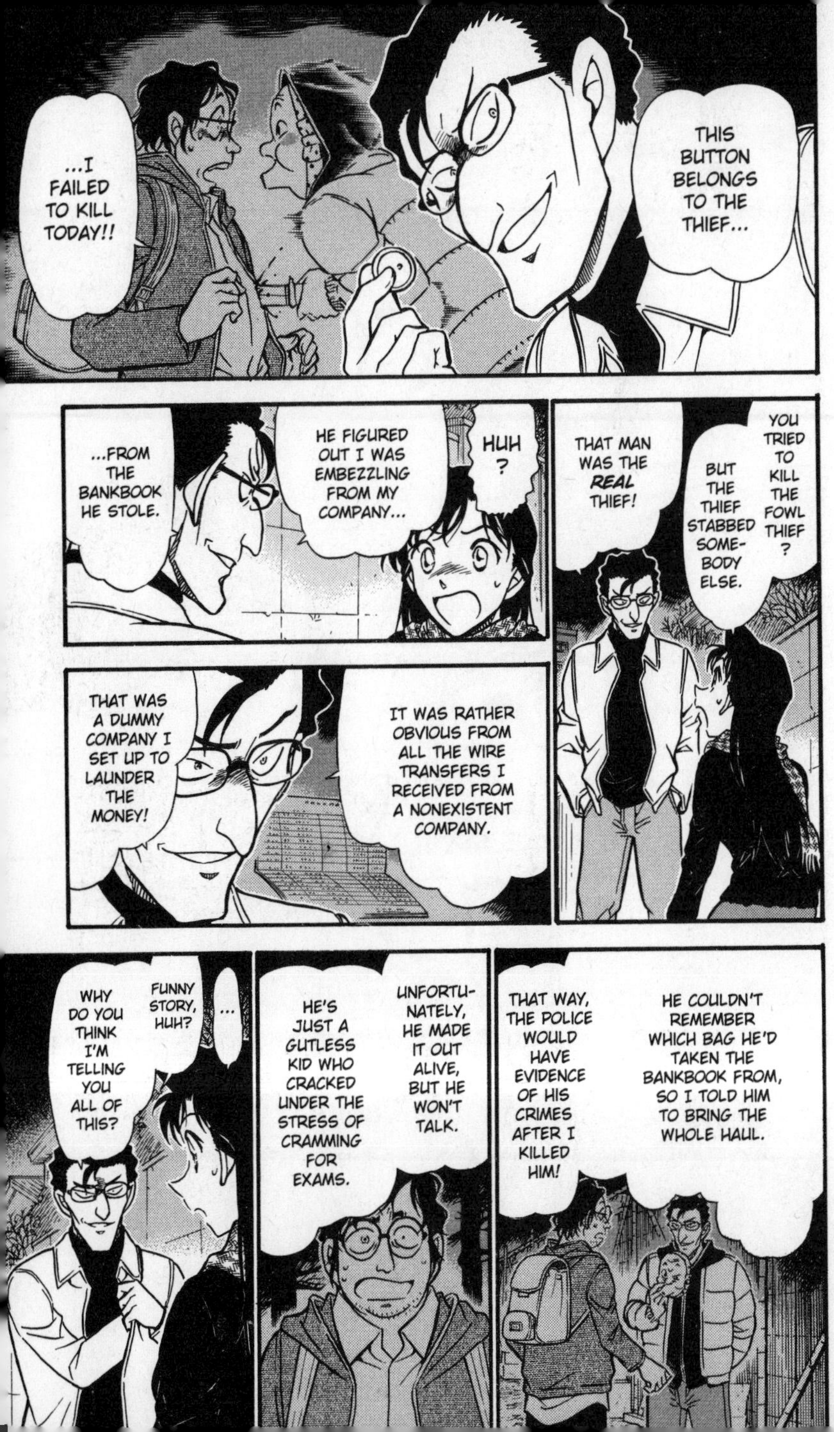
THIS BUTTON BELONGS TO THE THIEF...
...I FAILED TO KILL TODAY!!
YOU TRIED TO KILL THE FOWL THIEF?
BUT THE THIEF STABBED SOMEBODY ELSE.
THAT MAN WAS THE *REAL* THIEF!
HUH?
HE FIGURED OUT I WAS EMBEZZLING FROM MY COMPANY...
...FROM THE BANKBOOK HE STOLE.
IT WAS RATHER OBVIOUS FROM ALL THE WIRE TRANSFERS I RECEIVED FROM A NONEXISTENT COMPANY.
THAT WAS A DUMMY COMPANY I SET UP TO LAUNDER THE MONEY!
HE COULDN'T REMEMBER WHICH BAG HE'D TAKEN THE BANKBOOK FROM, SO I TOLD HIM TO BRING THE WHOLE HAUL.
THAT WAY, THE POLICE WOULD HAVE EVIDENCE OF HIS CRIMES AFTER I KILLED HIM!
UNFORTUNATELY, HE MADE IT OUT ALIVE, BUT HE WON'T TALK.
HE'S JUST A GUTLESS KID WHO CRACKED UNDER THE STRESS OF CRAMMING FOR EXAMS.
...
FUNNY STORY, HUH?
WHY DO YOU THINK I'M TELLING YOU ALL OF THIS?

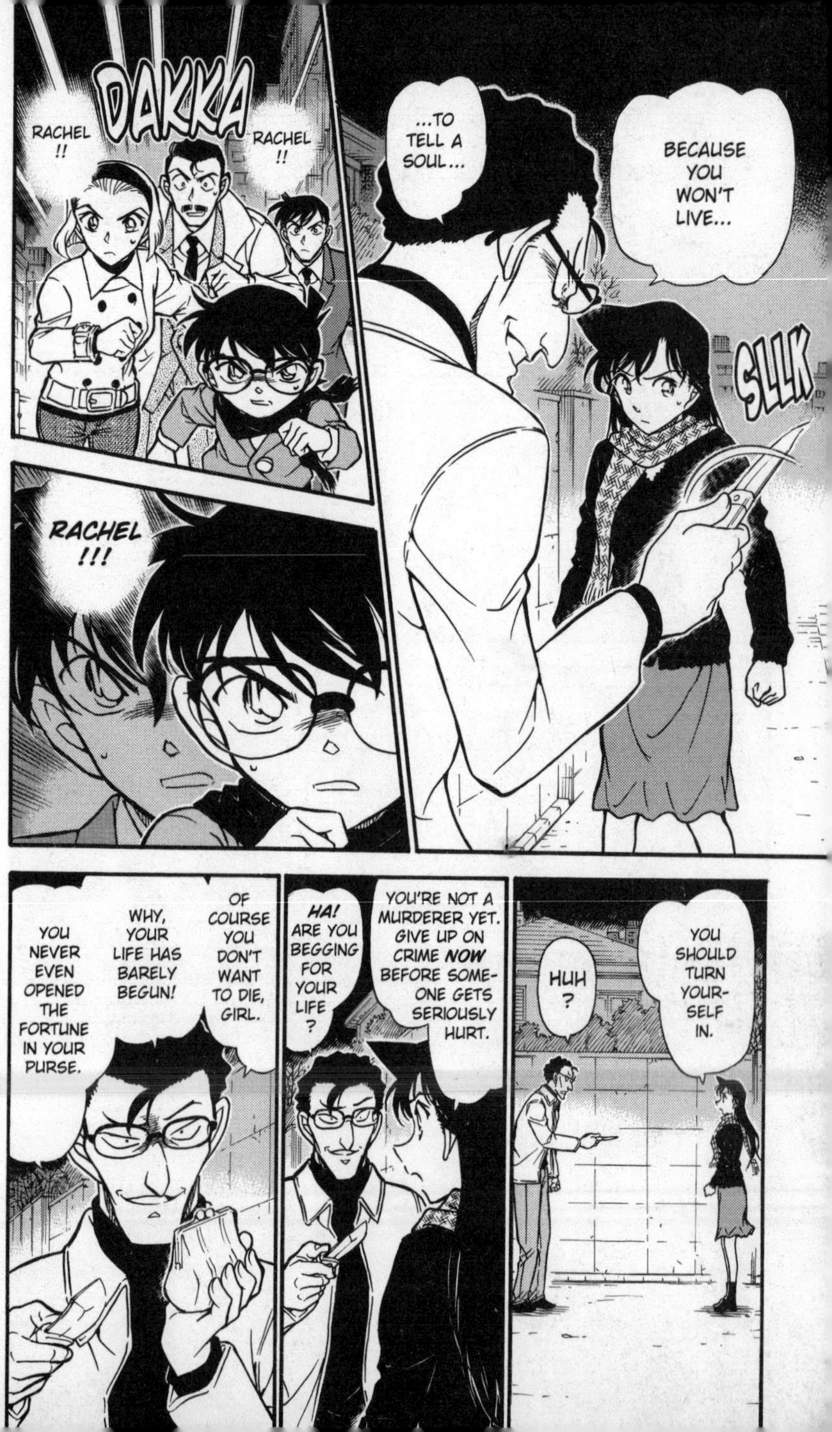
...TO TELL A SOUL...
BECAUSE YOU WON'T LIVE...
SLLK
DAKKA
RACHEL!!
RACHEL!!
RACHEL!!!
YOU SHOULD TURN YOURSELF IN.
HUH?
YOU'RE NOT A MURDERER YET. GIVE UP ON CRIME NOW BEFORE SOMEONE GETS SERIOUSLY HURT.
HA! ARE YOU BEGGING FOR YOUR LIFE?
OF COURSE YOU DON'T WANT TO DIE, GIRL.
WHY, YOUR LIFE HAS BARELY BEGUN!
YOU NEVER EVEN OPENED THE FORTUNE IN YOUR PURSE.

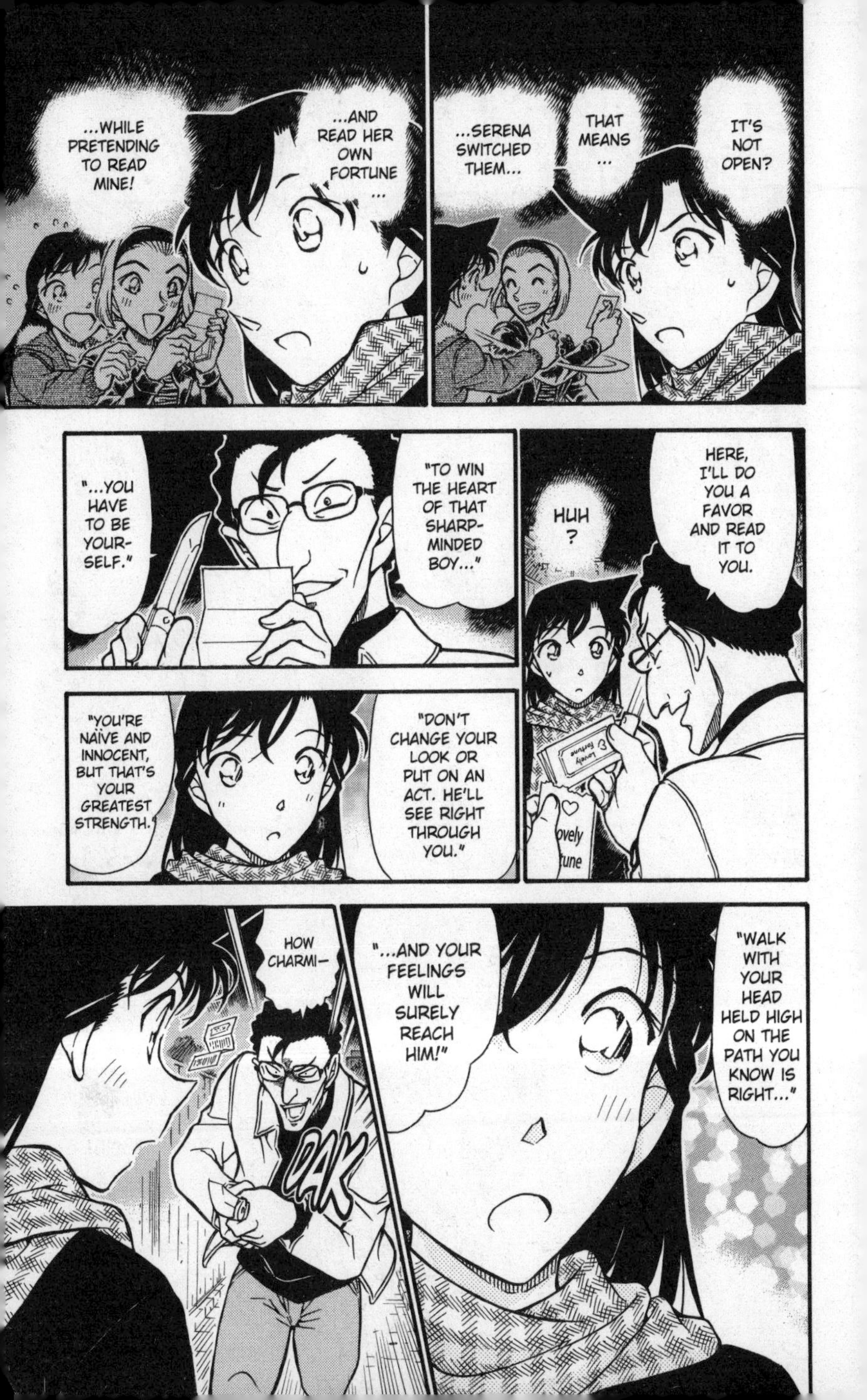
IT'S NOT OPEN?
THAT MEANS...
...SERENA SWITCHED THEM...
...AND READ HER OWN FORTUNE...
...WHILE PRETENDING TO READ MINE!
HERE, I'LL DO YOU A FAVOR AND READ IT TO YOU.
HUH?
"TO WIN THE HEART OF THAT SHARP-MINDED BOY..."
"...YOU HAVE TO BE YOURSELF."
"DON'T CHANGE YOUR LOOK OR PUT ON AN ACT. HE'LL SEE RIGHT THROUGH YOU."
"YOU'RE NAÏVE AND INNOCENT, BUT THAT'S YOUR GREATEST STRENGTH."
"WALK WITH YOUR HEAD HELD HIGH ON THE PATH YOU KNOW IS RIGHT..."
"...AND YOUR FEELINGS WILL SURELY REACH HIM!"
HOW CHARMI—

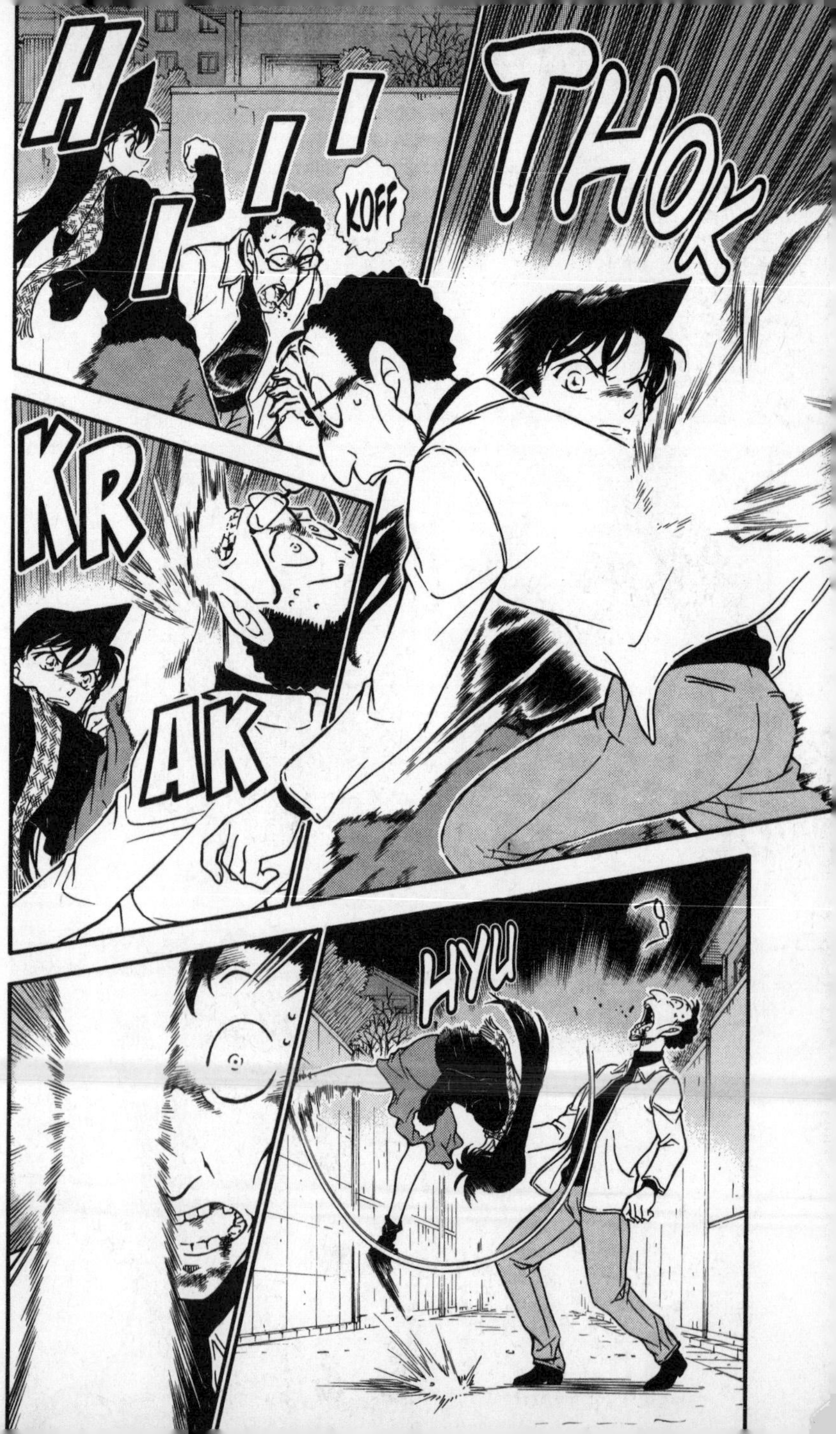
THOK
HIIII
KOFF
KR
AK
HYU

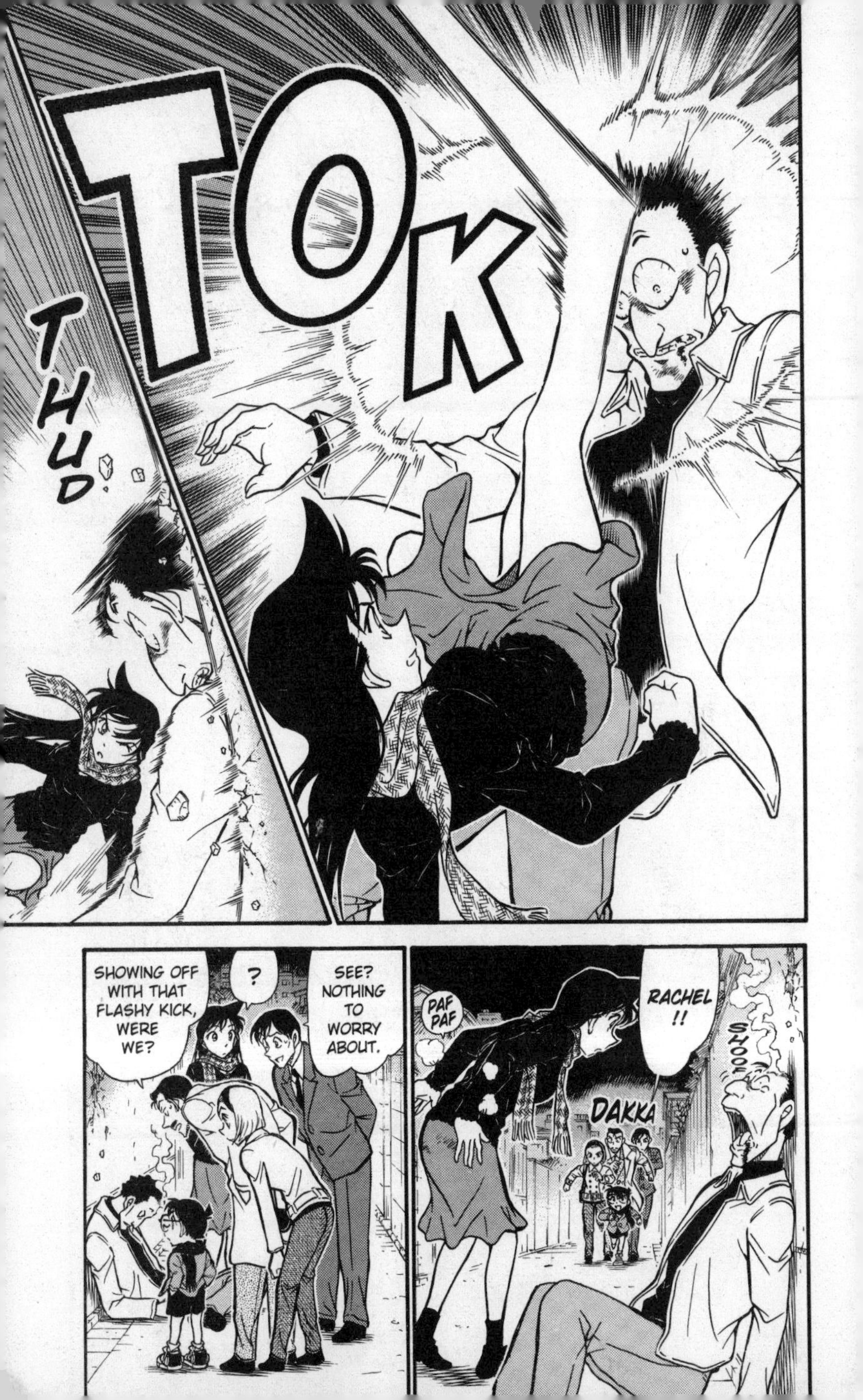
TOK
THUD
RACHEL !!
SHOOF
PAF PAF
DAKKA
SEE? NOTHING TO WORRY ABOUT.
?
SHOWING OFF WITH THAT FLASHY KICK, WERE WE?

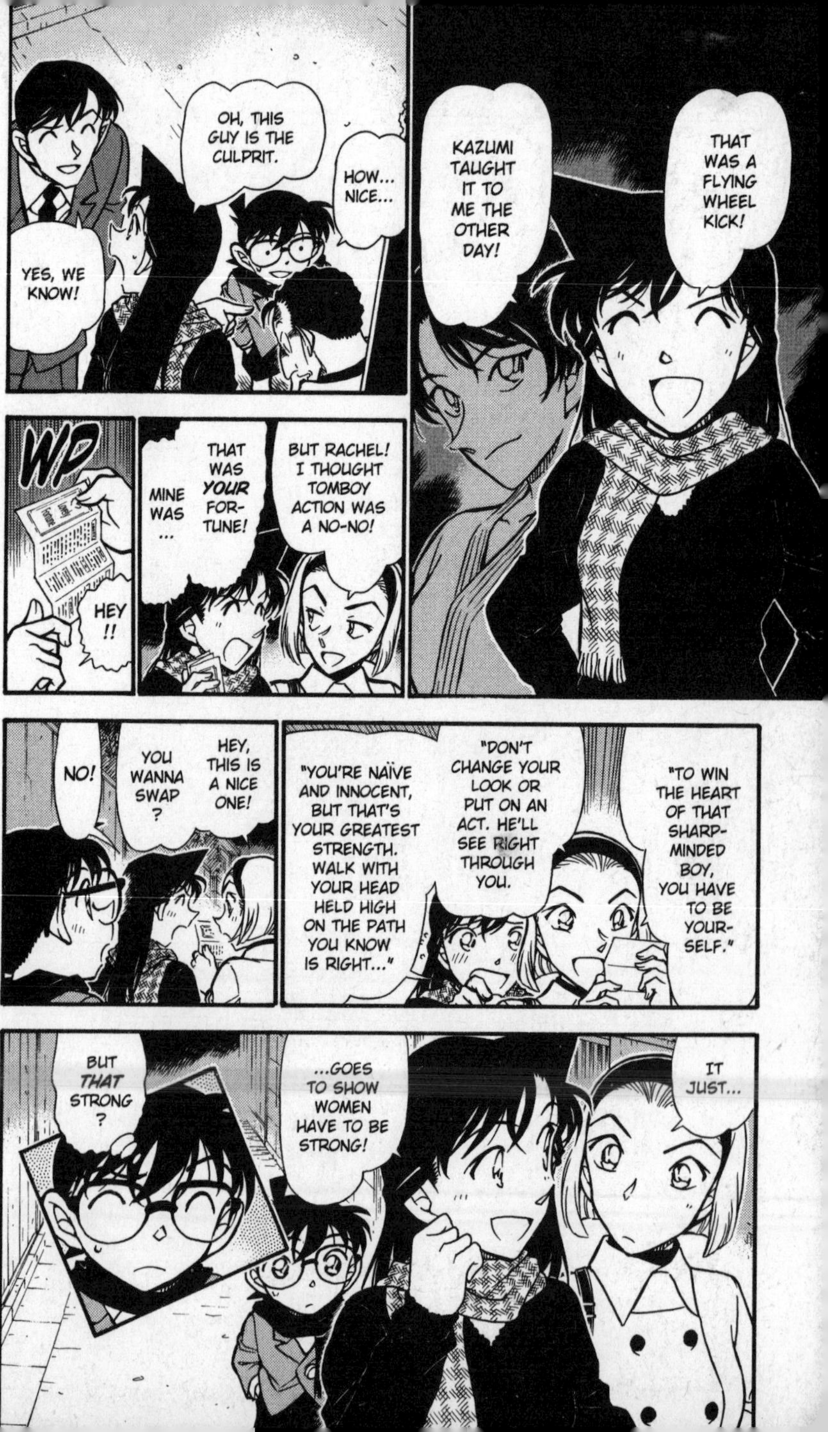
THAT WAS A FLYING WHEEL KICK!
KAZUMI TAUGHT IT TO ME THE OTHER DAY!
OH, THIS GUY IS THE CULPRIT.
HOW... NICE...
YES, WE KNOW!
BUT RACHEL! I THOUGHT TOMBOY ACTION WAS A NO-NO!
THAT WAS *YOUR* FORTUNE!
MINE WAS ...
WP
HEY !!
"TO WIN THE HEART OF THAT SHARP-MINDED BOY, YOU HAVE TO BE YOURSELF."
"DON'T CHANGE YOUR LOOK OR PUT ON AN ACT. HE'LL SEE RIGHT THROUGH YOU.
"YOU'RE NAÏVE AND INNOCENT, BUT THAT'S YOUR GREATEST STRENGTH. WALK WITH YOUR HEAD HELD HIGH ON THE PATH YOU KNOW IS RIGHT..."
HEY, THIS IS A NICE ONE!
YOU WANNA SWAP ?
NO!
IT JUST...
...GOES TO SHOW WOMEN HAVE TO BE STRONG!
BUT *THAT* STRONG ?

THE KILLER IS

Hello, Aoyama here!

Mechanical trick house, mechanical trick safe, mechanical trick storehouse, mechanical trick temple...the inventions of puppet master Kichiemon Samizu, genius of the Bakumatsu era, keep complicating Conan's cases!! His tricky devices always give Conan a hard time, but from his picture on the back cover you can see he's just a sweet, mischievous old man, right? *Heh...*

Gosho Aoyama's Mystery Library

68

BANNAI TARAO

Disguise is one of a detective's most important techniques, and Bannai Tarao is a master! A private detective who runs the Tarao Detective Agency, he's a middle-aged man with glasses, a mustache and a forgettable face. But once he begins his investigation he may turn into a gallant magician, a one-eyed driver or a mysterious fortune-teller! The disguises he uses to seek the truth behind baffling mysteries have earned him the nickname "The Man with Seven Faces." At the climax of each case, he reveals his true identity to the amazement of Taizo Fujimura, a once-infamous phantom thief who's turned over a new leaf to become an emissary of justice and truth!

The *Bannai Tarao* movie series starring Chiezo Kataoka made the character super popular with the ladies. Sheesh! Arsène Lupin, The Man with Twenty Faces, the Kaito Kid...masters of disguise are such heartthrobs. ♥

I recommend *Seven Faces*.

Hey! You're Reading in the Wrong Direction!

This is the *end* of this graphic novel!

To properly enjoy this VIZ graphic novel, please turn it around and begin reading from *right to left.* Unlike English, Japanese is read right to left, so Japanese comics are read in reverse order from the way English comics are typically read.

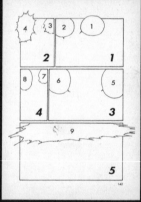

Follow the action this way

This book has been printed in the original Japanese format in order to preserve the orientation of the original artwork. Have fun with it!